Introducing Global Issues

SIXTH EDITION

Introducing Global Issues

edited by

Michael T. Snarr

D. Neil Snarr

LYNNE RIENNER PUBLISHERS

BOULDER
LONDON

Published in the United States of America in 2016 by
Lynne Rienner Publishers, Inc.
1800 30th Street, Boulder, Colorado 80301
www.rienner.com

and in the United Kingdom by
Lynne Rienner Publishers, Inc.
3 Henrietta Street, Covent Garden, London WC2E 8LU

Library of Congress Cataloging-in-Publication Data
Names: Snarr, Michael T., editor. | Snarr, Neil, 1933– editor.
Title: Introducing global issues / edited by Michael T. Snarr and D. Neil Snarr.
Description: Sixth edition. | Boulder, Colorado : Lynne Rienner Publishers, 2016 | Includes bibliographical references and index.
Identifiers: LCCN 2016000717 | ISBN 9781626375468 (pbk. : alk. paper)
Subjects: LCSH: World politics—1989– | International economic relations. | Social history—1970– | Ecology.
Classification: LCC D860 .I62 2016 | DDC 909.83/1—dc23
LC record available at http://lccn.loc.gov/2016000717

British Cataloguing in Publication Data
A Cataloguing in Publication record for this book is available from the British Library.

Printed and bound in the United States of America

∞ The paper used in this publication meets the requirements of the American National Standard for Permanence of Paper for Printed Library Materials Z39.48-1992.

5 4 3 2 1

For Emery Grace,
may you find and spread love in a troubled world

Contents

Part 2 Dimensions of the Global Political Economy

Part 3 Conclusion

Tables and Figures

Tables

Figures

Preface

MANY NEW ISSUES HAVE ARISEN AND MANY OLDER ONES HAVE EVOLVED since the previous edition of this book was published. ISIS has emerged as the most feared terrorist organization in the world, climate change cooperation has slowly progressed, technology has predictably created a more complex world, and more refugees have emerged as a result of climate and conflict. These issues and others receive increased attention in this edition, and each chapter has been updated to cover the most recent developments. A long-overdue chapter on agriculture and food is an entirely new addition, connecting with issues such as security, climate, hunger, and health. Some of the other significant changes include case studies on cyber-warfare and autonomous weapons; a new chapter on the role of women in development, including discussions of food security, political participation, and education; and a new chapter on health. Also, the entire book has been reorganized to better reflect its major themes. Ideas for improving the book, as well as general comments, are always welcome at michael_snarr@wilmington.edu.

* * *

We are indebted to those who made yet another edition possible. The two of us have spent a total of sixty-plus years studying and teaching global issues. As a result, this is a rewarding project. We feel fortunate to learn from and benefit from scholars and practitioners like those who have made valuable contributions to this edition, and we want to explicitly thank them for their devotion to their respective areas of expertise.

Sincere appreciation goes to Lynne Rienner, who agreed to publish the first edition of this book eighteen years ago and has continued to be a source of support. Special thanks goes to Megan Canfield, who spent an entire semester (as well as nearly a week of her Christmas break) helping with the citations, bibliography, and other important details involved in this edition.

As always, we can't thank our family enough for their unending support.

—Michael T. Snarr and D. Neil Snarr

1

Exploring Global Issues

Michael T. Snarr

RECORD-SETTING NUMBERS OF REFUGEES, BRUTAL BEHEADINGS BY TERrorists, abject poverty, the growing crisis of climate change, cruel human rights abuses, and widespread malnutrition and diseases. If you monitor the news, these are the headlines you will see. Unfortunately, as the statistics immediately below reveal, various global issues are threatening humanity.

- Approximately 200,000 people are added to the world's total population every day.
- Nearly 16,000 children die each day from hunger-related causes—one child every five seconds (WHO 2015k).
- There are 795 million hungry people in the world today (Gladstone 2015b).
- The world has more refugees now than any time since 1945 (Alexander 2015).
- Approximately one in nine people are undernourished globally (UN 2015a).
- Since 1990, global CO_2 emissions have increased 50 percent (UN 2015a).
- Approximately one in three people (2.4 billion) lack access to flush toilets or other forms of proper sanitation (Gladstone 2015a).
- Of the warmest fifteen years, thirteen have occurred since 2000 (Thompson 2015b).
- Scientists estimate that over the next several decades, 75 percent of animal species will become extinct (Neuhauser 2015).
- Nearly 40 percent of adults are overweight and 13 percent are obese (WHO 2015i).
- An area the size of South Africa (or twice the size of Texas) has been deforested over the past twenty-five years (Mooney 2015).

Though the news headlines today are often negative and the problems of the world often seem overwhelming, progress is being made on many global issues. Important strides have been made in the areas of education, war, health, and more. And through the hard work of states, international governmental organizations, nongovernmental organizations, and individuals, more improvements can be made. The list below offers some reasons for hope:

- War between countries has become very rare.
- The rate of global deforestation has been slowing (Mooney 2015).
- The global literacy rate has increased from 83 percent to 91 percent since 1990 (UN 2015a).
- On average, global life expectancies today are more than twice as high as they were a century ago.
- Over the past decade and a half, new HIV infections have dropped from 3.5 million cases to 2.1 million (UN 2015a).
- In the poorer countries, the percentage of hungry people decreased from 23.3 percent to 12.9 percent since 1990 (Gladstone 2015b), and the number of deaths of children under age five has declined by 53 percent (D'Urso 2015).
- The number of people consuming improved drinking water has increased to 91 percent from 76 since 1990 (UN 2015a).
- For the first time ever, the percentage of the world's population living in extreme poverty is less than 10 percent (World Bank 2015c).

Each of these items is related to a global issue discussed in this book, and many of them affect the reader. But what is a *global issue*? The term is used here to refer to two types of phenomena. First, there are those issues that are transnational—that is, they cross political boundaries (country borders). These issues affect individuals in more than one country. A clear example is air pollution produced by a factory in the United States and blown into Canada. Second, there are problems and issues that do not necessarily cross borders but affect a large number of individuals throughout the world. Ethnic rivalries and human rights violations, for example, may occur within a single country but have a far wider impact.

For the contributors to this volume, the primary goal is to introduce several of the most pressing global issues and demonstrate how strongly they are interconnected. Since these issues affect each and every one of us, we also hope to motivate the reader to learn more about them.

Is the World Shrinking?

There has been a great deal of discussion in recent years about globalization, which can be defined as "the intensification of economic, political, social, and cultural relations across borders" (Holm and Sørensen 1995: 1). Evidence of globalization is seen regularly in our daily lives. In the United States, grocery stores and shops at the local mall are stocked with items produced abroad. Likewise, hats and T-shirts adorned with the logos of Nike, Adidas, and the New York Yankees, for example, are easily found outside the United States. In many countries, Taylor Swift, Rhianna, and other US music groups often dominate the radio waves, the BBC and CNN dominate television screens, and *The Avengers* and other Hollywood films dominate the theaters. Are we moving toward a single global culture? In the words of Benjamin Barber, we are being influenced by "the onrush of economic and ecological forces that demand integration and uniformity and that mesmerize the world with fast music, fast computers, and fast food—with MTV, Macintosh, and McDonald's pressing nations into one commercially homogeneous global network: one McWorld tied together by technology, ecology, communication, and commerce" (1992: 53).

For the editors of this book, globalization took on a more personal face several years ago when we took a group of students to Mexico. As we sat on a bus bound for the pyramids of Teotihuacán, just outside Mexico City, we met a Canadian named Jag. We learned on the bus ride that Jag was a Hindu from India who lived in Montreal. His job was to assist the newly formed Inuit (Eskimo) government of Nunavet, a new Canadian territory created through negotiations with the Canadian government. Think about it: a Hindu Indian living in French-speaking Montreal, assisting the Inuit government, and visiting a pyramid built by the Teotihuacán peoples, while vacationing in Mexico City—now that's globalization!

Technology is perhaps the most visible aspect of globalization and in many ways is its driving force. Communications technology has revolutionized our information systems. CNN reaches hundreds of millions of households in over 200 countries and territories throughout the world. "Computer, television, cable, satellite, laser, fiber-optic, and microchip technologies [along with nano- and cyber-technology are] combining to create a vast interactive communications and information network that can potentially give every person on earth access to every other person, and make every datum, every byte, available to every set of eyes" (Barber 1992: 58). Technology has also aided the increase in international trade and international capital flows and has enhanced the spread of Western, primarily US, culture.

Thomas Friedman, in his boldly titled bestseller *The World Is Flat,* argues that the world is undergoing its third phase of globalization: "Globalization 3.0 is shrinking the world from a size small to a size tiny and flattening the playing field at the same time" (2005: 10). Whereas globalization in the past was characterized by companies becoming more global, this third phase is unique due to "the newfound power for *individuals* to collaborate and compete globally" (2005: 10). For instance, radiologists in India and Australia interpret CAT-scan images from the United States, telephone operators in India answer calls for major US corporations, and Japanese-speakers at call centers in China serve Japanese customers. Thus the playing field is being leveled and individuals and small companies from all over the world, including poor countries, can now compete in the global economy.

We can see a similar phenomenon occurring with global conflict. Steven Pinker and Andres Mack (2014) have discovered that while the media may lead us to believe the world is increasingly violent, we are actually living in a relatively peaceful time. Similarly, Joshua Goldstein (2011) has noted that over recent decades, wars have been diminishing in number and war deaths have been decreasing. Goldstein argues that governments, "by participating in an international community, . . . jointly achieve some mutually beneficial outcomes that could not be realized separately. The reduction of war worldwide is one of those outcomes" (2011: 8). In part, Goldstein recognizes the importance of shared global values that widely reject war and human rights abuses. Both the strengthening of the international community and shared values are evidence of a shrinking, increasingly homogeneous world.

Of course, Earth is not literally shrinking (nor flat), but in light of the rate at which travel and communication speeds have increased, the world has in a sense become smaller. Many scholars assert that we are living in a qualitatively different time, in which humans are interconnected more than ever before: "There is a distinction between the contemporary experience of change and that of earlier generations: never before has change come so rapidly . . . on such a global scale, and with such global visibility" (CGG 1995: 12). Or as Friedman puts it: "There is something about the flattening of the world that is going to be qualitatively different from other such profound changes: the speed and breadth with which it is taking hold. . . . This flattening process is happening at warp speed and directly or indirectly touching a lot more people on the planet at once" (2005: 46).

This seemingly uncritical acceptance of the concept of globalization and a shrinking world is not without its critics, who point out that labor, trade, and capital moved at least as freely, if not more so, during the second half of the nineteenth century as they do now. Take, for example, the following quote, which focuses on the dramatic changes that have taken place in the past three decades to make the world more economically interdependent: "The complexity of modern finance makes New York dependent on London, London upon Paris, Paris upon Berlin, to a greater degree than has ever yet been the case in history. This interdependence is the result of the daily use of those contrivances of civilization . . . the instantaneous dissemination of financial and commercial information . . . and generally the incredible increase in the rapidity of communication" (Angell 1909: 44–45). If this statement were to appear in a newspaper today, no one would give it a second thought. But it was written at the start of the twentieth century—illustrating the belief of some critics that globalization is not a new phenomenon.

Some skeptics caution that while interdependence and technological advancement have increased in some parts of the world, this is not true for the vast majority of third world countries (the terms "third world," "the South," "developing world," and "less-developed countries" are used interchangeably throughout this book in reference to the poorer countries, in contrast to "first world," "the North," "developed world," and "more-developed countries" in reference to the United States, Canada, Western Europe, Japan, Australia, and New Zealand). For example, Hamid Mowlana argues that "global" is not "universal" (1995: 42). Although a small number of people in third world countries may have access to much of the new technology and truly live in the "global village," the large majority of populations in the South do not.

Research on global Internet usage illustrates this point. Table 1.1 shows findings from a survey of geographic regions of the world. Utilizing Internet usage as an indicator of globalization, the table clearly shows large disparities among regions. Notice that in Europe (73.5 percent), North America (87.9 percent), and Oceania/Australia (72.9 percent), a majority of the population uses the Internet. However, Africa (27.0 percent) and Asia (38.8 percent) stand in stark contrast. North Americans are over twice as likely to use the Internet as are Asians, and over three times more likely than Africans. These trends over the past decade indicate that Asia, the Middle East, and especially Africa are rapidly increasing their Internet usage (nearly 7,000 percent in fifteen years); however, the gap between North and South will take many years to close. In other words, globalization is far from universal when measured by Internet usage.

Table 1.1 World Internet Usage and Population Statistics, 2015

	Estimated Population, 2015 (millions)	Number of Internet Users, 2000 (millions)	Percentage Increase in Internet Usage, 2000–2015	Percentage of Population Who Use the Internet, 2015	Regional Users as Percentage of Worldwide Users, 2015
Africa	1,158.4	4.5	6,839.1	27.0	9.6
Asia	4,032.5	114.3	1,267.6	38.8	47.8
Europe	821.6	105.1	474.8	73.5	18.5
Middle East	236.1	3.3	3,426.1	49.0	3.5
North America	357.2	108.1	190.4	87.9	9.6
Latin America and Caribbean	617.8	18.1	1,743.6	53.9	10.2
Oceania and Australia	37.2	7.6	255.6	72.9	0.8
Total	7,260.6	361.0	806.0	45.0	100.0

Source: IWS (2015).

Similarly, one can argue that the increased flow of information, a characteristic of globalization, goes primarily in one direction. Even those in the South who have access to television or radio are at a disadvantage. The globalization of communication in the less-developed countries typically is a one-way proposition: the people do not control any of the information; they only receive it. It is also true that, worldwide, the ability to control or generate broadcasts rests in the hands of a tiny minority.

While lack of financial resources is an important impediment to globalization, there are other obstacles. Paradoxically, Benjamin Barber (1992), who argues that we are experiencing global integration via "McDonaldization," asserts we are at the same time experiencing global disintegration. He cites the breakup of the Soviet Union and Yugoslavia, as well as the many other ethnic and national conflicts (see Chapter 4), as evidence of the forces countering globalization. Many subnational groups (groups within nations) desire to govern themselves; others see threats to their religious values and identity and therefore reject the secular nature of globalization. As a result, Hamid Mowlana argues that globalization "has produced not uniformity, but a yearning for a return to non-secular values. Today, there is a rebirth of revitalized fundamentalism in all the world's major religions, whether Islam, Christianity, Judaism, Shintoism, or Confucianism. At the same time the global homogeneity has reached the airwaves, these religious tenets have reemerged as defining identities" (1995: 46).

None of these criticisms mean that our contemporary world is not now different in some important aspects. There is widespread agreement that communications, trade, and capital are moving at unprecedented speed and volume. However, these criticisms do provide an important warning against overstating or making broad generalizations about the processes and effects of globalization.

Is Globalization Good or Bad?

There are some aspects of globalization that most will agree are good (for example, the spread of medical technology) or bad (for example, increased global trade in illegal drugs). The same technology that connects people throughout the world for good causes, such as the transmission of valuable healthcare products and information, also enables groups like ISIS to recruit via social media. Given globalization's complexity, it is useful to try to analyze the concept by considering different types of globalization.

Table 1.2 identifies three areas that are affected by globalization—political, economic, and cultural—and gives examples of positive and negative aspects of globalization. A key aspect of political globalization is the weakened ability of the state to control both what crosses its borders and

Table 1.2 Advantages and Disadvantages of Globalization

Effects of Globalization	Advantages	Disadvantages
Political	Weakens power of authoritarian governments	Unwanted external influence difficult to keep out
Economic	Jobs, capital, more choices for consumers	Exploitative; only benefits a few; gap between rich and poor
Cultural	Offers exposure to other cultures	Cultural imperialism

what happens inside them. In other words, globalization can reduce the state's sovereignty (its ability to govern matters within its borders). This can be viewed as good, because undemocratic governments are finding it increasingly difficult to control the flow of information to and from pro-democracy groups. Satellite television and the Internet in particular have eroded state sovereignty. But decreased sovereignty also means that the state has difficulty controlling the influx of illegal drugs and unwanted immigrants, including terrorists.

In the realm of economics, increased globalization has given consumers more choices. Also, multinational corporations are creating jobs in poor areas where people never before had such opportunities. Some critics reject these points, arguing that increased foreign investment and trade benefit only a small group of wealthy individuals and that, as a result, the gap between rich and poor grows both within countries and between countries. These critics point out that the combined wealth of the fifteen richest people in the world is more than the gross domestic product (the total goods and services produced in a given year) of sub-Saharan Africa (Parker 2002). Related to this is the argument that many well-paying, blue-collar jobs are moving from the North to the poor countries of Latin America, Africa, and Asia.

At the cultural level, those who view increased cultural contact as positive say that it gives people more opportunities to learn about (and purchase goods from) other cultures. But critics of cultural globalization see things differently. Samuel Huntington (1998) has argued that the shrinking world will bring a "clash of civilizations." In this scenario, clashes will occur among many civilizations, including the largely Christian West against Islam. Other critics are concerned with cultural imperialism, in which dominant groups (primarily wealthy countries) force their culture on others. A primary tool of cultural influence is the North's multibillion-dollar advertising budgets used to influence and to some extent destroy non-Western cultures. The fear of cultural imperialism is certainly a key component in the animosity of some Arabs toward the United States. Other critics are increasingly fearful that more and more national and minority languages will become extinct as foreign languages, especially English, penetrate borders. In response to cultural influences, countries like Iran have banned Western music from government radio and television stations in an attempt to stop unwanted outside influences. Even Western countries like France have adopted policies to regulate unwanted foreign cultural influences.

The degree to which cultural values can be "exported" is the subject of some debate. Huntington argues that "drinking Coca-Cola does not make Russians think like Americans any more than eating sushi makes Americans think like Japanese. Throughout human history, fads and material goods have spread from one society to another without significantly altering the basic culture of the recipient society" (1996: 28–29). Similarly, others, such as Hamid Mowlana, argue that globalization brings only superficial change: "McDonald's may be in nearly every country, but in Japan, sushi is served alongside hamburgers. In many countries, hamburgers are not even on the menu" (1995: 46). Thus the global product is often altered to take on a local flavor. The term "glocalization" has combined the words *global* and *local* to describe such hybrid products.

In sum, globalization offers a multitude of advantages to people throughout the world, from greater wealth to more choices in consumer products. At the same time, globalization exposes people to greater vulnerability and insecurity. Our jobs become less secure, diseases travel faster, and traditional family structures are weakened (Kirby 2006). It is left to the reader to determine whether globalization is having a positive or negative effect on the issues discussed in this book. Is globalization enhancing human capacity to deal with a particular problem? Or is it making it more difficult? Of course, each individual's perspective will be influenced by whether he or she evaluates these issues based on self-interest, national interest, a religious view, or a global humanitarian viewpoint. Readers must decide, based on what is most important to them, how to evaluate moral questions of good versus bad. For example, when considering the issue of free trade (Chapter 10), those concerned first and foremost with self-interest will ask, "How does free trade affect me?" For nationalist readers, the question will be, "How does free trade affect my country?" For religious readers, the question will be, "How does my religion instruct me on this issue?" Finally, global humanitarians will ask, "What is best for humanity in general?"

Interconnectedness Among Issues

As mentioned earlier, a primary purpose of this book is to explore the interconnectedness of the various issues discussed here. For example, the chapter on poverty should not be considered separate from the chapter on population, even though these two issues are treated separately. Here are several examples of how issues discussed in this book are interconnected:

- The growth in the world's population (Chapter 12) has been significantly affected, especially in Africa, by the AIDS crisis (Chapter 7).
- Many of the value judgments concerning trade issues (Chapter 10) are intricately linked to human rights issues (Chapter 5).
- Ethnic conflict (Chapter 4) (as well as other types of conflict) often leads to internal migration as well as international population movements (Chapter 12).
- One of the recommendations for reducing poverty (Chapter 11) is to educate women and give them more decisionmaking power over their lives (Chapter 13).
- Climate change (Chapter 15) is expected to have increasingly negative effects on health (Chapter 7), migration (Chapter 12), and conflict (Chapter 2).

The interconnectedness of these issues is even more extensive than these examples demonstrate. The recent events surrounding ISIS provide an appropriate case study. In 2014, reports came from Iraq and Syria about a ruthless terror group inspired by radical Islamic beliefs. This more radicalized offshoot of al-Qaeda sought to establish an Islamic-based country, or more specifically a caliphate, in the territory currently in the countries of Iraq and Syria. To some extent, the emergence of ISIS was enabled by the US invasion of Iraq in 2003 and the civil war in Syria. This civil war pits the leader of Syria, Bashar al-Assad, against diverse groups of rebels seeking to remove Assad from power. The civil war in Syria and the emergence of ISIS has led many countries to take sides. For instance, Iran and Russia support the Assad regime, while the United States and several Middle Eastern countries have offered varying degrees of support to rebels seeking to oust Assad.

Meanwhile, hundreds of thousands of refugees are flooding out of the region and seeking safe harbor in North Africa, Europe, North America, and elsewhere. In addition, millions of people are displaced within Iraq and Syria. It is believed that there are currently more refugees in the world than at any time since World War II (Nordland 2015). These refugees are subject to a host of related issues. Many have been relegated to refugee camps consisting of thousands of makeshift tents. Unfortunately, these camps often do not have adequate sanitation or access to clean water. Health officials point out that crowded conditions can lead to the spread of diseases like measles, typhoid, cholera, and polio. "High numbers of unvaccinated, malnourished people combined with unsanitary living conditions makes outbreaks among refugee populations very likely" (Welch 2015).

Unfortunately, governments and people of many of the host countries are reluctant or even vehemently opposed to allowing Middle Eastern refugees into their countries. The issues range from financial issues within the host country, to the fear that ISIS fighters may pose as refugees, to outright anti-Islamic feelings. Some European nations have even been accused of human rights violations against Middle Eastern refugees. For instance, the United Nations has accused the Czech Republic of human rights violations against migrants and refugees in an effort to dissuade them from entering the country (Calamur 2015).

This brief description of the catastrophic events surrounding the Syrian civil war and the emergence of ISIS reveals a network of interconnected events that, for the purposes of this book, are described in different chapters. Chapter 2, which discusses threats to global security and the changing nature of war away from *inter*state (war between countries) to *intra*state war (war within countries) is a natural home for cases like this one. Yet the nature of this issue extends beyond a single chapter. Chapter 12 addresses the issue of migration and refugees, while issues of poverty (Chapter 11), health (Chapter 7), and human rights (Chapter 5) are each discussed in separate chapters. Chapter 4 delves into how nationalism can pit one group against another—seen in the anti-immigrant sentiment just mentioned. Less visible in the Syrian civil war case is the connection to environment. Yet some observers argue that not only can we expect to see future increases in refugees due to climate change and extreme weather (see Chapters 6 and 15), but even argue that climate change is a contributing factor to the current refugee crisis (Baker 2015). Globalization (discussed in all chapters of this book) plays a significant role in many aspects of this case. For instance, globalization facilitates transportation and rescue attempts of refugees, as well as the communications ability of virtually all parties involved in the refugee situation. As mentioned earlier, increased communications speed due to globalization can be used for good and evil purposes. On the one hand, ISIS has been able to recruit fighters abroad more effectively through its savvy use of social media, but, in a humorous twist, hackers have used the same technology to ridicule ISIS by replacing its website with an advertisement for Viagra, the sex-enhancing drug (Chang 2015). In sum, readers should remember that even though the issues in this book are treated in separate chapters, many of them are inextricably linked.

Key Players

Of the key players or actors involved in these global issues, the most salient are countries. In the following pages, you will continually read about the countries of the world and their efforts to solve these various global issues.

Often, countries get together and form international governmental organizations (IGOs). The logic is that by cooperating through an IGO—like the United Nations, the World Bank, or the UN Children's Fund (UNICEF)—countries are better equipped to achieve a common goal, like preventing war or alleviating poverty, that they could not accomplish on their own. Goldstein (2011) argues that the UN's peacekeeping efforts have been a central factor in reducing war over the past few decades. The reader will notice that IGOs—especially the United Nations and its new Millennium Development Goals—are also mentioned throughout the book.

Nongovernmental organizations (NGOs) working on global issues are part of what is called civil society. For instance, in recent decades there has been a dramatic increase in the number of NGOs seeking to make the world a better place (NGOs are sometimes referred to as international nongovernmental organizations [INGOs]). NGOs, as their name implies, work outside the government and comprise individual citizens working together on one or more problems. There are many well-known NGOs working on global issues: the Red Cross, Greenpeace, Amnesty International, World Vision, and Doctors Without Borders are just a few of the thousands that exist. Because these NGOs are often made up of highly motivated people in the middle of a war or refugee camp, they can often achieve results that countries cannot. NGOs have become extremely active on all of the issues discussed in this book, and they often cooperate with IGOs and individual countries.

Other nongovernmental actors include businesses, often referred to as transnational corporations (TNCs). Nike, Apple, Toyota, and many other TNCs have gained increasing power in recent years to affect global issues. Many critics complain that, due to their economic strength and global networks, TNCs exercise too much power.

Celebrities can also play a role in resolving the global issues discussed in this book. A high-profile example was the 2015 Global Citizens Festival, which featured celebrities such as Beyoncé, Ed Sheeran, Pearl Jam, and Coldplay. The festival sought to raise money for several issues discussed in this book, including women's rights, hunger, and sustainable development. It is interesting to note that these celebrities partnered with some of the international organizations mentioned here. For instance, some of the well-known NGOs that partnered with the festival were CARE, KIVA, Heifer International, The Hunger Project, Oxfam, and UNICEF. IGOs such as the UN High Commissioner for Refugees (UNHCR) and the World Bank also supported the event. Transnational corporations such as Google and YouTube provided financial sponsorship.

Finally, individuals can have an impact on global issues as well. Leymah Gbowee provides an excellent example. Born in Liberia, Gbowee had a relatively unremarkable early life. However, as a teenager she experienced the first Liberian civil war. As the war drew to a close, she took part in a trauma-healing seminar sponsored by UNICEF. She later became a peace activist and led Muslim and Christian women in nonviolent, antiwar demonstrations. The protests gathered women in markets to pray and sing. She was also part of other creative nonviolent actions. For instance, in 2003, Gbowee and other women made their way into the hotel where Liberian leaders were holding peace talks. When the delegates tried to leave, the demonstrators blocked their exit and threatened to remove their own clothes. Since seeing an older or married woman naked is a great curse in their culture, the men remained in the hotel and continued negotiating. Based on these and other actions for peace in Liberia, Gbowee was a co-recipient of the Nobel Peace Prize in 2011.

Similarly, Malala Yousafzai, a Pakistani teenager, has raised attention and support for the rights of girls to receive an education. Her outspoken support of this human rights cause led a gunman from the Taliban to shoot Malala in the face. After many months of recovery, Malala continued her fight for the rights of girls and built an international movement. In 2014, at the age of seventeen, Malala became the youngest person ever to receive the Nobel Peace Prize. Several more examples of individuals like Gbowee and Malala, working to resolve various global issues, can be found in the following chapters.

Outline of the Book

This book is organized into three parts. Part 1 focuses on various dimensions of conflict and security. It considers some of the primary sources of conflict, such as weapons of mass destruction, nationalism, terrorism, and human rights abuses, as well as conflict over food security, health, and natural resources. The rationale for a broad view of "global security" is laid out in Chapter 2. Part 2 takes a broad view of the global political economy by including economic issues as well as social and environmental concerns. The content includes chapters on international capital flows, international trade, poverty, population and migration, the role of women in development, sustainable development, and climate change. Part 3 discusses possible future world orders, sources of hope, challenges in the coming decades, and innovative actions that are being taken to make a positive impact on global issues.

Discussion Questions

1. What examples of globalization can you identify in your life?
2. Do you think globalization will continue to increase? If so, in what areas?

3. Do you think globalization has more positive attributes or more negative attributes?

4. From which perspective (individual, national, religious, global humanitarian) do you tend to view global issues?

5. Can you think of additional examples of how the global issues discussed in different chapters are interconnected?

Suggested Readings

Barber, Benjamin R. (1996) *Jihad vs. McWorld.* New York: Ballantine.

Friedman, Thomas L. (2000) *The Lexus and the Olive Tree: Understanding Globalization.* New York: Anchor.

——— (2005) *The World Is Flat: A Brief History of the Twenty-First Century.* New York: Farrar, Straus, and Giroux.

Goldstein, Joshua S. (2011) *Winning the War on War: The Decline of Armed Conflict Worldwide.* New York: Dutton.

Iyer, Pico (2001) *The Global Soul: Jet Lag, Shopping Malls, and the Search for Home.* New York: Vintage.

Kirby, Peadar (2006) *Vulnerability and Violence: The Impact of Globalization.* Ann Arbor: Pluto.

Pinker, Steven (2011) *Better Angels of Our Nature.* New York: Viking.

Smith, Dan (2008) *The Penguin State of the World Atlas.* New York: Penguin.

Steger, Manfred (2009) *Globalization: A Very Short Introduction.* New York: Oxford University Press.

United Nations Development Programme (annual) *Human Development Report.* New York: Oxford University Press.

World Bank (annual) *World Development Indicators.* New York: Oxford University Press.

Worldwatch Institute (annual) *State of the World.* New York: Norton.

Part 1

Dimensions of Conflict and Security

2

Global Security: Old Issues, New Realities

Jeffrey S. Lantis and Michael T. Snarr

HUMAN HISTORY HAS BEEN MARKED BY BOTH TREMENDOUS ACCOMplishments and violent conflicts. Governments have launched astronauts into space, harnessed the power of water, wind, and sun for renewable energies, and worked through international organizations to help eradicate deadly diseases. At the same time, however, billions of people have suffered in militarized conflicts throughout recorded history. More than 200 million people died from wars and war-related causes in the twentieth century alone (Leitenberg 2011). This grim reality shows few signs of subsiding as conflicts rage on in countries such as Syria, Afghanistan, and the Democratic Republic of Congo.

This chapter establishes foundations for a broad exploration of global security in the twenty-first century. Just as warfare has evolved over time, so too have approaches to preventing conflicts. Historically, governments have focused on narrow national security approaches to war and war prevention. Yet with the end of the Cold War and increasing globalization, there have been more calls from policymakers, scholars, nongovernmental organizations, and even some in the military to pursue a security agenda that is more attentive to how people are affected by transnational threats to human health and prosperity. This approach, referred to as "human security," suggests a much broader view of security that addresses how people are affected by issues such as poverty, human rights abuses, and environmental degradation.

This chapter begins by exploring key actors involved in contemporary security issues. Next, historical approaches to security are examined, with a special emphasis on an emerging, broader focus on new dimensions of human security. Finally, the chapter explores current issues in security through case studies of the transnational threat of terrorism, autonomous weapons (killer robots), and cyber-security.

Key Actors

Global security is a multifaceted term. In the twenty-first century, our conception of global security recognizes a role for a variety of actors, including states (or countries), alliances, regional organizations, trade blocs, and international governmental organizations. This section highlights the rise of several of these actors over time as well as implications of their development for global politics.

Global security constitutes efforts by countries of the world to reduce conflict as well as promote individual prosperity. Global security can perhaps best be understood by contrasting it to state security. State security, which narrowly focuses on the security of countries, dates back to the evolution of the Westphalian political order, following the Thirty Years' War in Europe (1618–1648). This war pitted religious and political units against one another in a devastating conflict that swept across the continent. One of the central issues that sparked the war was whether kings and princes had the right to establish their own religious and political orders in their lands, or whether they should remain beholden to the Catholic Church. The groups fighting for more state autonomy won the conflict, and European leaders signed the Treaty of Westphalia to establish a new political order to ensure greater peace and stability in Europe.

Sovereignty became the cornerstone of state security after 1648. Sovereignty is the right of leaders to determine the rules, laws, and processes of civil society in their own territories. State security has become synonymous with the use of force (or the threat of the use of force) to regulate populations and to project power. Military capability and economic resources are often the primary measures of power in a state security model. Leaders seek to accumulate and hold on to these resources in a competitive, anarchic international system.

States do not stand alone in global politics, of course. Alliances also can help enhance state security. These are formal military relationships between two or more countries that typically include a mutual defense pact if one party comes under attack. Examples of military alliances in the twentieth century include the North Atlantic Treaty Organization (NATO) and the Southeast Asian Treaty Organization (SEATO). NATO was founded in 1949 to promote security cooperation between Canada, the United States, and Western European allies. Today, NATO has twenty-eight member states that engage in joint military planning and training for a variety of contingencies. The United States also helped form SEATO during the Cold War, an alliance that brought together the United Kingdom, France, Australia, New Zealand, Thailand, Pakistan, and the Philippines. In 1996, China spearheaded the creation of the Shanghai Cooperation Organization, an alliance with Russia and other former Soviet republics designed to counterbalance NATO expansion (Pressman 2008).

In addition, states have entered into trade pacts to promote economic well-being and maximize their power. Classic examples of trade arrangements include the modern-day European Union, which began as a customs union in the early years of the Cold War, and steadily expanded its membership and scope of activities. The Soviet Union also formed an economic trading bloc among its client states during the Cold War. Following their independence, a number of West African states formerly under British and French colonial rule established the Economic Community of West African States (ECOWAS). The North American Free Trade Agreement (NAFTA) was created in 1993 with the goal of elimination of tariff barriers to trade among Mexico, Canada, and the United States. In 2015, the United States negotiated the Trans-Pacific Partnership with Australia, Canada, Mexico, Japan, and several other Pacific Rim countries. Finally, states have established hundreds of international governmental organizations (IGOs) to promote cooperation in nearly every issue area imaginable. Some of the first IGOs were created for functional reasons, such as easing navigation on European waterways (the Danube River Commission of 1856) and establishing standards for international communication by telegraph (the International Telegraph Union of 1865).

The United Nations represents one of the strongest IGOs ever created. It was established in 1945 and comprises nearly 200 member states representing nearly every country in the world today. The UN was founded on the principle of collective security, an all-for-one security agreement implying a commitment for all member states to come to the aid of any member that is threatened. That is, any member state that experiences a violation of its sovereignty has the right to request the United Nations to come to its aid in a collective security operation. This arrangement also promotes a collective sense of security—members of the UN are committed to a broader definition of security than simply safety within their own borders. Global interests become state interests in this way.

The UN system operates on primary principles established in its Charter in 1945. A central focus of the UN is "maintaining peace and security," though it was also created to promote other principles, including human rights, self-determination, and economic development. With respect to conflict resolution, Chapter VI of the UN Charter requires critical disputes to be resolved through nonviolent means such as mediation, negotiation, or judicial settlement. If the conflict is not resolved, it can be referred to the UN General Assembly, which in turn makes nonbinding recommendations.

Chapter VII of the Charter gives the Security Council the ability to "restore international peace and security." In particular, Article 42 provides for UN military action, and Article 51 gives the Security Council responsibility "to take at any time such action as it deems necessary in order to maintain or restore international peace and security."

The UN comprises five principal organs, some with a more direct role in global security than others. All countries are members of the General Assembly, and each country possesses one vote. The General Assembly applies moral pressure on countries by passing resolutions; however, these resolutions are "nonbinding." In other words, the General Assembly cannot force countries to change their behavior.

In contrast, the second principal organ, the Security Council, wields coercive power. The Security Council comprises five permanent members—China, France, Russia, the United Kingdom, and the United States—plus ten nonpermanent, rotating members. The Security Council, as its name implies, focuses on issues of international peace and security. It is the only UN organ that can authorize military force. The permanent five (P-5) each have veto power and can block any Security Council action. Although the veto has stopped numerous Security Council actions in the history of the UN, the idea behind the veto is that the Security Council should have the full backing of the most powerful countries before recommending military action against a country or countries. Because this veto concept dates back to the founding of the UN in 1945, many have criticized the makeup of the P-5 as outdated. For instance, countries like Brazil and India have shown strong interest in joining this select group. It should be noted how active the Security Council is in the realm of global security. In 2014 alone, the Security Council dealt with conflict in several African and Middle Eastern countries, Iranian nuclear proliferation, and the Ebola outbreak, just to name a few.

Nongovernmental organizations (NGOs) also deserve a great deal of recognition in international relations today. NGOs working on global security issues have proliferated over the past few decades and have gained increasing stature. These organizations address all aspects of global security, from conflict reduction to nuclear nonproliferation to human rights issues to environmental security.

Some important global security (and human security) NGOs include the Friends Committee on National Legislation (conflict resolution and other issues), Doctors Without Borders (health), Amnesty International (human rights), and Oxfam (poverty and development). Global Zero, a relatively new NGO seeking to rid the world of nuclear weapons, has also generated a great deal of public support and attention. As noted earlier, many of these groups have been enabled to play a greater role in global security due to increasing communication speed (e.g., via e-mail and social media groups) and enhanced technology (e.g., webcameras, satellite phones, and smartphones).

Historical Approaches

Global security has involved both tragic conflicts and the progressive evolution of the global political agenda toward greater attention to the human condition.

The World Wars

Events of the twentieth century helped shape our modern conception of global security. World War I (1914–1918) was a catastrophic war that led to the collapse of major empires and a shift in the balance of power. Germany, the Austro-Hungarian Empire, and the Ottoman Empire aligned against allied powers including Great Britain, France, and Russia. The war included a series of major battles in Eastern Europe, the Balkans, the Mediterranean, North Africa, and Northern Europe. World War I ground to a bloody stalemate in trench warfare on the plains of Northern Europe, and bitter battles were fought over a few hundred meters of ground in the fields. States also introduced modern instruments of war such as chemical weapons (extensive use of mustard gas), machine guns, submarines, and tanks. In all, more than 9 million soldiers were killed during World War I.

World leaders gathered at the Palace of Versailles after the war to design a new blueprint for international cooperation. Among the initiatives for peace were plans for the readjustment of territories after the collapse of several empires across Eurasia, reparations to be paid by Germany, and the establishment of the League of Nations. While the primary focus remained traditional security, US president Woodrow Wilson also called for the principle of self-determination for all peoples, a theme that seemed to recognize critical concerns of the human condition. Unfortunately, Wilson was unable to secure ratification of the Treaty of Versailles and the League plan from an isolationist US Senate. For this and other reasons, the League lost a great deal of its legitimacy in the decade after World War I.

If modern warfare emerged in the first world war, the second major conflict in the twentieth century saw it rise to a terrifying level of maturity. The prelude to World War II came in the 1930s when Adolf Hitler of the National Socialist (Nazi) Party was elected chancellor of Germany and immediately began consolidating his authoritarian rule. Along with military allies Japan and Italy, the German "Third Reich" began its march to expand territory and influence across Europe, the Mediterranean, and North Africa. World War II officially began in Europe in 1939 when Nazi troops invaded Poland. In response, Great Britain and France declared war on Germany.

The United States joined the war after Japan's surprise attack on Pearl Harbor in December 1941, and by the end of hostilities in 1945 conflict had raged across five continents.

A major outcome of World War II was a weakening of traditional European powers. For example, France lost 500,000 soldiers and civilians and was occupied by Nazi forces for nearly five years. France's capitulation in World War II foreshadowed its loss of power and influence through the disintegration of its colonial empire after the war. Great Britain also lost 400,000 soldiers and civilians, but the psychological impact of the bitter struggle of war, the daily bombardment of London, and the fight against Nazi Germany revealed cracks in the British Empire. Germany lost more than 5 million soldiers and civilians. The Soviet Union suffered the greatest number of casualties, with nearly 20 million killed.

Casualty statistics illustrate another outcome of the war: greater attention to the human condition. World leaders recognized that major conflicts had devastating consequences for civilians as well. The international community was especially horrified by the Holocaust, an extermination campaign against Jews carried out by Nazi Germany that led to more than 6 million deaths. Governments organized massive relief operations for civilian refugees at the end of the war, and leaders came together in the following years to pass international conventions that prohibited genocide (the UN's Convention Against Genocide), promoted human rights (the UN's Universal Declaration of Human Rights), and protected prisoners of war and noncombatants (the Geneva Conventions).

The United States was the only great power whose home territory was left relatively unscathed by the war. In fact, the war was a catalyst for rapid economic development for the country. The United States also rose as a superpower after World War II due to the development of the atomic bomb. President Harry Truman ordered the dropping of two atomic bombs on Japan—the first on Hiroshima on August 6, 1945, the second on Nagasaki on August 9, 1945. After the war, possession of "the bomb" became a symbol of power, and a number of regimes strove to develop their own nuclear weapons. To the victims of the atomic bombings and the millions of citizens who lived under the shadow of the threat of nuclear attack in the decades to come, though, these weapons were a symbol of fear as well as a direct challenge to the human condition.

Cold War Security Imperatives

At the end of World War II, the wartime alliance fractured into two new rival blocs. On one side stood the United States, Great Britain, and allies in Western Europe (including the Western-allied zone of occupied Germany). On the other side stood the Soviet Union and client states (along with the Eastern-allied zone of occupied Germany). The capital of conquered Germany,

Berlin, was divided between East and West. Winston Churchill described an "Iron Curtain" that had descended across Europe. The United States and its allies formalized their military alliance in NATO and began economic reconstruction after the war. The Soviet Union established its own Warsaw Pact alliance, promoted economic reconstruction in some areas of devastated Eastern Europe, and began to order the region into a centrally planned economy. Meanwhile, both sides maintained hundreds of thousands of troops in the region, standing "toe-to-toe" in Berlin and beyond.

While the Cold War never led to a direct war between the superpowers in Europe (where many expected hostilities to break out), several major conflicts occurred on the periphery. The US commitment to South Korea—as well as the UN commitment to collective security—was tested by communist North Korea's invasion of South Korea in June 1950. The United States went to the United Nations for endorsement of a collective military response to this aggression and violation of sovereignty. US general Douglas MacArthur led an international military coalition to roll back the invasion, and conflict raged on the peninsula for nearly four years.

Another war soon erupted, this time in Indochina. A former French colony, Vietnam, was divided between north and south. Communist forces dominated the north, while the south was an ally of the United States. The Vietnam War simmered in the late 1950s and broke out into a major conflict in the mid-1960s. President Lyndon Johnson ordered the deployment of hundreds of thousands of US soldiers. The Vietnam War led to the death of more than 58,000 US soldiers. It eventually came to a close in 1975 when North Vietnamese forces took Saigon and unified the country.

Post–Cold War Security Frames

The Cold War ended when the Soviet bloc disintegrated in the late 1980s and early 1990s. The beginning of the end came with Mikhail Gorbachev's ascension to power in the Soviet Union in March 1985. Unlike his predecessors, Gorbachev recognized that the Soviet economy could no longer sustain the commitment to an expensive arms race with the United States. He believed that economic reforms and political liberalization were critical to the survival of the Soviet Union. Indeed, one could say that Gorbachev recognized that the needs of the human condition of Soviet citizens might outweigh the country's military agenda. Meanwhile, US president Ronald Reagan, the leader who had expressed his deep opposition to Soviet communism and labeled the country the "Evil Empire," saw an opportunity to improve relations. In 1986, Reagan and Gorbachev discussed the idea of completely eliminating nuclear weapons from their military arsenals. In 1987 they agreed to the Intermediate-Range Nuclear Forces Treaty, which eliminated an entire class of nuclear missiles from both sides and significantly stabilized the balance of power in Europe.

The late 1980s brought revolutionary changes to Eastern Europe with the collapse of the Soviet empire and transitions to democracy in many states. The George H. W. Bush administration was given an unprecedented opportunity to influence the new international order. While the president did achieve new arms control agreements with Russia, his presidency became focused on military engagements in Latin America and the Middle East. In August 1990 the Iraqi army, under the leadership of President Saddam Hussein, invaded and occupied Kuwait. Kuwait was a major oil-producing state and ally of many Western countries. The United States and the international community roundly condemned these actions as inflammatory. In November 1990 the UN Security Council issued an ultimatum to Hussein to withdraw Iraqi forces from Kuwait by January 15, 1991, or face military sanctions. That deadline passed unheeded, and Operation Desert Storm, a large-scale air and ground operation to liberate Kuwait, was launched. The first conflict of the "post–Cold War era" ended in February 1991. Unfortunately, the United States would be involved in Iraqi affairs, on and off, for decades.

The United Nations was another key actor in promoting global security in the twentieth century. UN peacekeeping operations began in the late 1940s and helped stabilize many hotspots, including Israel/Palestine, the Balkans, and the India-Pakistan border. Peacekeepers are neutral third parties sent by the United Nations to inhibit conflict by fulfilling one of two roles: as observers or as peacekeepers. In the former role, the UN deploys mostly unarmed observers from other countries who report violations of cease-fires. Peacekeepers can be tasked to separate warring combatants and help stabilize regional security challenges enough to foster negotiated settlements. These troops are usually lightly armed and authorized to use their weapons in self-defense. UN peacekeepers are often referred to as "blue helmets," a symbolic reference to their representation of the United Nations (and a direct reference to the color of their helmets and flag). Peacekeeping missions are authorized by the UN Security Council, and their operations are given consent by the host government and other key actors. As of 2015, over 90,000 peacekeeping troops and military observers were in the field taking part in sixteen different peacekeeping missions (UN n.d.).

Over time the role of UN peacekeepers has evolved to include more expansive responsibilities. In addition to being a relatively reactive third party with a mission to prevent outbreaks of violence, newer peace*making* operations have been ordered to provide humanitarian relief in war-torn regions, monitor elections, demilitarize combatants, and help rebuild post-conflict government institutions. In 2011, there were more than a dozen active UN peacekeeping operations.

In 1993, Bill Clinton became the first truly post–Cold War president. While Clinton preferred to focus on domestic policy priorities, his administration was forced to confront a series of foreign policy challenges. Many of them were based on a much broader notion of security than in the past. Some rivalries and political divisions had faded, leading the great powers and the United Nations to realize new opportunities for action. For the Clinton administration, confronting civil war and starvation in Somalia became one of the first missions of post–Cold War security order. In 1991, with the Somali government no longer in control of the country, the first United Nations Operation in Somalia (UNOSOM I), comprising 500 peacekeepers, was deployed. When it became apparent that lightly armed peacekeepers were no match for the local warlords, President George H. W. Bush sent 25,000 US troops to intervene and help secure food delivery. In 1993, Clinton extended Bush's military deployment in Somalia and turned the operation over to the United Nations. The mandate of the UNOSOM II mission was broader than that of most peacekeeping operations historically. Not only did it address humanitarian relief, but it also sought to hunt down the warlords perpetrating the violence. Clinton and other world leaders were adopting a wider frame for a new security order.

Another conflict was also raging in the former Yugoslavia, and European and US leaders wrestled with questions of when to intervene in ethnic conflicts that might include human rights violations. In 1992, the Security Council authorized the United Nations Protection Force for Yugoslavia (UNPROFOR), which, like the UNOSOM II operation, had a wide mandate. In addition to protecting ethnic minorities, UNPROFOR sought to "maintain a ceasefire, disband and demilitarize armed forces (both regular and irregular), ensure protection of basic human rights, and assist humanitarian agencies in returning refugees to their homes" (Mingst and Karns 2000: 98). As the civil war expanded, the UN intervention deepened as NATO air strikes supported the security operation in the former Yugoslavia. The participation of NATO marked the first time UN peacekeepers joined efforts with another IGO in a military alliance.

President George W. Bush faced similar challenges of global security following the September 11, 2001, terrorist attack in the United States. Those events prompted many to revisit traditional notions of security. Suddenly, innocent civilians inside the United States could be victims of terror attacks perpetrated by nonstate actors. The Bush administration authorized a new, more aggressive and proactive security posture that included a willingness to preemptively strike potential adversaries anywhere in the world. In the fall of 2001, an allied coalition invaded Afghanistan and overthrew the Taliban regime. In March 2003, the United States led an invasion of Iraq and overthrew the Baathist government led by Saddam Hussein. President Barack Obama, who assumed office in 2009, inherited the responsibility of these two wars—as well as the broader commitment to global security encompassed by the war on terror.

From State Security to Human Security

In the past, the term *security* primarily focused on national security or countries protecting themselves from external threats. The primary focus for policymakers (and most academic research) was on the state and military protection from foreign attacks. As the preceding discussion has shown, though, traditional definitions of security began to evolve toward a broader notion of "human security."

To be sure, the concept of human security was not new—the end of the Cold War enhanced the visibility of issues like human rights, the environment, and health. These increasingly became regarded as constituting security issues. Several factors are responsible for this broadened notion of security. First, policymakers and concerned citizens began to critically reexamine why the world tried to ignore the conflicts in Rwanda and the former Yugoslavia in the early 1990s. The genocide in Rwanda involved the massacre of more than 800,000 people in a three-month period in 1994. Ethnic cleansing in the former Yugoslavia in the early 1990s killed hundreds of thousands and displaced millions more. These were not "traditional" conflicts in the sense of great wars of empire; rather, they were internal struggles that produced mass civilian casualties and shocked the world into recognition of contemporary, multifaceted security challenges. In neither of these conflicts did a country come under attack from an external country, and so the world largely sat on the sidelines and watched the conflicts play out. Additional *internal* wars include those in Syria, Iraq, and Yemen. The devastating results have since prompted critical scrutiny. The increased importance of actors other than states has prompted a shift in thinking about security. Historically, a country's military and its size and strength were the primary factors considered in the security equation. Yet today, nongovernmental organizations are playing an increased role in security issues. Other nonstate actors, such as terrorist groups, also have come to the forefront of global security concerns as the rise of global terrorism has shifted the state-centered focus of security. Terrorist groups like al-Qaeda and the Islamic State (IS), also known as the Islamic State of Iraq and al-Sham (ISIS), represent a transnational network of cells spread across many states.

Many policymakers and analysts contend that the contemporary security situation is not zero-sum. In contrast to traditional security frames that minimize the role of shared interests and cooperation between states, experts on human security argue that since a civil war in one country can lead to a refugee crisis in a neighboring country, or that an outbreak of a given disease in one country can spread to other countries (not just neighboring countries), security is increasingly seen as interconnected. Simply put, countries are all in this together. Adopting such a perspective should lead to greater cooperation through international institutions, like the United Nations.

In addition, globalization is closely linked to new security frames. Globalization affords security actors greater access to technology, including greater communication and travel speed. This enables the potential for greater cooperation on these issues, and offers nonstate actors the ability to have greater impact. Globalization by its nature also facilitates the spread of diseases, enables refugees and migrants to travel farther and faster, and brings the attention of more people to human rights violations around the world.

Another important shift in thinking about security is the result of more practitioners, scholars, and policymakers acknowledging the importance of nonmilitary threats to security, including human rights abuses, environmental degradation (especially climate change), health issues, migration flows, overpopulation, poverty, and the like. Here the concepts of "negative security" and "positive security" capture the difference between national security and human security, with the former often referring to a lack of war or external threats and the latter placing more emphasis on human rights and the meeting of basic human needs like food, clean water, and healthcare. This emerging frame of human security was given clarity in the UN's 1994 *Human Development Report,* which encouraged moving "from an exclusive stress on territorial security to a much greater stress on people's security" and "from security through armaments to security through sustainable human development" (UNDP 1994: 24). While there is no agreement on a single definition for human security, the report gave a compelling description of its nature: "In the final analysis, human security is a child who did not die, a disease that did not spread, a job that was not cut, an ethnic tension that did not explode in violence, a dissident who was not silenced" (1994: 22).

The United Nations and other international organizations have helped to promote a shift in global priorities. Organizations like the World Health Organization call attention to the fact that some of the main causes of death today are *not* from wars. In poor countries, disease is the leading cause of fatalities. Millions of people die from lower respiratory infections (e.g., pneumonia), heart disease, diarrheal diseases, and HIV/AIDS each year. In the wealthy countries, people tend to die from heart disease, strokes, lung cancers, and lower respiratory infections (WHO 2014c). Table 2.1 summarizes the top ten causes of death worldwide. Disease is clearly one of the greatest killers. To put the table's numbers into context, in 2010 there were more than 13,200 fatalities from terrorism, but 1.46 million deaths from tuberculosis (CIA 2011). Hence, if countries truly want to ensure the security of their citizens, they must devote greater resources to combating health problems.

Table 2.1 Global Health Risks, 2014

	Numbers of Deaths (millions)	Percentage of Deaths
Ischaemic heart disease (coronary artery disease)	7.4	13.2
Stroke	6.7	11.9
Chronic obstructive pulmonary disease	3.1	5.6
Lower respiratory infection	3.1	5.5
Tracheal, bronchial, and lung cancers	1.6	2.9
HIV/AIDS	1.5	2.7
Diarrheal diseases	1.5	2.7
Diabetes mellitus	1.5	2.7
Road injury	1.3	2.2
Hypertensive heart disease	1.1	2.0

Source: WHO (2014c).

Many environmental issues also extend the traditional notion of security. Global warming threatens to raise the sea levels enough to severely disrupt coastal cities throughout the world or flood low-lying island nations in the South Pacific. A quick look at a world map reveals how many areas might be affected by rising sea levels. Evidence indicates that climate change already may be having an impact on agriculture in countries like Sudan and Bangladesh. There is increasing evidence that California's severe drought falls into this category as well. More important, climate change is expected to dramatically affect agriculture through increased desertification, droughts, flooding, and the like (World Bank 2011a). By 2020 in Africa alone, "between 75 and 250 million people are projected to be exposed to increased water stress due to climate change" (Cribb 2011: 140).

Resource scarcity is a related security issue. Many scholars expect conflict over resources to increase in the future as demand escalates due to increased levels of consumption and growing populations. Water scarcity has led to tensions in several other areas of the world as well. For instance, the Israeli-Palestinian conflict has intensified as Israeli settlements have been built on water aquifers in the West Bank. Similarly, Iran and Afghanistan are engaged in an ongoing conflict over the Hirmand River, on which both countries are dependent. Conflicts over oil are another example of how natural resources can fuel disputes. In the Gulf War (1991), Iraq invaded Kuwait in part to secure its oil resources. The United States, backed by the United Nations, launched a war to expel Iraqi forces from Kuwait months later. This had the effect of restoring both Kuwaiti sovereignty and stability in the international oil market.

Food security is another type of resource dimension included in human security. While there is more than enough food worldwide to feed the entire population of Earth, the food is not adequately distributed. So while some countries may have surplus food, others may experience starvation. War and inadequate infrastructure are both central reasons that can prevent food from arriving to starving populations. Food scarcity has led to uprisings in Latin America, South Asia, and throughout Africa. Since thousands of people die worldwide from lack of proper nutrition, food security is rightly considered a human security issue.

Current Issues in Global Security

In this section, three contemporary security issues are explored. Recent conflicts against terrorists and insurgents in Iraq and Syria illustrate the convergence of traditional military action with a concern for human security. Two other emerging issues—threats associated with autonomous weapons systems and cyber-security—are also examined. These issues stem from advancements in technology and are further complicated by globalization. They represent potential threats to both traditional and human security.

Terrorism

The United States and other great powers have begun to confront the scourge of international terrorism more directly in the past two decades. Western governments have committed hundreds of thousands of troops and billions of dollars to fight the global war on terror since the September 11, 2001, attacks. They have invaded countries they charged as sponsors of terror, such as Afghanistan and Iraq, and conducted military operations in many others. Nevertheless, hundreds more attacks have been carried out by al-Qaeda and affiliated groups since 2011, and Western countries also have been the targets of "homegrown" terror attacks. In recent years, the rise of the Islamic State and its virulent form of extremism appear to have further heightened terror threats and their potential to disrupt the global order. A US State Department report issued in 2014 revealed that the number of terrorist attacks had increased over the year prior by 35 percent, and total fatalities were up by 81 percent (Mallin 2015).

Modern terrorism presents a complex challenge. The US Department of State defines terrorism as "premeditated, political motivated violence perpetrated against noncombatant targets by sub-national groups or clandestine agents," usually intended to influence an audience (USDS n.d.).

Expert Peter Bergen (2001) says today's terrorism challenge is characterized by well-organized, global networks that perpetrate violence (see also Mockaitis 2007). Another expert, Mark Juergensmeyer (2000), suggests that the primary motivations of many modern terror groups include extremist fundamentalist and radicalized religious principles. Ethno-nationalism and separatism have sparked the rise of terror groups as well, but Bruce Hoffman (2006) believes that the combination of nationalism and religious fervor represents the most serious motivation for terrorism. In addition, new terror groups seem more willing to cause mass casualties in their attacks.

Although terrorist groups can be found throughout the world—and include Hindu, Christian, Jewish, and Muslim groups—al-Qaeda has been one of the highest-profile terrorist organizations of the past two decades. The group was founded by Osama bin Laden, the fugitive Saudi national who masterminded a series of terror attacks. Bin Laden was linked to attacks on US embassies in the 1990s and the September 11, 2001, strikes, as well as others. Greatly influenced by radical interpretations of the Quran, bin Laden began to organize terror cells to carry out offensive terror attacks against the enemies of Islam in the Middle East region and beyond. Bin Laden's grievances against the United States included its continued military presence on the Arabian Peninsula, tough sanctions and military actions in Iraq, and support for Israel in the struggle against the Palestinians. He exhorted all believers of Islam to kill Americans wherever and whenever possible (Lewis 1998). The war on terror in Afghanistan and Pakistan, plus the US commando raid that killed bin Laden in May 2011, dealt a significant blow to al-Qaeda.

Other terror groups also present threats to global security. Groups on the US State Department's official list of foreign terrorist organizations include Hezbollah, a radical Shiite group based largely in Lebanon with a mission to carry out the destruction of Israel. Hezbollah guerrillas have launched terror attacks in Israel and in 2006 were effectively at war with Israel during that country's invasion of Lebanon to root out the terrorists. Hezbollah is a transnational movement today and receives substantial financial backing from the government of Iran.

Two terror groups that have gained prominence in Africa are al-Shabaab, a radical Muslim organization based in Somalia, and Boko Haram in Nigeria. Al-Shabaab's senior leaders are affiliated with al-Qaeda, and the group has carried out a number of attacks in Somalia and neighboring countries. Boko Haram (an organization whose name translates as "Western education is forbidden") is based in northeastern Nigeria and is active in neighboring countries as well. The group practices its own version of Salafism (a fundamentalist belief in the need to return to the old ways and earliest interpretations of the Quran), and has been responsible for suicide bombings and mass kidnappings. Between 2009 and 2015, Boko Haram was responsible for the deaths of tens of thousands of civilians, the kidnapping of hundreds of school-aged girls, and the displacement of millions across the region.

The Islamic State is a transnational Sunni Islamist terrorist group. It rose to international attention in 2014 through a combination of violent extremism and widespread promotion of its horrific acts on the Internet. IS follows a nihilistic variant of extremist Islam. Its leader, Abu Bakr al-Baghdadi, called on all Muslims to join the cause and even welcomed the prospect of direct confrontation with the west. IS forces, which numbered an estimated 10,000 to 20,000 soldiers in 2015, included several hundred Westerners who were recruited through a vigorous online campaign (Wood 2015).

In June 2014, al-Baghdadi formally declared the establishment of a "caliphate"—a state governed in accordance with *sharia* law—in areas occupied by IS in Syria and Iraq. IS was able to gain control of parts of Syria due to a vacuum of power caused by the civil war raging there since 2011. IS members also include former Saddam Hussein loyalists and members of the Iraqi military. The group was able to gain control of territory in northwestern Iraq dominated by Sunni tribes, and it drove out Iraqi security forces that had been trained by the United States. By 2015, the group controlled a volume of resources and territory unmatched in the history of terrorist organizations: it controlled large cities in Iraq and Syria, made millions of dollars each day by selling oil on the black market, and fulfilled basic services for many living under its rule.

The Islamic State clearly represents a threat to global security. Al-Baghdadi has called on Muslims throughout the world to move to the caliphate and rise up against infidels. IS seeks to establish branches elsewhere and has attracted organized support in Egypt, Libya, Nigeria, Saudi Arabia, Yemen, and Afghanistan. It also appears to be inspiring attacks in the United States and Europe, such as the November 2015 attacks in Paris. The US government was on high alert starting in 2014 against attacks on the homeland. It also led a multinational coalition fighting ISIS using airstrikes, aiding guerrilla forces fighting against IS, and economic assistance to affected civilians in the region.

The terrorist threat today is widespread and multifaceted. Attacks carried out by these groups show that they represent a material threat to Western security. But the larger specter of terrorism also represents an existential threat to security. That is, the very presence of these groups and their ability to disrupt or even damage ways of life in many societies implies that terrorism itself has taken on a higher order of significance. The Obama administration's war on terror represents one response to this challenge, but all members of society are involved in a transition to understand and frame the threat today. In these ways, a material threat has become a virtual threat to our very conception of security in the twenty-first century.

Lethal Autonomous Weapons (or Killer Robots)

Technology has always played a role in security, whether it be local, national, or global. Recently, attention has begun to focus on developments in artificial intelligence (AI) and robots as an important but less traditional security challenge. Pop culture is likely where most people have encountered these issues. Hollywood has introduced us to the *Terminator* series, which pits humans against a computer system that achieves "self-awareness." In the movies, the AI computer system Skynet uses autonomous robots to exterminate humanity, which itself is viewed by the computer as a threat to global security. Other examples of movies dealing with these science fiction themes include *Ex Machina, Robocop, Transformers,* and a well-known precursor to all these films, *2001: A Space Odyssey.*

These types of advanced technologies do not just exist on movie screens. Computers today can concentrate better than humans, remember far more, and process information much faster. As a result, scientists are discussing, researching, and implementing a wide variety of new tasks for robots using AI. The effects will be wide-ranging. One immediate concern is the impact on human employment. Some experts argue that computers will replace lawyers, artists, pilots, economists, and more. Even politics might be impacted by AI. According to one expert: "With good statistics, valid social science theories, and the ability to read audience reactions in real time and with great accuracy, AIs could learn how to give the most convincing and moving of speeches" (Armstrong 2014: 14). In the economic realm "AIs could become skilled economists and CEOs, guiding companies or countries with an intelligence no human could match. Already, relatively simple algorithms make more than half of stock trades and humans barely understand how they work" (2014: 15).

In the military realm, advanced technologies are pushing the limits of warfare and sparking much excitement. Picture for instance a robot seeking out unexploded landmines. Such technology could save farmers cultivating land in former conflict zones from losing limbs or dying. Plans are also being made for the possible use of armed robots in conflict, which could save human lives. Conversely, many people are concerned about military uses of artificial intelligence, including weapons or robots guided by AI (sometimes called roboticized weapons). It is not hard to imagine why people are concerned. The thought of robots being used to kill humans is alarming. However, it is important to note that mechanized weapons already exist. Drones, for instance, also known as unmanned aerial vehicles (UAVs), are guided from thousands of miles away. Drones have been used over the past few years to kill people in remote areas. Since drones do not operate without humans, they tend to be referred to as "semiautonomous" weapons, as opposed to "fully autonomous," which generally are weapons that require little to no human control. Though there is some ambiguity about what actually constitutes human control, the focus generally seems to center on control over choosing the target and firing the weapon. It should be noted, however, that some extant weapons fit this description. The Iron Dome is an Israeli weapons defense system designed to automatically intercept missiles fired at Israel. It identifies incoming missiles and fires at the target without human intervention.

One typology that has emerged to try to classify autonomous weapons distinguishes between humans "in the loop," "on the loop," and "out of the loop." In the first case, weapons systems "engage individual targets or specific groups of targets that a human has decided are to be engaged" (Scharre and Horowitz 2015). When humans are "on the loop," the human can act to veto or stop the weapons system from selecting and attacking the target. In the "out of the loop" scenario, humans cannot intervene in the weapons system's activities. An increasing number of voices are demanding the creation of international policies to regulate autonomous weapons, especially the last category (Scharre and Horowitz 2015).

One such group is Human Rights Watch, a respected nongovernmental organization. In 2014, Human Rights Watch decided to aggressively seek a global ban on what it calls "lethal autonomous weapons," or less formally "killer robots." This ban would focus solely on fully autonomous weapons. At this point, many in the international community appear to agree with Human Rights Watch. In July 2015, nearly 3,000 AI researchers signed an open letter at the International Joint Conference on Artificial Intelligence, calling for "a ban on autonomous weapons that select and engage targets without human intervention" (CSKR 2015).

Of course, the future of any ban on autonomous weapons will depend on leading military powers like the United States, China, and Russia. Recently the US Department of Defense published the Unmanned Systems Integrated Roadmap for 2013–2038, which acknowledges the increasing autonomy of weapons systems (DOD 2013), and a Department of Defense Directive, which appears to directly address the future of human control over autonomous weapons. The directive states: "Autonomous and semi-autonomous weapon systems shall be designed to allow commanders and operators to exercise appropriate levels of human judgment over the use of force" (DOD 2012). But what does the term "appropriate" mean? If the DOD believes autonomous robots are better at selecting and engaging targets, then it could rationalize the development of "out of the loop" weapons systems.

Proponents of a ban on lethal autonomous weapons argue that leaders may be more inclined to declare war if robots are doing most of the fighting. They also argue that machines will not be as capable as humans to distinguish between combatants and noncombatants. For instance, will a robot be able to distinguish between a child with a toy gun or stick, and a soldier?

Those seeking a ban on lethal autonomous weapons also argue that robots will not be able to understand the concept of proportionality, which requires a balanced response in war rather than an excessive use of force. There is also justifiable concern about malfunctions leading to accidental war. At this point, opinion polls have found support for those seeking a ban, especially active military members (Wallach 2015).

Critics of a ban argue that using more robots in conflict will lessen the number of human casualties. They also argue that robots will be more efficient because they will avoid human error emanating from emotions and misperceptions. Critics also point to the difficulty of verifying if countries are complying with a ban on lethal autonomous weapons. In other words, it is much easier to verify if countries are developing nuclear weapons than it is to assess a country's work on autonomous weapons.

Some experts believe that artificial intelligence will advance to the extent that it can be designed to improve itself. In others words, someday a robot may not need humans to advance or evolve. It would be programmed for self-improvement and could redesign itself beyond the expectations of the humans who designed it. This phenomenon is termed "technological singularity." Notable scientists including Stephen Hawking have warned that singularity represents a dangerous possible future development, with vast implications for human security.

Cyber-Security

The development of the Internet and networks for digital communications by computer has opened another new frontier of challenges to global security. As technology advances, networked communications that were designed to offer "secure" connections for military command and control, scientific research, and data-sharing also have become portals for attacks on material and human security. Cyber-technologies similarly create the possibility of cyber-terrorism and cyber-crime. Because these technologies are inherently transgressive—constituting a violation of traditional boundaries of sovereignty, as well as a blurring of the lines between civilian and government concerns for security—they raise fascinating questions about international standards of behavior and the politics of security in the modern era.

The modern cyber-revolution began when the first programmable computing systems were designed for the US military in the 1930s and 1940s. The Defense Department started integrating computing technologies during the Cold War to help regulate complex areas of warfare such as artillery fire and aerial combat operations. In the late 1960s, the Defense Department began work on an experimental prototype network for linking computers called Arpanet. One goal was to create an alternative, secure means for military command centers to communicate during a nuclear war. Building on early success, researchers began working on new networks, rules, and procedures for the routing of messages between computers in the 1970s, which became known as Internet protocols. By the late 1980s and early 1990s, scientists, researchers, and average citizens began communicating through the system using electronic mail. In the early-1980s, perhaps 20,000 computers in the world were linked in some form; today, more than 3 billion people worldwide use the Internet to communicate with friends, family, and business partners. Merchants also depend on the Internet for supply-chaining and online sales, while consumers shop for and purchase products online, pay their bills, and track their shipments right to their front doors. From humble origins, the Internet has become a broad and deep ocean of global commerce and communications (Cavelty 2008; Deibert and Rohozinski 2010).

However, as the Internet has expanded and become ever more part of our daily lives, so too has vulnerability to cyber-attacks (Arquilla and Ronfelt 1997). Generally speaking, the US military embraced the early development of cyber-technologies in the knowledge that they gave the West significant advantages over its adversaries. Computers, Arpanet, Milnet, satellite-based ground location systems, and thousands of related technologies set the stage for a "revolution in military affairs" in the 1990s. The conduct of information warfare, or cyber-warfare, was an important dimension of the revolution in military affairs. The Defense Department defines information warfare as "actions taken to achieve information superiority by affecting adversary information, information-based processes, information systems, and computer-based networks while defending one's own information, information-based processes, information systems, and computer-based networks" (DOD 2011).

Cyber-attacks are easier to carry out than traditional military operations. They can be launched by state actors, state-supported groups, or rogue actors (ranging from terrorist groups to reckless teenagers). They may be designed to damage an adversary's infrastructure and material security, but they also can lead to collateral and indiscriminate damage that affects noncombatants. Expert Dorothy Denning (1999) has described several basic categories of cyber-security challenges in the modern era, including distributed denial of service (DDoS) attacks, which can be delivered by a virus or a worm to cripple the target's ability to operate Web content and communication by bombarding it with requests for information; hacking attacks, by which hackers can gain major access to the exploited computer and even link it to other compromised computers in a network termed a "botnet," through which the hacker is able to monitor Web traffic and communications, and gain access to confidential information from the entire network; and "phishing" attacks, which can be employed to download malware onto computers to gain access to their stored information. Broadly speaking, these instruments and techniques can be employed for cyber-warfare—or for cyber-crime, cyber-espionage, or cyber-terrorism (Denning 1999; Rollins and Wilson 2007).

Governments including those of the United States, China, Russia, and Israel are known to have carried out cyber-attacks. The US military's Cyber Command, headed by the director of the National Security Agency, conducts offensive as well as defensive operations. By 2011, a report by the Center for Strategic and International Studies said dozens of other states also were including cyber-warfare in their military planning and organization (Lewis and Timlin 2011). Cyber-attacks began in the 1990s and have expanded dramatically in recent decades. For example, Russian hackers struck Estonia in 2007 and Georgia in 2008, temporarily shutting down government computers and commercial servers. In 2013, a report stated that US intelligence agencies believe that thousands of breaches of US government and corporate websites have been launched by Chinese army officers and contractors (Sanger et al. 2013). In sum, cyber-warfare appears on the rise in the modern era, with the potential to impact billions of people around the world.

Nonstate actors also may become involved in cyber-terrorism. Indeed, the Internet has become a haven for criminals and terrorists by providing a measure of anonymity for their behaviors and secret communications. The number of websites and online activities linked to terrorist groups has grown dramatically in recent years. A research project at the University of Arizona called Dark Web tracks terrorist and extremist group activity in cyber-space and estimates that there are about 50,000 websites, chat rooms, blogs, and virtual interactive spaces sponsored by these groups today (University of Arizona 2015). According to expert Barbara Mantel (2015), terror groups use the Internet for at least five different purposes: fundraising, communication, training, media contacts, and radicalization and recruitment. Security analysts and law enforcement in Western countries attempt to follow such cyber-space activities carefully and keep one step ahead of extremists. Nevertheless, in today's complex environment, it is clear that determined states, state-sponsored groups, corporations, independent groups (such as Anonymous or LulzSec), or even individuals can use cyber-weapons like viruses or worms as a form of asymmetrical warfare against critical national infrastructures.

Finally, it is important to note that international response to the challenges of cyber-security has been mixed. For example, delegates to the first World Summit of the Information Society, held in 2003, debated whether multiple stakeholders, such as states, the computing industry, and nongovernmental organizations, should work together to govern the Internet, or if this dimension of security should be given over to the control of multilateral institutions with sovereign state members. Other key aspects of Internet governance include encouraging development of these technologies around the world and bridging the digital divide between less-developed countries and economically developed countries. While the global community agreed to a multistakeholder approach early in the twenty-first century, this posture came increasingly to be challenged by the governments of Russia and China, along with dozens of developing countries. Important efforts to shift international regulation to the control of the International Telecommunication Union or the United Nations (or both) continued throughout the first decade of the new century. While the George W. Bush administration opposed any consideration of multilateral management, President Barack Obama and Secretary of State John Kerry have entertained a broader dialogue regarding establishment of a new international code of conduct for the Internet and multilateral limits on national capacity building. Recent conventions on international telecommunications management, such as the World Telecommunication Development Conference in Dubai, have yielded greater progress toward developing a new consensus for governance.

Conclusion

This chapter has made the case that there are two broad dimensions of security worthy of further investigation: material/traditional security, typically associated with states; and human security, which is essentially a new way of looking at long-standing concerns in global politics. We argue that the concept of human security provides a much richer understanding of contemporary security issues. As traditional notions of security have evolved toward a broader, more inclusive concept, so too have traditional notions of sovereignty come under closer scrutiny, with the well-being of citizens receiving greater attention. Worldwide terror networks illustrate the emerging importance of actors not embedded in sovereign states. In the discussion of terrorism, ISIS has rejected sovereign borders and, at least in the case of Iraq and Syria, ignored elected leaders. The case of cyber-security highlights the extent to which technology can introduce new types of security issues—ones that are no longer simply the domain of states and military conflicts. The case of autonomous weapons is also an example of the role technology will play in the future of global security, even though it resembles traditional state security issues with its military applications.

To what extent these dimensions of security will continue to evolve remains to be seen. Certainly, increased globalization suggests that the world may continue to see security from a more global perspective—that is, with less attention to the political borders that separate us. A prime example is the heart-wrenching refugee crisis in the Middle East that is spreading suffering and human security issues throughout the region as well as into Europe and beyond. As climate change continues to make headlines, and widespread economic crises threaten increased global poverty, it is reasonable to assume that human security will gain increased attention in the future.

Discussion Questions

1. How does the concept of human security add to our understanding of contemporary security issues?

2. Do you think the number of wars in the future will decrease or increase?

3. What human security issues deserve the most global attention in the twenty-first century, and why?

4. What are the real causes of terrorism? Given these pervasive challenges, can you think of creative, alternative responses to recommend to policymakers?

5. Should there be legal or moral limits imposed on the autonomy of high-technology weapons systems in the twenty-first century? Why or why not?

6. Should traditional boundaries of sovereignty and control be enforced in the new global commons of cyber-space? If so, how would you define these boundaries to recognize dimensions of material and human security?

Suggested Readings

Caldwell, Dan, and Robert E. Williams Jr. (2006) *Seeking Security in an Insecure World.* Lanham: Rowman and Littlefield.

Cribb, Julian (2011) *The Coming Famine: The Global Food Crisis and What We Can Do to Avoid It.* Berkeley: University of California Press.

Goldstein, Joshua S. (2011) *Winning the War on War: The Decline of Armed Conflict Worldwide.* New York: Dutton.

Green, James A. (2015) *Cyberwarfare: A Multidisciplinary Analysis.* London: Routledge.

Homer-Dixon, Thomas (2006) *The Upside of Down: Catastrophe, Creativity, and the Renewal of Civilization.* New York: Island.

Kay, Sean (2011) *Global Security in the Twenty-First Century: The Quest for Power and the Search for Peace.* 2nd ed. Lanham: Rowman and Littlefield.

Reveron, Derek S., and Kathleen A. Mahoney-Norris (2011) *Human Security in a Borderless World.* Boulder: Westview.

Wallach, Wendell (2015) *A Dangerous Master: How to Keep Technology from Slipping Beyond Our Control.* New York: Basic.

Weiman, Gabriel (2015) *Terrorism in Cyberspace: The Next Generation.* Washington, DC: Woodrow Wilson Center Press.

3

The Threat of Weapons Proliferation

Jeffrey S. Lantis

THE PROLIFERATION OF WEAPONS IS ONE OF THE MOST SERIOUS CHALlenges to international security today. Confrontations with Iran and North Korea over their weapons of mass destruction (WMD) programs, the Iraq War (2003–2011), and threats of terrorist use of WMD all reflect modern proliferation concerns. World leaders have responded with a range of different policies and actions. For example, President George W. Bush launched a war on terror that focused, in part, on preventing proliferation of WMD. In 2009, President Barack Obama boldly announced his administration's goal "to seek the peace and security of a world without nuclear weapons." Permanent members of the United Nations Security Council launched negotiations with Iran to curb their ambitions for a nuclear weapons program that yielded a breakthrough agreement in 2015. Yet, given the pervasiveness of sensitive technologies and the motivations of some governments and nonstate actors, many proliferation threats remain.

Proliferation is not simply a distant problem for politicians and military leaders to solve. When governments choose to use weapons in conflict, they are exposing both soldiers and civilians to danger. When arms buildups occur in regions of high tension, the chances of even inadvertent military contact or accidental use of weapons systems increase. When governments devote funds to large armies or WMD, they are also diverting resources from other programs like education and healthcare. Whether or not they face imminent security threats, citizens of the world experience the effects of proliferation every day.

Types of Proliferation

Proliferation is best understood as the rapid increase in the number and destructive capability of armaments. As illustrated in Figure 3.1, there are four dimensions of proliferation to consider. Vertical proliferation is the development and stockpiling of armaments in one country. Horizontal proliferation is the spread of weapons or weapons technology across country borders. Conventional weapons are those systems that make up the vast majority of all military arsenals—including guns, tanks, most artillery shells and bullets, planes, and ships. Weapons of mass destruction are special weapons that have a devastating effect even when used in small numbers. Nuclear, chemical, and biological systems may be used to kill more indiscriminately than conventional weapons.

Figure 3.1 The Proliferation Matrix

	Vertical Proliferation	Horizontal Proliferation
Conventional weapons	Type I	Type II
Weapons of mass destruction	Type III	Type IV

Vertical Proliferation of Conventional Weapons

The buildup of conventional weapons arsenals is the oldest form of proliferation. While some might view this as the least-threatening, this type of proliferation can challenge global stability in several ways. First, arms stockpiling provides more weapons for governments and groups to engage in more conflicts. Conventional weapons have become more sophisticated (from automatic rifles to precision-guided munitions) and more destructive (from cannon balls to 2,000-pound bombs). Some believe that vertical conventional proliferation in an unregulated world market may contribute to conflicts. A second danger of conventional arms buildups is the social cost, which often includes trade-offs between defense and other programs, and cuts in social welfare spending by governments for citizens who can ill afford them.

More weapons mean more conflicts. Government programs to stockpile conventional armaments ensure that there are more weapons available to engage in more conflicts. Some experts believe that the simple availability of weapons systems and the development of military strategies increase the chances that a country will go to war. They argue that advances in conventional weaponry and offensive military strategies were contributing factors to the outbreaks of numerous conflicts, including both world wars and the Vietnam War. In this context, arms buildups are seen as one potential cause of war in the international system (Sagan 1986; Sivard 1991).

Before World War I, for example, Germany and Great Britain engaged in a race to build the most powerful warships. Adolf Hitler ordered research and development of surface-to-surface missiles and jet aircraft during World War II. In the Cold War, President Ronald Reagan called for the creation of a 600-ship navy, with an emphasis on strong aircraft carrier battle groups and advanced submarines. More recently, attention has turned to new technologies of warfare, including stealth planes and ships, armed unmanned aerial vehicles (UAVs) like the Predator drone, antisatellite weapons in space, and computer technology to give an edge to fighting forces in the twenty-first century.

The relationship between arms buildups and the likelihood of conflict is multiplied by the fact that conventional weapons have become more sophisticated and destructive. Today, "smart" bombs and precision-guided munitions allow militaries to hit targets more precisely from a long distance. Explosive devices triggered remotely by cell phones have enabled insurgent groups to attack unsuspecting soldiers in Iraq and Afghanistan. In 2014, an advanced Russian-made Buk missile launcher controlled by pro-Russian separatists shot down a civilian Malaysian Airlines flight over a conflict region in eastern Ukraine, killing all 298 people on board. Even now, scientists are working on long-distance hypersonic missiles, capable of precision conventional strikes on targets located anywhere in the world in less than an hour.

Finally, it is important to remember that conventional arms have been used repeatedly in conflict since the end of World War II. From landmines to fighter jets, conventional weapons have been blamed for roughly 50 million deaths in conflicts around the globe since 1945.

The social costs of arms buildups. Many governments have sizable conventional arsenals. Average annual US military expenditures have topped $350 billion over the past two decades, with most funds going to support troops and conventional weapons. Defense spending by the United States in 2014 was three times larger than that of its nearest potential competitor (China), more than five times larger than that of Russia, and represented 34 percent of total world military expenditures (Perlo-Freeman et al. 2015). Table 3.1 illustrates the broader context of changing levels of regional and global defense expenditures.

Table 3.1 World and Regional Military Expenditures, 2006–2014 ($ billions at constant 2011 values)

	2006	2008	2010	2012	2014
Africa	26.2	31.0	34.6	40.4	46.5
Asia and Oceania	276	313	356	388	423
Central America and Caribbean	5.6	6.3	7.5	8.5	9.8
Europe	375	396	394	392	391
Middle East	122	127	139	151	173
North America	607	671	741	691	596
South America	51.9	59.4	66.3	68.8	72
Total	1,464	1,604	738	1,740	1,711

Source: SIPRI (2015).

Note: Totals may not sum to the indicated numbers because of rounding conventions expenditure estimates. Data for some countries have been excluded because of lack of information.

Global defense spending levels rose steadily in the first decade of the twenty-first century, but the rate of increase appears to have leveled off in recent years. In 2014, the five biggest military spenders were the United States, China, Russia, Saudi Arabia, and France. The United States doubled its defense spending between 1998 and 2008, mostly associated with costs of the global war on terror, while spending levels have increased less dramatically since. Countries in Asia, the Middle East, and Europe also increased defense expenditures over that time.

Critics charge that there are dangerous social costs of military spending. In 1996, well before the global war on terror, world military expenditures per soldier equaled $31,480, while government expenditures on education were just $899 per student. Health expenditures per person were $231 in developed countries and just $22 in developing countries (Sivard 1996). The United States, which ranked first in the world in military spending in 2010, placed twenty-seventh in life expectancy (behind countries like Japan, Hong Kong, and Switzerland) and thirty-first for providing adequate food and shelter (behind Denmark, Singapore, and the Netherlands) (Legatum Institute 2011). In recent years there has been a sharp increase in the military expenditures of some countries as a share of their gross domestic product (GDP), presenting additional challenges for development. And when military expenditures rise in developing countries, studies have shown that the rate of economic growth declines and government debt increases (Nincic 1982). Rightly or wrongly, it sometimes seems that governments are more concerned with defending their citizens from foreign attack than they are with protecting them from social insecurities at home.

Horizontal Proliferation of Conventional Weapons

A second category of proliferation is the horizontal spread of conventional weapons and weapons technology across country borders. The main route of the spread of conventional weaponry is through arms sales. These are often legitimate transfers of weapons from sellers to buyers in the international arms market. However, the conventional arms trade is lucrative, and many experts are concerned that corporate greed may be driving the world more rapidly toward the brink of major conflict.

Arms dealers. The conventional arms trade is a very big business. The value of all arms deals completed in 2011 worldwide was $43 billion. The United States ranked first in the world for sales, with Russia and France a distant second and third respectively. From 2004 to 2011, these three supplier states were responsible for 70 percent of all international arms sales (Grimmett and Kerr 2012). Among these deals in 2011 were agreements by the United States to sell dozens of advanced fighter jets and large stocks of missiles and ammunition to Saudi Arabia, the sale of an advanced anti-missile shield and radar system to the United Arab Emirates (UAE), and a co-production agreement with Egypt for battle tanks. In 2011, Russia also signed arms agreements with Venezuela, Malaysia, Vietnam, Burma, and Indonesia (Grimmett and Kerr 2012). In addition, more and more countries are getting into the game of small arms production around the world, many with few regulations on their sales or use.

Arms customers. Who are the main customers for all of these weapons? US defense contractors sell most weapons to allies in the developing world. The Middle East and Asia have been the largest markets for arms sales in recent decades. For example, US defense contractors sell heavy weapons, equipment, and technology to Saudi Arabia, Egypt, Israel, Turkey, Oman, the UAE, and other countries. In Asia, allies such as Taiwan, South Korea, India, and Japan purchase large numbers of conventional weapons systems.

Arms are not always sold to countries considered traditional allies, however. In the 1980s the People's Republic of China spent more than $400 million on US weapons. These arms deals were stopped only after the Tiananmen Square massacre of pro-democracy activists in 1989. Iraq's leader, Saddam Hussein, built a massive conventional arsenal through the international arms market in the 1980s. Arms sales to Iraq by friends and allies came back to haunt the United States, however, during the Gulf War (1991) and the Iraq War (2003). In another ironic twist, the Islamic State (IS) terrorist organization seized thousands of new weapons provided by the United States to Iraq for postwar reconstruction when Iraqi soldiers fled the battlefield. Indeed, the sale of conventional weapons raises real concern about the potential for "deadly returns" on arms sales (Laurance 1992).

Legal and illegal arms transfers also have contributed to civil wars around the world in the past decade, including conflicts in Syria, Sierra Leone, Afghanistan, Algeria, Sudan, Colombia, Sri Lanka, Chechnya, and the Democratic Republic of Congo. In 2014, China was suspected of secretly selling arms to Libya, Sudan, and the Democratic Republic of Congo. Sadly, many of the casualties in these conflicts have been civilians. Children are especially at risk. According to the United Nations, millions of children have been killed, and millions more seriously injured, in civil wars and conflicts in recent decades, and as many as 300,000 children have been recruited as soldiers in dozens of conflicts. Another 23 million children have been forced to flee their homes because of conflict or human rights violations and are internally displaced or seeking refuge in neighboring countries. The Syrian civil war (2011–present) alone has displaced more than 9 million people from their homes and caused an estimated 207,000 deaths as of 2015 (Gladstone and Ghannam 2015).

Vertical Proliferation of Weapons of Mass Destruction

The vertical proliferation of weapons of mass destruction is another serious threat to international security. There are several important dimensions of this problem, including the types of WMD systems, incentives for states to build nuclear weapons, and patterns of vertical WMD proliferation.

There are three categories of weapons of mass destruction: nuclear, chemical, and biological. These are often examined as a group, but it is important to note that their effects—and potential military applications—are quite different.

Nuclear weapons. Nuclear weapons are devices with tremendous explosive power based on atomic fission or fusion. During World War II, President Franklin D. Roosevelt authorized a five-year, $2 billion secret research program known as the Manhattan Project that was first in the world to develop atomic weapons. On August 6, 1945, the United States dropped a 12.5-kiloton atomic bomb on Hiroshima, Japan. This weapon produced an explosive blast equal to that of 12,500 tons of TNT and caused high-pressure waves, flying debris, extreme heat, fires, and radioactive fallout, killing approximately 135,000 people. A second bomb was dropped on Nagasaki on August 9, 1945, killing 65,000. The Japanese government surrendered one day later.

The use of atomic bombs to end World War II was the beginning of a dangerous period of a spiraling arms race between the United States and the Soviet Union. The Soviet regime immediately stepped up its atomic research and development program, and detonated its first atomic test device. In response, the United States built more than 30,000 bombs and warheads during the darkest days of the Cold War in the 1960s. The Soviet arsenal was built up more slowly, but peaked in the 1980s with an estimated 27,000 nuclear weapons. Both superpowers also put an emphasis on diversification of their weapons systems. Land-based intercontinental ballistic missiles (ICBMs) were the symbolic centerpiece of arsenals, but the superpowers also deployed nuclear weapons on submarines, in long-range bombers, and even in artillery shells and landmines. And they were increasing the destructive capacity of nuclear weapons. During the Cold War, the Soviet Union deployed warheads with yields of 25 megatons (the explosive equivalent of 25 million tons of TNT)—thousands of times more powerful than the bomb that devastated Hiroshima (Arbatov 2009).

Chemical and biological weapons. Chemical weapons work by spreading poisons that incapacitate, injure, or kill through their toxic effects on the body. Chemical agents can be lethal when vaporized and inhaled in very small amounts or when absorbed into the bloodstream through skin contact. During World War I, mustard-gas attacks killed 91,000 soldiers and injured 1 million in 1917 alone. Chemical weapons were used again during the Iran-Iraq War (1980–1988), killing an estimated 13,000 soldiers (Spiers 2010). In 1995, a radical religious cult in Japan used the nerve gas Sarin against civilians in the Tokyo subway system, killing twelve and injuring thousands more. And in 2013, the Syrian military used chemical munitions against separatist fighters in a densely populated area, killing hundreds of civilians.

Chemical weapons are relatively simple and cheap to produce compared to other classes of WMD. Any group with some level of expertise could use a mix of chemicals to create dangerous weapons of mass destruction. Not surprisingly, this type of weapon has become popular with terrorist groups. In 2006, intelligence agents in Britain uncovered a plot to use chemicals hidden in drink bottles to build bombs that could blow up commercial aircraft. That same year, insurgents in Iraq began detonating bombs laced with chlorine gas in populated areas to maximize deaths and injuries.

As dangerous as chemical weapons can be, biological agents are actually much more lethal and destructive. Biological agents are microorganisms such as bacteria, viruses, or fungi that can be used to cause illness or kill the intended target. Anthrax is the most common example of a biological agent. Anthrax is a disease-causing bacterium that contains as many as 10 million lethal doses per gram. At the height of the Cold War, both superpowers had significant stockpiles of weaponized anthrax ready for use. In the aftermath of September 11, 2001, small amounts of anthrax were used in terrorist attacks through the US mail system—a case that remains unsolved at this writing.

Like chemical agents, biological and toxic weapons are relatively easy to construct and have a high potential lethality rate (if left untreated). Any government or group with access to a pharmaceutical manufacturing facility or biological research lab could develop biological weapons. And like the other classes of WMD systems, information about the construction of such systems is available in the open scientific literature and on the Internet.

Why build WMD systems? There are two primary reasons why countries build weapons of mass destruction: security and prestige. First, some government leaders genuinely believe that the security of their country is at risk without such systems. During the Cold War, the United States and the Soviet Union established large nuclear weapons stockpiles as well as arsenals of chemical and biological weapons. US policy on bioweapons development was finally reversed by President Richard Nixon in the early 1970s, but clandestine Soviet research and development continued for another decade. In the Middle East, Israel is suspected of having more than a hundred nuclear devices for potential use in its own defense. Indeed, the Israeli government secretly threatened to use them against Iraq during the 1991 Gulf War if Israel were to come under chemical or biological weapons attack.

The standoff between India and Pakistan is another prime example of the security imperative. After years of border skirmishes between the countries, India began a secret program to construct an atomic device that might swing the balance of regional power in its favor. In 1974, the Indian government detonated what it termed a "peaceful nuclear explosion"—signaling its capabilities to the world and threatening Pakistani security. For the next twenty-five years, both Pakistan and India secretly developed nuclear weapons in a regional arms race. In May 1998, the Indian government detonated five more underground nuclear explosions, and the Pakistani government responded with six test explosions of its own. Today, each country is estimated to possess more than sixty warheads.

Second, some governments have undertaken WMD research and development programs for reasons of prestige, national pride, or a desire for influence. It became clear to some during the Cold War that the possession of WMD systems—or a spirited drive to attain them—would gain attention for a country or leader. In the early 1990s, North Korea's drive to build a nuclear device drew the attention of the United States. After extensive negotiations, North Korea was offered new nuclear energy reactors in exchange for a promise to stop its bomb program. When it renounced the deal in 2002, world leaders scrambled to head off its program to develop more weapons. Nevertheless, the North Korean government successfully tested its first nuclear bomb in October 2006.

Some governments pursue the development of WMD arsenals because they believe it will help them gain political influence. For example, Libyan strongman Muammar Qaddafi launched a secret nuclear weapons program in the late 1970s, obtaining highly enriched uranium and all the necessary technology and components to build nuclear bombs through the black market. Libya did not face an immediate threat to its national security; rather, Qaddafi believed that nuclear weapons would bolster his country's profile in the region. A similar motive might explain clandestine Iraqi government efforts to develop a WMD arsenal from the 1970s to the 1990s. Iraqi leader Saddam Hussein ordered the creation of a secret WMD research and development program and began to acquire nuclear technology and materials from France, Germany, the United States, and other countries in the late 1970s. Hussein believed that a nuclear bomb would contribute to Iraqi prestige, power, and influence in the Middle East. In response, the Israeli government tried to stop Iraq's nuclear program by launching an air strike against Iraq's research reactor at Osiraq in 1981. But the determined Iraqi drive for WMD appears to have ended only with the work of the United Nations through its special commission to investigate and dismantle all Iraqi WMD programs following the Gulf War (Steinberg 1994).

Horizontal Proliferation of Weapons of Mass Destruction

The horizontal proliferation of WMD systems represents the fourth dimension of this challenge to international peace and stability. In fact, the spread of these weapons and vital technology across state borders is often viewed as the most serious of all proliferation threats. President George W. Bush famously warned that the gravest danger we face is that "the world's most dangerous people" will get their hands on "the world's most dangerous weapons."

Nuclear arsenals. The massive buildup of nuclear arsenals by the superpowers was not the only game in town during the Cold War. In fact, while the Soviet Union and United States were stockpiling their weapons, other countries were working to join the nuclear club. Today, the United States, Russia, France, Great Britain, China, India, North Korea, and Pakistan all openly acknowledge possessing stocks of nuclear weapons (see Figure 3.2). In 1952, Great Britain successfully tested an atomic device and eventually built a nuclear arsenal of about 200 weapons. France officially joined the nuclear club in 1960 and built a somewhat larger nuclear arsenal of an estimated 420 weapons. The People's Republic of China detonated its first atomic device in 1964 and built an arsenal of about 300 nuclear weapons during the Cold War (McGwire 1994).

Several developing countries began secret atomic weapons research and development projects after World War II. As noted earlier, states like India, Pakistan, and Israel pursued clandestine WMD programs because of concerns about security and prestige. The Indian government's detonation of its first nuclear explosion in 1974 symbolically ended the monopoly on nuclear systems held by the great powers. India obtained nuclear material for its bomb by diverting it from a Canadian-supplied nuclear energy reactor (that had key components originally made in the United States). Most

Figure 3.2 The Status of Nuclear Weapons in the World

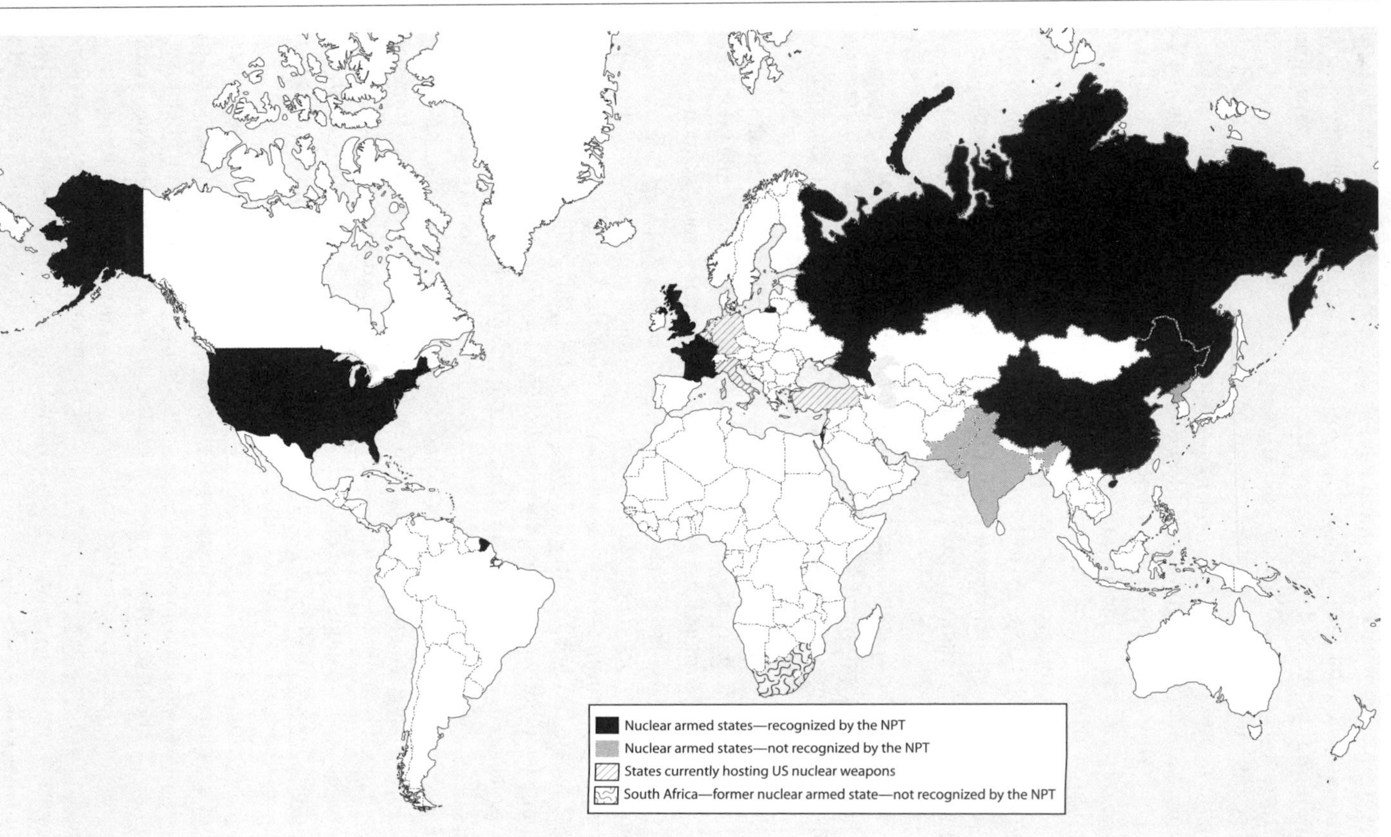

Source: ILPI (2015).

experts believe that India now possesses a stockpile of sixty to one hundred nuclear weapons. In the late 1970s, Pakistani research scientist A. Q. Khan stole classified information on uranium enrichment technology from a European consortium and became a national hero for directing Pakistan's weapons program. Today, Pakistan has scores of nuclear weapons that could be assembled quickly for use. The Israeli nuclear program was a derivative of research and development projects in the United States, South Africa, and, ironically, the Soviet Union. Like India, the Israeli government proved to be quite resourceful in adapting existing technologies to construct its arsenal (Cirincione, Wolfstahl, and Rajkumar 2002).

According to the Carnegie Endowment for International Peace, several countries are considered "high-risk" proliferants. North Korea is on the road to building up its arsenal since its 2006 test, and until the 2015 nuclear deal (discussed later) the Islamic Republic of Iran was also considered a potential breakout state. In 2004, it was revealed that Pakistani scientist A. Q. Khan had supplied both governments with the designs and technology to produce enriched uranium (Rohde and Sanger 2004). Experts now believe that North Korea has sufficient weapons material for at least a dozen nuclear bombs. World leaders are extremely concerned about the Iranian government's efforts to develop nuclear weapons.

Finally, it is important to note that some states have made political decisions to give up their WMD research and development efforts altogether. Included in this group are South Africa, Brazil, Argentina, Libya, and three former Soviet republics: Belarus, Kazakhstan, and Ukraine. The South African government admitted that it had constructed six nuclear devices for self-defense in the 1970s and 1980s, for example. But the government decided to destroy these weapons in 1990—unilaterally removing itself from the nuclear club. Argentina and Brazil renounced past efforts to develop nuclear arsenals. The three former Soviet republics had about 3,000 strategic nuclear weapons stationed on their soil after the breakup of the Soviet Union. Soon after gaining their independence, however, the three republics agreed to transfer all their nuclear warheads back to Russia in exchange for economic assistance from the United States (McGwire 1994). In December 2003, former Libyan leader Qaddafi surprised the world by announcing that his country, too, would give up its WMD research and development programs.

The spread of chemical and biological weapons. Dozens of countries are suspected to possess chemical and biological weapons. Those countries suspected of stockpiling biological weapons include Israel, North Korea, and Russia. Likewise, China, Egypt, India, Iran, Israel, Libya, North Korea, Russia, Syria, and the United States possess chemical weapons stockpiles. It should be noted that India, Libya, Russia, and the United States have each committed to destroying their chemical weapons.

WMD terrorism. The horizontal spread of WMD systems heightens concerns about the possible use of nuclear, chemical, or biological weapons systems in future terrorist attacks. Indeed, the 2001 anthrax attacks in the United States caused panic in many industrialized countries and increased public concerns about other potential threats, such as the use of smallpox or the plague as a terrorist weapon. Terrorist leader Osama bin Laden called it a "duty" for the al-Qaeda terrorist network to acquire a nuclear bomb to use against the West.

According to the database compiled by the Monterey Institute's Center for Nonproliferation Studies, some 100 chemical or biological attacks accounted for a total of 103 fatalities and 5,554 injuries in the twentieth century. More than two-thirds of all documented incidents occurred outside the United States (Tucker 2000). Many experts believe that the horizontal spread of nuclear weapons, materials, and expertise has increased the likelihood that a group or state will attempt an act of nuclear terrorism in the future. This is of particular concern given the chaos and instability surrounding the nuclear arsenal of the former Soviet Union, and there have been numerous reports of attempts to buy or steal nuclear warheads in that region. Finally, experts are concerned about the possibility that terrorists will combine radioactive materials with conventional explosives to create deadly radiological devices (also known as "dirty bombs"). All of these factors suggest that the threat of WMD terrorism has increased in the modern era.

Contemporary Challenges/Contemporary Solutions

The Nonproliferation Regime

Proliferation clearly represents a complex challenge to international security. World leaders have addressed proliferation threats through a series of regional and global initiatives, and the scope of initiatives to control and limit arms steadily increased from the 1940s to the 1990s. Some experts believe that these efforts have been extremely successful—that there are now even international taboos against the use of chemical, biological, and nuclear weapons (Tannenwald 2005; Paul 2000). However, governments are far from unified in their responses to the threat, and skeptics question the effectiveness of the nonproliferation regime in the twenty-first century.

The global nuclear nonproliferation movement actually began before the first use of atomic weapons in 1945. Scientists involved in the Manhattan Project recognized that such weapons were special and more dangerous than other systems. President Harry Truman, who had ordered the use of atomic bombs over Hiroshima and Nagasaki, later proposed that all nuclear materials and technology in the world be placed under United Nations control. While the plan did not receive widespread support, it demonstrated a first step toward global consideration of proliferation problems and set the stage for later progress on the issue. In the 1960s, world leaders agreed to new initiatives, including the Partial Nuclear Test Ban Treaty, which outlawed nuclear tests in the atmosphere, in outer space, and under water. In 1967 the Treaty for the Prohibition of Nuclear Weapons in Latin America created a large nuclear-free zone.

The Nuclear Nonproliferation Treaty. The centerpiece of the global nonproliferation regime, the Nuclear Nonproliferation Treaty (NPT) was an agreement to halt the spread of nuclear weapons beyond the five declared nuclear powers. Opened for signature in 1968, the treaty had ambitious goals for both vertical and horizontal proliferation. Article 1 of the treaty dictated that no nuclear weapons state (defined by the treaty as a state that detonated a nuclear explosive prior to 1967) would "directly or indirectly" transfer nuclear weapons, explosive devices, or control over these weapons to another party. Article 2 stipulated that no state without nuclear weapons capabilities could receive, manufacture, obtain assistance for manufacturing, or otherwise try to acquire nuclear weaponry. Another significant element of the treaty was Article 6, which required all nuclear states to pursue general disarmament under strict and effective international control. In many ways, the NPT represented the crowning achievement of global nonproliferation efforts during the Cold War.

Related nonproliferation initiatives. Several other significant agreements have followed in the spirit of the NPT. The Biological Weapons Convention of 1972 was the first major effort to gain some control over the world's deadly biological arsenal. More than 140 countries agreed to ban the development and stockpiling of biological agents. In 1993, the Chemical Weapons Convention (CWC) was opened for signature. This treaty committed all signatories to cease development and stockpiling of chemical weapons. In addition, it included a set of verification procedures somewhat more stringent than those under the NPT. These procedures supported the rights of a new CWC inspectorate to conduct rigorous investigations and surprise "challenge inspections" of suspected chemical weapons programs in signatory states.

In 1972, the United States and the Soviet Union negotiated their first major arms control treaties. The first Strategic Arms Limitation Treaty (SALT I) called for limits on the number of nuclear launch platforms, including missiles and strategic bombers. The Anti–Ballistic Missile (ABM) Treaty limited the deployment of defensive, ground-based antimissile systems. According to the treaty, each party pledged "not to develop, test, or deploy ABM systems or components which are sea-based, space-based, or mobile land-based" beyond allowed limits. Other bilateral agreements led to caps on the number of strategic warheads (the Strategic Arms Reduction Treaties) and even the elimination of an entire class of nuclear weapons (the 1987 Intermediate-Range Nuclear Forces Treaty).

In 1996, the Comprehensive Nuclear Test Ban Treaty (CTBT), another nonproliferation initiative, was opened for signature. Many UN member states voted to support the treaty and ban all nuclear testing. To become international law, the treaty required the signature and ratification of all forty-four countries known to possess nuclear reactors. However, the governments of both India and Pakistan refused to sign the treaty. India claimed that it wanted the CTBT to be stronger in order to force nuclear states' compliance with Article 6 of the NPT, and the Pakistani government stated that it would not sign the CTBT without India's cooperation. Their nuclear tests of May 1998 underscored their resistance to the regime. Other states, including Cuba and Syria, also remain reluctant to sign the treaty. However, the US position on the treaty was the most surprising of all. The treaty was met by a wave of conservative resistance, charging that the agreement was dangerous because it was not verifiable and would unduly restrict the United States while allowing rogue states to proceed with their programs. In a move that stunned the world, the US Senate rejected the treaty in October 1999.

Controlling Weapons at the Point of Supply

Given serious concerns about the implications of the spread of WMD technology around the world, governments have also tried to limit the supply of critical materials needed to build such weapons. Critics charge that the NPT was flawed because it did not prevent states from exporting "peaceful" nuclear energy reactors and other technology and materials that could potentially be converted for use in the development of WMD programs. To address such concerns, major supplier states formed the Nuclear Suppliers Group in the 1970s and established a "trigger list" of items that could be sold to other countries only under stringent safeguards. In the 1980s, supplier states established the Missile Technology Control Regime, which prohibited the transfer of essential technology for the development of ballistic missile systems.

Like the NPT, however, supply control efforts have had only marginal success. They have helped to limit missile development projects under way in South America and the Middle East, but some twenty countries still have acquired missiles. These supply controls did not prevent Iraq from manufacturing and modifying the Scud-B missiles that were used against Israel and Saudi Arabia during the 1991 Gulf War (which were also capable of carrying chemical warheads). Meanwhile, Pakistan developed its own ballistic missile, the Hatf, and acquired about thirty nuclear-capable medium-range missiles from China (McNaugher 1990). The North Korean government continues to develop a long-range ballistic missile that may have the potential to deliver a warhead to the continental United States, and is cooperating with Iran in ballistic missile research and development.

Finally, there has been significant progress on the conventional weapons front, as more policymakers, international organizations, and nongovernmental organizations recognize that arms transfers—even of small arms or light weapons like guns and antitank weapons—represent a fundamental threat to international security. In 1995, diplomats produced the Wassenaar Arrangement on Export Controls for Conventional Arms and Dual-Use Goods and Technologies, and Nobel Peace Prize laureates led by former Costa Rican president Oscar Arias called for the establishment of a conventional arms trade treaty throughout the first decade of the twenty-first century. The United Nations sponsored the first-ever Conference on the Illicit Trade in Small Arms and Light Weapons in All Its Aspects in 2001, and negotiations on the arms trade treaty continued from 2006 to 2013. Players argued that the trade of conventional weapons occurred largely in a moral and legal "vacuum," where lax laws were barely enforced and where leaders had not taken principled stances against this type of proliferation. Furthermore, many arms purchases were undertaken by countries with poor records of human rights (FAS 2002). In 2013, the United Nations finalized an arms treaty to regulate the international trade of conventional weapons and promote cooperation and transparency among states. The Obama administration signed the treaty, but officials knew it faced significant opposition at home, evidenced by the fact that the Senate has not ratified the agreement.

Negotiating a Nuclear Deal with Iran

The complicated case of nuclear ambitions of the Islamic Republic of Iran illustrates modern proliferation dilemmas. The government of Iran, led by President Mahmoud Ahmadinejad and Grand Ayatollah Ali Khameini, appeared to be on a collision course with the international community regarding its nuclear ambitions. A clandestine Iranian nuclear research program had taken off in the 1990s, with the help of technology acquired from Russia and China as well as bomb designs and technology from the A. Q. Khan network (Rohde and Sanger 2004). By the mid-2000s the Iranian government claimed to have made significant strides in its nuclear program but maintained that the research was for the peaceful production of nuclear energy. When the International Atomic Energy Agency (IAEA) concluded in 2006 that Iran was in serious violation of the NPT, Iranian president Ahmadinejad defied international will to halt the program or allow international inspections.

Western responses to these provocations were mixed. To the United States, this appeared to be another chapter in a complicated relationship that went back decades and included the taking of US hostages (1979–1981) and US support for Iraq in its war against Iran (1980–1988). President George W. Bush warned Iran not to pursue a clandestine nuclear weapons program and cobbled together a coalition of great powers to impose severe economic sanctions on Iran. There were also serious debates at the time regarding a possible preemptive Western military strike against suspect Iranian facilities (Kroenig 2012; Kahl 2012). When President Barack Obama entered office in 2009, though, he expressed a new willingness to negotiate with potential rivals, including the Iranian regime.

In 2013, permanent members of the UN Security Council joined with the European Union to negotiate a peaceful outcome to the standoff. Following twenty months of intense negotiations, the group announced in 2015 that they had reached an accord to significantly limit Tehran's nuclear ability for more than a decade in return for lifting sanctions on the Iranian oil industry and financial sector. President Obama hailed this as a major diplomatic achievement. The deal included restrictions on the amount of nuclear fuel that Iran could enrich and keep in its stockpile for the next fifteen years; it also required Iran to reduce its stockpile of low-enriched uranium by 98 percent (by shipping much of it to Russia). That measure, along with a two-thirds reduction in the number of centrifuges spinning at Iran's primary enrichment center at Natanz, would extend the amount of time it would take Iran to make enough material for a bomb should it ever abandon the accord and race for a weapon. The Iran deal officially went into effect in the fall of 2015. The United States and European Union started lifting sanctions, and in turn the Iranian government began decommissioning some uranium centrifuges and opening its facilities to enhanced international inspections (Sanger and Gordon 2015).

North Korea

Soon after the news of an Iran deal, North Korea's government announced that it had no interest in similar negotiations. North Korea's drive to build nuclear weapons began drawing the attention of the United States and other Western powers in the early 1990s. Under the leadership of President Kim Jong-un, North Korea is one of the world's few remaining communist dictatorships. Its nuclear reactors and a plutonium reprocessing plant were constructed at Yongbyon, in the country's north. The reactor produces enough plutonium to support the construction of one to two nuclear bombs a year, and this is exactly what the international community suspects that North Korea has been doing for more than a decade. In 1994 these tensions came to a boil, and the Bill Clinton administration considered the use of military force to halt North Korea's research progress. Conflict was avoided, however, with the negotiation of an agreed framework whereby North Korea would suspend its nuclear program in exchange for a package of benefits, including light-water nuclear reactors, oil shipments, and food aid.

By 2002 it had become clear that North Korea was not abiding by the terms of the agreement. It was revealed that North Korea also had acquired designs and technology for a nuclear weapons program through the A. Q. Khan network. In 2003, it formally withdrew from the NPT. The standoff intensified in February 2005, when the North Korean government acknowledged that it possessed nuclear weapons and would no longer negotiate with regional actors or the United States regarding the future of its program. Then, in October 2006, North Korea successfully tested its first nuclear bomb. Since then, Western governments and China have been engaged in negotiations to halt its enrichment program as well as ballistic missile development. North Korean officials meanwhile threaten new rounds of nuclear weapons tests and continue to defy the wishes of the international community.

* * *

The cases of Iran and North Korea represent examples of the challenges of proliferation in the twenty-first century. Optimists believe that international diplomacy may yield solutions such as allowing peaceful nuclear energy programs in exchange for pledges not to develop weapons. Pessimists warn, however, that these cases are just the tip of the iceberg of the contemporary threat and that any concessions to rogue states will surely multiply the number of developing countries seeking weapons in the future.

Contemporary Policy Debates: A Nuclear Zero?

The cases presented here illustrate different dimensions of what has been a long-standing political and philosophical debate about nuclear weapons development around the world. US presidents have taken very different approaches to the problem. To oversimplify, the debate over US nuclear strategy has experienced wild swings on a pendulum between "nuclear weapons are the greatest threat to mankind" to "nuclear weapons are the necessary guarantors of peace and security." President Harry Truman saw the value of atomic bombs in ending World War II, but was alarmed by their long-term implications; he endorsed an early plan to transfer all nuclear technology to UN control. Dwight Eisenhower increased funding and reliance on nuclear weapons for Western security in the Cold War, but also called for an international atomic energy agency to pursue peaceful uses of the technology. John F. Kennedy negotiated the Partial Nuclear Test Ban Treaty with the Soviet Union soon after the Cuban missile crisis. Richard Nixon led US negotiations with the Soviet Union that established the first major arms control treaties between the superpowers, SALT I and the ABM Treaty. In

1977, Jimmy Carter proclaimed that one of his goals would be the complete elimination of nuclear weapons, but Ronald Reagan championed nuclear deterrence as the centerpiece of US grand strategy in the 1980s.

While the end of the Cold War prompted new debates about US nuclear strategy, the September 11, 2001, attacks led some to conclude that nuclear weapons were essential to security. President George W. Bush appeared to have little faith in arms control agreements and focused instead on ways to enhance US nuclear leverage. His administration also argued that deterrence policy resting on mutual assured destruction (MAD) was a relic of the Cold War that should be jettisoned for preemption as a guiding principle for preserving US security. President Bush funded research and development of "mini-nukes" (or the Advanced Weapons Concept Initiative), "bunker-busters" (or the Robust Nuclear Earth Penetrator), and a revitalization program for nuclear warheads (Broad, Sanger, and Shanker 2007).

President Barack Obama tried to establish a coherent national security agenda in his first two years in office. The president pushed hard for Senate ratification of a new Strategic Arms Reduction Treaty (START) in 2010, sanctions on noncompliance with the NPT, interdiction programs for suspected illegal weapons shipments, and multilateral negotiation of a fissile material cutoff treaty. Obama's highest-profile initiative, though, was his April 2009 call for the complete elimination of nuclear weapons—to "seek the peace and security of a world without nuclear weapons" (White House 2009). While this call for disarmament echoed that of some of his predecessors and reflected a new political and intellectual movement—Global Zero—in favor of total elimination of nuclear weapons, skeptics charge that both the United States and the world have a very long road to travel toward this objective.

Prospects for the Future?

The proliferation of weapons is truly a major challenge to global security. One of the original catalysts of global proliferation was the Cold War arms race between the superpowers. But with that era now a distant memory, many scholars and politicians are taking a new look at incentives for proliferation in the twenty-first century. Some believe that we may be headed toward a nuclear-free world. They argue that a global build-down in tensions—a reverse proliferation—has occurred since the late 1980s. Skeptics warn, however, that many arms control initiatives are doomed to fail in a world where more countries are developing nuclear weapons, and the spread of civilian nuclear programs only exacerbates this problem. They truly doubt that President Obama's vision of a peaceful, nuclear weapons–free world will ever be realized.

Discussion Questions

1. Which of the four types of proliferation (as presented in Figure 3.1) do you think represents the most serious threat to international security?

2. Is the proliferation of conventional weapons a challenge that the global community can ever fully meet? Why or why not?

3. Is it possible that weapons proliferation could actually make the international system more stable in the twenty-first century? How might this occur?

4. What are some of the efforts that individual countries and international organizations have made to respond to the proliferation challenge? Which have been most effective, and why?

5. What are some implications of the trade-off between defense spending and social welfare spending?

6. What can governments do to confront threats of WMD terrorism? How have recent international developments changed the nature of horizontal WMD proliferation?

7. How might the trade in civilian nuclear technology contribute to weapons proliferation? Should technology-sharing be tightly curtailed in the twenty-first century? Why or why not?

8. Should governments use military force to stop would-be proliferators from threatening their security? Why or why not?

9. Do you believe that the Global Zero vision of a nuclear-free world is achievable in our lifetimes? Why or why not?

Suggested Readings

Cirincione, Joseph (2008) "Strategic Collapse: The Failure of the Bush Nuclear Doctrine." *Arms Control Today* (November).

Daalder, Ivo, and Jan Lodal (2008) "The Logic of Zero." *Foreign Affairs* 87, no. 6.

Einhorn, Robert (2015) "Debating the Iran Nuclear Deal." www.brookings.edu.

Fuhrmann, Matthew (2009) "Spreading Temptation: Proliferation and Peaceful Nuclear Cooperation Agreements." *International Security* 34, no. 1.

Joint Chiefs of Staff (2014) "Countering Weapons of Mass Destruction." www.dtic.mil.

Kroenig, Matthew (2010) *Exporting the Bomb: Technology Transfer and the Spread of Nuclear Weapons*. Ithaca: Cornell University Press.

Mueller, John (2010) *Atomic Obsession: Nuclear Alarmism from Hiroshima to al Qaeda*. London: Oxford University Press.

Perkovich, George (2006) "The End of the Nonproliferation Regime?" *Current History* (November).

Sagan, Scott D., and Kenneth N. Waltz (1995) *The Spread of Nuclear Weapons: A Debate*. New York: Norton.

Schell, Jonathan (2007) *The Seventh Decade: The New Shape of Nuclear Danger*. New York: Holt.

Stockholm International Peace Research Institute (2015) *SIPRI Yearbook: Armaments, Disarmament, and International Security*. Oxford: Oxford University Press.

4

Nationalism and the Clash of Identities

Lina M. Kassem, Anthony N. Talbott, and Michael T. Snarr

IN LATE FEBRUARY 1986, AS MANY AS 1 MILLION FILIPINOS LEFT THEIR homes in the middle of the night to form a human barricade around the Camp Crame military police base in Manila. The men, women, and children placed themselves in between the tanks of a vengeful dictator and a handful of coup leaders who had attempted to overthrow him. Catholic nuns, schoolchildren, dock workers, attorneys, farmers, business owners, and communist revolutionaries all joined together to stand in defiance of President Ferdinand Marcos. Why? What caused these wildly different people to unite? Was it some shared sense of purpose? Did a common destiny drive them? The answer is yes. The people of the Philippine People Power Revolution shared a common identity: Filipino. They saw themselves as belonging to a community, a community they imagined as encompassing all citizens of their country. They came together to rescue their country. They experienced a strong sense of *nationalism*. But what does this term mean?

Nationalism is a shared sense of identity based on important social distinctions that has the purpose of gaining or keeping control of the group's own destiny. Nationalism arises from many different sources. Shared ethnicity, language, religion, culture, history, and geographical proximity all generate feelings of comradeship and belonging to a certain group. As a result, human beings organize themselves into groups or communities. We are social beings. These communities determine how we interact with others and with whom we interact. They affect our perception of ourselves and of others. We consider other people either to be part of our group or to be outside of our group. Although we may have several identities (daughter or son, mother or father, spouse, club member, student, etc.), our nationality is one of the most important.

People unite into groups in pursuit of certain goals. Often this sense of shared identity becomes political. When the goal is self-determination for the group, the shared identification has become nationalism. In other words, when a group of sports fans identify with one another, but have no political aspirations, this does not constitute nationalism. But when a group of people seek to have political control over a given territory, then it becomes nationalism. Thus national self-determination is the main purpose of nationalism.

The shared identity of nationalism is often called an *imagined community,* because most citizens of a country, despite their strong feelings of fellowship, will never actually meet—let alone get to know—one another. But the feeling of unity remains. To understand nationalism, we must look at the origins of the nation and the state, how they have evolved, and the different shapes that nationalism takes in the world today.

The Evolution of the State

A state (also referred to as a country) is a political unit that has sovereignty over a geographical area. Sovereignty refers to the fact that the state is self-governing; that is, there is no external group or person that has authority over it. In other words, being sovereign means being "boss of your own turf." It is hard to imagine an alternative, but before the seventeenth century, states as we know them did not exist. Prior to the modern state, most people lived under political units referred to as empires. Empires usually included large swaths of land, encompassing many groups or nations. In Europe, between the fall of the Roman Empire and the beginning of the modern system of states, medieval feudalism was largely in place. Under feudalism, power was not as centralized as it was under the Roman Empire. Individual peasants had to answer to local nobles or kings, who in turn were loosely ruled by an empire. Lines of control and borders in medieval Europe were fuzzy at best. As Europe drew closer to the seventeenth century, the Catholic Church's power was increasingly called into question. The Protestant Reformation and secular authorities combined to challenge the Pope's authority. One tragic outcome was the Thirty Years' War (1618–1648), which pitted Protestants against Catholics and destroyed much of Europe.

The Treaty of Westphalia in 1648 ended this devastating war and recognized many independent, secular political units that would become modern states. One key distinguishing characteristic of these states was sovereignty. Unlike the earlier empires, which did not respect the right of other empires to govern their own territory, the new states recognized each other's sovereignty. In short, states were to govern themselves without outside interference. There was no distant secular emperor, king, or religious leader to control them. As a result, states slowly began to develop international law as a way to coordinate or govern relations between them.

The beginning of the modern state system did not happen overnight. It had begun to develop in Europe at least a century before the Treaty of Westphalia and slowly spread throughout the world in a process that is arguably still continuing today. In fact, most of the countries or states of today are relatively new.

The Role of Mapping and Geography

The next key factor in the development of our modern international system arose during the period of exploration and colonialism, from the fifteenth to the seventeenth century. It was mapping. Due to the desire by the British, Portuguese, Spanish, and other European powers to develop detailed navigational charts and to delineate their new colonial possessions, teams of surveyors and geographers were deployed to mark the precise locations and borders of the colonized territories. It is hard to overstate the importance of what we would consider to be this mundane act. Prior to the imposition of exact, national borders, large areas of land between states were in constant flux with few clear claims of control or ownership. States had frontiers, not borders. The power of a ruler usually diminished in direct proportion to the distance from the capital.

During this era, a ruler's power can best be viewed as a series of increasingly larger concentric circles radiating out from the capital. Each larger circle represents an area with a lesser degree of control by the ruler. Imagine a neighboring ruler's territory the same way. The areas that fell outside of the outer rings of power, or where the outer rings overlapped, were the frontiers or areas of disputed control. Once colonial officials drew and enforced precise borders between states, however, these frontiers vanished. This paved the way for rulers to exert control over every square inch of their territory and to attempt to compel the loyalty of every person living within their kingdom's borders. Think about the modern-day United States. Does the power of the American state diminish as one moves farther from Washington, D.C.? Does federal law become weaker in Maine or Alaska than in Virginia? Of course not. It was largely due to these precisely drawn borders that states could attempt to become sovereign and independent.

The Evolution of Nationalism

The creation of the modern state system and the reconceptualization of territory brought about by modern mapping paved the way for nationalism as we know it today. Prior to the spread of nationalism, most people were primarily concerned with local and personal affairs. People knew they were the subjects of powerful kings, queens, and emperors, but there were no serious attempts to foster a sense of common identity. Local rulers and feudal lords governed everyday matters. A vast gulf existed between rulers and those they ruled. Local people did not participate in government above the most basic levels. People knew only their family and others in the village. There was little sense of belonging to a larger, countrywide community. Slowly this began to change.

Although the roots of nationalism began before the end of the eighteenth century, most scholars point to the French Revolution as the defining moment for nationalism. Influenced by the Enlightenment, writers like John Locke and Jean-Jacques Rousseau argued that the people should govern themselves rather than being governed by kings or queens. Thus the concept of the divine right of kings was gradually replaced with the notion of the will of the people (known as popular sovereignty). The American (1776) and French (1789) revolutions greatly strengthened the idea that the people had the right to participate in their own governments. All rulers and governments seek legitimacy. When a government is legitimate, it means that the populace sees its rule over them as just, proper, and lawful. Legitimacy makes it much easier for rulers to govern their subjects, and the divine right of kings was a major source of this legitimacy. However, once the idea of popular sovereignty spread, it weakened the power of kings and queens by eroding the legitimacy of their rule.

Napoleon and the leaders of the French Revolution destroyed the French monarchy and tried to create a completely new state. They used popular sovereignty and the new sense of citizenship it fostered to create a psychological bond among the people that spread throughout France. For the first time, these varied people began to consider themselves as *Frenchmen* instead of members of a particular guild, religion, village, or region. This new identity led to many changes. People addressed one another as "citizen" rather than "sir," and a new flag was designed. France no longer had to pay mercenaries or force conscripts, but could now motivate an army of Frenchmen to fight for *their* country. United and empowered by nationalism, they did not merely fight for a ruler, they fought for France. The loyalty and fighting spirit this engendered made the French army nearly unstoppable. The kings and queens of Europe realized this, and soon after the French Revolution nationalism began to spread throughout Europe and gradually to the rest of the world.

With the erosion of the legitimacy of kings and queens brought about by the spread of popular sovereignty, and the great military advantage of having a nationalist army instead of merely mercenaries and conscripts, a new type of state began to arise. Kingdoms were gradually replaced by republics.

In a republic, legitimacy is not based upon heredity or the divine right of kings, but upon the consent of the governed. Nationalism is the glue that holds a republic together. But it can also be the force that rips a state apart.

Since the French Revolution, nationalism has been both a positive and a negative force in the world. It has united and divided peoples. It has brought peace and it has led to war. In one of its more negative forms, nationalism created a strong sense of superiority within Nazi Germany and led to the deaths of millions of innocent victims. Feelings of superiority and national pride within Europe also fueled the colonization of Africa and other parts of what we now call the South, or the developing world. In the case of Africa, colonization consisted of countries like Portugal, Great Britain, Germany, France, and others forcibly taking over and controlling the continent during the late nineteenth and early twentieth centuries. In what would become known as the "scramble for Africa," the European powers carved up the continent into colonies. These new political units ignored the existing tribal structure. In other words, very diverse groups, even enemies of one another, were forced together into colonies. The European colonial powers were able to take advantage of diverse groups living in Africa in a divide-and-conquer strategy that led to the subjugation of Africa. (Groups who identified with one another were sometimes split into separate units, as happened with the Somalis.)

Conversely, nationalism can often be a very positive force. For certain, nationalism offers many people a sense of belonging and meaning. In addition, it has rallied oppressed people to demand freedom. For example, in places like Africa, nationalism led to anticolonization. The colonized people of Africa and Asia (including the Middle East) eventually overcame their differences long enough to band together and overthrow their colonizers or persuade them to leave. The oppressive tactics of the colonizers ironically helped build a sense of shared identity among the diverse people within each colony that enabled them to build successful anticolonial movements.

Anticolonial nationalism had a dramatic effect on the world. As colonies rejected their colonizers, countries became independent, sovereign states. As a result, the decolonization of the twentieth century led to a dramatic increase in the number of states. Whereas in 1789 there were only 23 countries and in 1900 only 57, currently there are approximately 196 countries. These new countries were primarily formed in Africa and Asia, but other countries disintegrated, such as the Soviet Union and Yugoslavia. The new states led to smaller units that more closely resembled nation-states. For example, Croats and Slovenes, who formerly lived in a more multinational state (Yugoslavia), created more homogeneous countries named Croatia and Slovenia, respectively.

It is also interesting to note that during the short history of nationalism, many have predicted and called for its end or at least a reduction in its influence. After the death of millions in the two world wars, many argued that nationalism was too destructive. To a great extent, the League of Nations and the United Nations were designed to restrain the destructive tendencies of nationalism through international law. During the 1970s, as economic interdependence among countries increased, some argued that national allegiances would be reduced as the world's inhabitants interacted across country borders. At the core of this belief was the idea that, as countries became economically dependent on one another and cultural boundaries were frequently crossed, the strength of peoples' allegiances to their countries would erode. Needless to say, these predictions were premature—nationalism is alive and well today. To confirm nationalism's current importance, one need only look at the continuing struggle for some form of autonomy by the Kurdish communities in Turkey, Syria, Iran, and Iraq. The 2008 declaration of independence by Kosovo and the reaction of the Serbian minority there are other recent examples of the staying power of nationalism.

In sum, nationalism, mapping, and the modern state system, although different phenomena, all combined to lead to our current international system. As independent states began to form with newly defined borders, people living within these borders began to identify with one another. This process was aided by the concept of popular sovereignty, since people now had a stake in their government, and governments sought legitimacy for their rule. The natural result was what is called the nation-state.

The Nation-State

Although the term *nation-state* is generally used loosely to mean "country," it is technically defined as a single nation within the boundaries of a single state. It combines the concepts of *state, territory,* and *nation* (people) explained earlier. Very few modern countries are actually nation-states, but this is the ideal. For example, there exist nations that do not have a common state. One example would be Koreans, who are divided into peoples of North and South Korea. Another example is the Kurds, a group of people who identify with one another but are spread throughout northern Iraq, southern Turkey, western Iran, and other countries.

Similarly, there are dozens of examples of multinational states—single states within which multiple nations live. In many African countries, for instance, there are multiple tribes who historically fought one another but who now, since becoming united into sovereign countries in the last half of the twentieth century, live together within the same borders. Canada is another example. Within predominately English-speaking Canada sits the French-speaking province of Quebec. Nationalism in Quebec is so strong that nearly half of its citizens have voted to break away from Canada and create their own country. Also within Canada are several indigenous (native) groups who have resisted considering themselves Canadians. This is not uncommon. Throughout the world, thousands of indigenous groups are part of countries with which they do not identify. As a result, many of the contemporary countries cannot technically be considered nation-states.

Different Perspectives on Nationalism

Nationalism is a complex subject. Scholars disagree on when it first emerged and whether it is generally good or bad. There are also different ways to categorize nationalism. One of the most common ways is to consider nationalism as either civic or ethnic.

Civic vs. Ethnic Nationalism

If we define nationalism as a shared sense of identity based on important social distinctions that has the purpose of gaining or keeping control of the group's own destiny, then civic and ethnic nationalism are based on different sets of these social distinctions. Civic nationalism is associated with the Western experience and is based on citizenship rather than on ethnic linkages. The nation-state is seen as the core of civic nationalism. Its main role is to promote the principle that a society is united by territoriality, citizenship, and civic rights and legal codes transmitted to all members of the group. All members of this society, regardless of their ethnicity or race, are ideally equal citizens and equal before the law.

By contrast, ethnic nationalism arose in the East and the South as a response to the West. It is based on ethnicity. Ethnic nationalism draws its ideological bonds from the people and their native history. It relies on elements that are considered purely unique to a group, such as collective memory, common language and values, and shared religion, myth, and symbolism. It is dependent on blood ties, bonds to the land, and native traditions.

To understand nationalism, it is important to consider degrees of inclusiveness and exclusiveness. All nationalism is, by definition, exclusive—it excludes all people who are not members of that nation. In other words, how broadly defined is the nation? How many different subgroups make up the main group of people who compose the nation? History, culture, social-class structure, and form of government are all important. All of these influence how community is imagined and how nationalism is constructed. Civic nationalism is more inclusive than ethnic nationalism because anyone can potentially become a member of the nation. For example, Americans primarily experience civic nationalism, while Kurds are primarily ethnic nationalists. A Kurd could move to the United States and become a naturalized US citizen and, hence, a member of the American nation. In contrast, a non-Kurdish American who moved to northern Iraq could not change his or her ethnicity and would likely never be accepted as a member of the Kurdish nation.

Many scholars have treated these two types of nationalism as being diametrically opposed and have assigned value judgments to them. Civic nationalism is typically seen as the "good" form of nationalism. For instance, in most democracies of the world, an individual is a citizen not because of bloodlines, but because he or she believes in the ideals and symbols of that country and pledges allegiance to the country. Ethnic nationalism is viewed as having more negative characteristics, such as being more exclusive due to its emphasis on ethnic links between people. In other words, if you don't share the common history, language, and other ethnic ties, you are not part of the nation.

Although many scholars present these two categories of nationalism as being opposites, this is not always the case in practice. For example, the Philippine People Power Revolution, mentioned in the opening paragraph of this chapter, displayed elements of both civic and ethnic nationalism. Myth, race, religion, and citizenship all combined to unite and empower the people. As well, the civic nationalism of the United States has long displayed a strong ethnic component. Minority groups have struggled for many years to be considered full citizens with equal rights.

Pro-State vs. Anti-State Nationalism

Due to these issues, some scholars reject the civic and ethnic categories altogether. Instead, they see nationalism in terms of its primary purpose: Does it support or attempt to overthrow an existing government? Pro-state nationalism supports the existing state. It tends to originate in, or at least be guided by, the rulers of the state and is often termed *official nationalism*. It acts as the link between a unified people and their legitimate government.

Anti-state nationalism has the opposite purpose. It is the unifying ideology of a people who oppose what they see as an illegitimate state. This often takes the form of anticolonialism: a group of nationalists unite and organize their people in order to overthrow a foreign, colonial state. In post–World War II Indonesia, for example, nationalists created a new flag, a new language, and a new country in order to unite the diverse ethnicities of the Dutch East Indies and empower them to rise up in revolution against the Dutch colonial government.

Nationalism is often considered to be the most powerful political force of the twentieth century, and so far also of the twenty-first. At least since World War II, every successful war of independence and revolution has been driven by nationalism. During the same period, every government in power has used nationalism to gain the support of its people. Nationalism is a powerful tool that can liberate, oppress, or empower people.

Nationalism, Religion, and Violence

Nationalism and violence often go hand in hand. "United we stand, divided we fall" is the ultimate call to arms of the nationalist. The "us" versus "them" mentality operates in all types and sizes of communities—from rival villages arguing over grazing rights, to international coalitions involved in geopolitical disputes. Wars are fought for nationalist reasons. Nationalists overthrow governments. Often innocent civilians are targeted by nationalist groups claiming to be freedom fighters. Just as often, states also target civilians as collateral damage in pursuit of those they label as terrorists. The potential for violence often increases when the causes of nationalism and religion overlap. This is because nationality and religion are the two most powerful forms of identification in the world today. When people think about who they are, many, if not most, think of themselves as Americans or Turks or Thais, and as Christians or Muslims or Buddhists. Nationalism and religion are also the only two forces in the modern world that can legitimate social violence (as opposed to personal violence). A soldier who kills for her country is a hero. A person who dies for their religion is a martyr. Killing or dying in the name of your country or religion is not only accepted but also highly honored in most societies.

Although violence often accompanies nationalism, this is not always the case. Mahatma Gandhi's "Quit India" movement against the British was a remarkably nonviolent effort that relied on anti-state nationalism. The Philippine People Power Revolution also relied on peaceful means to achieve its goals. The nonviolent, antigovernment protests in Tunisia, Egypt, and Yemen during 2011's Arab Spring are also examples of nonviolent nationalism.

It should also be mentioned that while religion often intensifies nationalist feelings, it can also be a powerful motivator that transcends or even opposes nationalism. Take, for example, Osama bin Laden. If the traditional notion of nationalism were applied to him, one might have expected bin Laden to be a patriotic Saudi Arabian nationalist, since he was a citizen of Saudi Arabia. Yet this couldn't be further from the truth. Bin Laden's allegiance was not to Saudi Arabia or Yemen (his family's country of origin), but rather to Islam. He felt a far greater allegiance to Pakistani, Algerian, Jordanian, and even American Muslims who shared his interpretation of Islam, than he did to Saudi Arabians who did not share his religious beliefs.

Christianity in the United States is also an interesting case study. Some American Christians see the United States as a country favored by God and founded on Christian beliefs. To them, Jesus, US patriotism, and bellicose foreign policy decisions go hand in hand. Meanwhile, other Christians are horrified at the meshing of Jesus and US militarism. They focus on the New Testament's commands to "love one's enemy" and "turn the other cheek." In fact, an increasingly vocal group of American Christians argue that followers of Jesus in the United States should reconsider their national allegiances, as they may have more in common with fellow Christians outside the United States (including China and Iraq) than with non-Christians within the United States. Although these radical religious views do not immediately threaten nationalism as a whole, they have raised some interesting issues for people of faith.

* * *

In sum, nationalism is a tremendously important political force. From its origins in Europe, it has spread to every corner of the world. Nationalism is also a complicated concept that encompasses a wide range of expressions. It can be inclusive or exclusive, violent or nonviolent. It depends on the environment in which it develops, on the will of the leaders shaping it, and on how all the people involved imagine it.

The Israeli-Palestinian Conflict

The Israeli-Palestinian conflict provides an excellent case study of how nationalism works today. Palestinians are united by strong historical, territorial, and anticolonial forms of nationalism, while Israelis are motivated by a strong sense of religious nationalism. Self-determination is the guiding principle for both groups. How each of these two communities imagines itself affects how inclusive or exclusive it is. Ethnic nationalism is present for both Palestinians and Israelis. The total population of the state of Israel is slightly over 8 million. In 1950, the state passed the "law of return," which mandates that anyone who identifies themselves as Jewish qualifies for Israeli citizenship as soon as they arrive in the state, regardless of birthplace. This is significant, since a Jewish religious identity was all that is needed for citizenship, and it lends additional support to the state's definition of itself as a Jewish state, this definition excludes all the native Palestinian Arab population. Although international law does guarantee individuals the right to return to their homeland, Palestinians who were forced to flee their homes, as well as their dependents, were not allowed to return to their homes and their land was expropriated. Approximately 25 percent of Israel's citizens are Palestinian, including Muslims, Christians, and Druze. According to a 2014 study by the Palestinian Central Bureau of Statistics, the number of Palestinians and Jews in Israel and the occupied areas will be equal by 2016, but the number of Palestinians will exceed that of Jews by 2020 (PCBS 2014). These Palestinians are the descendants of the Arabs who lived in the area prior to the establishment of the state of Israel. Being non-Jews, it is difficult for them to identify with a state that defines itself

Table 4.1 Palestinian Demographics, 2014

	Number of Palestinian Arabs	Number of Israeli Jews
West Bank and East Jerusalem	2,790,331	300,000 settlers in East Jerusalem 350,000 settlers in West Bank
Gaza	1,760,037	
Israel	1,460,000 Palestinian Arabs with Israeli citizenship	5,336,985
Total	6,010,368	6,036,985[a]

Source: PCBS (2014).
Note: a. Approximately 19,000 Israeli Jewish settlers living in Israeli-occupied Golan Heights since 1967.

as a Jewish state. Although they live in Israel, and have lived on the same land for centuries, they do not enjoy the full rights of citizenship. To complicate matters, there are also Palestinians living under Israeli occupation, on land that Israel occupied as a result of the 1967 war (see Table 4.1). These Palestinians have been insisting on their right to self-determination, something that Palestinians have the right to according to the Universal Declaration of Human Rights. The conflict, which has now lasted nearly a century, has been expressed through both violent and nonviolent means. The terrorist tactics used by extremists on both sides, Israeli and Palestinian, are tragic examples of the violent potential of nationalism.

Historical Background

By the beginning of the twentieth century, European colonial powers effectively controlled over 85 percent of the world's natural resources as well as its peoples. Arab nationalism, which is at the center of the Israeli-Palestinian conflict, is a response to this European and foreign intervention. It was an attempt to assert Arab self-determination and independence from colonialism. In Palestine, Arab nationalism developed in response to another form of nationalism, Zionism. Zionists desired to create a homeland for Jews. Mostly born out of the European Jewish experience, Zionism was a response to the violent persecution that Jews suffered at the hands of Europeans. Russian persecution of Jews in the late nineteenth century resulted in the first wave of Jewish emigration to Palestine.

In the late nineteenth century, Theodor Herzl, widely regarded as the father of Zionism, came to the conclusion that the only solution for the plight of the Jews would be the creation of a Jewish homeland. Herzl, a secular, assimilated European Jew, considered several locations for a Jewish homeland, including possible locations in East Africa and South America. Other Zionists argued that the more religious Jews would join the Zionist project if the proposed homeland was in the biblical land of Palestine. The idea of establishing a Jewish state would also gain the support of Christian Zionists, who advocated restoration of the Jewish homeland based on their belief that the Bible promises it to the Jewish people. On the other hand, the Palestinians have inhabited the land for generations and see themselves as the descendants of the Canaanites, the original inhabitants of Palestine. They saw the new Jewish immigrants as a threat, since the latter did not intend to assimilate into the existing communities but rather to establish a competing claim to the land.

At the outbreak of World War I, the Arabs were under the control of the Ottoman Empire, which was allied with Germany. Britain, hoping to weaken the Ottomans from within, turned to the Arabs. In return for helping the British in the war effort, mostly by revolting against the Ottoman Turks, the Arabs of the region, including Palestine, were promised independence. This promise was articulated through a series of letters in 1915 between Hussein bin Ali, Sharif of Mecca, and Sir Henry McMahon, the British high commissioner in Egypt. The British were also very aware of the strategic importance of the region. Oil had already been discovered in areas of Iraq and Iran, and the Middle East represented an important strategic point on the trade route to India. Motivated by their strategic interest in the area, the British signed a secret agreement with the French that divided the entire Middle East into spheres of influence for the two colonial powers. This agreement, negotiated in 1916, became known as the Sykes-Picot Agreement, and contradicted Britain's earlier promises to the Arabs under the Hussein-McMahon letters, and would later also contradict another of Britain's pledges, this time to the Jews in the form of the Balfour Declaration.

In Palestine at the beginning of the twentieth century, Palestinians outnumbered Jews—both native and recent arrivals—about ten to one. Despite this, the British decided, for economic and political reasons, to support a Jewish homeland in Palestine. In 1917 the British issued the Balfour Declaration, which stated: "His Majesty's Government views with favor the establishment in Palestine of a national home for the Jewish people." Many books have been written in an attempt to decipher the true intentions of this declaration; however, it is clear that the British decided that it would serve their interests to support a Jewish homeland on territory where Palestinians had lived for centuries.

The Treaty of Versailles, which ended World War I, gave mandates to France and Britain to divide up the region into client states, under their domination. Palestine, during this mandate period (1919–1947), fell under the direct control of the British. This treaty opened the way for the Jewish National Fund (the Jewish land-purchasing agency of the Zionist movement) to start buying large amounts of land in Palestine, and Jewish settlers began building homes there. These large land acquisitions by the Jewish National Fund, coupled with the Balfour Declaration and Zionist aspirations, became increasingly threatening to Palestinian landowners and farmers. Palestinians feared that they might lose their land rights and become minorities in their homeland. As a result, fighting between the local Palestinian residents and Jewish settlers erupted.

During World War II, the Allied nations, including the United States, refused to open their borders to Jewish refugees fleeing the Holocaust. At the end of the war, when the horror and magnitude of the Holocaust were exposed, the Allies felt a great deal of sympathy for the Jewish people, along with a great deal of guilt. In late 1947, the United Nations decided to "partition" Palestine into two states, one Jewish and one Arab. The UN's partition plan gave 53 percent of the land to the Jews, who accounted for 30 percent of the population, and gave the remaining 47 percent of the land to the Arabs, who accounted for 70 percent of the population and had, until then, owned 92 percent of the land. The Arabs of mandate Palestine, made up of Christians, Muslims, and Druze, collectively known as Palestinians, felt that they were being forced to give up their historical land to compensate European Jews for crimes committed against the Jews by other Europeans. Immediately after the partition announcement, fighting broke out. Figure 4.1 briefly summarizes this war and three subsequent Arab-Israeli wars.

In the 1947–1948 war and the 1967 war, Israel acquired land beyond what the UN had given it (see Figure 4.2). These land acquisitions are especially important for understanding current land disputes. In 1964, the Palestine Liberation Organization (PLO) was formed by exiled Palestinian nationalists who had become disillusioned with the inability of other Arab leaders to liberate Palestine. Yasser Arafat emerged as its national leader, a role he held until his death in November 2004. The PLO helped unite both Palestinians living in exile and those living in the Occupied Territories, and gave voice to their hopes for self-determination and national independence, using a combination of diplomatic initiatives as well as armed struggle to gain international recognition for their national rights.

An important development was the first intifada, or uprising (1987–1993). In the West Bank and Gaza Strip, Israeli occupation became increasingly marked by human rights violations, including administrative detentions, land confiscations, and the destruction of Palestinian homes. Palestinians pointed to the fourth Geneva Convention's prohibition of these tactics. Israeli authorities argued that most of these actions were emergency measures to protect the security of Israeli citizens. Palestinians argued that these measures, such as home demolitions and land expropriations, were methods of acquiring more land for Israeli settlements.

The first intifada began in December 1987, following an incident in which four Palestinian workers were killed in Gaza. As a result, Palestinians took to the streets in protest. The intifada was symbolized by Palestinian youth throwing rocks at Israeli soldiers, who in turn retaliated with gunfire. The spontaneous uprising was a result of frustration over two decades

Figure 4.1 Arab-Israeli Wars

War of 1947–1948. As soon as the United Nations announced the partition plan in November 1947, fighting broke out. Subsequently, Jewish underground organizations (including several terrorist groups), being much more organized than any Palestinian resistance, achieved several strategic victories. Most Arab armies around Palestine were reluctant to intervene. On May 15, 1948, the state of Israel was declared. Over the next few days, armies from several Arab countries invaded Israel. At the end of the war, Israel had acquired close to 80 percent of the Palestine mandate. Jordan annexed what remained of Palestine (the West Bank), and Egypt took control of the Gaza Strip. Of the more than 1 million Palestinians, as many as 800,000 were forced to leave their homes. More than 500 Palestinian villages were either destroyed or depopulated. These Palestinians would become refugees, mostly in neighboring Arab states.

War of 1956. In 1956, Egyptian president Abdel Nasser nationalized the Suez Canal. Israel allied itself with Britain and France and invaded Egypt. The United States asked for and received a cease-fire, with UN peacekeepers maintaining a buffer zone between Israel and Egypt.

War of 1967 (Six Day War). The United Arab Republic (union of Egypt and Syria) asked for the withdrawal of the UN forces from the cease-fire lines. Israel, believing an attack from Egypt was imminent, launched a "preemptive" attack. Israel mobilized and attacked Jordan, capturing the West Bank and East Jerusalem (which had been annexed by Jordan in 1948). Israel also captured the Golan Heights (which was part of Syria), the Sinai Peninsula (which was part of Egypt), and the Gaza Strip (which had been annexed by Egypt in 1948). Following the war, the UN Security Council passed Resolution 242, requiring Israel to withdraw from the West Bank, Gaza, and all other areas it occupied as a result of the 1967 war.

War of 1973 (Yom Kippur War). Egypt and Syria attacked Israel in an attempt to reclaim Syrian and Egyptian territories occupied by Israel. Although the Egyptians were able to make strong advances early in the war, the Israelis rallied and pushed them back. Intervention by the United States and the Soviet Union led to a cease-fire. This war signaled the last major effort by Arab states to liberate Palestinian territory. In 1979, US president Jimmy Carter brokered a peace agreement between Egyptian president Anwar Sadat and Israeli prime minister Menachem Begin, which returned the Sinai Peninsula to Egypt. As a result, Egypt agreed to recognize the state of Israel as well as establish full diplomatic relations between the two states. The peace process was based on the acceptance by both parties of UN Security Council Resolution 242, which recognized the legitimacy of the state of Israel in its pre-1967 borders.

of Israeli occupation and systematic violations of human rights. The demonstrations and the rock-throwing were only a small part of it; the intifada would become a mass mobilization movement of mostly peaceful resistance to the Israeli presence. The intifada and the Israeli response had a

Figure 4.2 The Expansion of Israel

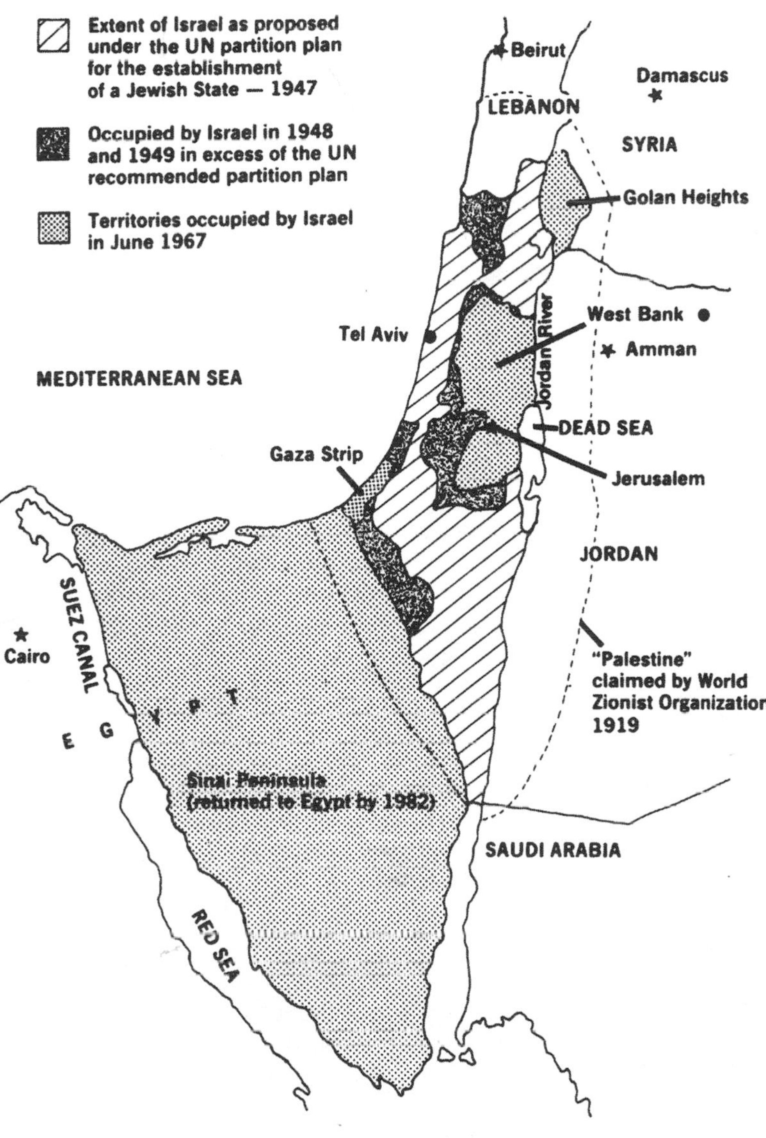

wide-ranging effect. For instance, when Israelis shut down Palestinian schools for three years, Palestinian students, teachers, and community leaders organized an alternative education for the students. Palestinians also organized boycotts of Israeli products.

Extremist groups on both sides feared the creation of a lasting peace, which might require compromise on both sides. In a dramatic illustration of the determined opposition on the Israeli side, a Jewish member of an extremist group assassinated Israeli prime minister Yitzhak Rabin in Tel Aviv in 1995. Just as Jewish extremists were using violence in an attempt to stop the peace process, Palestinian extremists also stepped up violent opposition in an attempt to destroy whatever was left of Israeli-Palestinian peace talks, known as the Oslo Accords (see Figure 4.3). Members of Palestinian extremist groups carried out suicide bombings in Jerusalem and Tel Aviv. Israelis blamed Arafat, who in 1996 was elected president in the first ever Palestinian elections. They were frustrated by the inability of his government, the Palestinian Authority (an administrative authority established after Oslo to administer some areas of the West Bank and the Gaza Strip), to control violent extremist groups, some of which had been responsible for attacks against Israeli civilians.

In September 2000, a visit by Israeli defense minister Ariel Sharon to the Temple Mount (the site of the al-Aqsa Mosque—the third holiest site in Islam) in East Jerusalem sparked widespread demonstrations, which resulted in the killing of six unarmed Palestinian demonstrators. This incident marked the beginning of a second intifada, which would become known as the al-Aqsa intifada, and increased militarization of the Occupied Territories. Whereas the first intifada was mostly a nonviolent resistance against the occupation, the second was shaped by the excessive use of violence on both sides. The continued military occupation of the West Bank and Gaza Strip facilitated the rise of extremist elements within Palestinian society. Groups such as Hamas increasingly resorted to terror attacks against Israeli civilians. Suicide bombers became their weapon of choice. Israelis began to undertake targeted assassinations of Hamas leaders and activists, often involving the death of innocent Palestinian civilians, including women and children. The Israelis continued to use other means of collective punishment, such as house demolitions, curfews, and mass imprisonment.

In 2002, Israel reoccupied all Palestinian areas it had withdrawn from as part of the Oslo process. Arafat was held responsible for failing to control Hamas and the other extremist groups, and was placed under house arrest in his headquarters in Ramallah (in the West Bank). Israel began construction of what it referred to as a "security fence" (actually a 403-mile-long, 25-foot-high concrete wall) within the West Bank, maintaining that this was an attempt to protect its citizens from terrorist attacks. The wall not only was built well into Palestinian territory, but also was an attempt to confiscate ad-

Figure 4.3 Israeli-Palestinian Peace Attempts

1988. A key development occurred in 1988 when Yasser Arafat accepted UN Security Council Resolution 242. This resolution called for the withdrawal of Israel from territories seized in the 1967 war as a basis for any just and lasting peace in the Middle East. This resolution has become the cornerstone of most international efforts to negotiate peace. Also in 1988, Arafat condemned terrorism for the first time and accepted Israel's right to exist.

1993. The Oslo Accords resulted from secret negotiations between Israel and the Palestine Liberation Organization. The basic principle of these negotiations was "land for peace," by which Israel would return land to the Palestinians, who in turn would halt attacks on Israel. As part of the peace accords, the Palestinian Authority was created and given limited home rule. Opposition emerged on both sides, and key issues such as Jerusalem, settlements, and the right of return for Palestinian refugees were left for later negotiations.

2000. Israeli prime minister Ehud Barak met with Arafat at Camp David, Maryland, and President Bill Clinton acted as the moderator. Although Barak was willing to return a larger part of the Occupied Territories (up to 80 percent) than any of his predecessors, he insisted that this portion be divided into several sections. This solution would leave Palestinians with small, unconnected areas of land, surrounded by areas controlled by Israel, making a Palestinian state impossible. The right of return for Palestinian refugees proved to be another major stumbling block.

2003. US president George W. Bush, supporting separate states for Israelis and Palestinians, announced his "roadmap for peace." The roadmap pushed for a stop to the building of Jewish settlements and to Palestinian violence. However, increased violence on both sides led to heightened frustration for Jews and Palestinians, and the US invasion of Iraq diverted attention away from the peace process.

2004. Israeli prime minister Ariel Sharon closed some settlements in the West Bank and all of the settlements in Gaza. However, Israel continued to control the airspace, territorial waters, and land passages of the West Bank and Gaza. Although Israeli public opinion appeared to support this dramatic move, it drew angry protests from within Israel. Palestinian critics argued that the targeted settlements represented only a fraction of Israel's settlements in the West Bank, and that they were already being replaced by additional new settlements in other areas of the West Bank. Most Palestinian and international critics argued that, although settlements in Gaza had been dismantled, Palestinians still lacked real sovereignty.

Palestinians often argue that Israel has never really been interested in Gaza, that it intends to withdraw only from Gaza, but not from most of the West Bank. More recently, Hamas's seizure of control of Gaza could be seen as a major blow to nationalist aspirations of having a viable Palestinian state in the areas occupied by Israel in 1967 (West Bank and Gaza).

(continues)

Figure 4.3 continued

2005. Israel announced a complete withdrawal from Gaza, though it still controlled borders and the territorial waters. Israeli prime minister Ariel Sharon ordered the complete evacuation of all Jewish settlements in Gaza, along with a complete troop withdrawal. This move was seen by some scholars as an Israeli strategy to gain greater concessions and create a situation that would be nearly impossible to reverse in the West Bank and East Jerusalem. In return for the withdrawal from Gaza, the Israelis did receive guarantees from the United States that they could keep some of the larger settlements in the West Bank in the final negotiations.

2006. Hamas won in the first election held after Israeli troops left Gaza. In response, several Western powers withdrew promised financial support to Palestinians. Israeli forces targeted Hamas-controlled police stations along with other facilities controlled by Hamas. A complete blockade of Gaza was enforced by the Israeli military. Ultimately the renewed confrontation culminated in a full Israeli invasion of Gaza in 2008. The invasion resulted in the death of over 1,300 Palestinians (mostly civilians according to the UN) and thirteen Israelis, three of whom were civilians.

2014. Israel again bombarded the Gaza Strip, which again resulted in heavy casualties among Palestinians, estimated at over 1,800. During the conflict, sixty-four Israeli soldiers and three Israeli civilians were killed. An independent UN commission was tasked to investigate possible war crimes during the war on Gaza, and the commission's report indicated that Israel had indeed committed war crimes. Even though the report did place some blame on Hamas fighters, Israel received the bulk of the blame. The chair of the commission, Justice Mary McGowan Davis, described the destruction in Gaza as "unprecedented" and said that it "will impact generations to come" and that "in the 51 day operation, 1,462 Palestinian civilians were killed, a third of them children"(UNHRC 2015c).

ditional Palestinian lands. Critics also point out that, in many cases, the wall separated Palestinian communities from their hospitals, schools, and farms. Although in 2004 the International Court of Justice ruled that the wall violated international law, Israel continued to build it.

In November 2004, Arafat died. In January 2005, Mahmoud Abbas was elected to replace him as president of the Palestinian Authority. The election of Abbas, along with the Sharm el-Sheikh summit, brought an end to the second intifada. In 2006, Hamas, which is currently on the US State Department's list of terrorist organizations, won a majority in the Palestinian Legislative Council elections. Others point to the Hamas victory as a clear sign of Palestinian resentment against a corrupt Palestinian Authority, which for some appears to be taking on the role of "prison guard" for the Israeli occupation, as well as a clear sign of disenchantment with continuous peace proposals that have not materialized, restrictions on their movement, and an illegal wall blocking access to their farmland.

In Gaza, Hamas was able to provide badly needed social services and the means for Palestinians to protest their worsening socioeconomic status. The major aid donors to the Palestinian Authority, the United States and several European Union nations, reacted to the election of Hamas by withholding all financial support. The justification was that Hamas had refused to abide by the three conditions imposed on it by the United States, the European Union, Russia, and Israel: recognize Israel's "right to exist," renounce violence, and accept the terms of all previous agreements between the Palestinian Authority and Israel. The first condition is particularly problematic, since by accepting Israel's "right to exist" Hamas would be agreeing to the legitimacy of the expulsion of about 800,000 Palestinians from their homes in 1948, something to which most, if not all, Palestinians would object. The Israelis tried to tighten the noose around the neck of Hamas by enforcing a tight embargo against the people of Gaza. This attempt to starve Hamas out of power had devastating consequences on the entire Palestinian population. The conflict escalated in December 2008 when Israel launched a full-fledged invasion of Gaza. The Israeli government, which code-named the invasion Operation Cast Lead, argued that this was a defensive operation to end rocket attacks being launched from Gaza. The Israeli campaign, which completely devastated Gaza, resulted in the death of more than 1,400 Palestinians and 13 Israeli soldiers. During the bombing attacks, schools, shelters, and a United Nations compound were hit, actions that were condemned by the international community, with the notable exception of the United States. This also highlighted the divisions between Hamas and the Fatah-led Palestinian Authority in the West Bank, with Hamas accusing Abbas and the Palestinian Authority of complicity with the Israelis and the Americans. Palestinians now fear that if the situation is not resolved soon, it could lead to two separate entities, neither of which, alone, could achieve sovereign status.

A majority of Israelis favor returning land in the West Bank and Gaza to the Palestinians if it would mean an end to the conflict. And the majority of Palestinians want an end to the occupation of the West Bank and Gaza and the establishment of a viable Palestinian state. However, there are disagreements over how to attain these objectives. Although Israel did withdraw from Gaza (but continued to control access to it) in 2005, no Israeli leadership has ever offered complete withdrawal from the West Bank and East Jerusalem (based on UN Security Council Resolution 242), and Palestinians argue that anything less will not allow them to establish a viable state.

Major Obstacles to Peace

Finding a lasting resolution to the Arab-Israeli conflict has proven to be extremely difficult. Some of the main obstacles have been illegal Israeli settlements, the right of return of Palestinian refugees, East Jerusalem, and terrorism.

Israeli settlements. A major stumbling block in Israeli-Palestinian negotiations has been what to do with illegal Israeli settlements in the West Bank. Approximately 547,000 Israeli settlers live in the West Bank (B'Tselem.org 2015), controlling more than 42 percent of the area (Hareuveni 2010). The area of land that falls under direct control of the Palestinian Authority in the West Bank currently constitutes less than 10 percent. Palestinians point out that the fourth Geneva Convention prohibits any occupying power from establishing settlements in occupied territories. Israel itself is divided on the issue of settlements—some favor moving settlers out of the territories, while others see such a move as betraying the Zionist cause. Even those in favor of moving the settlers acknowledge that it would be extremely difficult politically for the Israeli government to force Jewish settlers from their homes in the Occupied Territories. Israeli settlements continue to be a source of friction between Israeli leaders and even their close allies, including American officials. President Barack Obama is the most recent in a long line of presidents who have expressed their opposition to Israeli settlement policy. Israeli leaders continue to grant permission to more and more settlements, and for existing settlements to expand at the same time to continue to confiscate lands from Palestinians in order to accommodate the expansions of the settlements. This has been especially problematic in East Jerusalem, where the Israeli authorities are trying to establish "facts on the ground" by confiscating land from Palestinians in order to allow for the expansion of more Israeli settlements. This so-called Judaization of Jerusalem, is an attempt at eradicating Palestinian Arab presence from the holy city. As a result of these policies, Palestinians from Jerusalem (who have seldom participated in violent activities) have taken part in targeted attacks against Israeli soldiers and settlers.

Palestinian refugees' right of return. The right of Palestinians to return to their original homes has been a central issue to the larger Israeli-Palestinian conflict. Palestinians argue that Israel, despite international law, has consistently refused to allow Palestinians, who were forced to flee their homes in 1947–1948, to do so. To complicate matters, these Palestinian refugees are often not granted any rights in their host countries. In Lebanon, Palestinians are not allowed to own land or work unless through the United Nations Relief and Works Agency for Palestine Refugees in the Near East (UNRWA). Israel refuses to allow these refugees to return, arguing that it would be a demographic disaster for the Jewish state. If Palestinians were to return to their original homeland in Israel, they would outnumber Israelis, who are already concerned with the high birthrates of Palestinian populations compared to the much lower birthrates of Jewish populations.

East Jerusalem. Christianity, Islam, and Judaism have in common the patriarch Abraham, and all three consider Jerusalem to be holy land. Both the Israelis and the Palestinians lay claim to Jerusalem as their capital. Access to religious sites is a central issue in the conflict over Jerusalem. The Israeli occupation continues to restrict many Palestinians in the occupied West Bank from access to religious sites in occupied East Jerusalem. Security concerns have always been the rationale used by the Israelis for restricting access. Although international law rejects Israel's annexation of predominantly Arab East Jerusalem, which was part of Palestinian-controlled territory prior to the 1967 war, approximately 250,000 Israeli settlers live in occupied East Jerusalem. Palestinians continue to demand that Arab East Jerusalem become the capital of a future Palestinian state, while the Israelis refuse to divide Jerusalem, claiming that it should forever be the capital of the state of Israel. More recently as part of the Judaization of East Jerusalem, increasing numbers of Palestinians have been forced to leave their homes. The Christian community has been especially hard-hit, and according to Attallah Hanna (2009), the archbishop of Sevastia (of the Greek Orthodox Patriarchate of Jerusalem), the Christian population of the city "is down to 10,000 after being 40,000 in 1967 at the beginning of the Israeli occupation."

Terrorism. Israeli officials argue that a major obstacle to peace is the continuous threat of terrorism that the state must endure from extremist groups. Israel has blamed the Palestinian Authority for not being able to stop these groups, such as Hamas, from carrying out suicide missions. The Palestinian Authority is therefore, Israelis argue, not a legitimate negotiation partner. Palestinians reject the terrorism label and argue that they are engaged in armed struggle for liberation, which is legitimate under international law. They maintain that the occupation of Palestinian lands is the cause of these attacks, and if the occupation of the West Bank and Gaza Strip ends, then so too will the attacks. Palestinians also point out that the Israeli army engages in state terrorism against Palestinians, which perpetuates the violence. Recent statistics confirm that the number of Israeli civilian deaths caused by armed Palestinian groups is many times fewer than the number of Palestinian civilian deaths caused by the Israeli forces (B'Tselem.org 2014).

Internal Palestinian Division. Division among Palestinian groups, especially between Fatah and Hamas, has also undermined a peaceful resolution to the conflict. Currently Hamas has authority in Gaza, while the

Palestinian Authority, largely dominated by the Fatah faction (the faction that was founded by Yasser Arafat, and the faction of the current president of the Palestinian authority, Mahmoud Abbas) has authority in the West Bank.

It is important to note, however, that Palestinian resistance to Israeli occupation has also included nonviolent movements. One significant example, mentioned earlier, is the first Palestinian intifada, which began in 1987. Another example is the Boycott, Divestment, and Sanctions movement (BDS). BDS—a nonviolent movement organized by Palestinians that urges various forms of boycott against Israel until it ends its occupation of all Arab lands occupied in June 1967. This campaign wants the state of Israel to recognize the fundamental rights of all Palestinians, including the full equality of the Arab-Palestinian citizens of Israel. The movement also calls for the implementation of UN General Assembly Resolution 194, which calls for a right of return for all Palestinian refugees to their homeland. The campaign has three main strategies. The first is the boycotting of Israeli products and companies that are regarded as profiting from violating Palestinian rights. Similar to the campaign against apartheid South Africa, the Palestinian campaign also calls for a boycott of Israeli sporting, cultural, and academic events and institutions. It is significant to note that the BDS campaign was endorsed by the African National Congress of South Africa in 2012.

A second strategy employed by the Palestinian campaign is divestment from corporations seen as being complicit in the violation of Palestinian rights. This effort has gained significant support around the world, especially on university campuses. Students on US campuses, for example, have demanded that their campuses divest from companies that support continuation of the occupation of Palestinian lands. Successes have included the passage of resolutions in support of divestment at Stanford University and Princeton University, and on seven of the nine campuses of the University of California. This has taken a significant toll on Israeli foreign direct investment, which decreased 46 percent in 2014 compared to 2013 (Glantz 2014).

The third strategy used by the Palestinian campaign is international sanctions. This is especially effective, since it brands Israel as a violator of international law. Though this strategy has seen successes, they have been significant. Most recently, in 2014, seventeen European Union member states took action against businesses that have economic links to Israeli settlements. Among the most significant signs that the Palestinian campaign overall is succeeding is the labeling of the campaign by Israeli state officials, such as Prime Minister Benjamin Netanyahu, as a major strategic threat to the Israeli State.

Nationalism and the Future

Historically speaking, the state system and nationalism are relatively young. However, both have an extremely strong impact on our lives. As in the past few hundred years, nationalism will continue to play an important role in the world by bringing people together and shaping their identities. It will also play an important role where groups seek self-determination (e.g., Chechnya and French-speaking Quebec) and in areas ravaged by war (e.g., the Israeli-Palestinian conflict and the conflict in Iraq).

In light of the power of nationalism and state sovereignty, it will be interesting to see how they fare against the forces of globalization over the next few decades. In a system based on sovereignty, states will continue to seek control over their borders. Yet as the world continues to become more interconnected, states may find it more difficult to control their borders against external elements such as illegal drugs, weapons, and immigrants. Similarly, globalization may lead citizens to identify with groups in other countries (based on religion, popular culture, and the like) as much as, or even more than, they identify with groups in their own countries. For both nationalism and state sovereignty, changes will likely be gradual.

Discussion Questions

1. What are your primary allegiances? In other words, how do you identify yourself?
2. Has state sovereignty eroded over the past few decades? Do you think it will decline significantly in the future?
3. Do you think the force of nationalism will decline in the future? Why or why not?
4. Which do you think is a better way to categorize nationalism: civic versus ethnic, or pro-state versus anti-state?
5. What do you think would be a fair solution to the conflict between the Israelis and the Palestinians?

Suggested Readings

Alatar, Mohammed (2006) *The Iron Wall*. Video. Palestinian Agricultural Relief Committees and Palestinians for Peace and Democracy.

Anderson, Benedict (1991) *Imagined Communities: Reflections on the Origins and the Spread of Nationalism*. 2nd ed. London: Verso.

Chatterjee, Partha (1993) *The Nation and Its Fragments*. Cambridge: Cambridge University Press.

Chomsky, Noam, and Ilan Pappé (2015) *On Palestine*. New York: Haymarket.
Gellner, Earnest (1983) *Nationalism*. Ithaca: Cornell University Press.
Hobsbawm, Eric (1992) *Nations and Nationalism Since 1780: Programme, Myth, Reality*. New York: Cambridge University Press.
Hutchinson, John, and Anthony D. Smith, eds. (1996) *Ethnicity*. New York: Oxford University Press.
Khalidi, Rashid, L. Anderson, R. Simon, and M. Muslih, eds. (1991) *The Origins of Arab Nationalism*. New York: Columbia University Press.
Laqueur, Walter (1972) *The History of Zionism*. New York: Schocken.
Morris, Benny (1999) *Righteous Victims*. New York: Knopf.
Palestinian Central Bureau of Statistics. www.pcbs.gov.ps.
Pappe, Ilian (1992) *The Making of the Arab-Israeli Conflict, 1947–1951*. New York: Tauris.
Shavit, Ari (2015) *My Promised Land: The Triumph and Tragedy of Israel*. New York: Spiegel and Grau.
Simons, Lewis M. (1987) *Worth Dying For*. New York: Morrow.
Smith, Anthony D. (2001) *Nationalism: Theory, Ideology, History*. Malden: Polity.
Smith, Charles D. (2010) *Palestine and the Arab-Israeli Conflict*. New York: St. Martin's.
Stein, Yael (2010) "By Hook and By Crook." www.btselem.org.
Winichakul, Thongchai (1994) *Siam Mapped: A History of the Geo-Body of a Nation*. Honolulu: University of Hawaii Press.

5

The Quest for Universal Human Rights

Anthony N. Talbott, D. Neil Snarr, and Audrey Ingram

ALL OF US HAVE HEARD THE TERM *HUMAN RIGHTS*. BUT FEW OF US truly understand what human rights are or where they came from. Fewer still could name more than one or two rights that we believe are universal human rights. This chapter introduces human rights to the reader and traces their origin, development, and implementation. It covers how respect for human rights is greater now than at any time in history, but also details the many failings of human rights implementation. The world is rapidly changing. Advances in transportation and telecommunications technology, mass migration, the spread of international crime and terrorism, growing wealth and inequality, remarkable progress in health and education around the world, and a growing body of international law and norms of state behavior all have an impact on human rights. Many consider 1948's Universal Declaration of Human Rights (UDHR) by the newly formed United Nations to be one of the most significant moments of the twentieth century. It was the first time in human history that we recognized that all members of the human family are equal and possess the same rights.

The Origin of Human Rights

As long as there have been human civilizations, there have been rights. However, these rights were always restricted to certain privileged groups: citizens, males, property owners, nobles, priests, and the like. It was very rare for rights to extend beyond these groups. But the foundations of conceiving of rights as being universal to all human beings also existed. Over 2,500 years ago, Cyrus the Great of Persia proclaimed freedom, tolerance, and respect for all peoples. In ancient Rome, philosophers and jurists coined the term "natural law" to indicate a body of universal, eternal laws that human beings naturally followed. The great religions of the world proclaimed divine rules of behavior that applied to all persons. More recently, there are many key documents that arose from Enlightenment thinking and paved the way to the 1948 UDHR. The British Magna Carta (1215), the French Declaration of the Rights of Man and of the Citizen (1789), and the US Bill of Rights (1791) are just a few of these contributions. Late in the nineteenth century slave trading was outlawed, and early in the twentieth century slavery itself was outlawed. Later, humanitarian considerations in the conduct of war were agreed upon, and the treatment of workers and prisoners, the rights of women, of disabled persons, and of children became the subject of international agreements.

The true triggers for the establishment of universal human rights were the horror of over 50 million dead in World War II and the terrible atrocities committed, such as the Holocaust. The United Nations was established with the expressed purpose to ensure such events never happened again (see Figure 5.1). For the first time in human history, a set of rights that applied equally to all humans everywhere was declared.

The Universal Declaration of Human Rights

On December 10, 1948, the United Nations General Assembly (the UN body that includes all member states and meets each year in September in New York City) approved the Universal Declaration of Human Rights. There were no votes against the document, but eight countries abstained while forty-eight voted in its favor. It must be noted that there are presently nearly 200 member states of the UN, which means that a small number of countries initiated and approved this document in 1948. The countries that did not participate were not yet independent or sovereign states (countries). They were the areas of the world suffering the scourge of colonialism imposed by European states. They would become independent and begin participating in the UN in the 1960s and 1970s. Since that time, the UN has approved well over 200 documents that elaborate and expand these rights (such agreements are often referred to as conventions, treaties, or covenants). Since their inception, human rights issues have received tremendous attention.

During the popular uprisings in North Africa and the Middle East in the spring of 2011, the issues of human rights and state sovereignty permeated the news. Should heads of states who do not respect the human rights of their own citizens be permitted to continue to govern? Ban Ki-moon, Secretary-General of the United Nations, stated: "I am willing to take any measures when it comes to the fundamental principle of human rights" (*Christian Science Monitor* 2011). That was typical of the manner in which these events were perceived. Still, as we will see, and as critics point out, it is easier to endorse human rights agreements than to enforce them.

Figure 5.2 First Generation of Human Rights, UDHR Articles 2–21

2. Everyone is entitled to all the rights and freedoms set forth in this Declaration, without distinction of any kind, such as race, color, sex, language, religion, political or other opinion, nation of social origin, property, birth or other status. Furthermore, no distinction shall be made on the basis of the political, jurisdictional or international status of the country or territory to which a person belongs, whether it be independent, trust, non-self-governing or under any other limitation of sovereignty.
3. Everyone has the right to life, liberty and security of person.
4. No one shall be held in slavery or servitude; slavery and the slave trade shall be prohibited in all their forms.
5. No one shall be subjected to torture or to cruel, inhuman or degrading treatment or punishment.
6. Everyone has the right to recognition everywhere as a person before the law.
7. All are equal before the law and are entitled without any discrimination to equal protection of the law. All are entitled to equal protection against any discrimination in violation of this Declaration and against any incitement to such discrimination.
8. Everyone has the right to an effective remedy by the competent national tribunals for acts violating the fundamental rights granted him by the constitution or by law.
9. No one shall be subjected to arbitrary arrest, detention or exile.
10. Everyone is entitled in full equality to a fair and public hearing by an independent and impartial tribunal, in the determination of his rights and obligations and of any criminal charge against him.
11. (1) Everyone charged with a penal offence has the right to be presumed innocent until proved guilty according to law in a public trial at which he has had all the guarantees necessary for his defense.

    (2) No one shall be held guilty of any penal offence on account of any act or omission which did not constitute a penal offence, under national or international law, at the time when it was committed. Nor shall a heavier penalty be imposed than the one that was applicable at the time the penal offence was committed.
12. No one shall be subjected to arbitrary interference with his privacy, family, home or correspondence, nor to attacks upon his honor and reputation. Everyone has the right to the protection of the law against such interference or attacks.

(continues)

Figure 5.2 continued

13. (1) Everyone has the right to freedom of movement and residence within the borders of each State.

    (2) Everyone has the right to leave any country, including his own, and to return to his country.

14. (1) Everyone has the right to seek and to enjoy in other countries asylum from persecution.

    (2) This right may not be invoked in the case of prosecutions genuinely arising from nonpolitical crimes or from acts contrary to the purposes and principles of the United Nations.

15. (1) Everyone has the right to a nationality.

    (2) No one shall be arbitrarily deprived of his nationality nor denied the right to change his nationality.

16. (1) Men and women of full age, without any limitation due to race, nationality or religion, have the right to marry and to found a family. They are entitled to equal rights as to marriage, during marriage and at its dissolution.

    (2) Marriage shall be entered into only with the free and full consent of the intending spouses.

    (3) The family is the natural and fundamental group unit of society and is entitled to protection by society and the State.

17. (1) Everyone has the right to own property alone as well as in association with others.

    (2) No one shall be arbitrarily deprived of his property.

18. Everyone has the right to freedom of thought, conscience and religion; this right includes freedom to change his religion or belief, and freedom, either alone or in community with others and in public or private, to manifest his religion or belief in teaching, practice, worship and observance.

19. Everyone has the right to freedom of opinion and expression; this right includes freedom to hold opinions without interference and to seek, receive and impart information and ideas through any media and regardless of frontiers.

20. (1) Everyone has the right to freedom of peaceful assembly and association.

    (2) No one may be compelled to belong to an association.

21. (1) Everyone has the right to take part in the government of his country, directly or through freely chosen representatives.

    (2) Everyone has the right of equal access to public service in his country.

    (3) The will of the people shall be the basis of the authority of government; this will shall be expressed in periodic and genuine elections which shall be by universal and equal suffrage and shall be held by secret vote or by equivalent free voting procedures.

people's lives. Originating in seventeenth-century and eighteenth-century Western ideas, these rights found expression in the revolutions of France, Britain, and the United States.

The United States often refers to these politically oriented rights as civil rights or civil liberties. It is this category of rights that receives the most attention and which the US media typically portray as "human" rights. Such issues as genocide, widespread rape, and human trafficking immediately grab news headlines.

In 1966 the General Assembly considered an agreement that would expand and clarify this first generation of rights, called the International Covenant on Civil and Political Rights (ICCPR). As is the procedure for such a covenant to become adopted, a designated number of member states must sign it. In this case, thirty-five signatories were required and it took until 1976 to reach the designated number. Most countries also require that the appropriate legislative body ratify the treaty as well. Even with the strong support of US president Jimmy Carter in the late 1970s, the covenant was not ratified by the US Senate until 1992. It is important to note that the United States, for various reasons, has been reluctant to commit itself to many of the popular UN conventions. One key reason is that the United States does not like to relinquish its sovereignty and open itself to foreign criticism.

Social and Economic Rights

Second-generation human rights (see Figure 5.3) are referred to as social and economic rights, and also known as prescriptive or positive rights. Contained in Articles 22 through 26 of the UDHR, they stem from the Western socialist tradition. To some degree they have developed in response to what is considered to be the excessive individualism of the first generation of rights and the impact of Western capitalism and imperialism. They focus on social equality and the responsibility of one's government to provide for its citizens. In other words, they *prescribe* or advocate for specific government actions and programs. They require the positive *provision* of government services.

Rather than protecting the citizen from the government as the first-generation rights do, the second-generation rights necessitate a proactive government acting on behalf of its citizens. They establish an acceptable standard of living, or minimal level of equality, for all citizens. Like the International Covenant on Civil and Political Rights, which elaborated the first generation of rights, an agreement to expand and elaborate this second generation of rights was introduced to the General Assembly in 1955, titled the International Covenant on Economic, Social, and Cultural Rights (ICESCR). The United States has not ratified this covenant and has been reluctant to consider social and economic rights as universal rights. The two international covenants (ICCPR and ICESCR) plus the UDHR are often grouped together and referred to as the International Bill of Human Rights.

Figure 5.3 Second Generation of Human Rights, UDHR Articles 22–26

22. Everyone, as a member of society, has the right to social security and is entitled to realization, through national efforts and international cooperation and in accordance with the organization and resources of each State, of the economic, social and cultural rights indispensable for his dignity and the free development of his personality.
23. (1) Everyone has the right to work, to free choice of employment, to just and favorable conditions of work and to protection against unemployment.

    (2) Everyone, without any discrimination, has the right to equal pay for equal work.

    (3) Everyone who works has the right to just and favorable remuneration ensuring for himself and his family an existence worthy of human dignity, and supplemented, if necessary, by other means of social protection.

    (4) Everyone has the right to form and to join trade unions for the protection of his interests.
24. Everyone has the right to rest and leisure, including reasonable limitation of working hours and periodic holidays with pay.
25. (1) Everyone has the right to a standard of living adequate for the health and well-being of himself and of his family, including food, clothing, housing and medical care and necessary social services, and the right to security in the event of unemployment, sickness, disability, widowhood, old age and other lack of livelihood in circumstances beyond his control.

    (2) Motherhood and childhood are entitled to special care and assistance. All children, whether born in or out of wedlock, shall enjoy the same social protection.
26. (1) Everyone has the right to education. Education shall be free, at least in the elementary and fundamental stages. Elementary education shall be compulsory. Technical and professional education shall be made generally available and higher education shall be equally accessible to all on the basis of merit.

    (2) Education shall be directed to the full development of the human personality and to the strengthening of respect for human rights and fundamental freedoms. It shall promote understanding, tolerance and friendship among all nations, racial or religious groups, and shall further the activities of the United Nations for the maintenance of peace.

    (3) Parents have a prior right to choose the kind of education that shall be given to their children.

Solidarity Rights

The third generation of rights (see Figure 5.4) are referred to as solidarity rights, because their realization requires the cooperation of all countries. Contained in Articles 27 and 28 of the UDHR, these rights were articulated for those who came late to the wave of industrialization that swept the Western countries during the past two centuries. These are the peoples of

Figure 5.4 Third Generation of Human Rights, UDHR Articles 27–28

27. (1) Everyone has the right freely to participate in the cultural life of the community, to enjoy the arts and to share in scientific advancement and its benefits.
    (2) Everyone has the right to protection of the moral and material interests resulting from any scientific, literary or artistic production of which he is the author.
28. Everyone is entitled to a social and international order in which the rights and freedoms set forth in this Declaration can be fully realized.

the global South, or the third world, many of whom lived under the burden of colonialism and were not represented at the UN when the UDHR was approved. They constitute 80 percent of the world's population but receive a very small portion of its benefits. Third-generation rights work toward the goal of global redistribution of opportunity and well-being.

The third-generation rights do not have the status of other rights and are still in the process of articulation and implementation. Law professor Burns Weston says the following:

> [They] appear so far to embrace six claimed rights. . . . Three of these reflect the emergence of Third World nationalism and its demand for a global redistribution of power, wealth, and other important values: the right to political, economic, social, and cultural self-determination; the right to economic and social development; and the right to participate in and benefit from "the common heritage of mankind" (shared earth-space resources; scientific, technical, and other information and progress; and cultural traditions, sites, and monuments). The other three third-generation rights—the right to peace, the right to a healthy and balanced environment, and the right to humanitarian disaster relief—suggest the impotence or inefficiency of the nation-state in certain critical respects. (1992: 19–20)

As an example of the implementation of the third-generation solidarity rights, the General Assembly adopted the Declaration on the Right to Development in December 1986. As Winston Langley notes: "The Declaration confirms the view of the international community that the right to development is an inalienable human right by virtue of which every human person and all peoples are entitled to participate in, contribute to and enjoy economic, social, cultural and political development, in which all human rights and fundamental freedoms can be fully realized" (1996: 361).

The UN's Millennium Declaration of 2000 and its Millennium Development Goals (MDGs), together with the newly approved Sustainable Development Goals (SDGs) of 2015, bring together the environment, economic development, and human rights more strongly than ever before. In many ways, the SDGs set forth an agenda promoting solidarity rights to be achieved by 2030.

* * *

As mentioned, not everyone is content to divide human rights into these three categories. Some students of human rights merge the second and third generations. The UN has done this in its *Human Development Report,* published annually by the United Nations Development Programme (UNDP), arguing that human rights cannot be realized without human development, and that human development cannot be realized without human rights. Others argue that separating rights into the three generations leads to first-generation rights being valued more than second- or third-generation. The objective of human rights is to protect and promote the life and dignity of all. Stopping any actions violating any rights is an equally important obligation of states (Shue 1980). Other scholars have developed different categories of human rights. Johan Galtung (1994), for example, argues that human rights exist to serve human needs. Therefore rights are best categorized according to which need is being protected (survival, well-being, freedom, and so on). These debates show how the study of human rights is very much an active and evolving field of academic scholarship.

Following the third-generation rights, the final two articles of the UDHR, Articles 29 and 30 (see Figure 5.5), affirm the universality of and responsibility for the rights described in Articles 1–28.

Figure 5.5 UDHR Articles 29–30

29. (1) Everyone has duties to the community in which alone the free and full development of his personality is possible.

    (2) In the exercise of his rights and freedoms, everyone shall be subject only to such limitations as are determined by law solely for the purpose of securing the recognition and respect for the rights and freedoms of others and of meeting the just requirements of morality, public order and the general welfare in a democratic society.

    (3) These rights and freedoms may in no case be exercised contrary to the purposes and principles of the United Nations.

30. Nothing in this Declaration may be interpreted as implying for any State, group or person any right to engage in any activity or to perform any act aimed at the destruction of any of the rights and freedoms set forth herein.

Impact of Globalization on the UDHR

As mentioned, state sovereignty, which includes territorial integrity, self-determination, and nonintervention, was an accepted fact until the UDHR was approved in 1948. It was assumed that countries were self-governing and that external pressures were held at bay. But globalization has greatly changed the world since then, and many argue that it has eroded state sovereignty, which means that the state is now less able to control its destiny. We have moved away from a state-centric world and this directly impacts human rights. Of course, not all agree on the extent to which this move has taken place. Several clear changes, however, support this assertion.

First, multinational or transnational corporations can more readily move from country to country to avoid the economic, environmental, and human rights demands of their hosts. Some of these corporations have economic and political power that rivals that of many countries. Second, global economic agencies, especially the World Bank, the International Monetary Fund, and the World Trade Organization, have been granted the power to overrule the decisions of sovereign states. This manipulation generally results from the ability of these institutions to grant or withhold different types of support, such as resources for development. A third factor is the rise of what are called violent nonstate actors; examples include terror groups, warlords, and militias that have control over territory, such as in Syria and Somalia, and criminal gangs such as the "Mexican Mafia," which is moving into Central America, or the MS-13 street gang, which is active across North and Central America. Such organizations generally emerge due to the failure of the state in which they exist to provide adequate opportunity, security, or services. Finally, there are the nongovernmental organizations (NGOs) that have emerged throughout the world to help people, especially in the poor countries of the global South, cope with the many problems they face.

As the strength of these four actors increases, the power of the state to control and serve those living within its borders is diminished. The UDHR and the entire international human rights regime, or framework, is predicated upon the centrality of states as actors. International law mandates that states take responsibility to develop and protect human rights. Thus, with the erosion of state sovereignty, the context within which the UNDHR was conceived is changed and the entire human rights protection system is weakened. Historically, it was the sovereign state that was to address the issues within its borders, but the weakening of state power due to globalization has created the need for other groups to step in to fill the vacuum (Evans 2011).

At the same time, forces of globalization, especially advances in telecommunications, widespread gains in education and literacy, and the spread of a culture of respect for human rights, are working to strengthen human rights around the world. The rapid diffusion of cellular phones and other mobile devices and the billions of people using social media platforms have led to a near global peer-to-peer communications network that is able to circumvent traditional authoritarian roadblocks to free speech and organization. Mobile phones and Twitter were crucial in the popular uprising against Hosni Mubarak in Egypt in 2011 (part of the Arab Spring). In the United States and other countries, videos of police-based violence and other state abuses of human rights are recorded by ordinary citizens and shared instantly around the world. NGOs have joined individuals in this endeavor. For example, Witness is an international NGO that trains and supports people using video for human rights. Their slogan is "See it. Film it. Change it."

Human Rights: Universalism vs. Relativism

Clearly, human rights have not emerged onto the world's political agenda without controversy. At every step since the signing of the Universal Declaration of Human Rights, there have been delays and denouncements. There is no reason to believe that these controversies will cease anytime soon.

The UN Charter guarantees state sovereignty, self-determination, and nonintervention. It also proclaims that all individuals, regardless of their citizenship and status, have human rights. These principles are often found to be contradictory. The idea that everyone possesses these rights as found in the UDHR is referred to as *universalism.* On the other hand, some countries and cultures follow traditions that are considered inconsistent with the UDHR, and they claim exception for their traditions. This is termed *relativism* or *cultural relativism.* These governments or ethnic groups, and some scholars, say that the final authority in determining what is right for a citizenry lies with the people themselves or their government (state sovereignty). Accordingly, appropriate expectations for human rights are judged against, or relative to, local culture. In other words, certain customs that are thought by some to violate human rights are considered legitimate, long-standing cultural or religious practices by others. Customs such as the subordination of women, child marriage, and female circumcision (also known as female genital mutilation or female genital cutting) serve as examples of this.

In South Asia, young girls are often betrothed by their families to marry at an early age, without consideration of the desires of the child. Those supporting the universalist position generally consider this practice to be a violation of the child's rights, but it is often defended as a cultural (or relativist) tradition. For those who participate in this practice, the determining factor is tradition, not an abstract rule established by foreigners.

Female circumcision is practiced by millions of people throughout Africa and the Middle East, and has also been defended as a cultural practice that should not be subject to a universal human rights rule. Female circumcision involves a procedure that may include the complete removal of the clitoris and occasionally the removal of some of the inner and outer labia. It is estimated that this procedure has affected some 137 million women, mostly in Africa. Those who defend this practice culturally claim that it makes girls "marriageable" (because it ensures their virginity) and also diminishes their sex drives to prevent adultery.

UN agencies disagree with this relativist position and have begun to take steps to eliminate female circumcision. Many African countries, such as Egypt, Senegal, Eritrea, and Sierra Leone, have either declared themselves to be against the practice or passed laws in an effort to terminate it. But despite this seeming rush to eliminate female circumcision, the practice has also found its way into Western countries. It is estimated that more than 60,000 women in Britain have experienced the procedure and that an additional 20,000 girls are at risk. The British government has declared female circumcision a form of child abuse, but its perpetrators operate clandestinely and are difficult to stop (McVeigh 2010). Recently, the World Health Organization of the UN has made progress on this issue by framing it as a matter of public health and not specifically as a human rights issue. This has worked to counter some of the relativist arguments in support of the practice. As a sign of progress, in 2012 the UN General Assembly adopted a resolution on the elimination of female genital mutilation (WHO 2014b).

The UN has expended a great deal of energy in trying to diminish many cultural and traditional practices that subordinate women. As recently as July 2, 2010, the UN unanimously voted to merge four agencies with the purpose of achieving gender equality and women's empowerment. "The New UN Entity for Gender Equality and the Empowerment of Women—or UN Women—merged . . . the UN Development Fund for Women (UNIFEM), the Division for the Advancement of Women (DAW), the Office of Special Adviser on Gender Issues, and the UN International Research and Training Institute for the Advancement of Women" (UN 2011).

As the debate proceeds over what rights are universal, most decisions will fall somewhere between the two extremes of universalism and relativism. At the same time, however, there is general agreement that acts such as genocide (planned killing of an entire people, such as in Rwanda in 1994), modern-day slavery (human trafficking), torture, and summary executions are violations of human rights. Clearly, the UN has taken a universalist position on these.

Implementing Human Rights

The United Nations

It should be clear that human rights are a special domain of the United Nations. The 1948 UDHR was an undertaking of this international body; human rights agreements began there and much international monitoring emanates from its halls.

"For all its faults," says Darren O'Byrne, "the United Nations is probably the most important agency involved in the protection of human rights worldwide" (2003: 85). Tom Farer (2002) observes that the United Nations operates at four levels in supporting human rights. First, it formulates and defines international standards by approving conventions and making declarations. Second, it advances human rights by promoting knowledge and providing public support. At the third level, it supports human rights by protecting or implementing them. Although the task of directly enforcing human rights is primarily left to the states themselves, the UN does become involved in various means of implementation. During the 1990s and early 2000s, UN enforcement took on new meaning and controversy. The UN's efforts in the Persian Gulf, Somalia, Rwanda, the former Yugoslavia, and Afghanistan, often under pressure from the United States and its allies, are examples of this. They include boycotts of aggressor states, military action, military support for delivery of humanitarian aid, and protection of refugees.

Especially important in protecting human rights has been the task of peacekeeping. The UN currently has sixteen peacekeeping operations and one special political mission on four continents. Since 1948 it has operated in over sixty countries utilizing nearly a hundred thousand uniformed personnel. These uniformed personnel, sometimes referred to as "blue helmets," have been contributed by over a hundred different countries. These operations have had great success in protecting civilians as well as keeping belligerent groups at bay. For these operations to be undertaken, they must be approved by the UN Security Council and unanimously supported by the group's five permanent members (China, France, Russia, the United Kingdom, and the United States).

The fourth level that the United Nations operates at in supporting human rights is enforcement, through steps that some consider to be structural and economic aspects of human rights issues—that is, the second and third generations of rights, including economic development for poor countries as described previously. Though the UN has expended considerable resources on development, such efforts receive little public attention compared to more dramatic (such as military) actions. Many poor countries rely heavily on support and training provided by the UN.

A relatively new policy relating to UN direct enforcement of human rights is called the responsibility to protect (R2P). Unanimously adopted at the 2005 World Summit, R2P stresses that states have the responsibility to protect their populations from genocide, war crimes, ethnic cleansing, and crimes against humanity. It also maintains that the international community has a responsibility to intervene in these situations when a state fails to do so. Intervention can only be authorized by the US Security Council (UN 2013). R2P was used to authorize North Atlantic Treaty Organization (NATO) combat operations in Libya in 2011 and the French-led military operations in the Central African Republic in 2013.

Beyond the positive actions that the UN takes in supporting human rights, there is the significant criticism that human rights are often not enforced. Critics point out that some of the countries that have signed UN human rights conventions have made little progress toward instituting them. There are several reasons that countries may sign these conventions even if they have no apparent intention to enforce them. First, most countries want to appear to the world as though they treat their citizens justly. Second, some countries, regardless of their human rights records, are reluctant to subject themselves to the jurisdiction of world bodies such as the UN. The United States, which generally has a good human rights record, often fits into this category. These countries take the stance that what happens within their own borders is their own business and not the concern of other political bodies (an example of the principle of state sovereignty).

Third, the UN is not an independent body or a world government; it is subject to the whims of its members and has no more power or resources than it is given by its members. For instance, many UN decisions on human rights violations are made in the Security Council, in which any of the five permanent members can veto an action (the ten nonpermanent members do not have such veto power). Thus, all five permanent members must approve any action taken, a difficult task.

A final inhibiting factor is the availability of money for UN operations. The UN does not have its own, independent means of generating revenue. It was designed to be dependent upon the financial contributions of the member states. This is a means of control of the organization by the great powers. Further complicating the UN's financial woes is that several countries are either unable or unwilling to pay their rightful shares. For instance, under the George W. Bush administration the United States was over $1 billion in arrears, the largest amount owed by any country. In this case the cause was not lack of money, but rather opposition to UN actions and policies. This changed under President Barack Obama, who paid the debt for UN dues and peacekeeping operations. Under the UN Charter, a member state may be expelled from the UN General Assembly for failure to pay, although this is rarely even contemplated, much less carried out. As of this writing, five members are in arrears, but the General Assembly has passed a resolution to allow them to retain their voting privileges (UNGA 2015).

The International Criminal Court

During the Cold War (late 1940s to 1990), massive human rights violations were overlooked by the two superpowers. Geoffrey Robertson (2000) refers to this period as the "inglorious years," during which the United States and the Soviet Union were vying for support from countries while giving little attention to their human rights records. During that time, the United States supported many governments that were responsible for widespread human rights violations, but justified its support on the basis of fighting communism. The Soviet Union did the same thing, with different justification—fighting Western imperialism and capitalism.

At the end of the Cold War it was possible to shift attention to leaders of nations that were abusing the rights of their own peoples—abuses that were overlooked while the two superpowers were vying for support. Leaders of these abusing states came under the scrutiny of all groups that were concerned with human rights.

These crimes committed by states against their own peoples, which came to be known as crimes against humanity, were not new. At the end of World War II, many Germans and Japanese were charged with committing crimes against humanity, defined as "inhumane acts of a very serious nature committed as part of a widespread or systematic attack against a civilian population on political, ethnic or religious grounds. They may be committed in times of peace or of war" (Robertson 2000: 295). During the Cold War these crimes tended to be overlooked, as both East and West were scrambling to find political allies among the countries of Asia, Africa, and Latin America. As a result, serious criminals were allowed to walk free and often were even absolved of their crimes.

Things began to change, though, soon after the end of the Cold War. For instance, at the end of the Gulf War in April 1991, the UN Security Council passed Resolution 688, which permitted the establishment of temporary havens for refugees inside Iraq—without Iraq's permission. The rationale was that the Iraqi government's violent treatment of Kurds (a large ethnic group living in Iraq) threatened international peace and security. This move clearly contradicted the traditional understanding of state sovereignty. A more recent example of this shift was the establishment of international tribunals to try persons responsible for crimes against humanity. But the establishment of separate tribunals seemed a cumbersome approach; many cases needed to be dealt with and so the idea of a single, international criminal court emerged.

In early 1993 and again in late 1994, two international tribunals were established by the UN Security Council to deal with crimes against humanity, one in the former Yugoslavia and one in Rwanda. In the former Yugoslavia some 200,000 people had been killed in what was called "ethnic cleansing" (the "purifying" of a society ethnically through violent means), and in Rwanda approximately 800,000 had been massacred in tribal violence. The timing of these tribunals was especially important, because they were established before the end of the conflicts and thus constituted a form of early intervention. Also, these tribunals were established based on international law, which supersedes state sovereignty, at least in principle. Though their establishment was an important step in dealing with the impunity so pervasive until recent times, these were ad hoc tribunals—established for specific cases of crimes and for limited time periods.

In 1998 the International Criminal Court (ICC) was established via the Rome Statute. According to the ICC, it "is the first ever permanent, treaty based, international criminal court established to promote the rule of law and ensure that the gravest international crimes do not go unpunished. The ICC will be complementary to national criminal jurisdictions" (ICC 2004). The ICC Statute entered into force on July 1, 2002, after sixty countries had ratified it. The Court is an independent international organization, seated at The Hague in the Netherlands. As of January, 2015, 123 countries are parties to the Rome Statute. However, the United States, China, India, Indonesia, and other powerful countries have not joined.

President Bill Clinton signed the Rome Statute on December 31, 2000, the last day before signature expiration, but the US Senate did not ratify it. Later, George W. Bush "nullified" the US signature on the treaty by sending a letter to UN Secretary-General Kofi Annan on May 6, 2002, declaring that the United States would not be bound by treaty. Since that time, the United States has often sought to minimize the role of the ICC, and has pressured countries to sign bilateral agreements meant to ensure immunity for US citizens. Why does the United States feel so threatened by the ICC? One argument is that it does not want its past or future actions to be subject to international scrutiny. For instance, it is possible that the Court could charge high-ranking US officials with crimes for their behavior during the Vietnam War. However, since the ICC Statute, like other treaties, allows countries to register reservations upon signature, the United States could prevent such criminal charges against its citizens. Given this adamant opposition by the United States, it appears that this superpower largely objects in principle to opening itself up to legal criticism by a foreign court.

There is some evidence, however, that the US position toward the ICC is moderating. The administration of Barack Obama "has so far made greater efforts to engage with the Court. It is participating with the Court's governing bodies and it is providing support for the Court's ongoing prosecutions. Washington, however, has no intention to join the ICC due to its concern about possible charges against US nationals" (GPF 2016). In 2009, for the first time, the Obama administration sent a "nonparty" delegation to the ICC annual meeting and has since pledged to work with the Court on several side issues (BBC 2009). However, no moves have been made to "re-sign" or ratify the Rome Statute.

The United States is not the Court's only critic. The ICC is increasingly coming under fire from Africans that it is unfairly targeting Africans—specifically black Africans—in the cases being brought before it. Supporters of the Court claim that this is coincidental to the fact that most crimes against humanity are currently occurring on the African continent. Critics claim the Court is ignoring crimes against humanity that are being committed in the Middle East, Asia, and Latin America (Kimenyi 2013). To date, twenty-three cases in nine different situations have been brought before the ICC. All of these are in Africa.

Nongovernmental Organizations

Nongovernmental organizations are legally constituted, private organizations with public missions that generally operate independently from any government. There are hundreds if not thousands of such organizations in the world that focus on human rights. Some are global in focus, such as Amnesty International and Human Rights Watch, while others have narrower interests, such as Cultural Survival (focused on the rights of indigenous people to their land, language, and culture) and B'Tselem (Israeli Information Center for Human Rights in the Occupied Territories). Some receive funding from governments and others refuse government donations to avoid conflicts of interest.

In general, human rights organizations that deal with the first generation of rights refuse government money, as it could bias their research and findings. For instance, the United States and Britain have been found to use extreme rendition, which is defined as abducting and transferring a person illegally to another country for interrogation or torture. If human rights organizations had received funds from their governments for such investigations, they would be expected to turn a blind eye to such activity. Organizations that deal with the less controversial second and third generations of rights (e.g., humanitarian aid), however, often receive funds from several sources, including individuals, foundations, governments, and corporations.

Provisions have been made for NGOs to have official representation at the United Nations and at UN-sponsored conferences. Geoffrey Robertson, a scholar who has been quite critical of the UN, argues that experts from human rights NGOs should be eligible for appointment to UN committees and commissions: "The best way forward is to bring non-government organizations (which do most of the real human rights fact-finding) into the appointments process, thereby providing some guarantee that members are true experts in human rights, rather than experts in defending governments accused of violating them" (2000: 47). Most NGOs work with the Economic and Social Council (ECOSOC) of the United Nations. Over 4,300 NGOs have consultative status with the United Nations (ECOSOC 2015).

Celebrities

In the United States, and across the world, Hollywood carries a lot of weight. Some stars use this exposure to raise awareness of human rights issues. The UN capitalizes on the celebrity's power to mobilize with its UN Goodwill Ambassador program. Hundreds of actors, singers, authors, Olympians, and athletes represent dozens of UN programs and specialized agencies.

Angelina Jolie, George Clooney, and Bono stand out among their peers for their work on human rights issues. Jolie first learned about ongoing human rights issues following her trip to Cambodia in 2000 to shoot scenes for *Tomb Raider.* She worked through the UN High Commission for Refugees (UNHCR) before eventually becoming a UN Goodwill Ambassador. She has since been on field missions and met refugees and internally displaced persons in more than thirty countries. She covers her own costs on such trips and shares living conditions with UN staff (Look to the Stars 2015). The actress received the 2003 Citizen of the World Award from the UN Correspondents Association, the 2005 UN Association of the USA Global Humanitarian Award, and even Cambodian citizenship for her work. She has spoken at international refugee and economic conferences and has lobbied Congress repeatedly since 2003. Jolie also cochairs the Education Partnership for Children of Conflict and donates directly to a number of organizations and programs that work to promote human rights (Look to the Stars 2015). In her directorial debut, *In the Land of Blood and Honey,* Jolie focused on the impacts of war in the former Yugoslavia (Ramsdale 2013).

George Clooney founded the human rights organization Not on Our Watch with *Ocean's 11* costars Don Cheadle, Matt Damon, and Brad Pitt, and producer Jerry Weintraub. The organization's goal was to stop the genocide in Darfur, Sudan. On an early visit to the region, Clooney and his father, Nick Clooney, also an actor, smuggled cameras into a refugee camp to report on the situation (Look to the Stars 2015). More recently, Clooney paid to put a satellite in the air above Darfur. He runs the Satellite Sentinel Project with activist John Prendergast. It costs about $5 million per year to run the satellite. Clooney raises about $3 million through advertising campaigns for products including Nespresso coffee and Omega watches. He kicks in the other $2 million per year himself. In 2008, Clooney was made a UN Messenger for Peace. Early in Barack Obama's presidency, Clooney lobbied him to create an envoy position to be fully dedicated to Darfur. Obama was noncommittal in his responses until Clooney reminded him that reporters and cameras from several major networks would be waiting to talk to Clooney after he left the White House. Obama met briefly with his foreign policy adviser, and then told Clooney he would get his envoy (Bilmes 2014). In March 2012, Clooney and his father were arrested for protesting outside the Sudanese embassy in Washington, D.C. Clooney's *Ocean's 11* costar Matt Damon has also been active for various causes, including human rights. Damon began H2O Africa, now a part of Water.org, an organization that focuses on bringing water to villages in developing countries in areas including Africa, Latin America, and Asia. This access to water, not traditionally thought of as a human right, is nonetheless an important one, because it gives the villagers what they need to grow and develop, as well as survive. Damon also worked with Clooney to raise 4.5 million euros for Darfur and participated in the Ante Up for Africa poker tournament (Look to the Stars 2015).

U2 lead singer Bono is another well-known celebrity activist who primarily focuses on tackling poverty. The Irishman has been knighted for his efforts. In 2005, he appeared alongside Bill and Melinda Gates on the cover of *Time* magazine as Persons of the Year for philanthropic work. Bono credits Nelson Mandela as his inspiration to work to end poverty. He helped start the ONE Campaign, which has worked to tackle poverty and preventable diseases throughout the world. More recently, the campaign's leaders joined forces with Facebook and Wikipedia leaders with a goal to make Internet access universal by 2020 (Cohen 2015).

The rapid rise of Internet and social media billionaires has increased interest in another type of activism: venture philanthropy, sometimes called hacker philanthropy. Napster cofounder Sean Parker explained this strategy in a *Wall Street Journal* op-ed in which he decried large, safe monetary gifts to established institutions and instead urged the new rich generation to bet big on new philanthropic ideas the same way they take risks on new innovations in business. To demonstrate, Parker started a new foundation, bearing his name, and dropped $600 million into it with a goal of fighting allergies, malaria, and cancer in new ways (Massing 2015).

Bill and Melinda Gates have implemented venture philanthropy for more than a decade. The Bill and Melinda Gates Foundation has $41 billion in assets. Its work has focused on primary and secondary education and public health, funneling millions into research to beat polio, malaria, tuberculosis, and HIV/AIDS, among other diseases. The $15 billion it has so far funneled into public health has helped decrease measles deaths in Africa by 90 percent since 2000, tuberculosis deaths across the world by 45 percent in the past twenty-five years, and malaria cases by 30 percent over the past twelve years (Massing 2015).

New Technologies

Technology is always changing. Constant advancements offer many new techniques, tools, and devices in the global fight for human rights. The first and possibly most powerful of these tools is, of course, the Internet. The Internet has expanded exponentially since it first started to take off in the 1990s. It is a virtual library, providing detailed information on human rights abuses both historical and current. It provides instant communication between people in communities from around the world, people who might otherwise never meet. The increased speed of information transmission allows people to report, learn about, and act and react faster to news of a human rights abuse. The access the Internet provides to uncensored information and history is feared by undemocratic governments, because of the possibilities and power it can provide to the citizens under their regimes.

Naturally, with the Internet comes social networking. Sites like Facebook, Twitter, and YouTube are increasingly used to promote human rights, whether by those actually involved in human rights struggles or by outside activists. An example of the former can be seen in Egypt. In a country where two-thirds of the population is under age thirty and over 15 million have online access, Egyptian officials were confounded by the use of these technological tools by their opponents during the 2011 Arab Spring revolution. For instance, journalist Wael Abbas, one of Egypt's most prominent bloggers, used Twitter to post hundreds of videos of police brutality. Upon being arrested, he and a friend used Twitter to inform his followers, in real time, of his arrest by the Egyptian army and subsequent release. Such actions can alert thousands or more to human rights abuses, which in turn can embarrass or shame the authorities in charge (Cole and Schone 2011).

Others in Egypt used websites to post the names of abusive police officers, challenging state authority and forcing government action. One high-profile case was that of Khaled Said, who was dragged out of an Internet cafe and beaten to death by police officers. After an initial response in which officials cleared police of wrongdoing, activists used YouTube and Facebook to organize nonviolent protests against the government, with the nonviolent revolution gaining momentum in early 2011. The "We Are All Khaled Said" Facebook page is credited with being a central rallying point in the successful overthrow of the Hosni Mubarek regime (Afify 2011). As this case and others demonstrate, Facebook can be a powerful tool when it is used to link together groups with similar goals.

Facebook has also been used to address the issue of genocide. For example, the campus organization STAND (the student-led division of United to End Genocide, an NGO) is connected to the Great Lakes (United States) regional STAND organization and the national STAND organization. Suddenly, a handful of people on campus can be connected to thousands across the country, allowing coordination of protests and campaigns. The Facebook application Causes is used to allow people to support causes they are passionate about, or even create their own. The site contains 500,000 member-created causes. Two of the Causes sponsors include Save Darfur and

Global Justice. The application includes fundraising and petition elements. Over $40 million has been raised so far for 27,000 nonprofit organizations through this application. One petition has received over 3.7 million signatures (Causes 2011). Facebook also allows members to provide updates, messages, and bulletins to keep people informed on the latest developments, events, or initiatives. A more specific example of YouTube's effects on advocacy was evident at the 2009 national STAND conference. Part of the conference was a Pledge2Protect campaign in which local chapters videotaped testimonies from important members of their communities on why it was important to create genocide prevention legislation. These individual testimonies were uploaded to YouTube for all to see, also allowing coordinators at the national level to select testimonies from individual US states and create a unique copy of relevant testimonies for each US senator and representative, to be presented to him or her when students lobbied Congress on the last day of the conference.

In light of the importance of the Internet in communications and human rights, new technology is also allowing for Internet access to be provided to very rural developing areas in the third world. For example, Inveneo, a San Francisco–based nonprofit, developed a wireless, solar-powered Internet network. Relay stations can simply be bolted to trees, connecting four miles of personal computers. In the village of Nyarukamba in Uganda, the system gives the 800 or so inhabitants access to crop information and market values. It has helped the villagers increase their incomes, giving them greater buying power, better access to healthcare, and more opportunities to learn to read (Marsh et al. 2006). Other examples of bringing the Internet to less-developed countries are Internet.org, a collaborative effort led by Facebook, and Google's Project Loon. These efforts use mobile phones and high-tech weather balloons, respectively, to try to make the Web truly worldwide.

Cell phones are also increasingly being used in the area of human rights. Over 5 billion cell phones are in use worldwide, a significant portion of them in low-income communities. The Grameen Foundation is using cell phones to warn farmers about crop rot and to coach expectant parents in Ghana through successful pregnancy via text messages (Kang 2010). Meanwhile the Bill and Melinda Gates Foundation is supporting the development of electronic banking programs in Africa and Pakistan that will allow rural farmers to open savings accounts, even though the area is too rural and poor to attract a full-blown commercial bank (Kang 2010). The UN is also getting involved, testing a pilot project in Uganda that will allow refugees to register themselves and find their families, all using a cellular network (UN News Centre 2010). In California, at Berkeley's Soul of the New Machine conference in 2009, the first prize in the mobile-tool competition was awarded to an advocacy group that developed an anonymous phone that can conceal its user and data, allowing the individual to report human rights abuses from anywhere in the world without worrying about the perpetrators finding them or the signal (Net Squared n.d.).

The basic right to drinking water is another area being addressed through technological innovation. In South Africa, for example, one group of researchers recently developed a "tea bag" water filter, except the tea bag is coated with nanostructured fibers and filled with activated carbon instead of tea. When water is poured through it, it can actually stop and kill harmful bacteria, making the water safe to drink (Saenz 2010). Similarly, General Electric has developed a desalination technology that makes saltwater safe for drinking and irrigation.

Technology can also help battle diseases. Second-generation rights to health are often compromised in poor countries where citizens can't afford healthcare. Often, many die from preventable diseases, such as malaria. Though malaria is not only preventable but also curable, approximately one child in Africa dies every forty-five seconds from this disease. However, an experimental Novartis drug called NITD609 has been shown to clear malaria infection in mice with only one dose. If developed for humans, the one-dose cure would be much cheaper and much more affordable than the current cocktail that must be administered one to four times a day for up to seven days (Novartis 2010). HIV/AIDS is another example. In this case, instead of a new cure, an old technology, condoms, is being repackaged and marketed to help prevent the spread of this sexually transmitted disease. In Haiti and Rwanda, 10 percent and 30 percent of the population, respectively, are infected. However, condom sales have increased a hundredfold, showing that marketing and technology can encourage people to take preventative measures to protect their health (Dadian 2010). These are just a few of the many ways that technological improvements are helping to promote human rights in the world today.

However, technological advances are not always viewed positively, especially in regard to the information technology revolution in the third world. In *Third World Citizens and the Information Technology Revolution,* Nivien Saleh argues that this revolution is structured by and for the first world without input from those on the periphery (middle- and low-income societies). He argues that his book "documents how the World Bank, The European Commission, the US government, and transnational corporations reconfigured power relations within poor economies with the allurement of technology and how they reinforced social injustice by denying ordinary citizens the right to choose their own political institutions" (2010: 4). He says there are two reasons for this. First, third world citizens have little power, and second, these citizens must "bow to the dictates of creditor states, development agencies, and corporations" (2010: 5–6). Saleh's thesis supports the argument presented by Tony Evans (2011) in his book

Human Rights in the Global Political Economy regarding the emergence of globalization: the rich countries get richer and the poor countries get poorer. Despite the benefits of globalization, it is clear that most poor countries have not improved their standard of living—that second- and third-generation human rights are not being realized.

Assessing the Successes and Failures of the International Human Rights Regime

There are dramatically differing opinions about the success of the UDHR and international human rights. The topic of human rights covers so many domains, most of which are in constant flux, that a global assessment is virtually impossible. In one very broad and positive assessment, a well-informed scholar observes: "The human rights framework, with its international bodies, international courts, and international conventions, might be exasperating in its slowness to respond or repeated inability to achieve its ultimate goals, but there is no better structure available for confronting these issues" (Hunt 2008: 213). On the other hand, Amnesty International refers to the UDHR as a collection of unfulfilled promises, declaring that "world leaders owe an apology for failing to deliver on the promises of justice and equality in the Universal Declaration of Human Rights, adopted 60 years ago. In the past six decades, many governments have shown more interest in the abuse of power or in the pursuit of political self-interest, than in respecting the rights of those they lead" (2008: 3).

The well-respected human rights organization Freedom House evaluates the state of freedom in each of the world's countries. It annually utilizes a sliding scale to determine each country's level of civil, political, and human rights. In its 2015 report, Freedom House gravely states: "For the ninth consecutive year, *Freedom in the World,* Freedom House's annual report on the condition of global political rights and civil liberties, showed an overall decline. Indeed, acceptance of democracy as the world's dominant form of government—and of an international system built on democratic ideals—is under greater threat than at any point in the last 25 years" (Puddington 2015: 1). Though Freedom House focuses only on the first generation of human rights, this is a telling tale of the forces that those committed to human rights must face.

But what about the second- and third-generation rights—economic and social rights and solidarity rights? In 1990 the UN developed the Human Development Index (HDI), which measures many of the dimensions included in the second and third generations of human rights. Essentially, the HDI measures countries' average health, wealth, and education levels. The 2014 *Human Development Report* opens with a positive view of the progress being made: "most people in most countries have been doing steadily better in human development. Advances in technology, education and incomes hold ever-greater promise for longer, healthier, more secure lives" (UNDP 2014a: 1). However, the report goes on to say that many of the advances in human development are inherently fragile and vulnerable to structural, political, social, and environmental conditions. The authors call for more sustainable, secure, and resilient human development that can survive the many threats facing the world's vulnerable populations.

Thus we find a very mixed picture of the state of human rights in the world. Even as the international community comes together to support sustainable development and human rights through the UN's Sustainable Development Goals and its Agenda 2030, we find civil liberties, freedom, and democracy under siege by resurgent authoritarian regimes, terror groups, and transnational organized crime syndicates. It seems we take two steps forward and one step back. It is good to remember that the Universal Declaration of Human Rights is less than seventy years old, while human civilization is over 4,000 years old. When we take the long view, it seems clear that we have made remarkable progress in a relatively short time.

Discussion Questions

1. Which generation of human rights do you think is most important?
2. Why are UN-approved human rights so often not enforced?
3. Do you consider globalization to have more negative or more positive implications for human rights?
4. Which is more important: state sovereignty or universal human rights?
5. Considering the findings of the *Freedom in the World* and *Human Development* reports, what do you think will happen to human rights implementation around the world in the coming decade?

Suggested Readings

Amnesty International (annual) *Amnesty International Report*. London.

Evans, Tony (2011) *Human Rights in the Global Political Economy*. Boulder: Lynne Rienner.

Farer, Tom (2002) "The United Nations and Human Rights: More Than a Whimper, Less Than a Roar." In Richard Pierre Claude and Burns H. Weston, eds., *Human Rights in the World Community*. Philadelphia: University of Pennsylvania Press.

Hunt, Lynn (2008) *Inventing Human Rights: A History*. New York: Norton.

International Criminal Court (2004) "Historical Introduction" (December 1). www.icc-cpi.int.

Langley, Winston E. (1996) *Encyclopedia of Human Rights Issues Since 1945*. Westport: Greenwood.
O'Byrne, Darren J. (2003) *Human Rights: An Introduction*. London: Pearson Education.
Puddington, Arch (2015) *Freedom in the World 2015*. New York: Freedom House.
Robertson, Geoffrey (2000) *Crimes Against Humanity: The Struggle for Global Justice*. New York: Norton.
Saleh, Nivien (2010) *Third World Citizens and the Information Technology Revolution*. New York: Palgrave Macmillan.
Weston, Burns H. (1992) "Human Rights." In Richard Pierre Claude and Burns H. Weston, eds., *Human Rights in the World Community*. Philadelphia: University of Pennsylvania Press.

6

Conflict over Natural Resources

Deborah S. Davenport and Melissa M. C. Beaudoin, with Audrey Ingram

ACCORDING TO ECONOMISTS, NATURAL RESOURCES ARE THE FOUNDATION of the world economy; no wealth can be created without them. They may be defined as materials found in the environment—or nature—that are used by humans. Thus, natural resources are crucial not only for wealth but also for sustaining life itself. It is therefore not surprising that conflict can occur over natural resources. Indeed, virtually all wars may be said to have included an element of competition over one or more resources.

Natural resources are at the root of wars fought over territory historically. At least half of the interstate wars since the modern state-based international system was established in 1648 have been fought for control over territory (Johnson and Toft 2014). Why is this? Having control of a specific territory means having control of all of the land, people, and resources that are within it. States (countries) prefer not to be dependent on other states to provide needed or vital resources but, rather, to have enough resources to be completely secure on their own. Since few states are self-sufficient, they must either cooperate with other countries to obtain the resources they need or, if cooperation is not possible, resort to violent conflict as a viable alternative. Whether it is a state government or a nonstate group such as ISIS, one primary reason that a group of actors enters into violent conflict is to gain territorial control of a specific area so that the resources found there can be used to ensure security and survival.

The role of natural resources in conflict between states is reflected in the term *geopolitics*, which refers to the importance of geographic factors in international politics. But it is also a component of what has more recently been termed *environmental security,* defined by the Institute for Environmental Security in The Hague as "the maintenance of the regenerative capacity of life-supporting eco-systems . . . in order to safeguard essential conditions for peace and sustainable development" (IES 2015). Environmental security scholars argue that resource depletion or degradation will be a source of increased violent conflict in the future and attempt to identify the conditions in which violent conflict may appear to be the most reasonable course to ensure supply of that resource.

The issue of environmental security has come to the fore with ever more extreme warnings by scientists regarding the dangers this term connotes, such as a recent statement by James Hansen and colleagues that if global greenhouse gas emissions "continue to grow, . . . multi-meter sea-level rise would become practically unavoidable, probably within 50–150 years" and that the "social disruption and economic consequences of such large sea-level rise could be devastating. . . . [C]onflicts arising from forced migrations and economic collapse might make the planet ungovernable, threatening the fabric of civilization" (Hansen et al. 2016: 3799). Hyperbole? Certainly the issue is worthy of closer examination.

Explaining Conflict over Natural Resources

Conflict exists in any situation in which parties (states or other actors) disagree over preferred outcomes. For example, a pair of states sharing a river may always have conflicting views over how that river should be used. Each country may prefer that the other country draw no water from the river (so as to maximize its own potential access) and dump no pollution into the river (so as to maximize its own potential to use the river as a "sink" for the disposal of waste material). Conflict over shared resources is thus to some extent ever-present. This is particularly true between states, given that states would always prefer to have exclusive access and given that there is no entity with authority over states to regulate their behavior and compel interstate cooperation. States may in fact share an interest in preserving a natural resource that is under threat (such as Canada and the United States sharing an interest in the restoration of decreasing Pacific salmon stocks), but still disagree over how that shared goal is to be achieved and how the benefits and costs of pursuing that goal should be distributed.

Not all disagreement leads to violence or war. There are numerous factors that influence the potential for conflict over a particular resource, including the availability of the resource, difficulty in extracting or harvesting it, its necessity for human security or survival, its ability to regenerate, and indeed the complexity of interests in the resource itself. Many different groups may have some claim to a particular resource, and for different reasons—a particular resource such as a forest holds many values that may conflict with each other, as in the case of a forest's value for timber, fuelwood, nontimber forest products, habitat for other species, or simply as unoccupied land available for agricultural conversion.

The relationship between conflict and natural resources does not necessarily start with conflict over a particular resource in and of itself, but with what the resource and its context represent to the actors involved. The characteristics of the resource are critical in assessing whether competition for it may ultimately result in or contribute to violence or even war.

Necessity vs. Substitutability

The first consideration is whether the resource is necessary for survival or whether there are viable alternatives available. The question of whether a resource is needed for immediate survival or is substitutable can have an enormous impact on actors' motivation to engage in violent conflict to obtain it or to protect it from encroachment. Many resources that are necessary for survival, such as agricultural products, have been plentiful historically or available in sufficient varieties to be substitutable. For example, if corn is in short supply in a particular geographic region, it might be substituted by rice, potatoes, or wheat. While human life requires some source of nutrition, no single specific food is necessary to ensure survival (although it should be noted that many other life forms are less adaptable to changing food sources). In most cases, therefore, the greater the availability of other food for consumption, the greater the likelihood that actors will opt for a substitute rather than engage in violence.

This is not the case for water and air, however. Air and water are immediately necessary for life to be sustained beyond a short period of time and are not substitutable. When resources that are necessary for immediate survival are limited, restraints on violence are minimized. The effort to ensure survival can therefore foster violence. Lack of control over the growth, extraction, and use of a resource that is necessary for survival can have literal life-or-death implications, thus pushing actors into conflict. After all, who may be more willing to resort to violence than someone whose only other option is death?

The Nile River, the longest in the world, is shared by eleven states as it flows to the Mediterranean (Ofori Amoah 2014). The Nile is the only source of water for Egypt and is a constant source of tension between Egypt and its African neighbors. Because of this, Egypt openly includes use of military force as part of its policy to ensure that it has sufficient amounts of water. In 2013–2014, tensions over water mounted between Egypt and Ethiopia as Ethiopia moved forward with plans to build a dam on the Nile. Fearing loss of already limited water supplies, Egypt considered war and financing a rebel coup against the Ethiopian government to ensure water security (Hussein 2014; McGrath 2014; Pearce 2015).

Even if a resource is not an urgent necessity for minimum survival, a state or other group may be economically dependent upon it. This is particularly true of single-resource economies. A single-resource economy is an entity whose economic welfare is dominated by a specific commodity, either as a source of revenue or as a percentage of its gross domestic product (GDP). Single-resource economies can be dependent on any one of many economic sectors. This can include the agricultural sector with the growth of corn, cotton, or rice; the mining sector with the mining of coal, diamonds, or crude oil; or even the black market with the production and sale of illicit drugs. An example of the latter can be found in Latin America with the cocaine trade . The narcotics trade has been blamed for the rise of violence, assassinations, and rebel groups in Colombia and Peru. On the other hand, it has also been credited with helping to alleviate Colombia's negative trade balance, reduce costs for consumer goods and imports, and even shrink the country's foreign debt through the increased cash-flow associated with it (Ekonu 2015). Actors that depend on a single resource for economic survival can be threatened by changes in their ability to produce the resource for sale, changes in the global supply of the resource, or decreases in the dollar value of the resource, motivating them to engage in conflict to ensure economic survival.

Renewable vs. Nonrenewable Resources

The next question is whether the resource is renewable or not, which pertains to the availability of its supply. Renewable resources are those that regenerate themselves, such as trees, fish, and animals, unlike a nonrenewable resource such as copper. This distinction is not always simple, however. Most resources are actually renewable, but the question is whether the resource can be renewed over a comparatively short time in terms of human lifespan. For example, it takes sixty to ninety years for oak trees to reach economic maturity, whereas bamboo is considered a rapidly renewing resource with a maximum harvest cycle of ten years (Bamboo Grove 2008). On the other hand, while oil, as a fossil fuel derived from the remains of plants and animals, does regenerate, it takes hundreds of thousands of years to form crude oil (Leed 2010; Sherman 2013; Wu and Salzman 2014). For policymaking purposes, then, it is more accurate to consider oil and other fossil fuels as nonrenewable resources. Competition over oil is considered a huge potential source of violent conflict and indeed has already engendered war, as with the Iraqi invasion of Kuwaiti oilfields in 1990.

Theoretically, renewable and nonrenewable resources might have different impacts on the international system. Because renewable resources regenerate, states should have less need to fight over them. If states are unable to meet their own needs for a renewable resource, they can cooperate to meet those needs through trade agreements and economic integration. The potential for conflict is affected, however, by the rate of regeneration of a renewable resource. The likelihood of conflict increases when a renewable resource is overconsumed or "mined" at an unsustainable rate. Fishing and whaling conflicts thus seem similar to conflicts over nonrenewable resources, in that overconsumption leads to competition for dwindling stocks.

Boundary vs. Transboundary Resources

A resource can be characterized as either boundary, meaning that it occupies a fixed geographic region completely located within the boundaries of one state, or transboundary, meaning that the resource spans the borders of two or more states. A forest is an example of a boundary resource: most forests are located within one state's borders. Although a particular forest may occupy territory spread across more than one state, such as the Amazon rainforest, which covers territory in eight countries in South America, each of those countries has full authority over the part of the Amazon rainforest that lies within its borders. Conflict is considered less likely to take place over a boundary resource, because of the international principle of sovereignty: states have the sovereign right to control their own resources.

Most boundary resources are fixed and do not move across boundaries. However, the distinction between boundary and transboundary resources relates fundamentally to the clear ownership of the resource and associated property rights; a fixed geographic location alone does not result in the benefits associated with a boundary resource if that geographic location does not result in clear ownership, as with "commons" resources such as oceans. Even natural resources that are not commons but are bounded within a sovereign state may provide transboundary services, such as the benefits that tropical rainforests provide the atmosphere. Clear-cutting a forest may lead to less local rainfall, or even lead to second-order effects of global significance, such as climate instability due to the loss of a forest's carbon absorption capacity.

Second-order effects from overharvesting a forest reflect what are often called environmental or ecosystem services—intangible "goods" provided by the natural functions of a resource. These environmental benefits are rarely incorporated into the market value of a natural resource. Even if a natural resource is enclosed in a boundary that determines its physical ownership, it may provide transboundary environmental services. Claims to these benefits are usually trumped by the physical owners' (or sovereign state's) claims to dispose of the natural resource as they see fit, regardless of the second-order impacts, although disputes over legal title to the resources in question can engender physical conflict, as in the case of violence over conflicting claims to indigenous territories in the Amazon (Boekhout van Solinge 2010; Watts and Collyns 2014).

A fully transboundary resource, such as a river, may be more likely than a boundary resource to cause interstate conflict. A river may define a border between countries or may travel from one country to another; in either case, the river must be shared by two or more states. Similar to the situation of the Nile, the Danube River runs through ten European states as well as forming part of the border between Slovakia and Hungary, and Bulgaria and Romania. The possibility of conflict over a transboundary resource therefore hinges on whether the states that share it can cooperate.

Other Political Factors

The question of whether a resource is transboundary indicates that political factors, such as conflicting interests among different groups with claims to a resource, are a primary factor in judging the potential for violent conflict over resources. Most research supports the idea that other political factors, such as the capacity of states to manage group demands domestically or to negotiate an acceptable cooperative agreement with relevant neighbor states over a particular resource, are highly significant in determining whether natural resource scarcity will lead to violence. For example, groups competing for a resource must consider where the resource lies in terms of political control, such as where state borders lie and the power attributes of the state within whose borders the resource lies.

The determination of how critical a resource is for survival may be included among political factors. If having a resource is an immediate need for survival, parties will be more willing to accept the risk of conflict to secure it. If it is an exchangeable or nonnecessary resource, however, actors may be more willing to compromise and work together. Another political consideration is the ability of an actor to secure a resource. If a state is wealthy or has a strong military, it may be willing to accept the risk of conflict, or act unilaterally, to gain control of a resource—especially in the absence of an agreement with an enforcement mechanism. If a state is competing against other states that are stronger, however, it is more likely that they will seek cooperation through alliances or treaties.

The relationship between politics and resources goes in two directions, as well, because war ("politics by other means," to quote the famous Prussian military theorist Carl von Clausewitz) can sometimes result in extreme environmental damage. The more powerful the weapons that are developed and used, the more damage to the environment may occur. It may take generations or longer to recover from such damage, thus seriously hindering postconflict efforts both economically and socially and leading to new or renewed resource competition. If left unresolved, a renewal of violence can occur (Rustad and Binningsbo 2012). There is therefore a dual relationship between violent conflict and resources—the role that natural resources can have in provoking conflicts and the impact that war has on the quality and availability of resources after it has ended.

Global Trends

In the twenty-first century, resource competition is also affected by trends that have been identified at the global level in recent decades. Of particular importance is the human population "explosion" (Ehrlich and Ehrlich 1990), in combination with deterioration in the supply and quality of many natural resources and the global environment generally. Although these trends are seen at a global level, their impacts vary according to type of resource in question and the degree of local vulnerability. Thus the potential for violence may be exacerbated by these trends in some areas more than others. For example, extreme drought conditions have a greater impact on human survival in a poor country in Africa than in a rich country such as the United States, which can better afford to take expensive measures to reduce vulnerability.

Case Studies

The remainder of this chapter will cover three cases manifesting different degrees of conflict over natural resources, followed by a section discussing the loss of resources and violent conflict. The cases discussed diverge according to substitutability, renewability, location, other political factors, and vulnerability.

Fish

Fish are a renewable resource. Yet fish stocks are depleting throughout the world, due in part to technologies developed during the nineteenth and twentieth centuries that increased catch size and processing capabilities. The decrease in fish stocks particularly affects the billion people in the world who rely on fish as their main source of animal protein (Marine Stewardship Council 2015). As the world's population increases, the demand for inexpensive food sources such as fish is increasing as well, while increasing wealth in some countries also increases demand for high-value species such as salmon, tuna, and swordfish (Dey, Bose, and Alam 2008).

Many of the fish that are most in demand either live in the ocean, live in a global commons, or cross state boundaries at some point in their lives. The United Nations Convention on the Law of the Sea was in part intended to help resolve fishing conflicts by establishing a state's rights over resources found in waters up to 200 miles off its coast, an area called its exclusive economic zone. An exclusive economic zone is not part of the state, but the state has the exclusive right either to use all the ocean resources found in that area itself or to sell usage rights to others. Many people thought that the Law of the Sea Convention would prevent most conflicts over fishing rights, because worldwide recognition of 200-mile exclusive economic zones brought more than 90 percent of the world's commercially fished stocks under the jurisdiction of individual coastal states (Alcock 2002). Unfortunately, the Convention has been inadequate to resolve a number of fishing disputes, and fish stocks throughout the world continue to be overharvested, primarily because the Convention's enforcement mechanism is insufficient to punish states that do not abide by the treaty and because poorer states frequently lack the resources to adequately patrol their own waters.

The US-Canada salmon dispute. One example of a transboundary dispute over fishing rights is the dispute over salmon in the Pacific Northwest, ongoing since the nineteenth century. Although occasionally called a "war," it has not usually been characterized by violent conflict. Rather, the relationship between the United States and Canada over Pacific salmon has been one of contentious negotiations alternating with periods of cooperation. Occasionally, however, a decision by the government of either Canada or the United States, or actions by parties involved in the salmon fisheries, will spark a cross-national clash.

Technology has fueled this resource conflict. With the development of the canning industry in the early 1900s, salmon became a viable export and a rush to exploit this rich industry began (Ralston and Stacey 1997–1998). The expansion of fisheries within the Pacific Northwest's major river systems precipitated a long decline in the salmon population of the region. Since 1980 the situation has become critical, with a sharp fall in salmon populations in the region, particularly in the US states of Washington and Oregon (Barringer 2008; NOAA 2011).

Salmon are anadromous, meaning that they spawn in freshwater streams, migrate to the sea, where they feed and grow for two to four years, and then return to their stream of origin. This makes it necessary to conserve the salmon-spawning habitat (upstream), which takes place within national jurisdictions, even though the salmon fishing industry (downstream) is located in the open sea. It is also necessary to ensure that harvesting of mature salmon is limited, so that enough salmon can return to rivers and lakes to spawn sustainable populations. Harvests are currently managed through catch quotas, open and closed fishing seasons, minimum-size limits, and limits on the numbers of licensed commercial fishers (NOAA 2015b).

US-Canadian efforts to cooperate over Pacific salmon began with the Fraser River Convention of 1930. This agreement created an international commission to restore the Fraser River, the spawning habitat of the sockeye salmon, and divided annual harvests equally between the United States and Canada. Even this limited agreement took seventeen years to achieve, and covered only one species and one habitat. While it achieved its limited aims, it did not adequately address how to fairly allocate the costs of maintaining the spawning habitat of sockeye salmon (Knight 2000).

The Law of the Sea Treaty changed the international norm of ownership of high-seas resources from one that applied solely to caught fish, to one based on the "state of origin" of the fish. For salmon, the state in whose freshwater river the salmon spawn is now considered the owner of that resource. However, because salmon cross political boundaries during their migrations, it is impossible to separate them by country of origin. Hence, fishers from the United States and Canada catch, or "intercept," some of the salmon that originate in each other's rivers. This means that the fishing industries of both countries are mutually dependent, to greater or lesser degrees, on the conservation of habitat within each (Huppert 1995; Knight 2000; NOAA 2015b).

In 1985, in the aftermath of the Law of the Sea Treaty and after a fourteen-year effort, the United States and Canada signed the Pacific Salmon Treaty. This allocated harvests based on equitable distribution of salmon according to state of origin. If one country intercepts more than its fair share, this is offset by allocating an increased share of another stock to the fishers of the other country. For example, if Washington fishers intercept a larger number of Fraser River sockeye than allocated under the treaty, then Canadian fishers to the north can intercept more Columbia River (Alaska) chinook salmon (Knight 2000). Unfortunately, this solution to the political dispute further increased the harvesting of salmon and did not promote conservation.

Under the Pacific Salmon Treaty, the obligation to conserve salmon stocks is solely the responsibility of each country, and the United States gives authority for this implementation primarily to local governments, states, and Native American tribes, which are supposed to arrive at decisions on implementation through consensus (PSC 2014). Throughout the region, salmon are caught by competing fleets for competing purposes. Native American tribes harvest salmon for subsistence, ceremonial, commercial, and recreational purposes (Knight 2000; WDFW 2015). The weak decisionmaking framework in the United States, requiring consensus among all the various stakeholders in Alaska, Washington, and Oregon, eventually led to gridlock (Knight 2000).

By 1991, salmon stocks, which had formerly seemed inexhaustible, were in poor condition in all but 6 percent of their range within the continental United States, and were extinct in 38 percent of it. This meant that, while Canadian and Alaskan stocks remained relatively strong, the salmon stocks in Washington and Oregon were no longer viable (Knight 2000). Because of the practice of offsetting, not just the United States was affected by this loss. Canadian fishers depended on stocks from Washington and Oregon to offset interceptions by US fishing boats of Canadian salmon when they migrated to Alaskan waters.

At the regional level, the Convention for the Conservation of Anadromous Stocks in the North Pacific Ocean was signed by Canada, Japan, the Russian Federation, and the United States in 1992, entering into force in 1993 (South Korea joined in 2003). This convention established the North Pacific Anadromous Fish Commission, which promotes and enforces the conservation of anadromous fish stocks in the North Pacific Ocean. But even this was not enough to address the problem. The continuing decline in health of salmon stocks in Washington led to restrictions on their harvesting under US law, which dramatically reduced the number of interceptions of Washington-origin salmon by Canadian fishers.

Meanwhile, however, Washington and Alaskan fishers were still able to intercept salmon of Canadian origin. Washington fishers were willing to reduce their own catch of Canadian fish to address this inequity, but Alaskan fishers were not. Their harvests remained large while the rest of the Pacific salmon fishing industry was severely limited.

Canada responded by increasing its fishing off the coast of Vancouver to try to balance Alaskan interceptions of Canadian fish. Cooperation eventually broke down in 1994 when Canada instituted the requirement that US fishing vessels passing through Canadian waters obtain a permit. Then, in 1997, the dispute turned into a real "fish war," as newspapers labeled it, when Canada blockaded an Alaskan ferry and held it for several days to protest Alaskan interceptions of Canadian fish (Kenworthy and Pearlstein 1999; Nickerson 1997).

Clearly, a new agreement was needed. Negotiations were started in 1995 and took four years to complete. The 1999 agreement replaced one of the annexes, or side agreements, of the 1985 Pacific Salmon Treaty. It mandated the establishment of a new body to oversee salmon originating in the transboundary rivers of Canada and southeastern Alaska, funding to improve resource management and habitat restoration, and scientific cooperation.

The 1999 agreement brought conservation concerns to the fore in allocating harvest allowances but did not address the problems of consensus-based decisionmaking among US stakeholders that had led to cooperation failure in the 1990s. The Yukon River Salmon Agreement was signed in December 2002, forming another annex to the 1985 treaty and focusing on conservation of salmon stocks originating in the Yukon River in Canada (USDS 2002). Meanwhile, subnational implementation methods spawned proposals to cut fishing fleets in Alaska (Juneau Empire 2004) and spurred the rise of salmon farming. Controversy still exists, however, over whether hatchery-spawned salmon pose a threat to wild salmon—such as by infecting them with lice (Jones and Beamish 2011)—or are viable for release into the wild and inclusion in population numbers for allocation purposes (Wild Salmon Center 2004–2015).

Populations of wild salmon continue to decline due to water pollution, drought, loss of habitat, overfishing, dam construction and operation, water use for irrigation and other purposes, predation by other species, diseases and parasites, and climatic and oceanic shifts, as well as genetic and ecological risks posed by hatchery-produced salmon. Increased human consumption compounds all of these other problems. No one has yet devised a realistic technical solution to reverse the decline of wild Pacific salmon and ensure their survival beyond 2100 (Lackey 2008).

In 2008 the Pacific Salmon Treaty of 1985 was again amended. The new agreement, according to the Pacific Salmon Commission, "represents a major step forward in science-based conservation and sustainable harvest sharing of the salmon resource between Canada and the United States of America" (Gadsden 2008). Critics argued that the treaty lacked a comprehensive approach and was insufficiently focused on conservation (Trout Unlimited 2009). With the amendments in place, however, the United States and Canada have been able to expand their cooperative efforts to other types of salmon and have placed clearer fishing parameters on commercial and tribal fishermen. As a result, "global capture" rates have decreased (NOAA 2014; PSC 2014).

Can the current regime survive and lead to full cooperation and recovery of wild salmon in the future? Canada and the United States may be "managing" the conflict over Pacific salmon through political cooperation, but it remains to be seen whether they will succeed in actually managing to bring salmon stocks back to sustainable levels. While states see the wisdom of acting cooperatively to ensure the survival of a resource, no state wants to be taken advantage of by abiding to an agreement only to find that their cosignatories have been secretly "cheating" and breaking the terms of the agreement. No one likes to be played for a sucker. Similarly, states need to maintain their economies, not only for their own benefit, but also for the benefit of their population. It is difficult to place limits on (or reduce) the earning potential of fishers in your state only to see the earnings of the same industry in another state increase. This could have dire political and economic ramifications. Thus there is a delicate balancing act between acting for the public good and protecting the national interest.

Water

Water is usually considered renewable, but in fact more than three-fourths of underground water is nonrenewable, in that it takes centuries to replenish. Water may also be considered nonrenewable when irreparably polluted, for example by a chemical spill. In addition, freshwater sources may be used up during droughts, which can last many years. The water situation around the world is so serious that the United Nations declared 2003 the International Year of Freshwater and created a new refugee category, water refugees—those 25 million people who have faced social and economic devastation as a result of critical shortages of water.

Nowhere is the water situation more dire, nor its potential to contribute to conflict greater, than in the Middle East. This region remains one of the most arid in the world. Water scarcity is a rarely acknowledged factor in the continuing conflict between Israel and its neighbors.

States in the Middle East depend almost entirely on regional river systems for their water supply, none of which exist solely within one state's borders; 90 percent of all potable (drinkable) water sources are transboundary (Peterson 2000). Generally, upstream countries are in a stronger position, since they can control both the quantity of water (through dams) and the quality of water (by their industrial and agricultural actions). One glaring result of this imbalance in the Middle East is that Palestine and Jordan lack appropriate drinking water, while Israel has a freely flowing supply. This imbalance between upstream and downstream states heightens feelings of anger and frustration in an area that is already embroiled in conflict.

There is growing international legal debate over whether states should have absolute sovereignty over water resources found within their borders (the Harmon Doctrine) or, conversely, be obliged to ensure that their use of water resources does not adversely affect other states (the principle of "equitable utilization," as promoted by the United Nations).

The Jordan River Basin. In the Middle East, water problems are enmeshed with unresolved border issues, massive population increases, diminishing agricultural resources, and increasing industrialization. Because there are so many people living together and competing for finite resources within a small area, the differing religious, linguistic, and cultural traditions have exacerbated the conflict. In the case of the Jordan River, the situation has been exacerbated by the way that colonial Britain and France divided the territories surrounding it in the aftermath of several wars. The colonial legacy of the region has been so convoluted, in terms of water resources, that it was bound to lead to conflict (Wolf 2000).

The water problems that exist in the Jordan River basin exemplify tangled upstream and downstream relationships. The Jordan River empties into the Dead Sea. Along its route, it is shared by Syria, Lebanon, Jordan, Israel, and Palestine. The Jordan River is comprised of the primary river as well as its four tributaries, three of which arise in Syria or Lebanon, as seen in Figure 6.1. The Jordan River is modest in terms of length as well as flow. Yet it is the focus of intense attention, given the acute political tension in the area (Dolatyar and Gray 2000).

The Jordan River was able to supply the demand put upon it until the twentieth century. Significant increases in regional population (from under half a million in the late nineteenth century to over 10 million by the beginning of the twenty-first) have noticeably strained the Jordan River basin (Amery and Wolf 2000; Dolatyar and Gray 2000; Yaghi 2004). The upstream states, Syria and Lebanon, obtain only 5 percent of their water from the Jordan River basin. Jordan, however, has a serious water deficit and relies heavily on the Jordan River and one of its tributaries, the Yarmouk River, to satisfy its water needs. Israel obtains about one-third of its water supply from the Upper Jordan, and has severely restricted Palestinian use of water from the Jordan River directly, and from the aquifers (underground geological structures that can store water) underlying the West Bank of the Jordan (Dolatyar and Gray 2000; Deconinck 2004). Palestinians do not have a large enough supply of water to meet the World Health Organization's minimum standard of 100–150 liters per capita of daily potable water supply (Amnesty International 2009; Lendman 2014). Because of the environmental strain that the lack of water is putting on the region, the Dead Sea is shrinking at the rate of one meter per year (LaFond 2015).

Due to ongoing political hostilities, unilateral action by individual states has frequently been seen as the only strategy available to ensure their access to water. Each of the riparian (riverside) states along the Jordan River system moved to utilize as much water as it needed for itself, without regard to the others' needs. This has sometimes included military force. Whether water is a sustaining aspect of the conflicts in the Middle East or reflects other underlying tensions, it has clearly exacerbated the political situation (Morris 1996). Unlike textiles such as cotton or wool, there are no viable substitutes for water. Water is a resource that is necessary for survival. Therefore, it is a nonnegotiable resource.

On the other hand, states' mutual vulnerability to water scarcity could be a source of future cooperation rather than war (Dolatyar and Gray 2000; Coles 2004). The Jordan River is a vital resource for Israel, Palestine, and Jordan, making all three mutually dependent on one another in its adminis-

Figure 6.1 Jordan River Basin

tration. The 1994 peace treaty between Israel and Jordan contained promising language on ownership and use of mutually shared water resources (Morris 1996; Izenberg 1997).

Despite an increase in violence in the Israeli-Palestinian conflict since 2000, the governments of Israel and Jordan have worked collaboratively to ensure that the region's water needs are met and to halt the shrinking of the Dead Sea. In February 2015, Israel and Jordan signed an agreement that, if followed, will help alleviate the region's water crisis. In the agreement, Israel agreed to sell more water to Jordan's northern regions and to Palestine. Jordan has agreed to build pipelines providing saltwater from the Gulf of Aqaba to the Dead Sea. Jordan also agreed to build a desalination plant and to sell water to Israel's southern areas (al-Khalidi 2015; LaFond 2015). A few months later, a nongovernmental organization–led initiative, supported by the United States and Canada and 114 North American mayors, brought together government officials from Israel, Jordan, and the Palestinian Authority to develop a master plan to "convert a toxic river and highly depressed economic area into an international model for river rehabilitation and regional stability" (Balbo 2015; see also Lidman 2015). Because of cooperative efforts such as this, scholars and others hope that such collaborative efforts over water resources will increase the chances for regional peace and general cooperation (Dolatyar and Gray 2000; Hamrouqa 2013).

Minerals

Minerals are nonrenewable resources. It takes millions of years for minerals to be created, through natural geological processes within Earth's mantle and crust. Minerals on and near Earth's surface provide essential nutrients and conditions for plant and animal life; they have thus been key in the development of human societies throughout history. Indeed, the "ages" of humanity are actually defined by human use of mineral materials (e.g., the Stone Age, the Bronze Age, the Iron Age).

Because minerals are nonrenewable resources, most processes of mineral creation cannot be initiated or catalyzed by any human efforts. They are thus vulnerable to greater scarcity than are renewable resources, which can lead to competition and conflict, for several reasons.

First, minerals can be very valuable for the countries that possess existing mineral resources. The political influence gained by the states (or, at times, nonstate actors such as ISIS) that control the geographic locations where these minerals lie illustrates the concept of geopolitics. Countries that need mineral resources from another country must often adjust policies to accommodate the countries and governments that can provide the minerals. Where they are unwilling or unable to do so, many wars and conquests have occurred in pursuit of mineral resources.

Second, demand for minerals increases with economic development. Moreover, the globalization of the market creates international implications on political and social levels as demand rises: the mineral trade is very lucrative and there are vast profit opportunities, particularly if the mineral in question is rare. Also, as technology continues to develop, new uses for old resources are discovered, which may increase their value significantly.

Finally, because minerals are nonrenewable resources, their stores decrease as they are increasingly mined. As the scarcity of minerals in great demand increases, violence may result.

Armed conflicts over minerals have taken place between states, between militia groups and state governments, and between different militia groups within state boundaries. These have sometimes led to human rights abuses and refugee situations that may also force other countries or supranational organizations to become involved. Therefore, even when nonrenewable resources lie within clearly defined boundaries, they can still be key components, or causes, of violent conflicts both within and across those borders.

It should be noted that not all scarce minerals cause conflict, either nationally or internationally. Two key factors that influence whether or not a scarcity will lead to conflict is the willingness of parties competing over them to work together and compromise, and the strength of any overarching authority structure to enforce cooperation. A weak government may not be able to prevent the presence of armed militia groups within state borders, for example. Such groups are rarely recognized as legitimate powers at the international level and often have little inclination or interest in compromise. Without efforts to alter their motivation, the likelihood of success through negotiations is decreased. Even in countries with legitimate and powerful governments, leaders can still refuse to talk on the basis of religious or ideological differences that they believe will prevent them from compromising with one another. Many of these trends are illustrated today in the Congo region of Africa.

Conflict in the Congo. The Congo River basin has always been rich in raw materials, but as a result it also has a history rich in violence. Its resources made it much sought after by European interests, with Belgium colonizing the area now known as the Democratic Republic of Congo (DRC) in the late 1800s. Predating conflict over mineral resources in the region, rubber became a valuable commodity during the colonial era as its use increased for the production of tires for bicycles and then automobiles. The Congo area was "given" to King Leopold of Belgium in 1885, who became known as the Butcher of the Congo for causing the deaths of over 10 million people during his twenty-three-year effort to pull as much rubber as possible from the land.

This violence over rubber is the area's earliest example of conflict over a boundary resource. Though rubber is renewable over time, this case illustrates how even a renewable resource can be overexploited to the point that it mimics a nonrenewable resource. Because it can be "mined" much faster than nature creates it, the resource becomes scarce, fueling conflict in a manner similar to its nonrenewable counterparts.

Current conflicts in the Congo are over the minerals tin, tungsten, tantalum, and gold. These materials are used in the electronics and technology that are used on a daily basis, particularly in the global North. Tantalum stores electricity, enabling items like cell phones to hold a charge. Tungsten is used to give a cell phone a "vibrate" option. Tin is used as a solder in circuit boards, and gold is used to coat the wiring inside virtually all electronic devices. Finished products include cell phones, laptops, iPods, MP3 players, and gaming systems. There is a good chance that the international community is unknowingly contributing to a system responsible for massive human rights violations and environmental plunder given the economic value of these minerals.

Since the DRC gained its independence in 1960, internal Congolese conflicts have been exploited by foreigners motivated by an interest in these resources in particular. Additionally, conflicts from the Central African Republic, Uganda, Rwanda, and Angola have spilled over into the Congo, further complicating the DRC's own civil wars. These conflicts have also been at least partly influenced by the desire of various parties to control the Congo's rich resources or to deny those resources to others. In this case, it is not the necessity of the minerals for survival that drives conflict but their economic value, particularly as extracted minerals have funded past and current conflicts (Enough Project n.d.).

Armed rebel groups generated approximately $185 million through illegal mineral trade in 2008 alone. This money is often spent on arms to fight ongoing violent conflicts. Just as was the case with King Leopold's human rights abuses in the name of rubber, so too are these groups often guilty of extreme human rights abuses.

The "crisis in the Congo" has been cited as the most deadly conflict the world has seen since World War II. According to the International Rescue Committee, more than 5 million people in the Congo died in conflict-related deaths between 1998 and 2007 (Gettleman 2012). Despite cease-fire agreements, many Congolese still die each year due to a breakdown in the healthcare, economic, and education systems, which increases the hardships for innocent civilians. According to the United Nations High Commissioner for Refugees, the ongoing conflict in the eastern part of the country has internally displaced more than 2.7 million of these civilians (UNHCR 2015b). Many flee their homes to escape torture, death, wrongful imprisonment, rape, slavery, or forced conscription. Sadly, many who flee to neighboring states in hopes of avoiding the horrors of conflict fare little better, as host states are often ill equipped to meet the immediate needs of a new refugee population. In addition, violence and war can spill over into other countries with the fleeing population. In 2014, the United Nations reported that there were more than 500,000 Congolese refugees in the DRC's nine neighboring countries: Angola, Burundi, the Central African Republic, the Republic of Congo, Rwanda, South Sudan, Tanzania, Uganda, and Zambia (AMC 2014). The accounts of the refugees, especially the stories of the women and children, can be chilling.

Many nongovernmental organizations are working in the Congo region to stop this violence and assist victims, but another approach to end the violence is to stop the purchase of those resources fueling the conflict. This "conflict-free" campaign is similar to that against "blood diamonds," in which activists and organizations worked to stop the purchase of diamonds that were fueling similar violent conflicts and civil wars in Liberia, Sierra Leone, Angola, and the DRC in the late twentieth century (Global Witness n.d.). However, one of the greatest challenges to this approach is the difficulty of tracing where the individual minerals and ores originated. The minerals are smuggled out of the Congo and into neighboring countries such as Uganda and Rwanda by the armed militias. They are then smuggled or exported to smelting companies in China, Thailand, India, and Malaysia, where they are mixed with similar minerals from around the world. Then they become components that end up in our electronics (Enough Project n.d.).

Despite the difficulty involved in tracing these original resources, some action has been initiated. In July 2010, the US Congress passed the Dodd-Frank Wall Street Reform and Consumer Protection Act. One aspect of this law requires companies to trace the chain of custody of any imported mineral resources and disclose any that originated in a conflict zone or area, such as the Congo. The law requires independent audits of the supply chain for minerals to be reported to the US Securities and Exchange Commission. The law was implemented in 2012. Implementation cost roughly $140 million in 2014, significantly lower than the $3–4 billion estimated by lobbyists who opposed the bill (Enough Project 2015).

Loss of Resources and Violent Conflict

Conflicts over natural resources do not necessarily lead to violence. A violent outcome will result only if at least one side anticipates a better outcome from violence than negotiations. Clearly defined ownership of boundary resources can reduce conflicts over who has sovereign rights to the exploitation of a natural resource, while the transboundary nature of some resources creates competing sovereign claims. The extent to which a resource is renewable, and its rate of regeneration, can mitigate the severity of a conflict, with nonrenewable resources posing the highest stakes. However, there are always other important factors to consider, such as the existing relationship between states that are party to a natural resource conflict and the distribution of power among the parties involved, as well as trends in environmental degradation and resource decline due to various factors.

Throughout history, interstate conflicts have occurred over nonrenewable resources such as oil and minerals. While little empirical evidence has been found to suggest that violent interstate conflicts arise over renewable resources, freshwater resources have recently become a key factor in some interstate conflicts. Thomas Homer-Dixon (1991, 1994, 1999) discusses environmental change as a modern source of conflict. He sees such conflict as qualitatively different from those historical conflicts where increasing resource scarcities lead to deepened poverty, large-scale migrations, sharpened social cleavages, and weakened institutions, all of which have been linked to violence and conflict.

Moreover, environmental security scholars emphasize an indirect means by which scarcities of renewable resources can lead to violent conflict. As degradation or depletion of resources occurs, it can trigger large-scale population movements. The creation of ecological migrants or refugees subsequently interacts with existing group-identity conflicts, which can in turn spark violent subnational conflicts. These subnational conflicts may then spill over into cross-national conflicts. The Syrian refugee crisis is somewhat different in that it is Syrian refugees themselves who are exacerbating the shortage of water in Jordan (Sullivan 2015).

The ongoing conflict in the Darfur region of Sudan has been characterized as an environmental conflict by both UN Secretary-General Ban Ki-moon (Ban 2007; Borger 2007) as well as the United Nations Environment Programme, the latter of which linked the conflict to reduction in crop and grazing land and ultimately to climate change (UNEP 2007). Desertification led pastoral Arab Sudanese groups to move south, where they encroached on land farmed by sedentary agricultural African tribes in the Darfur region of Sudan. The conflicts between these two populations ultimately provoked the Sudanese People's Liberation Army (SPLA), a separatist organization, to attack police and Sudanese governmental forces. The central Sudanese government, preoccupied with other conflicts, chose to arm and encourage the creation of Arab Janjaweed militias. These Janjaweed militias targeted the pastoralist communities in retaliation for allegedly supporting the separatists. Additional factors were critical in this case, such as the complex interaction of activities by neighboring states (Chad and Libya), long-term economic marginalization of the Darfur region in favor of central Sudan, and actions of the Sudanese government in fostering the violent conflict (de Waal 2007). However, it is difficult to dispute the significance of desertification in creating tensions among populations competing for land. While it would not be accurate to say that resource scarcities always cause violent conflict, competition for scarce resources can serve as an underlying source of conflict among populations.

If resource competition exacerbates the onset of war, resource depletion can also be a result of war. The cost of war is often measured in terms of loss of lives or economic opportunity. Another "casualty" of war, however, can be the loss or reduction of the availability or quality of natural resources. Farmlands and crops in combat areas can be destroyed; resource delivery mechanisms (such as roads, railways, airports, or water transportation) can be damaged; crop planting seasons or harvests can be missed; and resource access or extraction can be deliberately sabotaged, all as an act of war. An example of this was the destruction of the Iraqi oilfields at the end of the Gulf War in 1991.

Iraq invaded Kuwait on April 2, 1990. The invasion is attributed to three issues of contention between the Baathist Iraqis and the Kuwaiti Emirate: the failure of Kuwait to forgive massive amounts of debt owed them by Iraq after eight years of war against Iran; Kuwait's exceeding of oil production quota levels as set by the Organization of Petroleum Exporting Countries (OPEC); and Kuwait's "stealing" of oil from Iraq's Rumaila Field by slant-drilling across international borders (Hayes 1990). Though the physical fighting of the war lasted less than two months, it caused enormous environmental damage. As Iraq withdrew from Kuwaiti territory, it "released more than 10 million barrels of oil into the Persian Gulf" (McCarthy 2010). In addition to this, more than 600 oil and natural gas wells were set ablaze (TED 2000). The fires burned for ten months before they were extinguished (Barkham 2010). For each day that the fires burned, an estimated 6 million gallons of oil and more than seventy cubic meters of natural gas burned (Shubber 2013). In all, 1.5 billion barrels of oil were released into the environment. As of this writing, it is the largest oil spill in human history. Tragically, it was a deliberate act of war perpetrated by a state as it was retreating in defeat.

The environmental impact of the burning of the Kuwaiti oilfields was enormous. Approximately 25,000 migratory birds perished from exposure to oil or polluted air (Barkham 2010; TED 2000). Oil lakes, some in excess of one meter deep, covered 50 square kilometers of Kuwaiti territory, some of which percolated into local water supplies (Enzler 2006). Over 400 miles of the Persian Gulf's coastline was covered in oil, resulting in the destruction of regional aquatic and marine life (TED 2000). Despite international cooperation to remove oil from the Persian Gulf, it was estimated that in 2012 over 1 million barrels of oil remained in the gulf (Gray 2012). In addition to the damage to the region's economic and environmental infrastructures, an increase in the rates of cancer in Kuwait has been attributed to fires set by Iraq in 1991 (Chilcote 2003).

The Need for Sustainability

There are several lessons to be drawn from the case studies presented in this chapter. Conflict over resources can be generated when resources are needed for survival. Resources may also be a source of conflict when they can produce wealth that is then linked to political power or used to fund war. Another lesson is that while resource loss or degradation is associated with causes of conflict, it is also exacerbated by it. Resources can be accidentally damaged or destroyed due to their spatial relation to physical combat, but they can also be lost through deliberate sabotage or destruction.

Conflict is less likely to occur over renewable resources when they can regenerate themselves to produce enough supply that extreme competition is avoided. Conflict is also less likely to occur over boundary resources, because there is less question of ownership and use rights when resources do not cross international boundaries. Conflict, particularly violent conflict, is more likely to occur in the presence of factors such as resource nonsubstitutability, resource scarcity, resource nonrenewability, distrust between parties, or transboundary location. In addition, competition over both renewable as well as nonrenewable resources can lead to conflict when those resources become depleted.

The avoidance of conflict may well require more sustainable use of natural resources. For populations and states in the global South, sustainability requires finding alternatives to many of the development techniques that are currently depleting resources, such as developing new ways to share water resources to meet basic human needs and finding energy sources to fuel development that do not exacerbate climate change. For the global North, sustainability means actively reducing emissions of waste products such as carbon and other greenhouse gases, but also reducing consumption in general, to create the "ecological space" for people in the rest of the world to increase their own consumption to at least the minimum standards necessary to live healthy, safe lives without continuing to overshoot the planet's capacity to support the human species. Both North and South need to cooperate to develop policies that are more efficient in ensuring the sustained provision of basic human needs around the world.

Discussion Questions

1. Do market-based solutions present appropriate responses to water shortages?
2. Are salmon a critically important resource?
3. What is the role of technological development in the exploitation and conservation of natural resources?

4. What impact do natural resources have on current conflicts in the Middle East? Are Israel and Jordan's cooperative efforts sufficient to ease water tensions between the two countries?

5. What actions should the international community take to ensure that natural resources are not damaged or destroyed as a result of war?

6. Should countries' security policies address environmental security?

Suggested Readings

Cone, Joseph (2014) *A Common Fate: Endangered Salmon and the People of the Pacific Northwest*. New York: Holt.

Homer-Dixon, Thomas F. (2010) *Environment, Scarcity, and Violence*. Princeton: Princeton University Press.

Klare, Michael (2012) *The Race for What's Left: The Global Scramble for the World's Last Resources*. New York: Picador.

Knight, Sunny (2000) "Salmon Recovery and the Pacific Salmon Treaty." *Ecology Law Quarterly* 27, no. 3.

Mikhail, Alan (2012) *Water on Sand: Environmental Histories of the Middle East and North Africa*. New York. Oxford University Press.

Moss, Todd (2012) "The Governor's Solution: How Alaska's Oil Dividend Could Work in Iraq and Other Oil-Rich Countries." Washington, DC: Center for Global Development.

Negewo, Bekele D. (2012) *Renewable Energy Desalination: An Emerging Solution to Close the Water Gap in the Middle East*. World Bank.

Petiere, Stephen C. (2004) *America's Oil Wars*. Westport: Praeger.

7

Ensuring Health

Michael D. Newman and Christina L. Veite

A BUTTERFLY FLAPPING ITS WINGS IN CHINA CAN INFLUENCE THE weather in New England. This notion is known as the butterfly effect (NECSI 2011). Taken literally, this concept is farfetched; however, we are becoming increasingly aware that small events in one location can have a large impact elsewhere. This idea is consistent with a growing concept in global health: a framework that emphasizes a unified transdisciplinary approach to global health issues. A "one medicine, one health" approach recognizes that everything in our world is interrelated (Kahn, Clouser, and Richt 2009).

Recent examples highlight this notion. Deforestation in Guinea led to increasing interactions between expanding urban populations and a species of fruit bat that harbors a deadly virus. The Ebola epidemic was born (Saéz et al. 2015). Many infectious diseases are of zoonotic origin: they come from animals. A recent study suggests there may be a link between exposure to a bovine leukemia virus and breast cancer in humans (Buehring et al. 2015). Another more well-known example is the "bird" flu, in which domestic poultry (and in a few cases, humans) are infected by wild birds. Factors in one geographical area affect our entire world; animal health issues are intertwined with human health issues; environmental changes affect us all.

In 2000, world leaders gathered at the United Nations in New York and adopted the Millennium Development Goals (MDGs) (UN 2015a), eight goals to be reached by 2015. Each of the goals has a relation to health or illness; however, five are specifically directed to the global eradication of health problems:

- Reduce the rate of child mortality among children under five by two-thirds.
- Reduce maternal mortality by three-quarters.
- Halt and begin to reverse the spread of HIV/AIDS and the incidence of malaria and other major diseases.
- Reduce by half the proportion of people without access to safe drinking water, and achieve significant improvement in the lives of at least 100 million slum dwellers (the latter by 2020).
- Develop a global partnership for development, one part of which calls for providing access to affordable essential drugs in developing countries.

In 2015, the Millennium Development Goals were reassessed. Of the five goals listed here, the most substantial improvements were in reducing the rate of child mortality for children under the age of five. Since 1990, the mortality rate has decreased by more than half; however, despite this improvement, the two-thirds reduction goal was not met. Correspondingly, substantial improvements have also been made to the other set of goals since 1990, but they fall short of the original goals established in 1990.

Maternal mortality has decreased by approximately 45 percent worldwide. In addition to fewer maternal deaths, the number of assisted births with trained health professionals has increased by 12 percent. There has also been a significant reduction in the transmission of HIV/AIDS and malaria. Though the spread of HIV/AIDS has not been halted, the number of instances reported has decreased by approximately 40 percent. As well, antiretroviral therapy has saved approximately 7.6 million lives (UN 2015a). Malaria instances have also decreased greatly, because of the increase in insecticide-treated mosquito nets given to countries greatly affected by malaria. This increase in access to healthcare and medicinal treatment has greatly helped to reduce the loss of life since the 1990s.

There has also been success in increasing water availability, but not to the extent that was desired in the Millennium Development Goals. Nearly 2.6 billion individuals now have access to safe drinking water, but many people still have to rely on unsafe drinking water. The same is true with the development of a global partnership for the reduction of cost and barriers for those needing essential medicines. While major improvements have been made since the creation of these health goals, there is still a lot of work to do in the developing world (UN 2015a).

Illness is caused by many factors that are often geographically and culturally specific. Malaria is not present in most Northern and Western Hemisphere countries (although eight cases were found in the US state of Florida in 2003), because either the climate is too cold to sustain the parasite-bearing mosquito or the mosquito has been eradicated. Japan and Nigeria have very low incidences of colon cancer; this may be due to dietary habits and lifestyle (Sung et al. 2005). River blindness, caused by a parasite, occurs mainly in Africa, South and Central America, and Yemen; the parasite does not occur in other areas. Multiple sclerosis is found primarily in the northernmost latitudes of both the Northern and Southern Hemispheres and is potentially caused by genetic and environmental factors (Rose, Houtchens, and Lynch n.d.).

War zones are particularly unhealthy, more so for women and children than for fighters. In modern warfare, women, youth, and children suffer the greatest number of casualties; many more die during conflicts than those actually fighting the war. Almost 80 percent of those displaced during conflicts are women, children, and youth. Displacement can lead to malnutrition, lowered resistance to disease, and mental health problems. Refugees fleeing from Syria and other Middle Eastern countries have experienced many of these problems.

The availability of medical services and treatment also varies widely from country to country; more than a dozen countries have fewer than 0.5 doctors per 10,000 people, while Qatar (77), Monaco (71), and Cuba (67) have the largest health work forces (WHO 2015e). In many developing countries, nurses and community health workers supply most of the medical treatment. Transportation to a clinic or medical office, or lack of ability to pay for treatment, often stops people from seeking help; this is true in developed as well as developing countries. When people are not able to access basic healthcare, disease often progresses to the point that radical, expensive intervention is required. These realities have an important effect on life expectancies throughout the world (see Table 7.1).

Table 7.1 Estimated Life Expectancy at Birth, Selected Countries, 2015

Monaco	89.5
Japan	84.7
Singapore	84.7
United States	79.7
Cuba	78.4
China	75.4
Syria	74.7
Pakistan	67.4
Mozambique	52.9
Somalia	52.0
Afghanistan	50.9
Chad	49.8

Source: CIA (2012).

There are two main categories of ill health or disease: infectious and noninfectious. Infectious diseases are those that are spread from person to person, as with the flu; from animal to human, as with rabies; or from the environment to human, as with tetanus. Noninfectious diseases are those that are not spread; they either originate within one's body, such as cancer or lupus, or result from an external event, such as assault.

Due to the vastness of the subject, this chapter focuses on physical and mental health, including infectious and noninfectious health concerns; even with this limitation, we can barely begin to scratch the surface of global health. Other types of health not addressed here include intellectual, social, spiritual, environmental, and occupational health. We begin with nutritional health, a noninfectious disease, then consider several infectious diseases, and then return to some salient noninfectious diseases.

Nutritional Health

The World Health Organization states that "nutrition is an input to and foundation for health and development" (WHO 2015h). It is this broad definition that leads one to wonder what constitutes "good" nutrition and what factors affect the nutritional health of an individual or a community. The connotation of the word *nutrition* itself differs greatly when comparing developed nations to developing nations. In a rich nation, the term conjures images of low-carbohydrate diets, fortified cereal, and foods that are free of trans-fats. In the context of the poverty, disease, and extreme weather conditions that affect so many developing nations, different pictures arise, such as the swollen belly of an undernourished child in Africa or the goiter on a South American woman who is iodine-deficient.

For the purposes of this chapter, good nutrition signifies the presence of an appropriate amount of calories, protein, fats, vitamins, and minerals in the diet to ensure proper growth and health. The absence of any one of these factors has a wide array of effects on the individual's body and on the community as a whole. In order to better understand nutritional health and its effect on the global community, one must focus on those factors that have an influence, such as population density, food production, violent conflict, and climate change.

Food Security

The term *food security* describes the ability of a family or household to obtain enough food to sustain its members, which is dependent on both the amount of land available for agricultural use and the population of the region or nation.

Table 7.2 Food Security, Selected Countries, 2014

	Total Population (millions)	Percentage of Arable Land	Percentage of Undernourishment in Total Population
China	1,367.5	11.3	9.3
India	1,251.7	52.8	15.2
Nicaragua	6.0	12.5	16.6
United States	321.4	16.8	< 5.0
Zambia	15.1	4.8	47.8

Sources: FAO (2015d), CIA (n.d.).

Table 7.2 compares food security across five nations. The United States represents the Northern world (rich and developed); China and India represent two sides of a rapidly developing Asia; Zambia is an African nation fighting infectious disease and poverty; and Nicaragua is a Central American country plagued by poverty. As can be seen, although a developing nation may use a large percentage of its land for agriculture, sometimes that country is unable to adequately feed its people. This results in undernourished children and a weakened population. India is a primary example: while close to 53 percent of its land is arable land (capable of producing crops), 15 percent of its total population is undernourished. This is due primarily to the overwhelming population, as the number of people has surpassed the availability of arable land.

Prolonged international and civil conflict should also be considered when evaluating food security: access to land in times of war or strife. In these areas, travel is unsafe and food sources are often compromised. Over the past decade, violent conflict has led to malnourishment in countries such as Afghanistan, Iraq, Somalia, and Sudan.

Issues of climate-related food security are also becoming increasingly relevant, as these natural patterns compound significant issues of chronic poverty and food insecurity in politically volatile regions. For instance, in December 2015 the Famine Early Warning Systems Network identified Ethiopia, South Sudan, and Yemen as key endangered areas, citing extreme drought and violent conflict, for the widespread concern (FEWS NET 2015).

Under- and Overnutrition

Undernutrition. In 2008, *The Lancet* cited undernutrition as the "underlying cause of 3.5 million preventable maternal and child deaths each year," stating that undernutrition was also "responsible for 35 per cent of the dis-

Figure 5.1 Preamble of the UN Charter

We the peoples of the United Nations determined
- to save succeeding generations from the scourge of war, which twice in our lifetime has brought untold sorrow to mankind, and
- to reaffirm faith in fundamental human rights, in the dignity and worth of the human person, in the equal rights of men and women and of nations large and small, and
- to establish conditions under which justice and respect for the obligations arising from treaties and other sources of international law can be maintained, and
- to promote social progress and better standards of life in larger freedom,

And for these ends
- to practice tolerance and live together in peace with one another as good neighbours, and
- to unite our strength to maintain international peace and security, and
- to ensure, by the acceptance of principles and the institution of methods, that armed force shall not be used, save in the common interest, and
- to employ international machinery for the promotion of the economic and social advancement of all peoples,

Have resolved to combine our efforts to accomplish these aims
Accordingly, our respective Governments, through representatives assembled in the city of San Francisco, who have exhibited their full powers found to be in good and due form, have agreed to the present Charter of the United Nations and do hereby establish an international organization to be known as the United Nations.

What rights have been identified as human rights? One way to approach this question is to divide the UDHR of 1948 into three generations, or categories. These three generations have different origins and represent different views of human rights. While this way of understanding human rights has many adherents, many others see categorizing human rights as a potentially harmful endeavor. This debate will be covered later. Since the UDHR was approved, these rights have been expanded and elaborated, and still serve as a place to initiate discussion.

Civil and Political Rights

Following the UDHR's introductory statement is the first generation of rights, often referred to as civil and political rights They are contained in Articles 2 through 21 of the declaration (see Figure 5.2). They focus on the rights of the individual and emphasize the responsibility of governments to refrain from unjustly interfering in the lives of their own citizens. These rights are also known as proscriptive rights or negative rights. In other words, they *proscribe* or prohibit certain government actions and they are considered *negative* because they are based on the *absence* of government interference in ease burden in children under the age of five" (Black et al. 2008). Children who are undernourished often experience stunted growth (below standard height for their age) as a result. Africa and Asia are the worst-affected by undernourishment. Approximately 25 percent of children under five suffer from stunted growth. The majority of these children live in poor regions like sub-Saharan Africa. Between 2000 and 2013, however, stunting worldwide declined from 199 million to 161 million children (UN 2015a).

Undernutrition is a form of malnutrition, which simply means "bad nourishment," and is a major concern in most developing nations (WHO 2006). Undernutrition can be classified into two main types: protein and energy malnutrition, and micronutrient deficiency. The first occurs when the body lacks sufficient amounts of protein to sustain bodily functions. Protein is responsible for building tissues in the body and acts as an enzyme in many life-sustaining biological reactions; the absence of protein is detrimental to health. As stated in *Critical Issues in Global Health:* "Recent data supports the hypothesis that lasting risks for the development of diet-related diseases in later life, including hypertension, diabetes, obesity, and heart disease, are associated with fetal and infant under-nutrition" (Koop, Pearson, and Schwarz 2002: 232).

Micronutrient deficiency is the lack of certain necessary vitamins and minerals in the diet. When referring to global health, the micronutrients most commonly mentioned are iodine, Vitamin A, and iron. Iodine deficiency is the most common cause of brain damage and can cause goiter, a growth on the thyroid. Iodized salt is an easy prevention method, but even with this relatively cheap supplement, people in many countries remain iodine-deficient. Vitamin A deficiency is a major cause of blindness in developing countries, and anemia, brought on by iron deficiency, affects developed and developing nations alike.

The ramifications of undernutrition are far-reaching and often deadly. Protein and micronutrient deficiencies affect the health and immunity of the individual and subsequently the economic and social well-being of the community. At the individual level, poor nutrition increases the rate of death. In those testing positive for HIV (human immunodeficiency virus), nutrient deficiency can quicken the onset of AIDS (acquired immunodeficiency syndrome) and affects the safety and effectiveness of AIDS treatment by increasing the body's susceptibility to opportunistic infections. Inadequate nutrition also increases the probability of death in malaria patients. At the community level, undernutrition affects the individual's ability to contribute to society; it reduces worker productivity by limiting mental and physical capacity, simultaneously increasing the burden on government healthcare systems.

If malnutrition is to be overcome worldwide, a significant focus on preventative, rather than curative, healthcare is vital. As a global community, we need to refocus research and education on preventing the causes of undernutrition and overnutrition in order to see a significant decrease in chronic diseases.

Overnutrition. Overnutrition has recently become much more prevalent in the developed world as well as in the developing world. The "global obesity pandemic" is related to increased consumption of high-fat, high-calorie foods that are low in fiber and nutrients. Many factors have contributed to the spread of obesity, including poor diet, decreased physical activity, globalization, and urbanization. The prevalence of "Westernized" diets that are high in saturated fats, sugar, and refined foods has increased worldwide, greatly affecting developing countries in the midst of economic transition. Due to the availability of modern transportation and the widespread use of technology, there has been a severe decrease in physical activity, which means that instead of burning excess calories, the body stores them as fat. As regions become more industrialized, reliance on factory-made foods increases, and people move away from more balanced diets based on local foodstuffs. This shift has altered the geographic distribution of obesity; rates of obesity in poorer countries are now more quickly approaching the rate of obesity in the United States.

There are many ramifications of overnutrition: Type 2 diabetes (also known as adult-onset diabetes), cardiovascular disease, stroke, and cancer are just a few of the chronic conditions associated with obesity. These diseases, once considered "diseases of the affluent," are now becoming major health concerns for developing nations. According to the World Diabetes Foundation, diabetes has now reached "endemic proportions" (WDF 2011). Consequently, the nations most affected are India and China, with 67 and 96 million cases of diabetes in 2014 respectively (IDF 2015a, 2015b). This corresponds to information provided by the International Diabetes Federation, which states that 80 percent of diabetes deaths occur in developing countries (WHO 2015b). Economic impacts stem from the burden these diseases place on the healthcare system. According to a report from the Congressional Budget Office, 36 percent of the US adult population in 2015 was obese, and medical-care costs for obesity was $3,508 higher per person than for those of normal weight (Stilwell 2015).

To define overweight and obese ranges, a weight-to-height ratio called the body mass index is used. The index can be calculated by dividing an individual's body weight (kilograms) by the square of his or her height (meters). In adults, a body mass index of 25.0 to 29.9 is considered overweight, while an index of 30.0 or greater is considered obese. For example, an adult who is 5 feet, 9 inches tall and weighs 169 to 202 pounds is considered overweight. High body mass index is a major risk factor for noncommunicable diseases, such as cardiovascular diseases (heart disease and stroke), which were the leading cause of death worldwide in 2012 (WHO 2015i).

Infectious Disease

Tuberculosis: A Human-Made Problem

Tuberculosis (TB) is a disease caused by the bacteria, Mycobacterium tuberculosis. This bacteria likely spread to humans from cattle around 5000 B.C.E. In the eighteenth century, TB caused the death of one in five adults. One of the most meaningful achievements of modern medicine was the development of antibiotic regimens that, when used properly, could cure TB. In 2013, 9 million people around the world became sick with TB, and there were 1.5 million TB-related deaths worldwide (WHO 2015c).

Mycobacterium tuberculosis is difficult to treat in humans. The bacterium can evolve traits that make it resistant to certain antibiotics. Resistance develops more quickly when only one antibiotic is used to treat the disease. Successful treatment requires multiple antibiotics for an extended period of time. It can lie dormant and then cause disease when poor nutrition, overcrowding, or HIV/AIDS weakens one's immune system. Inadequate treatment in an individual increases the likelihood that a strain with mutations that confer resistance to multiple antibiotics will survive. The epicenter of the development of drug-resistant strains of TB was likely a prison system in the former Soviet Union. Prisoners were treated with insufficient drug regimens for inadequate time periods. When they were released from prison, they ultimately spread these resistant strains of TB worldwide (Reichman and Tanne 2002).

Multidrug-resistant TB is becoming an increasing worldwide health concern. The environmental factors that led to the evolution of drug-resistant strains were manmade (Davies and Davies 2010). The same processes have also occurred with other infectious diseases. The problem is exacerbated by overuse and misuse of antibiotics worldwide.

Ebola

The "index case" or the start of the most recent Ebola epidemic has been identified as a young child who was playing outside of his house in Guinea on December 26, 2013. This child came into contact with a fruit bat species that is one of the natural reservoirs for the Ebola virus. The virus rapidly spread to the boy's family members and others living nearby. The virus was definitively identified on March 19, 2014, in Gueckedou, Guinea, two miles from the border with Liberia in Western Africa. The outbreak was different from others because it quickly spread to population centers and was not isolated or containable in a remote location (Saéz et al. 2015).

Before this epidemic, the health infrastructure of Western Africa had been decimated by poverty and civil war. In 2005, for example, Guinea had 1 physician per 10,000 individuals, whereas the United States had 24 (WHO

2014a). As the Ebola epidemic spread, numerous healthcare workers contracted Ebola and died, further depleting the healthcare systems, which were already near collapse. External aid agencies intervened and in the summer of 2014, Médicins Sans Frontières (Doctors Without Borders) president Joanne Liu appealed to the World Health Organization, the United Nations, and foreign governments for more involvement. Help and assistance were slow to arrive. This example illustrates that having a coordinated global response is crucial in facing major health issues. When there is a leadership vacuum, the results can be devastating. "As of August 23, 2015, there were 28,041 Ebola cases and 11,302 deaths had been reported worldwide" (*The Economist* 2015a).

Smallpox: A Story of Success

Smallpox attacks the lungs, heart, liver, intestines, eyes, and skin. This infamous disease is known for the lesions and pustules it causes in addition to disfiguration, blindness, and often death. On average, smallpox proved deadly in 25 percent of cases, killing roughly 500 million in the twentieth century alone. It was still widespread just four decades ago—infecting nearly 15 million annually and killing 2 million (Koplow 2003).

After the discovery of an effective smallpox vaccine in the late eighteenth century, prevention of the disease became possible. In 1958, Victor M. Zhdanov of the Soviet Union proposed to the eleventh World Health Assembly that smallpox could be completely eradicated, and what became known as the Intensified Smallpox Eradication Program was born. By improving international communication, providing a system for identifying and reporting cases of infection, and developing mass quantities of vaccine, the world did indeed succeed in eradicating smallpox, as officially announced on December 9, 1979 (Koplow 2003).

The success of this campaign rested on the ability of countries to unite against a common enemy. Many of these nations were in the midst of civil war and racial strife, caught between the feuding superpowers of the late twentieth century. The United States and the Soviet Union, despite their entrenchment in the Cold War, and together with over seventy other nations, overcame political sensitivities and contained a virus that was unhindered by borders (Koplow 2003).

Polio: The Eradication Initiative Continues

The success of the smallpox campaign led the forty-first World Health Assembly to adopt a similar resolution for the worldwide eradication of polio. Poliomyelitis, as polio is formally known, is a highly infectious disease that attacks the nervous system and can paralyze its victims in just a few hours. This paralysis is permanent in 1 out of 200 infections, and in some cases affects the muscles involved in breathing, thus proving deadly. Symptoms of the virus include fever, fatigue, headache, nausea, and stiffness in the neck and limbs. While there is no cure for polio, a vaccine administered several times throughout the first year of infancy effectively immunizes a child for life. This vaccine has served as the world's main weapon in combating polio.

The Global Polio Eradication Initiative, led by the World Health Organization, Rotary International (a nongovernmental organization), the US Centers for Disease Control and Prevention, and the United Nations Children's Fund, have outlined three central objectives: interrupt transmission of the polio virus, achieve certification of its eradication, and contribute to and strengthen global healthcare systems. The core strategies of the initiative include infant immunization, supplementary immunization of children up to five years of age, increased surveillance of all polio cases among those less than fifteen years of age, and "mop-up" campaigns for specified locations where the polio virus has been isolated. This campaign has achieved tremendous results. When the initiative began in 1988, the disease was endemic to 125 nations and paralyzed a thousand children every day; however, in 2014 the disease was endemic to only two countries, with only 359 cases reported worldwide (GPEI 2015).

The job is far from complete, however, as "no country is safe from infectious diseases unless all countries are safe" (Koop, Pearson, and Schwarz 2002: 232). As with smallpox, polio knows no borders, and can even reinfect populations due to international food importations. While only two countries remain polio-endemic, a "funding gap" still remains. It will take continued volunteer efforts and global financial support to finally eradicate this disease.

HIV/AIDS: The Epidemic Rages On

While polio captures a relatively small media audience, HIV/AIDS has drawn worldwide attention in the past several years. The human immunodeficiency virus attacks the body's T-cells (which fight off infections), thereby weakening the immune system and allowing the onset of additional opportunistic infections. For an HIV patient, even an otherwise minor opportunistic infection, such as the common cold, can be extremely hazardous. In virtually all cases, HIV progresses to AIDS. HIV/AIDS has had devastating repercussions throughout the world, in both developed and developing countries. In 2014 there were 2 million new HIV infections, with about 36.9 million people living with HIV infection around the world and more than 1.2 million people in the United States living with HIV (CDC 2015).

Transmission. Unlike smallpox and polio, which can be transmitted through simple person-to-person contact, HIV is transmitted solely through bodily fluids. There are three primary routes of transmission: sexual intercourse, blood and blood products (e.g., contaminated drug needles, transfusions), and from mother to child (during birth and through breast milk). Sexual transmission is by far the most common, resulting in 80 percent of HIV infections worldwide (Marks, Crepaz, and Janssen 2006).

Prevention and treatment. The Millennium Development Goals specifically addressed HIV/AIDS, seeking to halt and reverse its spread by 2015. This ambitious task has been strengthened through worldwide consent; in June 2001 (the year following the Millennium Summit), heads of state and government representatives from 189 nations convened for the first time at a special session of the United Nations General Assembly on HIV/AIDS. This meeting resulted in the adoption of the Declaration of Commitment on HIV/AIDS. The Joint United Nations Programme on HIV/AIDS (UNAIDS) has united the efforts of many international governmental organizations and nongovernmental organizations in order to effectively combat the effects of this horrifying pandemic (UNAIDS 2007).

While treatment is often the primary focus of scientific research, prevention will prove our greatest ally in combating HIV/AIDS. There are more cases of HIV infections each year than there are deaths due to AIDS. This specialized UN coalition has developed a framework for prevention: "comprehensive HIV prevention requires a combination of programmatic interventions and policy actions that promote safer behaviors, reduce biological and social vulnerability to transmission, encourage use of key prevention technologies, and promote social norms that favour risk reduction" (UNAIDS 2007). Primary methods of prevention target sexually transmitted HIV and include increased distribution and use of condoms and education concerning safe sex practices, the advantages of abstinence and monogamy, and the advantages of male circumcision. The latter method has shown promise: the results of three randomized trials conducted throughout Kenya, Uganda, and South Africa have shown a 60 percent reduction in the risk of heterosexually acquired HIV infection in men (WHO 2012). Recent research in the United States indicates an effective prophylactic medication regimen for high-risk populations. Preexposure prophylaxis with antiretrovirals may enhance traditional risk reduction practices (Krakower, Sachin, and Mayer 2015).

Since the introduction of antiretroviral drugs in 1996, HIV/AIDS treatment has become increasingly cheaper and more effective; this improvement has extended the life expectancy of those diagnosed with HIV and has heightened their quality of life. Antiretroviral drugs disrupt the life cycle of HIV by inhibiting replication, halting entry into the host cell, and blocking the release of enzymes critical to its integration into the host cell's genetic material. Antiretrovirals are most effective when administered in a combination "cocktail" (the virus mutates rapidly and has quickly developed resistance to most uniform drugs). This drug combination is known as "highly active antiretroviral therapy" and has proven successful in suppressing the virus (NIAID 2007), especially when applied early (Karim 2015; Fauci and Marston 2015).

Global progress. Table 7.3 compares the impact of HIV/AIDS on different regions of the world and the state of the epidemic in 2001 and 2014. While tremendous efforts have been made in combating HIV/AIDS, the epidemic persists. Despite advances in therapy and the latest antiretroviral treatment, the disease continues to take the lives of millions and is now recognized as the leading cause of death for those between fifteen and fifty-nine years old. In order to slow and eventually halt this devastating disease, prevention education is vital. Sadly, those areas that are the worst affected by the infection are also the least likely to have access to prevention education. This is not uncommon, as many of those affected by the disease live in remote locations of the world and not only are unaware of the virus, but also have little or no knowledge of or access to condoms. If the global community wishes to halt this silent killer, education, accessible medications, and increased government funding must become the top priorities.

Malaria: A Tropical Disease?

As the global community continues to fight polio and works to educate people on HIV transmission and AIDS treatment, another deadly disease persists throughout the tropical world and is infecting millions of people. Malaria infection is caused by a parasite transmitted by the Anopheles mosquito that initially causes fever, headache, chills, and vomiting. It can progress to cause anemia, respiratory distress, multiple organ failure, and death. Malaria is endemic in ninety-seven nations, causing approximately 500,000 deaths each year, 90 percent of which occur in Africa (WHO 2015f).

Malaria incidence (the rate of new cases) decreased by 37 percent globally between 2000 and 2015. Death rates decreased in the same period by 60 percent. Progress is being seen, particularly in prevention methods using insecticide-impregnated mosquito nets, and in treatment methods using newer combinations of antibiotic regimens (WHO 2015f).

The first widely used drug to treat malaria was quinine. From an interesting historical perspective, two important antimalarial drugs are derived from plants whose medicinal values had been noted for centuries: quinine from the cinchona tree used in South America in the seventeenth century, and artemisinin from the Qinghaosu plant used in China in the fourth century. Artemisinin has become a current mainstay in the antimalaria treatment regimen. Tu Youyou won the Nobel Prize in Medicine in 2015 for her elucidating artemisinin research (Callaway and Cyranoski 2015).

Table 7.3 Regional Effects of HIV/AIDS, 2001 vs. 2014

	Number of People Living with HIV		Number of AIDS-Related Deaths	
	2001	2014	2001	2014
Sub-Saharan Africa	20,300,000	25,800,000	1,400,000	790,000
Middle East and North Africa	180,000	240,000	8,300	12,000
Asia and Pacific	4,179,000	5,000,000	246,000	240,000
Central and Latin America	1,100,000	1,700,000	53,000	41,000
Caribbean	240,000	280,000	19,000	8,800
Eastern Europe and Central Asia	760,000	1,500,000	18,000	62,000
Western and Central Europe and North America	1,830,000	2,400,000	37,300	26,000
Total	28,589,000	36,920,000	1,781,600	1,179,800

Source: UNAIDS (2015a).

Current treatment regimens frequently include artemisinin-based combination therapy. Multiple medications are given together in an effort to avoid the development of resistance. This strategy has not been entirely successful. Resistance has been seen in strains primarily in Cambodia and Thailand (Ashley et al. 2014; Bosman et al. 2014). Resistance has also been linked to insecticides used in mosquito nets. There is concern that this resistance pattern could spread to other regions of the world, mirroring the evolution of the multi-drug-resistant TB problem discussed previously. Regardless, progress has been made, as deaths have decreased from 839,000 to 438,000 annually in fifteen years (Kelland 2015), but continued increased diligence and globally coordinated strategic efforts to combat malaria are needed (Ouattara and Laurens 2014).

Cholera in Haiti: A Modern-Day Scourge

On January 12, 2010, Haiti, the poorest nation in the Western Hemisphere, experienced a devastating earthquake that resulted in the deaths of about 230,000 and the displacement of several million. Many of those people who were robbed of their homes by this natural disaster flocked to Port-au-Prince, the nation's capital, for shelter and aid, habitating dozens of makeshift "tent cities" that became temporary homes for hundreds of thousands; the population density, inadequate sewage control, and lengthened residency of victims created a situation ripe for widespread disease. On

February 19, one month after the earthquake, the *New York Times* argued this point in an article with the headline "Poor Sanitation in Haiti's Camps Adds Disease Risk" (Romero 2010). It forewarned that the buildup of waste was cause for health concerns, particularly outbreaks of typhoid, cholera, and other diarrheal diseases.

In October, many property owners began to feel that victims camping on their land were overstaying their welcome and over 140,000 threats of eviction ensued (Sontag 2010). With nowhere to go, victims remained in the camps. Later that month, fears of disease became a reality: on October 23 the first cases of cholera were confirmed. Within three days, nearly 300 victims had already lost their lives to this disease, resulting in a multinational medical operation to control the outbreak. Cholera, a waterborne diarrheal disease, is easily spread in unsanitary conditions. Research has indicated that the strain of cholera encountered was brought to Haiti by UN representatives from Nepal, originating in the Artibonite region north of Port-au-Prince (Walton and Ivers 2011). It quickly spread to the central province as well, with a few isolated cases in the capital. Unfortunately, in a nation with no sewage-treatment plants and hundreds of thousands of people living in dense camps without latrines, the disease spread quickly. With over 3,000 cases reported within the first week, a nationwide outbreak was feared (Delva 2010).

Cholera has continued to wreak havoc in Haiti. The disease has taken over 20,000 lives and infected over 700,000 people (O'Malley 2015). And the staggering truth amid the chaos is that cholera is easily treated with correct and timely medical attention. Nigel Fisher, the UN humanitarian coordinator ad interim in Haiti, is quoted as saying that aid workers need "doctors, nurses, water purification systems, chlorine tablets, soap, oral rehydration salts, tents for cholera treatment centers and a range of other supplies," and yet the response has been "lackluster." Haiti has the worst water security (access to clean drinking water and adequate sewerage) in the world. Short-term interventions need to evolve into longer-term plans to deal with underlying problems of this nature (Walton and Ivers 2011).

* * *

Infectious disease will continue to plague our world until we overcome these social, economic, and political obstacles. In order to halt the scourges of the twenty-first century, it is imperative that we begin to see ourselves as a global community rather than a divided world of North and South. As evidenced by the success of the smallpox campaign, the world can overcome political rivalries and break down the walls of economic and social differences in order to eradicate disease.

Reproductive Health

Reproductive health may be the most controversial area of healthcare in the world. Contraception, the "morning after" pill, abortion, stem cells, gender-based violence, and sexually transmitted infections are all within the realm of reproductive health, and all are divisive subjects. The World Health Organization states:

> Reproductive health . . . implies that people are able to have a responsible, satisfying and safe sex life and that they have the capability to reproduce and the freedom to decide if, when and how often to do so. Implicit in this are the right of men and women to be informed of and to have access to safe, effective, affordable and acceptable methods of fertility regulation of their choice, and the right of access to appropriate healthcare services that will enable women to go safely through pregnancy and childbirth and provide couples with the best chance of having a healthy infant. (WHO 2007)

Though the main focus of reproductive health is women, its purview also extends to men through responsible parenting, respect for and equal treatment of women, the use of condoms to prevent pregnancy and sexually transmitted infections, including HIV/AIDS, as well as the concern about breast and testicular cancers.

Articles 16 and 25 of the Universal Declaration of Human Rights, in particular, speak to reproductive rights:

- *Article 16.* Men and women of full age, without any limitation due to race, nationality or religion, have the right to marry and to found a family. They are entitled to equal rights as to marriage, during marriage and at its dissolution.
- *Article 25.* Motherhood and childhood are entitled to special care and assistance. All children, whether born in or out of wedlock, shall enjoy the same social protection.

Family Planning and Contraception

The word *contraception* can trigger some of the most virulent debates around the world. What is the role of women in a culture? In a family? Who defines what a family is? What do Christianity, Judaism, Islam, and Hinduism say about childbearing? What are the "gender rules" in Buddhist, Animist, and other religious traditions? What role does the state have in determining the availability of contraceptives? Should abortion be a method of family planning? When does life begin? Whose life is more important, a mother's or her baby's? Should human embryonic tissue be used for stem cell research?

Over 222 million women of childbearing age in the developing world have an unmet need for contraception (Guttmacher Institute 2013). What might this mean for a young woman? In regions of the world where women marry at very early ages, this will likely mean that she will begin bearing children immediately after marriage; there will be no other option for her. Whether or not her body is developed enough to bear children will not matter, even though complications and death during pregnancy, particularly during delivery, are significantly higher the younger the woman. It will also likely mean that the young woman will no longer be able to attend school, if she was attending at all.

Contraception and education are inextricably linked. Internationally, boys are favored over girls to attend school. Girls often must stay home to watch younger siblings or to work; many families believe that educating girls, who will inevitably "just get married and have children," is a waste of time and resources. Girls in families that have fewer children are more likely to be sent to school, and to stay in school longer, because resources are available. Educating girls has many societal and health impacts, the most significant of which is improving child health and reducing infant mortality; educated women marry later, use contraception, and have fewer and healthier children. Another factor is economic: educated women have improved nutritional levels and better health, including contraceptive and prenatal health, allowing them to provide greater economic contributions to their household.

In 2014, 225 million women in developing countries, wanting to avoid pregnancy, were not using an effective contraceptive method. If unmet needs for modern contraception were met, unintended pregnancies would drop by 70 percent, from 74 million to 22 million per year. Unsafe abortions would also decline by 74 percent, from 20 million to 5 million (Simmons and Rodriguez 2015; Guttmacher Institute 2014).

Reproductive health is often considered a "woman's issue"; however, local reproductive education and intervention programs for boys and men can help to change this cultural view. Contraception, education, and enlisting men as reproductive health partners provide the foundation for brighter futures for children, and for society as a whole.

Maternal Health

In East Africa there is a saying: "Every pregnant woman has one foot in the grave." This is because maternal mortality rates in developed countries average 12 deaths per 100,000 live births, while in sub-Saharan Africa they average 546 deaths per 100,000 live births (Alkema et al. 2015).

Pregnancy and giving birth are the leading causes of death around the world for women of childbearing age: deaths due to hemorrhage; sepsis; complications of unsafe abortion; prolonged or obstructed labor; hypertensive disorders including edema; delays in the decision to seek care; and lack of transportation to a healthcare facility and receiving appropriate care at a healthcare facility (WHO 2015g).

The Reproductive Health Response in Conflict consortium, a nongovernmental organization, has developed intervention strategies and policies to decrease maternal mortality in situations of conflict. Through planning and preparation, existing facilities can be enhanced to meet emergency conditions. Training and provision of clean delivery kits to midwives, and providing emergency transport from refugee camps to local hospitals, are two ways of reducing maternal mortality (RHRC 2011).

The fifth UN Millennium Development Goal, to improve maternal health, which committed the international community to decreasing maternal mortality by 75 percent between 2000 and 2015, has also helped generate greater attention for maternal health; between 1990 and 2015, maternal mortality decreased by 44 percent (WHO 2015f). Additionally, in January 2011 the United Nations established the Commission on Information and Accountability for Women's and Children's Health, which tracks how maternal and child health resources are spent and establishes an evidence base for successful, life-saving programs (UN 2010). Though the current reduction in maternal mortality is a significant achievement, it is clear that much more needs to be done to achieve the new Sustainable Development Goal of reducing maternal mortality to 70 deaths per 100,000 live births by 2030 (WHO 2015f).

Mental Health

Defining Mental Health and Mental Illness

Mental health is paramount to an individual's overall health, yet globally, mental health issues are defined by a "legacy of neglect and marginalization" (Becker and Kleinman 2013). Universal stigma attached to mental illnesses regrettably persists. Metrics are ill defined and nebulous, making scientific analysis problematic. A dramatic shortage of clinicians exists. More than 75 percent of people with mental health problems in less-developed countries do not receive treatment. These shortfalls are mirrored in mental healthcare in the United States (*PBS Newshour* 2014).

What is mental health? Over the past decade or so, mental health has come to be associated with treatment options for people with mental illness; however, this significantly limits the concept of and right to mental health. A person who is mentally healthy can be seen as "having a positive sense of well-being, resources such as self-esteem, optimism, sense of mastery and coherence, satisfying personal relationships and resilience or the ability to cope with adversities" (WHO 2007). It is important to understand mental health as separate from, and at the same time inextricably linked to, mental illness, each being one side of the same coin.

Most broadly, mental health disorders include several types: mental illness, neurological disorders, behavioral disorders, and substance abuse. Defining mental illness can be tricky, for many reasons. Unlike discrete diseases that most often have specific, limited symptoms and manifestations (e.g., lung cancer or measles), many mental illnesses present overlapping symptoms, making diagnosis difficult. A person can suffer from depression, anxiety, bulimia, and substance abuse all at the same time. Some symptoms may be behavioral, requiring psychological treatment, while others may be physiological, requiring medical treatment.

A second difficulty is that the definition of an "illness" dictates treatment. Western countries tend to focus on the individual when treating mental illness, while other countries and regions tend to focus on the group or community. This is particularly relevant to intervention. In some cases, one-on-one psychotherapeutic approaches may be antithetical to healing, and traditional healing ceremonies that link the individual with the group may be much more appropriate and successful.

A third difficulty is that "diagnosis" of mental illness can be used to quell dissent in a society. Much has been said on this subject, from Sidney Bloch and Peter Reddaway's *Psychiatric Terror: How Soviet Psychiatry Is Used to Suppress Discontent* (1985), to a speech about the criminalization of dissent in the Soviet Union by New York Law School professor Michael Perlin, who said:

> Placing dissidents in psychiatric hospitals rather than prisons served three points: it avoided the already limited procedural safeguards of a criminal trial, stigmatized people to subordinate them, and confined dissenters indefinitely. By 1989 conditions had begun to improve in the Soviet Union, but tools of coercive psychiatry still were used in what some call the "criminalization of dissent." And this practice was not limited to Russia; the expression of political opinions was perceived as delusional throughout the Soviet bloc. (2006)

Today, depression is a leading cause of disability in the world. Depression affects about 350 million people internationally and is associated with almost 800,000 suicides annually. This disease is treatable with appropriate interventions, including traditional healing such as ritual cleansing or purification ceremonies, as well as with medication and therapy; however, less than 25 percent of those affected have access to treatment services (WHO 2015a; Becker and Kleinman 2013).

Schizophrenia affects about 21 million people around the world; 90 percent of people with untreated schizophrenia reside in developing countries. Schizophrenia is a chronic and potentially deeply debilitating disease; people with schizophrenia often don't realize that they have the illness or don't want to take medication (at a cost of about $2 per month) due to significant side effects and stigma. A WHO report (2015j) indicates that people with schizophrenia can be treated providing the following are in place: appropriate training of primary-care health personnel, provision of essential drugs, strengthening of families for home care, referral support from mental health professionals, and public education to decrease stigma and discrimination.

The Burdens of Mental Illness

Mental illness, unlike other illnesses, brings two burdens: an undefined burden and a hidden burden. The undefined burden includes the economic and social impacts of mental illness for families, communities, and countries that result from decreased or lost productivity, as well as from premature death due to suicide.

The hidden burden of mental illness includes both stigma and violations of human rights and freedoms; this burden is borne more by the individual. People with mental illness often experience rejection by friends, family, and society, and they tend to suffer from other illnesses as well, including vascular disease, diabetes, cancer, and HIV/AIDS, resulting in shorter lifespans (WHO 2001a). People with mental illness are also often denied basic human rights. The World Health Organization has developed a framework of violations and legislative actions that can be taken to ensure that these violations are rectified, as shown in Table 7.4.

Table 7.4 Mental Health and Human Rights

Human Rights Violation	Legislative Solution
Lack of access to basic mental health care and treatment	Mandate and fund mental health services at the community level
Inappropriate forced admission to or treatment in mental health facilities; violations within psychiatric institutions	Develop and implement monitoring bodies to ensure that human rights are respected in all mental health facilities
Discrimination against people with mental disorders, largely due to stigma	Develop and enact laws to ensure anti-discrimination in all areas of life, including work, housing, and education
Inappropriate detention in prisons	Mandate that people with mental disorders be diverted to mental health facilities instead of prisons

Source: WHO (2001b).

A Holistic Approach to Mental Illness

People with mental illnesses need to be seen as people first. Saying that someone "is a schizophrenic" is very different from saying that he or she "is a person who has schizophrenia." The first stance equates the person with their illness. The second recognizes the dimensionality of the person, something most everyone wants, resulting in better interventions and legislation regarding mental illness.

Since mental illness and mental health affect overlapping areas of a person's life, interventions must involve entire societies and governments, as well as communities. According to the World Health Organization, respect for the individual and his or her needs and values—social, cultural, ethnic, religious, and philosophical—must be maintained. Care and treatment should be provided in the least-restrictive environment and should seek to promote the individual's self-determination, personal responsibility, and highest attainable level of health and well-being (WHO 2001b).

Conclusion

According to international institutions, health is not merely the absence of disease, but also the maintenance of a state of well-being. Health is a human right, guaranteed around the world, but not yet universally upheld, even in developed countries. Health is determined by multiple, globally interlinked factors, such as climate change, food security and production, the cost and availability of medication, and nutrition. Therefore, improved health requires the creation and implementation of inclusive, cross-border solutions. This includes work at the policy level as well as research and development of vaccines and medications for all people, not solely the ones who can afford them. On the ground, it mandates the availability and affordability of quality health services. Health as a human right requires immediate work on climate change, with a forward-looking approach to determine the impacts of and solutions for the new health problems that will occur.

Although many battles remain to be fought, the crusade toward global health has achieved many victories. Smallpox, once an uncompromising killer, has been eradicated. Children are receiving vaccines to prevent measles, mumps, and tetanus. Improvements have been made to combat malaria. Once-a-day medications for HIV/AIDS have been developed, and generic drugs are being used to help make treatment more available. As global issues increasingly affect an individual's health, global health requires a multidisciplinary, coordinated effort for future advancement. We need to stay focused and at the same time adopt a broader vision.

Discussion Questions

1. Do you consider health to be a human right?

2. To what extent is political and economic will central to creating a healthy world?

3. What impact does culture have on health?

4. What would you do, globally, to reduce under- and overnutrition?

5. Who should provide global health leadership and why is this important?

6. With respect to health, to what extent should wealthy countries aid poorer countries?

Suggested Readings

Eckstein, Gustav (1970) *The Body Has a Head*. New York: HarperCollins.

Kawachi, I., and S. Wamala, eds. (2007) *Globalization and Health*. New York: Oxford University Press.

Koop, C. E., C. E. Pearson, and M. R. Schwarz, eds. (2002) *Critical Issues in Global Health*. San Francisco: Jossey-Bass.

Koplow, D. (2003) *Smallpox: The Fight to Eradicate a Global Scourge*. Los Angeles: University of California Press.

Moon, Suerie, et al. (2015) "Will Ebola Change the Game? Ten Essential Reforms Before the Next Pandemic." *The Lancet* (November 22).

Timberg, Craig, and Daniel Halerin (2013). *Tinderbox: How the West Sparked the AIDS Epidemic and How the World Can Finally Overcome It*. New York: Penguin.

United Nations (2015) *The Millennium Development Goals Report 2015*. www.un.org.

Verghese, Abraham (2009). *Cutting for Stone*. New York: Vintage.

8

Ensuring Food Security

Coreen H. Cockerill

THE CHALLENGES PLACED ON FARMERS TODAY ARE ONEROUS—TO produce food in a changing and volatile climate, faced with limited resources and spaces suitable for production, in order to feed a growing population, expected to hit 9 billion by 2050. The task seems almost insurmountable.

Some of these challenges are driven by natural forces or factors, for example the natural distribution of productive soils (natural glacial deposits), or climate patterns that affect food production (such as El Niño, localized droughts, or hurricanes). Others are nonnatural, or anthropogenic, and are caused, produced, or amplified by humans. Examples of such anthropogenic factors include soil loss and degradation from farming marginal lands, the increased use of dwindling underground water reservoirs for irrigation purposes, and increased demand among developing nations for energy-intensive meat proteins. It is the nature of farming as a system, or a complex convergence of factors—both natural and anthropogenic—that makes its challenges seem so difficult to address.

The Food and Agriculture Organization (FAO) of the United States classifies a "farming system" as having the following attributes:

> Available natural resource base, including water, land, grazing areas and forest; climate, of which altitude is one important determinant; landscape, including slope; farm size, tenure and organization; and dominant pattern of farm activities and household livelihoods, including field crops, livestock, trees, aquaculture, hunting and gathering, processing and off-farm activities; and taking into account the main technologies used, which determine the intensity of production and integration of crops, livestock and other activities. (n.d.)

These attributes are diverse and variable over time and space. They define, influence, and shape the food system. Consequently, these attributes must be considered all together in discussions and analyses of agriculture. Where systems are complicated, so are the solutions to problems within them. This chapter explores such food and farming systems from a global perspective.

Natural Factors

Geography and Population

Land is an asset required in food production, yet its availability has reached a critical state. Farmers who raise crops (fruits, vegetables, and grains) and livestock depend on the availability of land suitable for agriculture. Suitability can be determined by a number of land characteristics, including but not limited to soil type, topography or slope, water availability (groundwater, surface water, and precipitation), drainage capacity, availability of macro- and micronutrients, and tract size. Certainly, some land is not suitable for production, whether because it does not possess any or all of these characteristics ideal for agriculture or because it has already been developed. Rapid development or conversion of land by way of urban expansion is also happening across the globe in an attempt to accommodate growing populations. These lands are being converted into residential spaces, building lots, paved highways and parking lots, schools, and the like, rendering them no longer suitable for agriculture. Land as a resource for food production is becoming increasingly scarce. Some researchers question whether Earth has already reached its carrying capacity, or the maximum population an area can support as determined by its food requirements (Harris and Kennedy 1999). Understanding land as both an asset and a limitation to growth in agriculture is critical to the analysis of the food system.

The global population is expected to reach 9 billion by 2050, up from 7 billion today, placing increasingly more pressure on land resources. According to the FAO, most population expansion will occur in developing countries, with sub-Saharan African populations expected to grow the fastest. Populations will become more urbanized, leaving farm operations in rural areas to be managed by fewer individuals. Simultaneously, urbanization is expected to result in economic growth among developing countries, thereby creating an expanded global middle class (FAO 2009).

Typically, as per capita income increases, so does the demand for more nutritious food—including meat proteins (e.g., eggs, chicken, pork, beef). According to an article published by the Stanford Woods Institute for the Environment: "Meat production is projected to double by 2020 due to increased per capita global consumption of meat and population growth. Most of this increase in production will come through industrialized animal production systems" (SWIE n.d.). At present, poultry production dominates the global growth market, followed by pork and eggs. Because meat production requires extensive land, water, and waste-removal capacities, this growth is expected to strain, and perhaps damage, natural resources. A recent study revealed that "beef produces five times more heat-trapping gases per calorie, puts out six times as much water-polluting nitrogen, takes 11 times more water for irrigation and uses 28 times the land" (*CBS News* 2014). The Livestock, Environment, and Development Initiative cites an example out of Asia where physical and political capacities are limited in response to increased production of livestock: "Key forces encouraging this trend are subsidized concentrate feed, poor infrastructure and weak regulations. Where roads are inadequate and transport costs high, industrial units are usually located close to urban centres. This has happened in Asia, for example, where industrial livestock production has developed very quickly and where a weak regulatory structure compounds the risks to human health" (FAO 2015a).

In short, population growth between 2020 and 2050 will surely stretch the production limits of the food system, and will likely add significant strain to the livestock and feed production sectors. So, how much growth is too much? At what point does agricultural expansion become unsustainable?

While there is no consensus on how much land would need to be in production in order to sustain a population of 9 billion, researchers estimate it would require raising food production by 70 percent. At current rates, production in developing countries would need to double (FAO 2009). However, production increases cannot come by land expansion alone, as previously discussed. According to the FAO, available land that is suitable for production "is concentrated in a few countries in Latin America and sub-Saharan Africa . . . and much of the potential land is suitable for growing only a few crops that are not necessarily those for which there is the highest demand" (2009: 2–3). Some countries may have already reached limits on land available for production purposes—either crop or livestock—particularly in the Near East/North Africa and South Asia. Nearly 40 percent of Earth's surface land is being utilized already for production agriculture (Foley et al. 2005). Tropical forests were being converted to farmland in the Southern Hemisphere at a rate of 5.2 million hectares (12.8 million acres) per year (roughly the size of West Virginia) between 2000 and 2010, down from 8.3 million hectares (20.5 million acres) per year between 1990 and 2000 (FAO 2010). Deforestation for agricultural purposes is declining among some countries, including in Brazil and Indonesia, but continuing at high rates in the regions of southern Africa and southern Asia (FAO 2010). The loss of forests impacts the environment in a number of ways, most significantly through loss of wildlife habitat; loss of water-absorption and evaporation capacity; loss of canopy or cover, which helps maintain Earth's surface temperature; and loss of carbon sequestration capacity—or the ability for forests to absorb excess pollutant greenhouse gases.

So far, agricultural expansion (most recently by way of deforestation) and intensification (increasing crop yields) has provided sufficient production to meet current global per capita food demand, according to most researchers (Cassman and Wood 2005). Agriculture continues to be the "principle driving force of the rural economy and, for those developing countries without substantial mineral resources, often the whole economy" (FAO 2002: 13). Research and development in biotechnology and expanded use of inputs (e.g., fertilizers, herbicides, pesticides, fungicides) has allowed for continued advancements in crop yields, including grains used in livestock feed. But can this growth be sustained? Optimists suggest the answer to sustained production in the face of a growing population will come primarily through technological advancement. Whether advancements in science and technology can stretch Earth's carrying capacity remains uncertain.

Climate

In addition to the production limits of shrinking land and expanding populations, Earth's climate has introduced a number of new and unique challenges for agriculture. As discussed in Chapter 15, Earth's temperature is rising. According to the National Oceanic and Atmospheric Administration (NOAA), global surface temperatures have increased 1.4 degrees Fahrenheit since the early twentieth century. This change is most notable when examining average temperatures since 1981, during which NOAA has recorded the twenty warmest years since national records began in 1895. In fact, September 2015 broke all previous records as the warmest September ever documented. With warming surface temperatures also comes warming sea temperatures, driving Arctic ice-melting and sea-level rise. Global sea levels have risen an average 1.7 millimeters per year over the past hundred years, with an increase to 3.5 millimeters per year since 1993, according to NOAA (n.d.). These increases impact agriculture in unique ways, not only based on temperature changes, but more importantly based on changes in precipitation events.

More than 80 percent of farm operations globally are classified as rainfed agriculture, or production that relies on rainfall as its primary water source. This percentage varies by region, but is concentrated in developing countries. According to the FAO, rainfed agriculture accounts for more than 95 percent of farmed land in sub-Saharan Africa, 90 percent in Latin America, 75 percent in the Near East and North Africa, 65 percent in East Asia, and 60 percent in South Asia (UNEP 2009). These rainfed systems account for 60 percent of global food production. Changes to precipitation—particularly in the regions noted here—can therefore have a drastic effect on production capacity. These changes are likely to vary significantly across the globe, from severe lack of precipitation leading to drought in some regions and increased precipitation leading to flooding in others. Neither condition is ideal for food production.

Research conducted in 2008 by the Iowa State Extension Service examined the likely impact of climate change on the suitability of rainfed production systems. By estimating both increases and decreases in rainfall using data from the Intergovernmental Panel on Climate Change (IPCC), researchers were able to identify areas that would experience significant decreases in production suitability based on a "suitability index," which factored in precipitation, suitability of soils, and terrain. Key findings (Takle 2008):

- The central United States will likely experience a modest decrease in precipitation, particularly in the Great Plains.
- Mexico and Central America will likely experience a significant decrease in rainfall events. This decline in precipitation is a feature of all global climate models. Because of the magnitude of this impact on Mexico and Central America, US policymakers should monitor climate change over this region through the coming years.
- Brazil, Uruguay, and Argentina might see an increase in rainfall that likely will be beneficial.
- Southern and eastern Europe likely will see a substantial decrease in precipitation.
- Central Africa likely will see an increase in precipitation and in southern Africa, a decrease.
- India probably will experience an increase in precipitation.
- China and East Asia will probably experience an increase in precipitation. However, the likelihood of extreme increases in precipitation in these areas may be detrimental to agricultural production.
- Australia is projected to see an increase in precipitation in the east and a decrease in the west.

Climate change may also affect agriculture in its impact on the spread of pests and pathogens (e.g., fungi, insects, bacteria, viruses) among crops and livestock. It is estimated that nearly 15 percent of crops grown for food and feed are lost each year to pest and disease outbreaks. Current rates of loss amount to enough food to feed 8.5 percent of today's population (Bebber, Ramotowski, and Gurr 2013). Changing weather patterns can shift or altogether change the movement and distribution of pests and pathogens. Researchers from the Universities of Exeter and Oxford in 2013 examined historical crop pest/pathogen distribution data since 1960, looking for trends in movement or spread. While more than 600 organisms were examined, each demonstrating varied distribution, most were found to be shifting away from the equator and toward the North and South Poles at an average rate of 2.7 kilometers per year. The researchers contend that warmer global temperatures have allowed pests and pathogens to survive at higher latitudes, encouraging winter survival and spread. "If climate change will make it easier for crop-destroying organisms to spread, renewed efforts to monitor the occurrence of pests and diseases and control their transport will be critical in controlling this growing threat to global food security" (Bebber, Ramotowski, and Gurr 2013: 987).

Such research provides a compelling case for adaptation strategies to be developed and implemented among farming systems. Whether adapting to increased precipitation, decreased precipitation, or extreme variations and related issues of new pests or pathogens, crop farmers will have to modify their practices or adopt new technologies or biotechnologies better suited for new or changing climate conditions. Such technologies may come in the form of tillage tools, irrigation systems, or drainage mechanisms designed to better address weather variations. Biotechnologies may include drought-, flood-, or disease-resistant seed varieties developed through natural selection or genetic modification. Likewise, livestock producers will face challenges unique to each species. According to the FAO: "Climate change has direct effects on livestock productivity as well as indirectly through changes on the availability of fodder and pastures. It determines the type of livestock most adapted to different agro-ecological zones and therefore the animals that are able to sustain rural communities" (2012). The production of fodder, or course grains, hay, straw, forage, or compressed pellets fed directly to livestock, and the use of pastures, can be inhibited by either too much or too little rainfall. For example, a recent case study out of Monteverde, Costa Rica (see Figure 8.1), identifies the complex challenges of livestock production in a delicate ecosystem facing significant changes in localized climate.

In summary, the threats to the global farming system of population growth and expansion and climate change persist and are expected to intensify in the decades to come. And yet agriculture, too, must persist. Food is essential to survival. Although researchers currently work to develop predictive models for changes in both population and climate, they cannot project with certainty the direct or indirect effects of either variable on global food security—or the availability of adequate food supply to meet global dietary needs. In short, the population is unstable, the climate is unstable, and these factors increase vulnerability in the farming system. Farmers must adapt to these vulnerabilities in order to sustain a future in food production. Most contemporary research looks to and critically analyzes possible reactive or adaptive scenarios, such as the following:

Figure 8.1 Case Study: Cattle-Farming Operations in the Monteverde Region of Costa Rica

Monteverde is a region of Costa Rica located in the northwest highlands with an elevation of near 4,500 feet. Its ecosystem is characterized as a cloud forest, which features persistent low-lying cloud or fog cover conducive to the growth and support of many species of flora and fauna. The region was settled in the mid-1950s by a small group of Quakers from the United States seeking refuge from US war drafts in a country that had abolished its military. The Quakers brought with them knowledge of farming and, once settled, established dairy farms throughout the area. Eventually they expanded from milk to cheese production, building the first cooperative factory, which transported cheese to the central valley of San Jose. The region experienced a proliferation of farms between 1960 and 1990—both Quaker and native Costa Rican—that gave rise to a thriving cash economy. Dairy farmers were commended in research literature for their use and protection of blocks of cloud forests standing between pastures, intended as wind blocks, and their daily pasture rotation systems, ideal for the region's porous volcanic soils (Mondrus-Engle 1982).

Today, Monteverde farmers are facing a multitude of challenges brought on mostly by climate change. Although the cheese factory still supports local milk and cheese production, dairy farmers are struggling with increasing drought conditions, pasture management issues, and decreased milk production by their cattle. The once green pastures of East African stargrass (*Cynodon nmenfluensis*) and white clover (*Trifolium repens*) are now dry and sparse as temperatures climb and rainfall diminishes. A biologist studying bats in the cloud forest since the 1970s has documented an increase of 3 degrees Celsius (37.4 degrees Fahrenheit) in average minimum temperatures from 1990 to 2000 (LaVal 2004). Another study on the mist in the cloud forest, which works to keep the temperatures down, found a significant decline in mist presence since the 1970s (Pounds, Fogden, and Campbell 1999). This dramatic change to the microclimate of the region has rendered pastures virtually unable to support grazing livestock, especially during the dry season. Many farmers have resorted to the importation of silage from lowland regions, though the practice adds cost to production due to the limited availability of silage and the country's poor roads and lack of transportation options. Furthermore, the quality of silage is often poor, as it can rapidly deteriorate in tropical climates. As a result, farmers have reported a decrease in milk production by their cattle, up to 50 percent less than at peak productivity, devastating this once-thriving dairy industry.

Newsweek has declared Monteverde the world's fourteenth of 100 places to visit before it disappears. Because of the delicate nature of the cloud forest ecosystem, even slight changes to temperature or precipitation can have dramatic effects on its ability to support flora and fauna. As the region becomes warmer and dryer, the cloud cover has begun to dissipate or recede to higher elevations, leaving the once plush pastures of Monteverde brown and brittle, unable to support plant and animal life. What was once the dominant industry and main source of income and sustenance for the people of Monteverde, dairy farming has now become a dwindling and threatened practice—likely to disappear with the clouds in the near future.

• *Rely on technology as a fix.* Invest in new technologies or biotechnologies to solve issues associated with crop/livestock yield, pest or pathogen outbreaks, precipitation extremes, limitations to micro- and macronutrient availability, and the like, in order to enhance productivity and therefore food security.

• *Influence consumption patterns.* Drive consumption patterns away from crops/livestock that are resource-intensive, or those requiring higher use of inputs (water, nutrients, fuel for machinery) per land area. This approach is intended to reduce the increasing need for additional inputs that are either limited in supply or that add stress to the natural system.

• *Diversify production.* Work to develop a more diverse system of food production that utilizes local assets and resources, and that is designed to be more resilient than single, monoculture (single-crop/species) systems. Diversification is expected to minimize risk associated with crop or livestock failure (whether risks brought on by climate occurrences, pest or pathogen outbreaks, or natural resource limitations) by maintaining a more resilient system of multiple crop or livestock species—called polyculture.

• *Do nothing.* This approach relies on a restabilization of climate conditions (whether via natural processes or human mitigation), and a wait-and-see approach to population growth and expansion.

Anthropogenic Factors

Modern Farming Practices and Biotechnology

The domestication of agronomic plants (or those grown in open fields), mainly barley, wheat, peas and lentils, began nearly 12,000 years ago within the Fertile Crescent area comprising present-day Iraq, Kuwait, Syria, Lebanon, Jordan, Israel, Palestine, Cyprus, Egypt, Turkey, and Iran, surrounding the Tigris and Euphrates rivers. During the period known as the neolithic revolution or agricultural revolution, hunter-gatherers began planting and harvesting crops using primitive tillage and irrigation systems. The production of food allowed for growing populations, which expanded to larger settlements, and eventually cities. Agriculture changed very little between the earliest era to approximately 1700 C.E. Developments in food production during that time came primarily in the form of advanced planting and harvesting tools and the use of horses as a source of power. Some 90 percent of the population was engaged in the production of food.

Modern industrial agriculture emerged between the sixteenth and nineteenth centuries, significantly reshaping the farming system. Mechanization, brought on by the invention of the plough, seed drill, and threshing machine, redefined agriculture as an industry. British farmers adopted agronomic crop rotation systems that would allow for greater quantities and varieties of crops. The development of the steam engine and subsequent railway system advanced the marketing and transportation of crops for trade purposes. Mechanized farming practices facilitated a surplus of grains that could also be traded internationally and moved by ships or barges. Although such advancements led to greater efficiencies on farms in terms of capital, labor, and distribution, many people still abandoned rural farm life in exchange for jobs in urban areas that were less labor-intensive and offered higher wages. During this period, between 70 and 90 percent of the global labor force was represented by farmers.

Indeed, the industrialization of agriculture represented a total revolution of all aspects of the farming system, altogether transforming who produced what products and how. The revolution brought with it a number of trends that remain today—primarily the proliferation of technology and reduction of rural or farm populations. Currently, less than 35 percent of the global labor force is engaged in farming. That percentage is less than 4 in most developed countries, including Australia (3.6 percent), Canada (2.0 percent), Germany (1.6 percent), Norway (2.2 percent), Sweden (2.0 percent), Switzerland (3.4 percent), the United Kingdom (1.3 percent), and the United States (0.7 percent) (CIA n.d.). Globally, farms are becoming smaller and more mechanized, but still increasing in productivity. According to the FAO, the majority of farms worldwide are "small or very small." Worldwide, farms of less than one acre account for 84 percent of all farms, but control only 12 percent of all agricultural products. In contrast, only 1 percent of all farms in the world are larger than thirty acres, but control 65 percent of agricultural products globally (FAO 2014). The effort to reap higher yields on increasingly smaller farms has prompted extensive use of inputs, or enhancement products, including fungicides, herbicides, insecticides, fertilizers, and genetically modified organisms (GMOs) or seeds.

Three cereal grains—wheat, rice, and corn—represent more than 50 percent of the global food supply, making them the three most abundant plants on earth (Awika 2011). In other words, these grains make up more than half of calories consumed by humans worldwide. It is the abundance of these three grains and lack of plant diversity that has caused increased biological pressures on these crops in the form of weeds and pests. Single or continuous cropping systems—also called monocultures, where single plant species are grown in the same place at the same time—are more vulnerable to disease, pests, weeds, and weather, putting the bulk farming system at risk. Excessive weed pressure can choke out desired plants, negatively impacting yield. Simultaneously, encroaching insects, fungi, and molds can compromise plant health in ways that significantly reduce productivity. This practice is rising in popularity in the western United States, including in Illinois, where some producers have most, if not all, of their fields in corn every year. Crops that used to be incorporated into rotations, including oats, hay, and wheat, have been replaced by corn and soybeans—but predominantly corn, which typically offers higher yields and higher market prices than do other grains (Nafziger 2009).

For this, plant biologists have worked since the late 1960s on these specific crops to strengthen plant genetics in order to improve agricultural outcomes. For centuries prior, farmers utilized selective breeding as a natural process of breeding plants with ideal traits to those expressing less-than-ideal traits. Modern biotechnology, driven by the discovery of deoxyribonucleic acid (DNA) and recombinant DNA in 1935 and 1973 respectively, found ways to isolate genes to be used for specific purposes. The first GMO patent in the United States was issued in 1980 to General Electric for a proprietary bacterium developed to aid in oil spill clean up. In 1982, the US Food and Drug Administration (FDA) approved the first GMO available in the public market, Humulin, an insulin developed from another hearty bacterium (Altman 1982). Advancements in breeding technologies have since led to the development of GMO plant species that have been genetically enhanced for more desired outcomes.

GMO varieties of all three of the major grains have been developed, though only GMO corn is available in the global market. Trials of both GMO rice and GMO wheat have been conducted in the United States, the United Kingdom, and China, but neither product is available for public consumption. Likely with time and additional trials, these products, too, will become available to the public. Most GMO corn varieties have been developed to do one or more of the following: resist herbicides sprayed directly on and around the plant to kill weeds; resist pests by emitting a protein that, when ingested by insects, causes sickness or death; and tolerate stresses caused by drought. The ability for farmers to produce robust crop yields by eliminating the stresses of weeds, pests, and drought is therefore enhanced through the use of GMO varieties. According to David Tilman and colleagues: "Breeders have been successful at improving resistances to abiotic stresses, pathogens and diseases, and at deploying these defenses in space and time so as to maintain yield stability despite low crop diversity in continuous cereal systems" (Tilman et al. 2002: 674). Proponents of the use of biotechnology have deemed GMOs a major success toward a future of food production in an environment stressed by climate and with increasing demand to achieve global food security.

While GMOs have persisted in the scientific realm, they have not been well received by the public and are often the target of media attacks. Although the figures shift regularly, approximately twenty-six countries currently employ total or partial bans on GMOs. Another sixty countries have GMO restrictions in place (Bello 2013). Underlying public concern, primarily, is a lack of transparency or understanding of the genetic modification process—in other words, the current drivers of GMO production. At present, there are no federal labeling laws in the United States that identify which food products on the market contain GMOs. Some states, including Vermont and California, have passed local or state labeling laws, though the legislation is currently being challenged in courts by a number of major food corporations. At the root of the issue in the United States is the definition of a food product containing GMOs. According to the FDA, which in part oversees the development and approval processes of GMOs on the public market: "Labeling, by law, is limited to identifying significant changes in a food's composition, and it must not mislead consumers" (House Hearing 1999). In short, the FDA contends that where there is no nutritional difference between a GMO-containing product and its non-GMO counterpart, labeling is not necessary.

Nevertheless, there is substantial support in the public realm for the mandatory labeling of GMO products. A 2013 poll conducted by the *New York Times* found 93 percent of respondents said they wanted labels on foods containing GMO ingredients. That same poll found that two-thirds of respondents had concerns about the unknown or potentially negative health effects of GMO-containing foods (Kopicki 2013). In addition to issues of trust and concern for human health, the FAO has identified further public concern over GMOs to include the impact of GMOs on the environment, and the impact of GMOs on the livelihood of small-scale farmers (FAO 2001). See Table 8.1 for a list of public concerns most often found in both scientific literature and the media.

A theme across most of the risk factors is a lack of knowledge of or transparency with both processes and potential outcomes. The Pew Research Center, which conducts opinion polls on the topics of the Internet, science, and technology, reported in 2015 the gap between citizens' and scientists' perceptions of GMO safety at 51 percent—the largest opinion difference between the public and scientists in that poll (Funk and Rainie 2015). While social media have facilitated more digital conversations among diverse consumers and constituents, it is often in the absence of scientific conversation. Public media have played into public fears by amplifying risk messages associated with GMOs that often have no scientific backing. For example, the media have adopted biased phrasing when reporting on GMOs, like using the term "Frankenfoods," which was even added to the online *Oxford Dictionary* in 2012. Tina Andersen Huey discusses this divergence between the public, food conglomerates, and scientists:

> The plot of the GM food story is that not only are consumers at the mercy of a multinational, unaccountable conglomerate, but they are also at the mercy of unintelligible forms of knowledge. Biotechnology is discursively set up as abstract, remote, and vested, in contrast to farmers' knowledge (specific, local, and diverse) or consumers' knowledge (autonomous). Genetic engineering, like any advanced technology, sharpens the divide between insiders and outsiders on the basis of comprehension. (2015: 271)

Table 8.1 Overview of GMO Risk Factors: Practices and Outcomes

Area of Public Concern	Trend or Practice	Risk Outcomes
Environmental	Using increasing amounts of herbicides sprayed onto and around resistant GMO plants	Excessive herbicides in the environment may cause damage; herbicides may build up in the soil; herbicides may kill unintended plant species
Environmental	Using increasing amounts of same herbicides over time	Can lead to development of herbicide-resistant weeds (sometimes called superweeds) that can be managed only with additional chemicals
Environmental	Planting pest-resistant GMO seeds	May have negative unintended impact on insect species; development of resistant insects that form a tolerance
Environmental	Planting GMO seeds adjacent to non-GMO seeds	Can lead to possible cross-pollination in non-GMO-containing fields
Human health	Consuming GMO-containing foods	May involve unknown risks to human health; risk is amplified by inability to control consumption choice without labels on products
Human health	Inserting genetic material from other species in order to create new GMOs	Genetic-modification process is not transparent and therefore could lead to insertion of allergens or toxins into foods
Social	Purchasing proprietary GMO seeds	Small-scale farmers, particularly in developing countries, may not be able to afford GMO seeds; farmers cannot save seeds to be planted in subsequent years due to patent controls

Ultimately, Huey (2015) calls for transparency of channels of financing, production, and distribution, as well as pressure on researchers to engage both consumers and producers in productive dialogue, backed by science. But what agency or entity will take on the task of uniting rhetoric, public opinion, and science? Who will reinforce the transparency that will be required to overcome the gaps in knowledge and transparency? Awareness of the gap is a starting point, but society has a long way to go to find resolution in the GMO debate.

Resources: Soil, Water, and Nutrients

Food cannot be produced without adequate soil, water, and nutrients. These are all factors that serve as limitations to production. As mentioned earlier, access to high-quality soils, sufficient freshwater supplies, and nutrients readily available for plant uptake is restricted in many parts of the world, and yet increased food production requires increasingly more of each resource. More than 80 percent of water consumption in the United States can be attributed to agriculture, the majority of which is tied up in irrigation systems in the western region (Schaible and Aillery 2012). This is the same region where more than 2,000 types of soil support more than 400 varieties of crops, including not just corn and wheat, but also almonds, artichokes, dates, figs, raisins, kiwi fruit, olives, clingstone peaches, pistachios, dried plums, pomegranates, sweet rice, ladino clover seed, and walnuts. California, specifically, grows nearly half of the fruits, vegetables, and nuts consumed in the United States, and 82 percent of almonds consumed globally (USDA 2013). It is in regions like this where entire states and even global societies rely on the productivity of a relatively small natural system of water, soil, and available nutrients. When that system becomes limited or stressed, those populations become less food-secure. An important case study comes out of California, which experienced in 2015 its most significant drought in nearly a century (see Figure 8.2).

Water and soil are limitations not only in terms of their availability, but also in terms of their integrity. Water quality is compromised when wastes—residential, industrial, and agricultural—are carried off land, move with water, and pool in freshwater reservoirs, such as ponds, lakes, gulfs, and even oceans. Waste in agriculture comes from a variety of sources, but can include excess nutrients or fertilizers, residual pesticides (e.g., herbicides, insecticides, fungicides), and animal waste or manure. When these wastes or toxins enter the water system, they often accumulate as they travel from many small tributaries to larger creeks or rivers, and eventually to larger basins where such wastes are concentrated.

Concentrated chemicals or nutrients can have a harmful effect on aquatic systems. In the case of both nitrogen and phosphorous, common fertilizers applied to enhance crop yields, excess nutrients not taken up by plants often leave the system during rainfall or runoff events. Nutrient runoff that accumulates in basins can facilitate the growth of algae—a process called eutrophication. When the algae die and sink to the bottom, they are decomposed by bacteria, a process that depletes dissolved oxygen from the water. This process often pushes the aquatic system into a state of hypoxia—or low oxygen—which can destroy aquatic life. According to a study produced by the World Resources Institute, there are 415 areas around the world identified as experiencing eutrophication. Additionally, "a staggering 78 percent of the assessed continental US coastal area and ap-

Figure 8.2 Case Study: When California Has a Drought, Everyone Has a Drought

The year 2015 marked a state of emergency in California, a state gripped by drought for a record-breaking four consecutive years. Brought on by the lowest snowpack ever recorded in the mountains surrounding the California central valley, increased temperatures, and lack of adequate precipitation, the water situation had reached a crisis point. Much of California's water comes from the Colorado River basin, which also provides water to six other states—Arizona, Colorado, Nevada, New Mexico, Utah, and Wyoming—supporting 40 million people and 15 percent of the nation's food supply. In April 2015, California's governor, Edmund G. Brown Jr., with the cooperation of the State Water Resources Control Board, implemented the first ever mandatory water reduction in cities and towns and on farms across the region, with the goal of reducing water consumption by 25 percent. As a result, all new homes were mandated to use drip irrigation systems with nonpotable water for lawn irrigation; venues with substantial lawn-care practices like golf courses, cemeteries, and college campuses were required to limit the frequency and longevity of waterings; and rebate programs were established to encourage the purchase of water-efficient appliances for existing homes.

But the greatest impact of both the drought and the mandatory water restrictions was felt by the state's agricultural sector, which accounted for 80 percent of the state's water use. According to a drought impact report by the University of California–Davis Center for Watershed Sciences, both employment and cropland in production decreased by 30 percent in 2015 as compared to 2014 (Howitt et al. 2015). That equated to a loss of more than 10,000 seasonal jobs, which caused high unemployment rates and economic depression in rural communities in the central valley. Domestic (residential-use) well water disappeared, as farmers began relying more on deeper wells and heavier pumping to secure water needed for crop irrigation. Reliance on groundwater caused some overdrafting, where groundwater use exceeded replenishing in underground reservoirs or aquifers, a practice that can compromise water quality and deplete future water reserves. The University of California–Davis study also projected that more than half a million acres of land would go fallow—removed altogether from food production—and remain abandoned until the drought situation ends.

There seems to be no end in sight for the California water crisis. Climatologists estimate another year of drought to come in 2016. This will likely mean additional cuts to the agricultural labor force, additional strains on the dwindling water resources, and additional land left fallow. Also likely is a subsequent rise in the cost of food for consumers. According to an Economic Research Service report by the US Department of Agriculture: "Owing to higher production costs, insufficient water, or both, producers may opt to reduce total acreage, driving up prices not just this year but for years to come. At this point we have started to see this happen" (USDA 2015). The implications of California's persistent drought on the larger global food system may not be felt for years. But given that this single state produces the world's ninth largest agricultural economy, the reverberations, worldwide, could be dramatic.

proximately 65 percent of Europe's Atlantic coast exhibit symptoms of eutrophication" (Selman 2008: 1). Of all the global systems found to be eutrophic, 169 have become hypoxic, and are commonly called "dead zones." The two most well-known hypoxic areas are the Gulf of Mexico and the Black Sea, both of which support substantial commercial fisheries. While the Black Sea has been "in recovery" since the 1990s, due mostly to reductions in fertilizer use, the hypoxic zone in the Gulf of Mexico continues to expand, now measured at about 22,000 square kilometers, up from 5,000 square kilometers in 2000 (Selman 2008). Efforts to stabilize nutrient runoff have become a priority of organizations like the US Environmental Protection Agency (EPA), the US Department of Agriculture, and federal, state, and local farm-bureau organizations.

In addition to chemical or fertilizer wastes, animal-waste runoff from farming systems can carry bacteria and parasites that also compromise water quality. The majority of animal-waste runoff issues stem from the practice of clustering a large number of animals in or on relatively small spaces called animal feeding operations (AFOs). The EPA defines AFOs as "farms or feedlots where animals are kept and raised in confined areas for at least 45 days over a 12-month period" (EPA n.d.). Where animals are concentrated, so is the waste or manure they produce. Thus, waste management becomes a priority for those who operate AFOs. Often, manure is spread on fields of crops as a natural fertilizer. Some farmers, especially in developing countries, have incorporated biodigesters as a waste management system. Biodigesters are vessels or containers that hold liquid manure, called slurry. Anaerobic bacteria work within the vessels to break down the manure, thereby producing biogas, or a mix of methane and carbon dioxide. Farmers then harvest the biogas for various uses, primarily as a fuel for cooking, heating, or powering engines. These tend to work well for smaller operations. Waste management plans for larger livestock operations, however, are sometimes inadequate. Improper management or storage of manure can result in environmental contamination. Unlined waste containment ponds or corrals can allow contaminated wastewater to leach into groundwater systems. The size and placement of manure storage systems can also lead to runoff issues, especially those systems that are exposed or vulnerable to flooding from heavy rains or snow melts (EPA n.d.). Such flood conditions can wash wastewater into nearby waterways or streams, compromising those aquatic systems. Careful management of waste must become a priority if livestock production is expected to expand in order to meet growing consumer demand for meat proteins, as previously discussed.

The stability of soil is also uncertain in many parts of the world. Soil integrity is a critical factor in the global farming system, but is jeopardized by soil erosion. Soil erosion is the loss of the top layer of soil by way of wind, water, or ice. Because soil is the foundation that serves as an anchor to all plants, and because it supports a delicate balance of animals and microorganisms, its health is a primary concern for farmers. According to Ted Napier and Coreen Henry Cockerill (2014), erosion is taking place in every country on this planet, though it varies across regions and soil types. A number of natural factors can cause erosion (e.g., flooding that removes soil along riverbeds and banks, glacial movement, heavy winds, gravity); however, agriculture remains the single largest contributor to the increase in erosion rates globally (CSA 2010). The specific practice of soil tillage—or breaking up the soil into smaller particles in preparation for planting—is at the root of the issue. Soil that is tilled, or loosened, makes an ideal seed bed, but becomes more vulnerable to wind or rain events. As Humberto Blanco-Canqui and Rattan Lal explain: "Control and management of soil erosion are important because when the fertile topsoil is eroded away the remaining soil is less productive with the same level of input. While soil erosion cannot be completely curtailed, excessive erosion must be reduced to a manageable or tolerable level to minimize adverse effects on productivity" (2008: 3).

Replacing valuable and productive topsoil can be done, but the process is often slower than its removal via erosion. Determining the threshold where soil erosion is occurring at an unsustainable rate can be difficult, however. Some soils are well developed, dense with organic matter, and contain deep profiles, while others are shallow, thin, or sloping. Erosion assessments must take place locally, based on the local conditions of the soil. How erosion will impact the future of food production, therefore, will depend on the quality of specific local soils in production; and the impacts of localized climate conditions on those soils. Napier and Cockerill contend that "some of the highest rates of soil loss occur on cropland in lesser-scale societies where subsistence farming is most frequently employed and on soils that can least sustain such levels of soil loss without serious declines in productivity" (2014: 350). Thus, stretching the production limits of those soils—especially in Latin America and sub-Saharan Africa, where agricultural expansion is possible and likely to occur—may be impaired by excessive erosion.

Fuel Crops

Some crops are grown not for food or feed, but rather for fuel, also known as biofuel. Two specific biofuels can be found in the global market today—ethanol, made from corn, sorghum, or sugar cane; and biodiesel, made from vegetable oils or animal fats. Significantly more ethanol is produced worldwide than biodiesel. Biofuels are generally produced to achieve two goals: energy independence or a weaning away from dependency on foreign oil; and reduction of carbon dioxide (CO_2) and other greenhouse gas emissions. Fuels that burn cleaner than conventional fossil fuels emit fewer greenhouse gases into the atmosphere. Because CO_2 is a greenhouse gas that, when concentrated in the atmosphere, radiates the sun's energy back to Earth's surface, it is noted as a significant contributor to the rise of global temperatures.

While researchers have found biofuels to burn cleaner than fossil fuels, they have failed to find consensus on whether the production and use of biofuels reduces overall CO_2 emissions, as compared to the production and use of fossil fuels. This is mostly due to variations in biofuel production processes, which presently require a front-loading of CO_2 in the mechanics of tilling, planting, and harvesting the biomass (crops, in this example). In other words, crops must first be planted and harvested before they are available to be processed into fuel. This results in front-end emissions from machinery, vehicles, and heavy equipment used in the planting and harvesting processes. In short, because the production of crops to be refined into biofuels is carbon-heavy, it may not yet result in a cumulative reduction of CO_2 as compared to fossil fuel extraction and use. This, combined with global food shortages and food insecurity, has sparked a recent controversy in the media, often referred to as the "food versus fuel debate," which posits the question of whether the growth of plants for fuel competes directly with food production. If fuel production is in conflict with food production, what are the implications, especially where governments are encouraging, specifically, the production of biofuels by way of government tax incentives, subsidies, low-interest loans, and grants? Could the demand for fuel compromise the ability of farmers to produce food?

Aided by recent scientific advancements in biofuel production, some farmers have quelled the food-versus-fuel debate by moving toward the development of cellulosic biofuels—commonly referred to as second-generation biofuels. The manufacturing of cellulosic fuel from grain crops involves only the use of excess plant material (e.g., stalks, leaves, stems, cobs), or those left over from food production. This allows for a simultaneous production of food and fuel, though one that is still carbon-heavy on the front end. Other perennial plant materials, such as grasses, may prove to be even more efficient than grain crops. According to a study released by the National Academy of Sciences, "switchgrass produced 540% more renewable than nonrenewable energy consumed," with an estimated 94 percent reduction in greenhouse gas emissions when compared to gasoline (Schmer et al. 2008: 464). A third generation of biofuels is in development, spurred by the use of biomass materials, such as algae, produced not in crop fields but instead in dedicated reservoirs. While there are no biorefineries yet able to manufacture either switchgrass- or algae-based biofuels in mass quantities, continued support from governments, research institutions, and new markets could make these fuels more viable. How quickly these cleaner and greener biofuels enter the market will also depend on economic viability. Where coal, oil, and natural gas reserves are cheaper to extract and process than biofuels, manufacturers, processors, and consumers will likely show preference for the cost savings.

Food Waste

Even if we were able solve all of the issues we have with access to sufficient water, fertile soils, and necessary nutrients, and were to remove the tension on both sides of the food-versus-fuel debate, we would still mitigate much of this success through wasted food. According to the FAO, more than 25 percent of global farmland is used to produce food that is wasted. More specifically, globally, 30 percent of cereals; 40–50 percent of root crops, fruits, and vegetables; 20 percent of oil seeds, meat, and dairy; and 35 percent of fish produced never reach dinner plates (2015c). Furthermore, the FAO reports that "every year, consumers in rich countries waste almost as much food (222 million tonnes) as the entire net food production of sub-Saharan Africa (230 million tonnes)" (2013). Where food is being wasted, so are the resources that go into food production. As discussed previously, those resources (soil and water, chemical and fertilizer inputs, and labor) are valuable and often limited in quantity or access. So, when researchers quantify the socioeconomic impacts of food waste, they must incorporate, too, both energy and resources lost. Such losses translate eventually into lost income for small farmers and higher food prices for poor consumers. Environmental losses, or degradation at the cost of food production, are more difficult to assess.

Most of the food wasted in developing countries stems from technical constraints in harvesting, storing, or cooling produce. These constraints could be addressed through improvements in infrastructure, transportation, and packaging—all facets internal to the farming and distribution system. In contrast, most of the food wasted in developed countries is due to consumer assessment of quality standards that emphasize appearance or freshness—facets external to the farming or distribution system. Thus, consumer behavior plays a major role in perpetuating waste. Addressing this issue is challenging, as it involves changing attitudes and behaviors, and perhaps even hard-to-break habits or cultural practices (e.g., overloading plates with more food than is desired or consumed, as often happens at food buffets). For example, when examining food waste at a small liberal arts school in Ohio in 2015, observers found students and food service workers, combined, threw out nearly 6,000 pounds of food in a standard workweek. Much of the waste came from students' emptying of leftovers into trash bins as well as food service workers' throwing out any food that had already been plated or prepared (e.g., salad bars and desert bars) (Cockerill 2015). These are all behaviors that would need to be changed in order to reduce wasted food. The FAO estimates that "even if just one-fourth of the food currently lost or wasted globally could be saved, it would be enough to feed 870 million hungry people in the world" (2013). So, when considering approaches to meeting the nutritional needs of 9 billion people by 2050, we must consider the global issue of food waste. The World Resources Institute contends:

> If the current rate of food loss and waste were cut in half from 24 percent to 12 percent by the year 2050, the world would need about 1,314 trillion kilocalories (kcal) less food per year than it would in the business-as-usual global food requirements scenario. . . . That savings—1,314 trillion kcal—is roughly 22 percent of the 6,000 trillion kcal per year gap between food available today and that needed in 2050. Thus, reducing food loss and waste could be one of the leading global strategies for achieving a sustainable food future. (Lipinski et al. 2013)

Conclusion

Identifying the most appropriate or most likely path forward for future food systems requires critical analysis of the challenges and opportunities facing food producers and consumers. Most practices related to food production cannot be easily categorized as right or wrong, good or bad, effective or ineffective. Instead, production practices are best analyzed on a continuum, as they are constantly changing and adapting, impacted by external forces (natural) and internal decisions (anthropogenic), and often best assessed at a local level. If we analyze only the duality of agricultural systems, we ultimately pitch conventional farming against organic; GMO technologies against non-GMO; industrial practices against local; food against fuel; and so on. This duality perpetuates the tendency of the public and the media to take sides, which implies that there will be winners and losers. Examining these aspects on a continuum instead of as competing categories facilitates a vision of the future where many diverse practices can be engaged simultaneously, for example a food system where both organic produce is offered at a local level, and environmentally suited GMO grains are delivered at the global level.

Furthermore, what is sustainable for one system may not be for another. There is not a single best approach at feeding 9 billion people. Instead, local problems are best met with local (often called indigenous) solutions that integrate appropriate technologies or biotechnologies, consider domestic resource (soil, water, and nutrient) availability and requirements, and acknowledge local sociopolitical or economic environments. Thus, sustainability is a modular and multifaceted concept, though this is often ignored in the media or in everyday conversation, where it is vaguely or narrowly defined. When we define sustainability, we should do so based on several factors, including:

environmental integrity, social responsibility, economic viability, and production efficiency. These facets can be examined exclusively or in concert with each other. So, when we critically examine specific practices, such as the employment of AFOs, persistent monocropping systems, or practices that result in nutrient runoff, for example, we must consider all facets of sustainability in order to determine extent and impact. In most contemporary agricultural applications, we will find a deficiency in one or more of the facets of sustainability, which implies the practice cannot be continued without potentially irrevocable damage to the environment, society, economy, or production practice.

Agriculture is not constant—it is dynamic and thus will change with climate; consumer demand; advancements in technology and biotechnology; water, soil, and nutrient availability; and government influence. And while much of agriculture is shaped by natural forces, we do play a role as global consumers in both understanding the system, and influencing or shaping it. We are all partners and allies in the future global food system—because we eat. Our preferences can and will drive markets. The increased presence of organic foods, farmers' markets, locally raised produce and meats, farm-to-table meals, backyard gardens, community supported agriculture, and canning and preserving, to name a few, represents the purchasing power of consumers. If we demonstrate an awareness of food-system functions that are unsustainable in one or many areas—and adjust our preferences accordingly—production practices will follow, and trends will shift. It begins with the prerequisites of awareness and engagement. That is the immediate and necessary charge if we are to achieve global food security.

Discussion Questions

1. Aside from relying on technology as a fix, influencing consumption patterns, diversifying production, or doing nothing, can you think of other possible scenarios for addressing the effects of population growth and climate change on agriculture?
2. Which anthropogenic factors affecting global farming systems do you think are the most critical to resolve in order to achieve global food security by 2050?
3. Which of these factors do you think will be the most difficult to resolve, and why?
4. Which of these factors do you think will be the easiest to address, and why?
5. Do you believe it is possible to achieve global food security by 2050?

Suggesting Readings

Committee on 21st Century Systems Agriculture (2010) "Toward Sustainable Agricultural Systems in the 21st Century." Washington, DC: National Academies Press.

Food and Agriculture Organization (2001) "Genetically Modified Organisms, Consumers, Food Safety, and the Environment." Rome: Viale delle Terme di Caracalla.

Gardner, Brian (2013) *Global Food Futures: Feeding the World in 2050*. New York: Bloomsbury Academic.

Lengnick, Laura (2015) *Resilient Agriculture: Cultivating Food Systems for a Changing Climate*. Gabriola Island, Canada: New Society.

Lipinski, B., et al. (2013) "Reducing Food Loss and Waste" (June). Washington, DC: World Resources Institute.

Ronald, Pamela C., and R. W. Adamchak (2010) *Tomorrow's Table: Organic Farming, Genetics, and the Future of Food*. New York: Oxford University Press.

Saltin, Joel (2012) *Folks, This Ain't Normal: A Farmer's Advice for Happier Hens, Healthier People, and a Better World*. New York: Center Street.

Tilman, D., et al. (2002) "Agricultural Sustainability and Intensive Production Practices." *Nature* 418.

White, Courtney (2014) *Grass, Soil, Hope: A Journey Through Carbon Country*. Burlington: Chelsea Green.

Part 2

Dimensions of the Global Political Economy

9

The Evolution of the Global Political Economy

Mary Ellen Batiuk and Joe Lehnert

FOR THE PEOPLE IN ANY COUNTRY TO PROSPER, IT IS CRITICAL THAT THEY have *capital,* in the form of goods, services, and money. Economic productivity and trade most often generate this capital, but some countries also receive loans and aid (official development assistance [ODA]) from other countries in order to increase the supply of capital. In addition, private corporations can invest directly into a country by building a company there (foreign direct investment [FDI]), or invest in the stock market in that country (foreign portfolio investment [FPI]). These flows of money into a country through trade, loans, aid, and investments are critical to the ability of any country to develop. Of course, capital also flows out of all countries in the form of payments for goods and services and to reduce debt. Government officials, business leaders, and citizens all want to see more capital flowing into their country than out, so as to foster growth and development.

But in today's world the gap between those countries that have experienced significant development (the more-developed countries [MDCs]), and those countries still trying to develop (the less-developed countries [LDCs]), remains extremely large. For example, in 2014, total FDI in the United States amounted to about $413 per capita (the total amount invested divided by the number of people in the country) (World Bank 2015a). By contrast, FDI in Kenya was about $21 per capita (World Bank 2011b). By this measure, people in the United States have a lot more financial capital to work with—capital that helps create the jobs that eventually support literacy, healthcare, and a higher standard of living. In 2014, annual per capita gross national income (GNI) in the United States was $55,860, compared to $2,940 in Kenya (World Bank 2015b). Gross national product (GNP) was used by reporting agencies until 2000, when it was replaced by GNI, which equals gross domestic product (GDP) (the total of goods and services produced in a given year) plus any foreign income, minus any interest or debt payments.

Generally speaking, the more financial capital flowing into a country, the better off the country will be. Today, most investment capital flows between the more-developed countries. In 2015, the developed economies accounted for about 41 percent of all global FDI inflows, down from about 69 percent before the 2008 global financial crisis. In contrast, developing countries in Africa received only about 4.4 percent of all FDI in 2014 (UNCTAD 2015). Countries with too much capital flowing out and not enough coming in fail to develop over time.

Global Capital Flows Before World War II

This current development gap between LDCs and MDCs has had a long history—one that dates back before World War II to the system of colonialism that dominated global capital flows at that time.

Economic and Political Structure of Colonialism

Colonialism is a political, economic, and social system in which one group of people, the core or dominant group, controls the political and economic lives of another group of people, the peripheral or dominated group. Colonialism usually signifies direct political control as well as economic control of another group. Colonies usually provide the core countries with cheap labor, raw materials unavailable at home, cheap commodities, and markets for goods produced in the core country. Typically, vast revenues flow out of the periphery while relatively little investment flows in. Colonialism has been around for a long time. The Greeks and Romans possessed colonies in the ancient world, and the Chinese and Japanese also historically possessed many colonies in the Asia Pacific. During the period 1500–1900, however, much of the world's population lived in colonies controlled by Western Europeans—primarily English, Spanish, French, Belgian, German, Dutch, and Portuguese. Even after US independence, European economic and political control extended throughout the Americas, Africa, Asia, and eventually the Middle East.

From 1500 to 1800, mercantilist trade policies and the slave trade dominated trade between the core and periphery. From the point of view of the colonizer, the idea was to protect industry at home and extract as much profit from the colony as possible. Colonizers ignored traditional native claims to property and created huge plantations for commodities like sugar, coffee, tobacco, cotton, and rice. Along with these agricultural commodities, lumber, furs, gold, and silver flowed out of the periphery and into the core. Additionally, some 9–15 million Africans were forcibly transported to the Americas during this time as slaves—forming what has come to be known as the Triangular Trade (see Figure 9.1). The slave trade was also incredibly profitable. Slaves made huge agricultural plantations possible because native populations often escaped when pressed into

Figure 9.1 Capital Flows in the Triangular Trade, 1500–1800

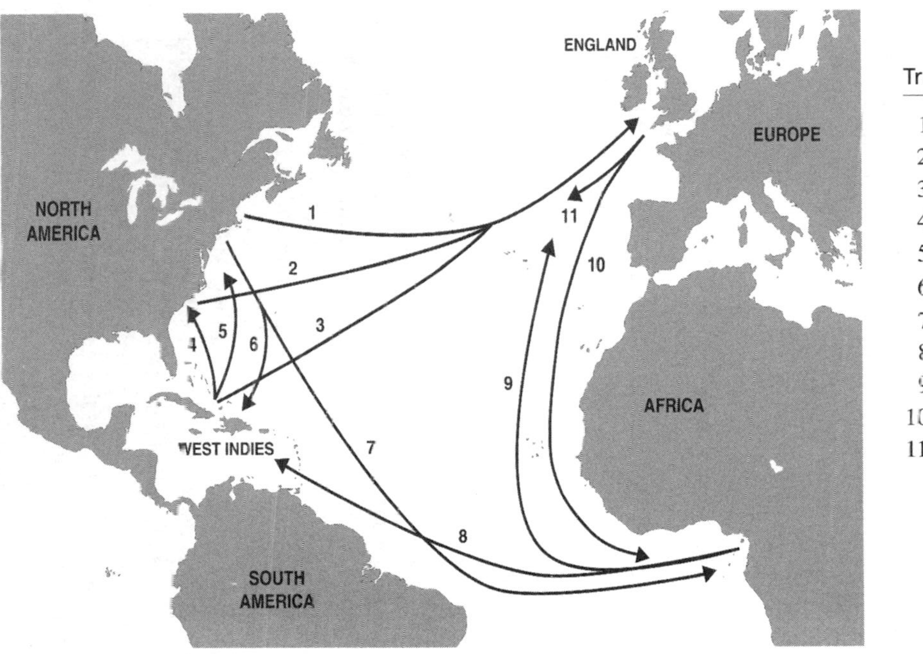

Trade Routes

1 whale oil, lumber, furs
2 rice, silk, indigo, tobacco
3 sugar, molasses, wood
4 slaves
5 slaves, sugar, molasses
6 fish, flour, livestock, lumber
7 rum, iron, gunpowder, cloth, tools
8 slaves
9 gold, ivory, spices, hardwoods
10 guns, cloth, iron, beer
11 manufactured goods, luxuries

Source: National Archives (2003).

service. In addition, native populations had no natural defenses for diseases like smallpox and measles that the colonists brought with them. Colonies in the Americas were especially lucrative. Money flowing into Europe from these colonies financed industrial development, personal luxury, and eventually war.

Early in the nineteenth century the slave trade was abolished by many European countries, which later outlawed slavery itself. European powers turned their attention to Africa, Asia, and the Middle East for new sources of capital in an era of colonial expansion. By 1856, most of India was under the control of the British East India Company, and by the end of the 1800s a "scramble for Africa" had begun. England had already laid claim to vast territories in North and South Africa. One of the most aggressive African colonizers was the king of Belgium, who personally gained control of 568 million acres of land in Central Africa (Hochschild 1999). That is seventy-five times the size of Belgium, and about one-quarter the size of the United States.

At the Berlin Conference of 1884, those European nations already in Africa officially divided the continent among themselves—without much regard to the tribes, kingdoms, and ethnic divisions already present on the continent. Boundaries were constructed to temporarily resolve European disputes about who owned what. No Africans were at the table, and the borders that were drawn (for example, straight lines that bisected natural boundaries like rivers) made little sense in terms of the indigenous populations.

Economic, Political, and Social Consequences of Colonialism

The consequences of colonialism were mixed for both the core and the periphery. For the peripheral territories (not yet countries), colonialism left a legacy of capital drain, exploitation, bureaucratic corruption, and ethnic and religious rivalries. Colonies were most often developed to provide one particular resource, or cash crop, to the dominant country. Instead of evolving diverse and resilient economic systems, colonial economies were actually quite fragile. If a population in the periphery produced primarily cotton, and global cotton markets collapsed, the indigenous people had little else to fall back on and suffered bitter consequences.

At the same time, peripheral peoples in the Americas, Africa, and Asia were introduced to European models of government and European ideas about individualism, equality, and justice. The English poet Rudyard Kipling wrote in 1899 about "the white man's burden" of bringing civilization and Christianity to indigenous (native) populations. Whether they liked it or not, and often under extreme duress, indigenous peoples around the globe succumbed to the influence of the developed world (Rodney 1983).

Europeans drained their colonies of human capital, commodities, and money. Commodity revenues that could have been used for the internal development of Africa by Africans were lost forever in the race for European profits. On the other hand, Europeans did develop considerable infrastructure in their colonies in the form of roads, shipyards, railways, and cities. After all, commodities must be collected, stored, and shipped, workers must be supervised, and life for the colonizers must be supported.

But how did a relatively small number of Europeans control such vast territories, markets, and capital flows? Core countries used both direct and indirect methods to rule the periphery. *Direct rule* created strong centralized bureaucratic administrations in the urban areas populated by Europeans. These bureaucracies generally followed European norms of property, individual freedom, civil rights, and justice. Indigenous peoples participated in urban colonial bureaucracies, but only at the lowest levels, with little hope of advancement. Direct rule was founded on principles that were clearly racist and was brutally enforced with advanced industrial weaponry. *Indirect rule* ceded power in the rural areas to local indigenous chieftains and warlords. In doing so, indirect rule created deep divisions among ethnic groups, tribes, and villages, as these strong and ruthless leaders were both armed and granted almost unlimited powers by colonial governments. In rural areas, systems of brutality and corruption became a way of life, supported and reinforced by distant urban administrators. Direct and indirect rule worked more or less side by side to enable a relatively small group to exert control over a much larger population. Terror, corruption, racism, and ethnic tensions turned out to be powerful tools that the core countries used to divide, conquer, and exploit their vast holdings in the periphery. All the while, capital kept flowing back to the core (Mamdani 1996).

Breakdown of Colonialism

Ironically, colonial revenues and rivalries ultimately fueled political tensions already simmering among Europeans themselves. Throughout the late 1800s, European leaders tried to keep a "balance of power" among themselves. But since each country wanted a military edge over its rivals, what really resulted was a huge arms buildup paid for in part by colonial revenues. Of all the countries in Western Europe, only Germany was without significant colonies in Africa and Asia. Lack of colonies meant lack of access to markets and raw materials. War appealed to some as an opportunity for colonial realignment and increased capital flows from abroad.

World War I (1914–1918) was the most expensive and deadly war in history up to that point. Flush with colonial capital, Europeans mustered armies, artillery, and firepower on a scale not seen before. Although US president Woodrow Wilson came to the 1919 peace talks in Paris promising to work for a "free, open-minded and absolutely impartial adjustment of all colonial claims," postwar colonial boundaries remained remarkably similar to those that had been established before the war. In addition, the victorious Allies of 1919 carved up the defeated Austro-Hungarian and Ottoman Empires as recklessly as they had Africa in 1884. While fragile independent Eastern European countries emerged, Britain and France gained control over much of the Middle East and began to exploit its oil wealth.

In the end, World War I settled nothing. Capital flows from the periphery to the core resumed their prewar patterns, which would continue to worsen inequality between countries, and cause poverty rates to rise in colonies around the globe. War wounds continued to fester, which would carry over into World War II. Colonial competition between Japan and China also became aggravated in Asia. A worldwide economic crisis (known as the Great Depression in the United States) crippled global economies in the 1930s and increased tensions among Europeans, and World War II began, less than twenty years after the so-called war to end all wars.

World War II was even more devastating than its predecessor in both military and civilian deaths. The economies of Europe and Asia all but collapsed because of the extent and severity of the aerial bombing. Following the destruction of World War II, the United States was able to achieve economic superiority, through such initiatives as the Marshall Plan, which was a comprehensive aid package that helped rebuild Europe and Japan. The end of World War II also saw the Union of Soviet Socialist Republics, or Soviet Union (now known as Russia), become a world power, which set the stage for the Cold War. Finally, without European armies and capital to support colonial domination, populations in the periphery saw their chance to achieve sovereignty. Through rebellion and negotiation, many colonies would eventually seek and achieve independence over the next twenty-five years.

Global Capital Flows After World War II

Rebuilding the Industrialized World

World War II ended the formal colonial systems that had so strongly influenced global capital flows for 500 years. By the end of the war, it was clear to many leaders that new institutions needed to be created to help rebuild the economies of Europe and Asia and restore stable capital flows around the world. For the first time, the United States took a leadership role in these global negotiations, and in 1944 hosted the United Nations Monetary and Financial Conference among the Allied nations in Bretton Woods, New Hampshire. These meetings resulted in the Bretton Woods agreements.

The organizers of the Bretton Woods agreements believed that liberal economics, freely flowing capital, and open markets held the keys to a more secure and peaceful world. Instead of secret alliances and trading blocs that resulted in nations fighting over raw materials and markets for finished goods, tariffs and protectionism would be minimized and all nations would have equal access to markets. There were three basic tasks to be accomplished under the agreements: stabilizing all national currencies, creating institutions and mechanisms for nations to manage their currency valuations, and financing the reconstruction of the battered European economies. Most of the resultant new rules and institutions offered advantages for the US economy. At the end of World War II, after all, the United States had by far the strongest economy. Having built up considerable industrial capacity during the war, the United States clearly wanted more trade and needed access to markets that had been artificially limited by prewar colonial systems and trading blocs. Bretton Woods helped make that possible.

In the Bretton Woods agreements, the first order of business was to stabilize currencies by means of fixed exchange rates. Fixed exchange rates facilitate trade by giving all nations the confidence that the currencies they hold today will continue to have a stable value tomorrow. Connecting the value of a currency to an independent commodity like gold could solve the problem. In fact, a gold standard had existed in Europe before World War I, but was abandoned when countries started printing money to finance that war. After World War II, gold production was not sufficient to guarantee all existing currencies, so they were instead pegged to US dollars, which were redeemable nominally in gold at $35 to one troy ounce.

But currencies naturally tend to fluctuate whenever countries experience severe budget imbalances. So the second creation of the Bretton Woods agreements was an institution called the International Monetary Fund (IMF), to advise countries and loan them money to help pay their debts and balance their budgets. Before the IMF, when countries owed money to other countries, they were tempted to devalue their currencies (usually by printing more money). This left their creditors holding nearly worthless currency. Through financial subscriptions and quotas from member countries, the IMF amassed a pool of money to be used for loans to help cover these debts and prevent devalued currencies. Though countries then became indebted to the IMF, national currencies remained stable. To aid nations in paying off their debts, the IMF would also make recommendations for cost-cutting measures that would free up money in national budgets for debt repayment. The original ten country members of the IMF were known as the Group of 10 (G-10) and still meet periodically today (now as the Group of 12).

Third, the Bretton Woods agreements created the International Bank for Reconstruction and Development (IBRD), to aid in the reindustrialization of Europe. The IBRD would eventually become part of a group of institutions known simply as the World Bank Group, or World Bank. Initially, however, the IBRD was underfunded, and greater flows of capital were needed to jump-start the economies of Europe. A plan developed by then–US secretary of state George Marshall, called the Marshall Plan, sent billions of extra dollars ($17 billion between 1948 and 1954) in grants to sixteen Western European countries. The decision to help rebuild even the economies of defeated Germany and Japan shows the degree to which US economic growth in this period depended on these rebounding markets. Without markets, economies simply cannot continue growing.

Finally, to keep the Bretton Woods negotiations an ongoing part of international financial stability, the Allied countries resolved to keep meeting to make adjustments to the Bretton Woods agreements as needed. This resolution became known as the General Agreement on Tariffs and Trade (GATT). Twenty-three countries signed the first GATT treaty in 1947, and eventually 125 countries participated in the 1986–1994 GATT rounds of negotiations. These negotiations eventually ended with the creation of the World Trade Organization (WTO) in 1995, whose mission is to eliminate any current barriers to trade.

For those who participated in them, the Bretton Woods agreements, coupled with the ambitious Marshall Plan and other development aid programs, succeeded in rebuilding war-torn economies and sustaining US levels of production.

Cold War Politics and the Periphery

While Bretton Woods represented a big step forward in international financial cooperation and coordination, some major parts of the world remained outside of these capital flows. Russia, China, and former colonies in Africa and Asia never became fully integrated into these new economic arrangements, largely because of the Cold War, which dominated international politics from the end of World War II (1945) through 1991. During that period, the Cold War had as much impact on post–World War II international capital flows as did the Bretton Woods agreements.

In 1917, at the end of World War I, Vladimir Lenin successfully led a communist revolution in czarist Russia, which eventually consolidated that empire into the Union of Soviet Socialist Republics (USSR)—a totalitarian socialist state. In 1949, Mao Zedong orchestrated a similar revolution in mainland China, creating a Chinese communist state. Both the USSR and the People's Republic of China (PRC) were communist states, and as such they committed to the overthrow of worldwide capitalism. Pure communism would be an economic system completely controlled by all citizens (see Figure 9.2).

At the end of World War II, the Bretton Woods agreements fashioned a global arena for capitalist free trade and open competition for markets that was in direct opposition to the Soviet economic system. As a result, the Soviet government moved decisively to further extend its economic and political power into larger and larger "spheres of influence." It seized the territories that its armies had liberated at the end of World War II, moving to take economic and political control of Eastern Europe, and as Winston Churchill observed, an "iron curtain" fell between Eastern and Western Europe. In 1949, when communism also spread to the PRC, which embarked on its own program of political domination and consolidation in Asia, the United States assumed a new global role as the defender of free trade and open capitalist markets worldwide. The official US policy from the 1950s through the 1980s would be to

Figure 9.2 Communism vs. Capitalism

While both the Soviet Union and the People's Republic of China claimed the label "communist," they were in fact totalitarian socialist states. Pure socialism is an economic system in which the state owns and controls all the capital used in the production of goods and services. Almost all individuals are employed directly or indirectly by the state, and government assumes the major responsibility for employment, education, healthcare, and living conditions. By contrast, pure capitalism is an economic system in which almost all capital is owned and controlled privately, and incentives for increasing social wealth are directly linked to the personal desire to increase one's individual fortune. Government primarily acts as a watchdog to prevent abuses, and employment, education, and healthcare are largely private concerns. Both systems can and do exhibit excesses. In socialism, governments can assume totalitarian powers over the individual that threaten human freedom and stifle individual innovation. In capitalism, the private drive for individual wealth and profit can override community interests and endanger the common good.

"contain" the spread of communism in general, and Soviet and Chinese power in particular. The West and East were locked in a new "cold" war.

From the 1950s through the 1970s, the United States and USSR averted direct, and potentially nuclear, confrontation. But the Cold War in fact bubbled up in a series of small "hot" wars all over the global periphery. Both the United States, through its newly formed CIA, and the Soviet Union, through its similar agency the KGB, sought to control postcolonial development in the periphery. Throughout the periphery, they pitted old colonial chieftains and warlords against one another, setting the stage for decades of civil strife, destruction, and instability. Operatives for both East and West disrupted elections, assassinated or plotted to assassinate elected officials, and financed ongoing civil wars with the "aid" of massive military firepower. In these battles, both East and West relied heavily on strong but often ruthless dictators to control postcolonial populations whose expectations for freedom and prosperity ran high. Unfortunately, these conflicts brought any real economic development in the periphery to a standstill. Both East and West tolerated crimes and corruption on the part of these dictators as long as the new nations remained in the "right" camp. While some newly sovereign nations declared their neutrality and did their best to maintain it, political forces of the East-West Cold War largely prevented that.

So while the United States and the Soviet Union never directly fired a shot at each other, they did engage each other all over the world for control of minds and hearts certainly, but also for the markets, raw materials, and cheap labor abundant in the periphery. Alongside the very real accomplishments of Bretton Woods, the Cold War created a new, increasingly unstable global arrangement. Populations in the core generally lived secure and increasingly abundant lives. Populations in the periphery lived increasingly with civil war, corruption, and underdevelopment.

Global Capital Flows After the Cold War

After the 1970s, patterns of capital flows began to shift again, through the end of the twentieth century. There were several reasons for this shift. First, Cold War tensions gradually began to ease. In the 1970s, the United States and the Soviet Union entered into a period of détente and began to trade art and culture, as well as some goods and services. The Strategic Arms Limitation Treaty (SALT), together with the Anti–Ballistic Missile (ABM) Treaty, offered hope that relations between the two countries could become less militaristic. By 1989, the Russian people demanded an end to the Soviet system, the Berlin Wall fell, and formerly Soviet countries sought more integration into the world trading system. In 1972, Richard Nixon became the first US president to visit China, which opened the door for greater global recognition for China. Gradually new Chinese leaders began to introduce freer markets in that country as well. Trade increased between the United States and both Russia and China.

Second, Japanese and European economies not only had recovered from World War II, but also were becoming major exporters to the United States. By 1971, President Nixon reasoned that since foreign banks held more dollars than US gold reserves could back, the gold standard was no longer feasible. Essentially the United States was not holding enough gold reserves to back up every US dollar. The US and world economy had grown too large to be tied to one precious metal, and it was Nixon's hope that the US and world economy could expand almost endlessly. Taking the United States off the gold standard inaugurated a system of floating exchange rates, which remains today. When exchange rates float, world currencies, including the US dollar, can fluctuate in value. Financial markets take on an increased importance, as buying, selling, and speculating on the price of currencies becomes as much a part of everyday economic activity as buying, selling, and speculating on the price of wheat. Ensuring global financial stability—the job of the International Monetary Fund—becomes critical in such a system, and after 1971 the IMF became a more powerful force in regulating world finance.

Third, the struggling nations of the periphery began to attract some systematic attention from the rest of the world. After centuries of colonial brutality, two world wars, and decades of corruption and civil strife, it was becoming clearer that development in the periphery needed to become a part of a global agenda. In the 1970s, a consensus began to form around the belief that the

World Bank and IMF, with help from the United States, could replicate in the less-developed countries what had happened between 1950 and 1970 in Europe and Japan. By the 1980s, this approach became widely known as the Washington Consensus. Essentially, advocates of the Washington Consensus argued that opening markets in the developing world to unrestricted free trade, initiating programs for fiscal responsibility, and encouraging privatization and foreign investment would be the best approach to bringing the economic periphery into the twentieth century. The MDCs of the core felt that they could do for the LDCs of the periphery what Bretton Woods had done for Europe and Japan.

But there were problems with the Washington Consensus from the very beginning. Europe and Japan had already been well-established and diversified economies prior to receiving post–World War II financial aid from the World Bank. Their work forces were highly educated and highly skilled, and their legal systems protected individual private property rights and fought systematic corruption. Little of this existed in the LDCs, where agricultural, cash-crop economies remained fragile, work forces were primarily rural and uneducated, and legal systems had been corrupted repeatedly during centuries of colonialism and Cold War manipulation.

Nevertheless, GATT negotiations reflected the main principles of the Washington Consensus and moved forward with an aggressive program of trade liberalization, which can be defined as the removal or reduction of the free exchange of goods between countries, in the LDCs. The World Bank, official development assistance, the IMF, and foreign direct investment all played important and interlocking roles in this process.

The World Bank, Conditionality, and Comparative Advantage

The World Bank reasoned that developing exports in the less-developed countries required sizable loans for large-scale infrastructure and agricultural investments. While the LDCs were eager to obtain financial capital, the money itself was offered only if certain conditions were met—a process called *conditionality.*

The most basic condition of any loan is interest. Many LDCs were encouraged by the World Bank to borrow heavily during the 1970s, and hoped that inflation, which was high during this period, would eat away at the real interest they owed. For example, if a loan is taken at a nominal interest of 5 percent, and inflation is 6 percent, the real interest owed is actually a *negative* 1 percent—the loan is paid back with money that is worth less than the money borrowed. With inflation in the 1970s outpacing interest rates, borrowing heavily seemed to be a good bet. But the LDCs lost their gamble when inflation slowed in the 1980s, and real interest rates began to climb. A side effect of growing interest rates was that the economies in many of the more-developed countries entered a recession, and so those MDCs purchased fewer products from the

LDCs, leaving the latter with less foreign currency to pay off their loans. Finally, in the 1970s the Organization of Petroleum Exporting Countries (OPEC) significantly raised the price of oil. The LDCs were forced to borrow even more money to meet their petroleum needs, and their debt kept mounting. Many private banks flush with oil profits from the Middle East loaned vast sums to the LDCs and created even greater debt burdens.

A more important aspect of conditionality was the World Bank's power to decide precisely what projects would receive funding. In doing this, the World Bank employed the principle of *comparative advantage,* which maintains that if one country has a lower relative cost in producing a certain commodity, then it is to the advantage of all trading partners that the specializing country produces that commodity. Thus LDC economies became tied to rather rigid terms of trade, where they were encouraged to specialize in agricultural products like cotton and peanuts and use the export profits (foreign exchange) to buy whatever else they needed. This made sense because agriculture tends to be labor-intensive and LDCs generally have a surplus of labor. As another condition for the loans, the World Bank required that the LDCs remove most tariffs for imports, and most subsidies for exports—that is, develop free and completely open markets.

But these particular World Bank policies put the LDCs at a global disadvantage in at least five ways. First, land that had formerly been used for domestic food production was placed into highly specialized and more mechanized commodity crop production. In this process, many poor farmers lost their livelihoods as small plots of land were consolidated into large agricultural complexes. These displaced farmers often migrated to overcrowded cities that were unable to absorb this new influx of people into the existing industrial base, infrastructure, or education and healthcare systems. Without jobs or education, these individuals became a permanent underclass plagued by poverty, illiteracy, and disease.

Second, this intense industrialized agriculture demanded specialized seed, fertilizer, pesticides, herbicides, and machinery that had to be purchased from the MDCs, adding to already ballooning debt. Third, planting the same crop over and over often degraded fragile ecosystems. In some LDCs, land began to lose fertility. Fourth, many LDCs became net importers of food with no effective means of national food distribution. Famine claimed more and more lives in the LDCs, not necessarily because there was no food, but because displaced peasants were too poor to buy relatively expensive imported food. Ironically, both food production and hunger grew globally during this time.

Fifth, the LDCs never fully realized enough profit from their agricultural exports, because although the World Bank required them to drop all tariffs and subsidies, many of the MDCs they wanted to trade with continued to heavily subsidize their own domestic agricultural commodities in order to protect MDC farmers from cheap imports. For example, the United States continued to subsidize its cotton farmers, making US cotton some of the cheapest cotton in the world. Most LDCs, no matter how efficiently they produce any commodity, cannot compete with heavily subsidized commodities from MDCs. And LDCs cannot enact their own subsidies without alienating the World Bank and IMF. Without sufficient foreign exchange from trade to pay their bills, debt in the LDCs kept growing throughout the 1980s and 1990s.

In addition to these reasons, corrupt leaders in many LDCs robbed their own governments and people of needed capital. Political expediency during colonialism and the Cold War had not fostered strong democratic regimes in most of the LDCs. On the contrary, throughout the end of the twentieth century, ruthless dictators and warlords gained power and engaged in corruption as a part of standard economic practice in too many LDCs. These dictators siphoned off and redirected capital coming into foreign bank accounts in MDCs—a process called *capital flight*. As a result, in too many LDCs there was often little to show for years and years of continued loans and mounting debt.

Finally, poverty in some LDCs led to crime and social unrest, which came to dominate local government policies. Illegal crops like poppies in Afghanistan or coca in Latin America fueled a worldwide drug trade. Some individuals in LDCs who felt their land had been taken from them unjustly, openly rebelled. Some famine-stressed countries erupted into civil war. Thus, crime and civil strife have led some governments to purchase arms and weapons for controlling the violence. At a time when education, healthcare, and jobs are desperately needed, many countries have used precious foreign exchange and even borrowed more heavily to arm themselves against rebels and criminals. All the while, the debt in the periphery has continued to mount.

Structural Adjustment and Foreign Direct Investment

By 1991 the LDCs had accumulated almost $1.4 trillion of total external debt to the World Bank, the International Monetary Fund, and other creditors, and were not experiencing sufficient economic growth to service their debt (meet interest payments), let alone retire it. In fact, debt was running at about 127 percent of total exports of goods and services. Some MDC economists began to fear that international economic crises might result if the LDCs defaulted on their debts (Hertz 2004). This is exactly what happened in Argentina in 2002, when the country defaulted on $93 billion. Foreign investment fled and the Argentine economy collapsed.

The IMF, fearful that global economic crises might become epidemic if the less-developed countries unilaterally devalued their currencies, began an aggressive series of loans to the LDCs with even stricter conditions. These new conditions imposed by the IMF are often collectively called *structural adjustment programs*. Such programs have become very controversial in recent years, because through them the IMF has directly influenced the internal budgets of sovereign nations. Specifically, structural adjustment programs have required some national governments to make large budget cuts in education and healthcare programs. Some countries have been instructed by the IMF to cut their education and social service budgets by as much as 40 percent, to enable them to balance their budgets and make greater payments on their debts. At the very least, these kinds of cuts create severe hardships for the poorest of the poor, and at worst they can exacerbate the types of social unrest many LDCs experience.

In addition, the IMF has pushed countries toward privatization, which often means countries are encouraged to sell the development rights to their own natural resources, like oil, to private corporations. Often, these private corporations are foreign multinationals located in the MDCs. Social services, like education and healthcare, are also privatized. As a result, the privatization of common resources and community services has increasingly become a byproduct of trade liberalization. Both privatization and liberalization envision a world where private corporations have unlimited access to internal domestic economies.

During the 1980s and 1990s, for example, oil production in Africa and Latin America became dominated by large multinational oil corporations like Exxon-Mobil (the United States), Royal Dutch Shell (the United Kingdom, the Netherlands), British Petroleum (the United Kingdom), and Chevron-Texaco (the United States). Relatively few LDCs (Saudi Arabia, Venezuela, Iran, Mexico) operated their own large oil corporations. In the 1990s, Shell-Nigeria, which accounted for slightly more than 50 percent of the total oil production in that country, became embroiled in accusations of environmental degradation and massive corruption. Unfortunately, LDCs had little power against these corporations. With trade liberalization policies as part of structural adjustment programs, LDCs were encouraged to grant huge concessions to multinational corporations, in the process often ceding not only profits, but environmental and social controls as well.

Structural adjustment programs have also called for the privatization of public services like healthcare, education, and even public utilities like water. Without financial support from the government, the cost of these services can rise beyond the reach of individuals with even moderate incomes, jeopardizing their well-being.

Until recently, trade liberalization was required by the World Bank and IMF as part of the conditionality for receiving needed capital through loans. LDCs could avoid these conditions by opting out of the loan process altogether. But in 1995, during the last round of GATT talks, the World Trade Organization was created. The purpose of the WTO is to negotiate all global trade disputes with the goal of moving the entire global economy toward greater trade liberalization. Since the WTO now has global jurisdiction and a mandate to enforce trade liberalization on a worldwide scale, the Washington Consensus has in effect become the international law of trade.

Foreign Aid

Foreign aid, or official development assistance, has not really solved the financial problems of the LDCs in the past. Three explanations are most often given for this. First, some argue that there has simply not been enough of it to really help. Jeffrey Sachs has continually argued (2005, 2008) that LDCs ideally need large infusions of untied capital to break the cycle of borrowing and debt, and to develop an adequate social and industrial infrastructure to compete fully in the global economy. As early as 1970, the UN General Assembly urged each economically advanced country to increase its ODA to reach a net amount of 0.7 percent of its gross national product by the middle of the decade. This same goal was repeated in the UN's Millennium Development Goals (MDGs) in 2000. But to date, the twenty-two largest MDC economies (collectively known as the Development Assistance Committee [DAC]) are averaging only 0.31 percent of gross national income (ONE 2011).

As of 2014, the United Arab Emirates maintained the world's highest ODA as a percentage of GNI (1.17 percent), followed by Sweden (1.10 percent), Norway (0.99 percent), Denmark (0.85 percent), and the United Kingdom (0.71 percent). While the United States remains the leader in overall ODA in absolute numbers (over $32 billion in 2014), as a percentage of GNI it ranks near the bottom of the DAC countries with an ODA of 0.19 percent of GNI (OECD 2015). However, given the global financial crisis of 2008 (known in the United States as the Great Recession), it is likely that these levels will remain stagnant or even drop at least in the near future, as the United States and other MDCs begin to address issues of unemployment, education, healthcare, and growing external debt at home.

Second, official development assistance is too often used as a tool of foreign or economic policy on the part of the donor nation. John Perkins (2005, 2009) has argued that ODA is often tied to projects that directly benefit the donor nation at least as much as the intended LDC. This type of aid is sometimes called "phantom aid" and is often tied to debt relief, projects, and technical assistance in which capital flows in a circular fashion. A hypothetical example of this would be an MDC supporting a project in an LDC to build a dam for generating electricity. The money (given as ODA) is used to purchase supplies, technical assistance, and expertise from the MDC. The LDC may or may not ultimately benefit from the dam depending on the level of expertise already existing in that country and the infrastructure needed to utilize the electricity that is created. But the multinational corporations located in the MDC do benefit directly through purchases of labor, materials, and technical assistance by the LDC. Even humanitarian food aid (which is not included in most ODA totals) often benefits the donor MDC more than the LDC. In 2007, one of the world's largest international relief agencies, CARE, declined $45 million in food aid from the United States because it believed that the aid would hurt the poor in LDCs more than it would help them (Dugger 2007).

Cheap food from MDCs, often subsidized by their own governments, can drive local farmers in LDCs out of business—exacerbating problems of food production in very poor countries.

Third, some feel that ODA has not really succeeded because it actually fosters a climate of corruption, dependency, and capital flight. Dambisa Moyo (2009) argues that it is not clear that much real development has resulted from the estimated $2 trillion in aid transferred from MDCs to LDCs since World War II. However, the Organization for Economic Cooperation and Development noted that ODA from the Development Assistance Committee countries totaled $135.2 billion, which was level with the all-time high of $135.1 billion in 2013. This rise was a rebound after two years of falling volumes, as a number of governments stepped up their spending on foreign aid (OECD 2015). Countries provided a total of $134.8 billion in net ODA, marking a rebound, as a number of governments stepped up their spending on foreign aid. If bilateral aid (between two countries) is examined, a slightly different picture emerges. Bilateral aid to sub-Saharan Africa was $26.2 billion, a decrease of 4 percent in real terms from 2012. Overall, aid to the African continent fell by 5.6 percent to $28.9 billion. Bilateral net ODA to all LDCs rose by 12.3 percent in real terms to around $30 billion, though this does factor in debt relief. The OECD projects that ODA to middle-income countries—such as Brazil, China, Chile, Georgia, India, Mexico, Pakistan, Sri Lanka, and Uzbekistan—will remain stable, while ODA to low-income countries, particularly those in Africa, is expected to fall (OECD 2014). While these figures offer conflicting views, there are positive trends.

Current Trends and Future Prospects

What does the future hold for the developing world? What role will states play in determining how to approach development? How has neoliberalism, an economic philosophy maintaining that government should have limited involvement in the economy, altered the way the state operates? This section addresses the role of the state in providing resources to its citizens. Equally essential to this puzzle is the changing relationship between development and environmental concerns, as developmental issues such as climate change pose severe threats to our future (see Chapter 15). How countries, like China, determine who to financially support in the development process, and why, also warrants consideration.

Neoliberalism: The Diminishing Role of the State?

The founding figures of neoliberal thought took political ideals of human dignity and individual freedom as fundamental, as the "central values of civilization." These values, they held, were threatened not only by fascism, dictatorships, and communism, but also by all forms of state intervention that substituted collective judgments for those of individuals free to choose (Harvey 2005). Neoliberals believe that markets should have limited direction by the governments of states. The restructuring of the global economic institutional order, via the Bretton Woods agreements, was designed to prevent a return to the catastrophic conditions that had contributed to causing the Great Depression in the 1930s. Another related issue is privatization of state services (such as welfare), which means that private companies are responsible for providing these services. Should governments continue to provide social services, or is the influence of corporations better for individuals that need to access these services? Limiting the role of government has other consequences as well, such as environmental degradation and destruction. As we move forward, the potential diminishing role of the state, and the increasing influence of multinational corporations (MNCs), are things to be watched. Potential issues include the privatization of natural resources, which poses serious consequences for developing countries. Will MNCs behave in a responsible manner and take into account environmental concerns? Countries, especially developing ones, may not receive the economic benefits that natural resources can provide if the pursuit of economic growth does not take into account issues of environmental sustainability.

Development and the Environment

As mentioned, neoliberalism can have dangerous consequences for the natural world. Natural resources are finite, yet they are continually exploited, which further demonstrates the need to protect natural resources, especially as it relates to the needs of developing LDCs. Environmental concerns, particularly around climate change, and development are key issues that are currently being taken up by international governmental organizations (IGOs), such as the United Nations.

One of these key issues is sustainable development (discussed in greater detail in Chapter 14), which first made its way into policy discussions in the 1980s. While there is a great deal of contention as to what it actually is, most proponents of sustainability take it to mean the existence of the ecological conditions necessary to support human life at a specified level of well-being through future generations (Lele 2013). Two examples of trying to reach this goal include focus on sustainable development on the part of the United Nations Environment Programme (UNEP), and new climate change initiatives being pursued by the United Nations.

The institutionalization of sustainable development has continued to progress. UNEP has articulated fifteen Sustainable Development Goals (SDGs), which were finalized in September 2015. This list of goals is one example of the growing importance of incorporating environmental concerns into questions of economic development. Another example of this relationship is the Climate Change Adaptation and Development (CC Dare) initiative, which is administered by both UNEP and the United Nations Development Programme (UNDP). The program is intended to help countries address climate change issues and develop national legislation that assists in combating these issues. Individual countries are the primary participants in this program. Presently, there are eleven countries involved: Benin, Ethiopia, Ghana, Malawi, Mozambique, Rwanda, Senegal, Seychelles, Tanzania, Togo, and Uganda. Examples of initiatives adopted in these countries include rainwater harvesting (Seychelles), protecting forest resources (Tanzania), and improving land quality for agriculture (Rwanda). The protection of natural resources and addressing of climate change are important issues for developing countries. Programs such as the CC Dare initiative are promising changes.

Politics and Development

Increasingly, efforts such as the SDGs and the CC Dare initiative signal that key policymakers are beginning to think more broadly about economic development. Are developing countries taking the lead on these issues? One example is that of the BRIC countries—Brazil, Russia, India, and China (South Africa has recently also been added to this group, in the BRICS configuration). These countries offer an alternative perspective on development issues compared to the perspectives of the Group of Eight (G8) highly industrialized nations (Canada, France, Germany, Italy, Japan, Russia, the United Kingdom, and the United States), countries that have traditionally pushed neoliberal economic policies.

In a recent report commissioned by the US-based Citigroup bank, South Africa was ranked as the world's richest country in terms of its mineral reserves, worth an estimated US$2.5 trillion. South Africa is investing the equivalent of $36 billion into expanding and improving its railways, ports, and fuel pipelines, as a catalyst to help unlock the world's greatest mineral wealth.

The inclusion of South Africa among the BRIC countries is important not only for the recognition of African countries on a global scale, but also because the BRIC countries, notably China, have begun investing in African countries and establishing trade partnerships that could remake the economic and political landscape in Africa. Also of importance is China's attempt to create an alternative to the World Bank, which is known as the Asian Infrastructure Investment Bank (AIIB). The World Bank is composed of five international organizations: the International Bank for Reconstruction and Development, the International Development Association, the International Finance Corporation, the Multilateral Investment Guarantee Agency, and the International Center for the Settlement of Investment Disputes. The imbalance in voting shares between countries like China and the United States (in the IBRD for example, China has 4.82 percent of the vote, while the United States has 16.10 percent) makes the creation of an alternative like the AIIB significant, as it indicates China's desire to become more involved in the global political economy. China has also used its considerable foreign reserves to invest heavily in Africa. In 2012, China doubled its 2009 financial commitment to $20 billion in financing to African countries. Most of China's economic involvement on the African continent is based on infrastructure projects (building roads, dams, and the like) in return for the extraction of natural resources (Sun 2015). The extent of China's involvement in economic development on the continent of Africa, and elsewhere, is something to monitor, as it may have significant effects on global economic development.

Progress

Despite the problems posed by climate change, neoliberal-inspired economic practices, and general global economic institutional inequality, there are examples of progress. Addressing climate change through initiatives such as CC Dare puts it on the global agenda, and integrating environmental concerns in development is essential to achieving true sustainability. Further developments include increasing literacy rates and rising levels of democratization and openness throughout much of the world. The Arab Spring signaled the importance of tools such as the Internet and social media for individuals pressing for democratic change within developing countries. Changes like these signal the importance of focusing on all aspects of development, not just those related to economic development. Development involves a variety of issues and concerns. From addressing the effects of climate change to increasing literacy rates, the ability to close the inequality gap between the developed world and the developing world is possible. These are examples of the growth of targeted programs emphasizing change from the bottom up. Focusing on development from the bottom up will help those most in need, because it entails looking at development from a broader perspective than that of just development of a state's economy. Abhijit Banerjee and Esther Duflo (2011) argue that targeted programs that are in touch with everyday needs and sensibilities of populations on the ground, and that are rigorously evaluated before being replicated in other populations, hold the most promise for making significant inroads into poverty in the future.

Discussion Questions

1. What are the lasting effects of colonialism on the flow of capital in today's world?
2. How did the politics of the Cold War impact less-developed countries?
3. Are current World Bank and IMF policies helping or hurting less-developed countries?
4. Do more-developed countries have a responsibility to assist less-developed countries? Why or why not?
5. What economic role do you think that China and India will play in the developing world in the coming century?

iomics: A Radical Rethinking of
licAffairs.
) "China's Direct Investment in
kings Institution.
orest Countries Are Failing and
Jniversity Press.
'unds for Food Aid." *New York*

Vhy the West's Efforts to Aid the
New York: Penguin.
sm. Oxford: Oxford University

Why We Need a Green Revolu-
Macmillan.
d Intentions: How a New Eco-
'ork: Dutton.
evelopment Is Succeeding and
York: Basic.
Development." *Current History* (November).

Moyo, Dambisa (2009) *Dead Aid: Why Aid Is Not Working and How There Is a Better Way for Africa.* New York: Farrar, Straus, and Giroux.

Organization for Economic Cooperation and Development (2014) "Aid in Developing Countries Rebounds in 2013 to Reach an All-Time High." www.oecd.org.

Sachs, Jeffrey (2008) *Common Wealth: Economics for a Crowded Planet.* New York: Penguin.

United Nations Conference on Trade and Development (2015) *World Investment Report 2015.* http://unctad.org.

10

Dilemmas of Free Trade

Bruce E. Moon

INTERNATIONAL TRADE IS OFTEN TREATED PURELY AS AN ECONOMIC matter that can and should be divorced from politics. This is a mistake, because trade not only shapes our economy but also determines the kind of world in which we live. The far-reaching consequences of trade pose fundamental choices for all of us. Citizens must understand those consequences before judging the inherently controversial issues that arise over trade policy. More than that, we cannot even make sound consumer decisions without weighing carefully the consequences of our own behavior.

The Case for Trade

The individual motives that generate international trade are familiar. Consumers seek to buy foreign products that are better or cheaper than domestic ones in order to improve their material standard of living. Producers sell their products abroad to increase their profit and wealth.

Most policymakers believe that governments should also welcome trade, because it provides benefits for the nation and the global economy as well as for the individual. Exports produce jobs for workers, profits for corporations, and revenues that can be used to purchase imports. Imports increase the welfare (well-being) of citizens, because they can acquire more for their money as well as obtain products that are not available from domestic sources. The stronger economy that follows can fuel increasing power and prestige for the state in international affairs. Further, the resultant interdependence and shared prosperity among countries may strengthen global cooperation and maintain international peace.

Considerable historical evidence supports the view that trade *can* improve productivity, consumption, and therefore material standard of living (Moon 1998). Trade successes have generated spurts of national growth, most notably in East Asia. The global economy has grown most rapidly during periods of trade expansion, especially in the years after World War II, and has slowed when trade levels have fallen, especially during the Great Depression of the 1930s. Periods of international peace have also coincided with trade-induced growth, while war has followed declines in trade and prosperity. Globally, trade has grown from 12 percent of gross domestic product (GDP, defined as the total of goods and services produced in a given year) in 1960 to 30 percent today, and average incomes are more than two and a half times larger.

Yet trade is no panacea, as witnessed by patterns of trade and economic growth since the end of World War II. Global growth exceeded 5 percent per year for the first thirty-five years of that period, when trade averaged under 15 percent of GDP. However, during the globalization era since 1980, marked by trade levels of about 25 percent of GDP, growth fell to under 3 percent. Furthermore, the groups of countries that have lagged behind over this period began as the most active traders in the world. Sub-Saharan Africa's trade levels were more than twice the global average in 1960, but for half a century per capita income in Africa has grown barely half a percentage point per year. At this pace, Africa will not reach the income level that rich countries had attained by 1960 for nearly 400 years. Meanwhile, the rich countries, which historically relied much less on trade, have grown almost four times as fast (World Bank 2015d). This mixed record suggests that trade can have either positive or negative consequences.

Still, the private benefits of trade have led individual consumers and producers to embrace it with zeal for the past half century. As a result, trade has assumed a much greater role in almost all nations, with exports now constituting over a third of the economy in most countries and over half in many (World Bank 2015d). Even in the United States, which is less reliant on trade than virtually any other economy in the world because of its size and diversity, the export sector now constitutes more than 10 percent of GDP.

Since World War II, most governments have encouraged and promoted this growth in trade levels, though they have also restrained and regulated trade in a variety of ways. All but a handful of nations now rely so heavily on jobs in the export sector and on foreign products to meet domestic needs that discontinuing trade is no longer an option. To attempt it would require a vast restructuring that would entail huge economic losses and massive social change. Furthermore, according to the "liberal" trade theory accepted by most economists, governments have no compelling reason to interfere with the private markets that achieve such benefits. The reader is cautioned that the term *liberalism,* as used throughout this chapter, refers to liberal economic theory that opposes government interference with the market and is not to be confused with the ambiguous way the term *liberal* is applied in US politics, where it often means the opposite.

From its roots in the work of Scottish political economist Adam Smith (1723–1790) and English economist David Ricardo (1772–1823), this liberal perspective has emphasized that international trade can benefit all nations simultaneously, without requiring governmental involvement (Smith 1910). According to Ricardo's theory of *comparative advantage* (1981), no nation need lose in order for another to win, because trade allows total global production to rise. The key to creating these gains from trade is the efficient allocation of resources, whereby each nation specializes in the production of goods in which it has a comparative advantage. For example, a nation with especially fertile farmland and a favorable climate can produce food much more cheaply than a country that lacks this comparative advantage. If it were to trade its excess food production to a nation with efficient manufacturing facilities for clothing production, both nations would be better off, because trade allows each to apply its resources to their most efficient use. Liberals contend that no action by governments is required to bring about this trade, since profit-motivated investors will see to it that producers specialize in the goods in which they have a comparative advantage, and consumers will naturally purchase the best or cheapest products. Thus, liberal theory concludes that international trade conducted by private actors free of government control will maximize global welfare.

Challenges to the Liberal Faith in Trade

Though trade levels have grown massively in the two centuries since Adam Smith, no government has followed the advice of liberal economic theorists to refrain from interfering with trade altogether. That is partly because governments also have been influenced by a dissenting body of thought known as *mercantilism,* which originated with the trade policy of European nations, especially England, from the sixteenth century to the middle of the nineteenth.

While mercantilists do not oppose trade, they do hold that governments must regulate it in order for trade to advance various aspects of the national interest. The aspirations of mercantilists go beyond the immediate consumption gains emphasized by liberals, to include long-term growth, national self-sufficiency, the vitality of key industries, and a powerful state in foreign policy.

They are especially wary of trade patterns that offer immediate benefits but constrain long-term growth. For example, the slow-growing African economies specialize in the export of mining and tropical agriculture products that do not require either skilled labor or high technology. Because neither the products themselves nor their production techniques have changed much in decades, such specializations are developmental dead-ends. Furthermore, many poor countries are dangerously reliant on just a few such products. Two-thirds of African countries generate more than half of their export revenues from just three or fewer products. In six African countries, one product accounts for more than 85 percent of exports.

Contrast the resultant stagnation with the spectacular burst of new products and processes that have emerged from the digital revolution in computer and information technology. Developed nations that export such products derive high profits, well-paying jobs, and dynamic economic and social change. Clearly, the value of trade depends heavily on its composition.

Because most states accept the mercantilist conviction that trade can have negative as well as positive consequences, they try to manage it in a fashion that will minimize its most severe costs yet also capture the benefits claimed for it by liberal theory. It is a fine line to walk.

Mercantilists also observe that the rosy evaluation of trade advanced by Smith and Ricardo was predicated on their expectation that any given nation's imports would more or less balance its exports. However, when a nation's imports are greater than its exports—meaning that it buys more from other nations than it sells to them—mercantilists warn that this trade deficit carries with it potential dangers that may not be readily apparent. On its face, a trade deficit appears as the proverbial free lunch: if a nation's imports are greater than its exports, it follows that national consumption must exceed its production. One might ask how anyone could object to an arrangement that allows a nation to consume more than it produces. The answer lies in recognizing that such a situation has negative consequences in the present, and dangerously adverse repercussions in the future.

For example, the United States has run a substantial trade deficit for four decades, with imports surpassing exports by nearly $10 trillion over that period, including more than $500 billion per year since the turn of the century (US Bureau of Economic Analysis 2015). That trade deficit allowed US citizens to enjoy a standard of living more than $1,500 per person higher than would otherwise be possible. But mercantilists observe that these excess imports permit foreigners to obtain employment and profits from production that might otherwise benefit US citizens. For example, in the decades after the US trade deficit began to bloom in the 1970s, the massive sales of Japanese cars in the United States transferred millions of jobs out of the US economy, accounting for high levels of unemployment in Detroit and low levels of unemployment in Tokyo. Just since the normalization of trade relations with China in 2000, US manufacturing jobs have declined by a third, as the trade deficit in manufactured goods alone has averaged about $450 billion per year (Nager and Atkinson 2015; Pierce and Schott 2012). Corporate profits and government tax revenues also accrue abroad rather than at home.

However, the longer-term impact of trade deficits produces even greater anxiety. Simply put, trade deficits generate a form of indebtedness. Just as individuals cannot continue to spend more than they earn without eventually suffering detrimental consequences, the liabilities created by trade deficits threaten a nation's future. Unfortunately, the consequences of trade imbalances cannot be evaluated easily, because they trigger complex and unpredictable flows of money, including some that occur years after the trade deficit itself.

To understand this point, consider that the trade deficit of the United States means that more money flows out of the US economy in the form of dollars to pay for imports than flows back into the US economy through payments for US goods purchased by foreigners. The consequences of the trade deficit depend in large part on what happens to those excess dollars, which would appear to be piling up abroad.

In fact, some of these dollars are, literally, piling up abroad. About $500 billion of US currency is currently held outside the United States (Judson 2012). However, this cash held abroad is a mere drop in the bucket compared to the $10 trillion that has flowed out of the United States to pay for the excess of imports over exports since 1985. That year—the last time that Americans owned more assets abroad than foreigners owned of US assets—marked the transformation of the United States from a net creditor nation to a debtor nation. Most of that $10 trillion has already found its way back into the US economy as loans to Americans and purchases of US financial assets. For example, the US Treasury has borrowed over $2 trillion from foreign citizens and more than $4.1 trillion from foreign governments by selling them US Treasury bonds and other securities. Not only must this debt be repaid someday, but foreigners now also receive over $100 billion in interest payments annually from the US federal government. US businesses owe foreigners another $3.2 trillion as the result of the sale of corporate bonds. About $6.4 trillion in stocks—about 15 percent of outstanding US equities—are owned by foreigners (US Treasury 2015). Such capital flows can offset a trade deficit temporarily and render it harmless in the short run, but they create future liabilities that only postpone the inevitable need to balance production and consumption. The United States is being sold to foreigners piece by piece to finance a trade deficit that continues to grow.

Economists disagree about whether these developments ought to raise alarm. After all, the willingness of foreigners to invest in the United States and to lend money to Americans surely is an indication of confidence in the strength of the US economy. More generally, as revealed in Chapter 9, capital flows can be beneficial to the economy and its future. Indeed, foreign capital is an essential ingredient to development in many third world countries. Whether capital inflows produce effects that are, on balance, positive or negative, depends heavily on the source of the capital, the terms on which it is acquired, the uses to which it is put, and the unpredictable future behavior of foreign lenders and investors.

For example, should foreigners decide to use their $500 billion holdings in US currency—about half of all dollars in circulation—to purchase US goods, the result could be catastrophic: the increased demand for US products would bid up prices and unleash massive inflation. Alternatively, should they try to exchange those dollars for other currencies, the increased volume of dollars available in currency markets would constitute excess supply that could trigger a violent collapse of the external value of the dollar. If owners of US Treasury certificates—including Japan ($1.2 trillion) and China ($1.3 trillion)—sell their dollar-denominated holdings and invest in euro- or yen-denominated assets, US interest rates would rise and the dollar would plummet. In July 2007, Chinese officials threatened to use their dollar-denominated holdings to achieve political leverage in negotiations with the United States over other matters. In August 2011, an editorial in *People's Daily,* the official newspaper of the Central Committee of the Chinese Communist Party, called for halting purchases of US Treasury bills to force the United States to abandon plans to sell arms to Taiwan.

Even if none of these scenarios occur suddenly—as they did in Mexico, Argentina, Russia, Thailand, Malaysia, Indonesia, Korea, and Greece in recent years—over time the excess supply of dollars is bound to erode the value of the dollar more gradually. No one can predict the timing or severity of this decline, but it has been long under way already: the dollar was once equivalent to 360 Japanese yen, but traded at about 120 yen late in 2015. The dollar declined from 1.18 euros in 2000 to 0.88 euros by 2015. As the purchasing power of the dollar declines, the prices paid by Americans for foreign products, services, and investment assets will continue to increase, and the net worth of Americans—that is, US national wealth—will decline.

Thus a trade deficit provides immediate benefits but also risks reducing the standard of living for future generations. Americans who have grown accustomed to consuming far more than they produce will be forced to consume far less. Because these consequences are uncertain, nations vary somewhat in their tolerance for trade deficits, but most try to minimize or avoid them altogether, as counseled by mercantilists.

Options in Trade Policy

To achieve their desired trade balance, nations often combine two mercantilist approaches. They may emphasize the expansion of exports through a strategy known as *industrial policy*. More commonly, they emphasize minimizing imports, a stance known generally as *protectionism* (Fallows 1993).

Protectionist policies include many forms of import restriction designed to limit the purchase of goods from abroad. All allow domestic import-competing industries to capture a larger share of the market and, in the process, to earn higher profits and to employ more workers at higher wages. The most traditional barriers are taxes on imports called *tariffs*, or import duties, but they are no longer the main form of protectionism in most countries.

In fact, declining from their peak in the 1930s, tariff levels throughout the world are now generally very low. In the United States, the average tariff rate reached a modern high of 59 percent in 1932 under what has been called "a remarkably irresponsible tariff law," the Smoot-Hawley Act, which has been widely credited with triggering a spiral of restrictions by other nations that helped plunge the global economy into the Great Depression of the 1930s. The average tariff rate in the United States was reduced to 25 percent after World War II and declined to about 2 percent after the Uruguay Round of trade negotiations concluded in 1994. Most other countries have followed suit—and some have reduced rates even more—so that average tariff rates above 10 percent are now quite rare.

However, in place of tariffs, governments have responded to the pleas of industries threatened by foreign competition with a variety of nontariff barriers, especially voluntary export restraints. In the most famous case of voluntary export restraints, Japanese automakers "voluntarily" agreed to limit exports to the United States in 1981 (had Japan refused, a quota that would have been more damaging to Japanese automakers would have been imposed).

A favorable trade balance also can be sought through an industrial policy that promotes exports, especially in products that offer the strongest growth prospects. The simplest technique is a *direct export subsidy*, in which the government pays a domestic firm for each good exported, so that it can compete with foreign firms that otherwise would have a cost advantage. A variety of other policies can be used to encourage promising industries—like those that spurred the Internet and information technology—trusting that export gains will eventually follow. Such policies have at least three motivations. First, by increasing production in the chosen industry, they reduce the unemployment rate. Second, by enabling firms to gain a greater share of foreign markets, they give them greater leverage to increase prices (and profits) in the future. Third, increasing exports will improve the balance of trade and avoid the problems of trade deficits.

Liberals are by no means indifferent to the dangers of trade deficits, but they argue that most mercantilist cures are worse than the disease. When mercantilist policies affect prices, they automatically create winners and losers and in the process engender political controversies. For example, to raise the revenue to pay for a subsidy, the domestic consumer has to pay higher taxes. As noted earlier, protectionism also harms the consumer by raising prices even while it benefits domestic firms that compete against imports.

The Multiple Consequences of Trade

As nations choose among policy options, they must acknowledge liberal theory's contention that free trade allows the market to efficiently allocate resources and thus to maximize global and national consumption. Nonetheless, governments almost universally restrict trade, at least to some degree. That is because governments seek many other outcomes from trade as well—full employment, long-term growth, economic stability, social harmony, power, security, and friendly foreign relations—yet discover that these desirable outcomes are frequently incompatible with one another. Because free trade may achieve some goals but undermine others, governments that fail to heed the advice of liberal theory need not be judged ignorant or corrupt. Instead, they recognize a governmental responsibility to cope with all of trade's consequences, not only those addressed by liberal trade theory. For example, while trade affects the prices of individual products, global markets also influence which individuals and nations accumulate wealth and political power. Trade determines who will be employed and at what wage. It determines what natural resources will be used and at what environmental cost. It shapes opportunities and constraints in foreign policy.

Because trade affects such a broad range of social outcomes, conflict among alternative goals and values is inevitable. As a result, both individuals and governments must face dilemmas that involve the multiple consequences of trade, the multiple goals of national policy, and the multiple values that compete for dominance in shaping behavior (Moon 2000).

The Distributional Effects of Trade: Who Wins, Who Loses?

Many of these dilemmas stem from the sizable effect that international trade has on the distribution of income and wealth among individuals, groups, and nations. Simply put, some gain material benefits from trade while others lose. Thus, to choose one trade policy and reject others is simultaneously a choice of one income distribution over another. As a result, trade is inevitably politicized: each group pressures its government to adopt a trade policy from which it expects to benefit.

The most visible distributional effects occur because trade policy often protects or promotes one industry or sector of the economy at the expense of others. For example, in response to pleas from the US steel industry,

President George W. Bush imposed a temporary 30 percent tariff on various types of imported steel in 2002. Because the import tax effectively added 30 percent to the price of steel imports, the US steel industry could benefit from this protection against foreign competition by increasing its share of the market, by raising its own prices, or by some combination of the two. A larger market share or higher prices, or both, would certainly increase the profits of US steel firms, which would benefit steel executives and stockholders, and perhaps permit higher levels of employment and wage rates, which would benefit steelworkers. Steel producers argued that the respite from foreign competition brought idled mills back online and kept teetering plants from shutting down, resulting in the resurrection of 16,000 steel jobs.

Distributional effects are often regional as well as sectoral. The entire economy of steel-producing areas would be boosted by the tariff, because steel companies would purchase more goods from their suppliers, executives and workers would purchase more products, and the multiplier effect would spread the gains in jobs and profits throughout the regional economies where the steel industry is concentrated—Pennsylvania, Ohio, and West Virginia. In fact, critics contended (and White House officials only halfheartedly denied) that the main purpose of the tariff was to boost the president's reelection prospects in those key electoral states.

However, these gains represent only one side of the distributional effect, because there are losers as well as winners. For example, by making foreign-produced steel more expensive, the tariff also harmed domestic automakers, who had to pay higher prices for the steel they used. Indeed, the representatives of auto-producing states like Michigan and Tennessee denounced the tariff. The president's own economic advisers, led by Treasury secretary Paul O'Neill, also opposed the tariff, bolstered by liberal theory's contention that the total losses would outweigh the total benefits. A report by the International Trade Commission estimated the cost to industries that consume steel at more than $680 million per year (USITC 2003). This episode illustrates that most barriers to trade harm consumers because of higher prices, a point always emphasized by proponents of free trade.

Trade policy also benefits some classes at the expense of others, a point more often emphasized by those who favor greater governmental control. For example, the elimination of trade barriers between the United States and Mexico under the terms of the North American Free Trade Agreement (NAFTA) forces some US manufacturing workers into direct competition with Mexican workers, who earn a markedly lower wage. Since NAFTA guarantees that imports can enter the United States without tariffs, some US businesses move to Mexico, where production costs are lower, and US workers lose their jobs in the process. Facing the threat of such production shifts, many more US workers will accept a decline in wages, benefits, or working conditions. The losses from such wage competition will be greatest for unskilled workers in high-wage countries employed in industries that can move either their products or their production facilities most easily across national boundaries. But these losses also affect skilled workers in industries like steel and autos. Others, particularly more affluent professionals who face less direct competition from abroad (such as doctors, lawyers, and university professors), stand to gain from trade because it lowers prices on the goods they consume. Of course, the greatest beneficiaries are the owners of businesses that profit from both lower wage rates and expanded markets.

Proponents of free trade tend to de-emphasize these distributional effects and instead focus on the impact of trade on the economy as a whole. That is partly because liberal theory contends that free trade does not decrease employment but only shifts it from an inefficient sector to one in which a nation has a comparative advantage. For example, US workers losing their jobs to Mexican imports should eventually find employment in industries that export to Mexico. Proponents of free trade insist that it is far better to tolerate these "transition costs"—the short-term dislocations and distributional effects—than to protect an inefficient industry. Workers are not so sure, especially because short-term effects seem to last a lot longer to those who actually live through them, and because future prospects rarely compensate for present losses when security, stability, and peace of mind are factored in.

Because these distributional consequences have such obvious political implications, the state is also much more attentive to them than are economic theorists. That is one reason why all governments control trade to one degree or another. Of course, this does not mean that they do so wisely or fairly, in part because their decisions are shaped by patterns of representation among the constituencies whose material interests are affected by trade policy. In general, workers tend to be underrepresented, which is why trade policies so often encourage trade built on low wages that enrich business owners but constrain the opportunities for workers. Moreover, as the discussion of trade deficits has indicated, the economic activities shaped by trade policies tend to affect current generations very differently from future ones—and the latter are seldom represented at all.

The Values Dilemma

These distributional effects pose challenging trade-offs among competing values. For example, the effects of NAFTA were predicted to include somewhat lower prices for US consumers but also job loss or wage reduction for some unskilled US workers. The positions taken on this issue by most individuals, however, did not hinge on their own material interests; few could confidently foresee any personal impact of NAFTA, since the gains were estimated at well under 1 percent of GDP, and job losses were not expected to exceed a few hundred thousand in a labor force of more than 100 million. However, the choice among competing *values* was plain: NAFTA meant gains in wealth but also greater inequality and insecurity for workers. Some citizens acceded to the judgment of liberal theory that the country as a whole would be better off with freer trade, while others identified with the plight of workers, who were more skeptical of liberal theory simply because for them the stakes were so much higher. After all, it is easy for a theorist to postulate that job losses in an import-competing industry would be matched by job gains in an exporting firm, but it is far harder for workers who have devoted their lives to one career to pack up and move to a strange town, hopeful that they *might* find a job that requires skills they may not possess in an unfamiliar industry. In the final analysis, NAFTA became a referendum on what kind of society people wished to live in. The decision was quintessentially American: one of greater wealth but also greater inequality and insecurity. Other nations, which assess the trade-off between values differently, might have chosen an alternative policy toward trade and domestic inequality.

Of course, distributional effects gave rise to other value choices as well. Since the gains from NAFTA were expected to be greater for Mexico than for the United States, the conscientious citizen would also weigh whether it is better to help Mexican workers because they are poorer or to protect US workers because they are US citizens. As Chapter 11 implies, such issues of inequality in poor societies can translate directly into questions of life or death. As a result, the importance of trade policy, which has such a powerful impact on the distribution of gains and losses, is much higher in poor, dependent nations where trade constitutes half of the economy than in the United States, where it is closer to 10 percent.

Perhaps the most challenging value trade-offs concern the trade policies that shift gains and losses from one time period to another. Such intergenerational effects arise from a variety of trade issues. For example, as discussed earlier, the US trade deficit, like any form of debt, represents an immediate increase in consumption but a postponement of its costs. The Japanese industrial policy of export promotion fosters a trade surplus, which produces the opposite effect in Japan. The subsidies the Japanese government pays to Japanese exporters require Japanese citizens to pay both higher prices and higher taxes. However, the sacrifices of Japan's current generation may benefit future ones if this subsidy eventually transforms an infant industry into a powerful enterprise that can repay the subsidies through cheaper prices or greater employment. Similarly, Chinese currency policy has helped to expand exports and build future industrial capacity, while increasing prices for current Chinese consumers. The spectacular growth of the Chinese economy would not have been possible without accepting those short-term sacrifices.

The values dilemma encompasses much more than just an alternative angle on distributional effects, however (Polanyi 1944). The debate over competitiveness, which began with the efforts by US businesses to lower their production costs in order to compete with foreign firms, illustrates how trade considerations may imply a compromise of other societal values. Companies could lower their costs if the abolition of seniority systems or age and gender discrimination laws allowed them to terminate employees at will. But that would leave workers vulnerable to the whim of a boss. Labor costs would be reduced if the minimum wage and workplace safety regulations were cut, if collective bargaining and labor unions were outlawed, and if pensions, healthcare, paid vacations and holidays, sick leave, and worker compensation for accidents were eliminated. But such actions entail a compromise with fundamental values about the kind of society in which people want to live. Government regulations that protect the environment, promote equality and social harmony, and achieve justice and security may add to production costs, but surely achieving economic interests is not worth abandoning all other values. Choosing between them is always difficult for a society, because reasonable people can differ in the priority they ascribe to alternative values. Still, agreements on such matters can usually be forged within societies, in part because values tend to be broadly, if not universally, shared.

Unfortunately, trade forces firms burdened by these value choices to compete with firms operating in countries that may not share them. This situation creates a dilemma for consumers, forcing them to balance economic interests against other values. For example, continuing to trade with nations that permit shabby treatment of workers—or even outright human rights abuses—poses a painful moral choice, not least because goods from such countries are often cheaper. During a 2011 debate over a trade agreement, Richard Trumka, president of the American Federation of Labor and Congress of Industrial Organizations (AFL-CIO), asked: "Would we approve an agreement with Colombia, where 51 trade unionists were assassinated last year?"

As Chapter 5 documents, foreign governments have often declared their opposition to human rights abuses but have seldom supported their rhetoric with actions that effectively curtailed abusive practices. In fact, maintaining normative standards has fallen to consumers, who must unwittingly answer key questions daily: Should we purchase cheap foreign goods like clothing and textiles even though they may have been made with child labor—or even slave labor? Of course, we seldom know the conditions under which these products were produced—or even where they were produced—so we ask government to adopt policies to support principles we cannot personally defend with our own consumer behavior.

Where values are concerned, we cannot of course expect everyone to agree with the choices we might make. Child labor remains a key source of comparative advantage for many countries in several industries prominent in international trade. We cannot expect them to give up easily a practice that is a major component of their domestic economy and that is more offensive to us than to them. Unfortunately, if trade competitors do not share our values, it may prove difficult to maintain these values ourselves—unless we restrict trade, accept trade deficits, or design state policies to alleviate the most dire consequences. After all, it is hard to see how US textile producers can compete with the sweatshops of Asia without creating sweatshops in New York. That point inevitably animates a complex debate over whether eliminating sweatshops would really benefit the poor, a dilemma of international trade that cannot be avoided merely by refusing to think about it.

Foreign Policy Considerations: Power and Peace

Some of the most challenging value choices concern the effect of trade on the foreign policy goals pursued by states, especially power, peace, and national autonomy. Policymakers have long been aware that trade has two deep, if contradictory, effects on national security. On the one hand, trade contributes to national prosperity, which increases national power and enhances security. On the other hand, it has the same effect on a nation's trade partner, which could become a political or even military rival. The resulting ambivalent attitude is torn between the vision of states cooperating for economic gain and the recognition that they also use trade to compete for political power. The rise of China as a military and political competitor to the United States is a direct consequence of US policy to encourage trade with China.

While a market perspective sees neighboring nations as potential customers, the state must also see them as potential enemies. As a result, the state not only must consider the absolute gains it receives from trade, but also must weigh those gains in relative terms, perhaps even avoiding trade that would be more advantageous to its potential enemies than to itself. For this reason, states are attentive to the distribution of the gains from trade and selective about their trade partners, frequently encouraging trade with some nations and banning it with others.

While understandable, such policies sometimes lead to open conflict. In fact, US president Franklin Roosevelt's secretary of state, Cordell Hull, contended that bitter trade rivalries were the chief cause of World War I and a substantial contributor to the outbreak of World War II. Both were precipitated by discriminatory trade policies in which different quotas or duties were imposed on the products of different nations. Hull, who believed that free multilateral trade would build bridges rather than create chasms between peoples and nations, thus championed the nondiscrimination principle and urged the creation of international institutions that would govern trade in accordance with it. Moreover, the Great Depression of the 1930s made it plain that international institutions are required to establish the rules of trade and create the international law that embodies them.

In response, the United States sponsored the Bretton Woods trade and monetary regime, centered on the General Agreement on Tariffs and Trade (GATT), the World Bank, and the International Monetary Fund (IMF). Since 1946, GATT, which evolved into the World Trade Organization (WTO) in 1995, has convened eight major negotiating sessions (referred to as "rounds") in which nations exchange reductions in trade barriers. This bargaining is necessary to overcome the inclination of most nations to retain their own trade barriers while hoping other countries will lower theirs. The World Bank supports the effort by lending money to nations that might otherwise seek trade-limiting solutions to their financial problems. The IMF facilitates trade by providing a stable monetary system that permits the easy exchange of national currencies and the adjustment of trade imbalances. The result has been a dramatic increase in global trade.

However, the pace of global trade negotiations has slowed dramatically in recent decades. The issues most eagerly pursued by rich countries—those that offer them the greatest benefits without requiring much sacrifice—have already been resolved. The remaining ones pose stark trade-offs that activate formidable political resistance, many surrounding the sensitive question of agriculture, which is a fragile and highly protected sector in most rich countries. Poor countries, which rely very heavily on agriculture, have not been able to achieve progress in reducing either the import barriers or the subsidies enacted by rich countries that prevent their agricultural products from entering the most lucrative markets.

Since the advent of the WTO, only one round of trade negotiations has convened at all, and since it commenced in Doha, Qatar, in 2001, it has remained hopelessly deadlocked. As of late 2015 no progress was in sight. The Doha Round was supposed to have advanced a development agenda to benefit poor countries, especially in agriculture, but that priority has withered to the point that the World Bank has estimated that the plan on the table would net benefits of less than a penny a day to citizens of poor countries and actually harm most of Africa. With further progress in global trade agreements unlikely, the United States has instead used its economic and political might to negotiate arrangements with twenty individual countries as of 2015 as well as the Trans-Pacific Partnership (discussed later).

In between negotiating rounds, the GATT/WTO dispute resolution mechanism has provided a forum for diverting the inevitable skirmishes over trade into the legal arena rather than the military realm. Immediately after the controversial steel tariff introduced by President Bush in March 2002, the European Union (EU) lodged a complaint that was upheld by the WTO. This episode demonstrated that if mercantilist policies are controversial in the nations that enact them, they are met with even greater hostility by the nations with which they trade.

Despite the presence of international institutions, trade disputes are generally resolved as much by power in service to economic interests as by institutions that champion principles. The United States has been locked in a dispute with Brazil (and more than a dozen other countries plus the EU), which since 2002 has won three WTO judgments that US subsidies of its cotton production violate free trade obligations. These subsidies have allowed the United States to become the largest cotton exporter in the world, while depressing global cotton prices and displacing production by poor farmers in many countries. Oxfam has estimated that eliminating these illegal subsidies would provide revenue to feed a million children per year, especially in West Africa (Alston, Sumner, and Brunke 2007). In bilateral negotiations finally concluded in 2010, Brazil accepted an annual cash payment to settle the dispute, but congressional action on the 2012 farm bill deleted the necessary appropriation. Theoretically, free trade can bind nations together in peaceful interdependence, but actual trade practice is fraught with conflict.

At the regional level, a similar belief in the efficacy of free trade as a guarantor of peace was an important motivation for the initiative that eventually led to the creation of the European Union. In both the EU and Bretton Woods, policymakers saw several ways that an open and institutionalized trading system could promote peace among nations. The institutions themselves could weaken the hold of nationalism and mediate conflict between nations. Trade-induced contact could break down nationalistic hostility among societies. Multilateralism (nondiscrimination) would tend to prevent the development of grievances among states. Interdependence could constrain armed conflict, and foster stability, while the economic growth generated by trade could remove the desperation that leads nations to aggression.

European integration was launched in 1951 with the founding of the European Coal and Steel Community (ECSC), which internationalized an industry that was key not only for the economies of the six nations involved but also for their war-making potential. With production facilities scattered among different countries, each became dependent on the others to provide both demand for the final product and part of the supply capacity. This arrangement fulfilled the liberal dream of an interdependence that would prevent war by making it economically suicidal. In fact, the ECSC was an innovative form of peace treaty, designed, in the words of Robert Schuman, to "make it plain that any war between France and Germany becomes, not merely unthinkable, but materially impossible" (Pomfret 1988: 75). The most recent step to encourage European trade was the creation of a new regional currency, the euro, to replace national currencies in 2001. Freed from the complications of multiple currencies that fluctuate in value, trade and investment flourished, but the Greek debt crisis (discussed later) demonstrates that the resulting interdependence can transmit negative conditions like financial instability across national borders just as surely as it can spread prosperity.

Institutional efforts to secure global peace require the exercise of power. According to hegemonic stability theory, one dominant nation—a hegemon—will usually have to subsidize the organizational costs and frequently offer side benefits in exchange for cooperation. For example, the massive infusion of foreign aid provided to Europe by the United States under the Marshall Plan in the late 1940s was a key inducement in the creation of the Bretton Woods system. Maintaining the capability to handle these leadership requirements entails substantial costs. For example, US expenditures for defense, which have been many times higher than those of nations with which it has competed since World War II, erode the competitiveness of US business by requiring higher tax levels; they constrain the funds available to spend on other items that could enhance competitiveness; and they divert a substantial share of US scientific and technological expertise into military innovation and away from commercial areas. The trade-off between competitiveness and defense may be judged differently by different individuals, but it can be ignored by none.

International Cooperation and National Autonomy

International institutions may be necessary to facilitate trade and to alleviate the conflict that inevitably surrounds it, but they can also create conflict. Institutions require hegemonic leadership, but many critics complain that the United States benefits so much from its capacity to dictate the rules under which institutions operate that they have become extensions of US imperialism. Institutions seek to maintain fair competition among firms in different countries—which is essential to the international trading system—but they must also do so without undermining the national sovereignty and autonomy that are central to the modern state system.

Trade disputes test the capacity of institutions to balance these imperatives, because one nation will often defend its policy as a rightful exercise of national sovereignty, while another challenges it as an unfair barrier to trade. Since governments have many compelling motives for enacting policies that affect trade, clashes of values often appear as struggles over the rightful boundaries of sovereignty. Such disagreements can be settled by appeal to GATT or, more recently, to the WTO, but not even the WTO's chief sponsor, the United States, accepts the dominion of the WTO without serious reservations about its intrusion into affairs historically reserved for national governments.

Indeed, even though the US administration strongly supported the creation of the WTO in 1995 to prevent trade violations by other nations, a surprising variety of US groups opposed its ratification because it might encroach on US sovereignty. Environmental groups such as Friends of the Earth, Greenpeace, and the Sierra Club were joined not only by consumer advocates like Ralph Nader but also by conservatives such as Ross Perot, Pat Buchanan, and Jesse Helms, who feared that a WTO panel could rule that various US government policies constituted unfair trade practices, even though they were designed to pursue values utterly unrelated to trade. For example, EU automakers have challenged the US law that establishes standards for auto emissions and fuel economy. Buchanan said, "WTO means putting America's trade under foreign bureaucrats who will meet in secret to demand changes in United States laws. . . . WTO tramples all over American sovereignty and states' rights" (Dodge 1994: 1D). Because the WTO could not force a change in US law, GATT director-general Peter Sutherland called this position "errant nonsense" (Tumulty 1994), but the WTO could impose sanctions or authorize an offended nation to withdraw trade concessions as compensation for the injury.

Soon thereafter the United States found itself on the other side of the clash between fair competition and national sovereignty when it appealed to the WTO to rule that the EU's prohibition of beef containing growth hormones violated the "national treatment" principle contained in GATT's Article 3. Since almost all cattle raised in the United States are fed growth hormones and very few European cattle are, the United States contended that the EU rule was simply disguised protectionism that unfairly discriminated against US products. The EU contended that such beef was a cancer risk and that as a sovereign power it had the right—indeed the responsibility—to establish whatever health regulations it chose to protect its citizens. The WTO ruled in favor of the United States, incurring the wrath of those who saw this as an example of national democratic processes being overruled by undemocratic global ones. Can it be long before Colombia challenges US drug laws as discriminating against marijuana while favoring Canadian whiskey?

Neither can regional agreements avoid this clash between fair competition in trade and national autonomy. The first trade dispute under NAFTA involved a challenge by the United States to regulations under Canada's Fisheries Act, established to promote conservation of herring and salmon stocks in Canada's Pacific Coast waters. Soon thereafter the Canadian government challenged US Environmental Protection Agency regulations that require the phasing out of asbestos, a carcinogen no longer permitted as a building material in the United States (Cavanaugh et al. 1992).

Similarly, critics of the EU worry that its leveling of the playing field for trade competition also threatens to level cultural and political differences among nations. Denmark, for example, found that free trade made it impossible to maintain a sales-tax rate higher than neighboring Germany's, because Danish citizens could simply evade the tax by purchasing goods in Germany and bringing them across the border duty-free. Competitiveness pressures also make it difficult for a nation to adopt policies that impose costs on business when low trade barriers force firms to compete with those in other countries that do not bear such burdens. For example, French firms demand a level playing field in competing with Spanish firms whenever the French government mandates employee benefits, health and safety rules, or environmental regulations more costly than those in Spain. In fact, free trade and the institutions created to sustain it pressure nations to harmonize many policies, but not without significant risks.

Together with the elimination of tariff barriers, the creation of the euro certainly facilitated increased trade among European nations, but also allowed the ballooning of trade deficits in several countries by enabling the capital flows that financed them. By 2009 the resultant debt left Greece—whose imports were three times higher than its exports—teetering on the brink of default on loans from European banks. Before the Greek drachma was replaced by the euro, Greece could have eased trade deficits by allowing the drachma to decline in value, which would have increased exports and discouraged imports. With that option foreclosed, Greece instead sought to dampen imports through austerity policies that shrank the economy by a quarter and pushed unemployment over 25 percent. Threatening the stability of European banking systems, the Greek collapse spread to Italy, Spain, Portugal, and Ireland, among others. By the end of 2015, only stop-gap measures had prevented continentwide disaster, but the underlying problem remained unresolved. Tight interdependence offers familiar trade benefits but also risks crisis contagion.

Some trade barriers are designed to protect unique aspects of the economic, social, and political life of nations, especially when trade affects cultural matters of symbolic importance. For example, France imposes limits on the percentage of television programming that can originate abroad, allegedly in defense of French language and custom. The obvious targets of these restrictions, US producers of movies and youth-oriented music, contend that the French are simply protecting their own inefficient entertainment industry. They argue that programming deserves the same legal protection abroad that the foreign television sets and disc players that display these images receive in the United States. But if we restrict trade because we oppose child labor or rainforest destruction, how can we object when other countries ban the sale of US products because they violate *their* values—such as music and Hollywood films that celebrate sex, violence, and free expression of controversial ideas, or even blue jeans, McDonald's hamburgers, and other symbols of US cultural domination?

The Trans-Pacific Partnership

The most recent effort to expand trade is the Trans-Pacific Partnership (TPP), negotiated between 2008 and 2015 by twelve nations including the United States, Japan, Canada, New Zealand, and Australia, but also Mexico, Peru, Chile, Singapore, Malaysia, Vietnam, and Brunei. As of late 2015, the ongoing ratification processes in all twelve countries reflected the dilemmas discussed earlier, dominated by arguments that were eerily similar to those that surrounded previous multilateral trade agreements.

The distributional effects implicit in all trade—that some will gain and others will lose—drove the politics of ratification. Proponents emphasized export expansion through tariff reductions. The Barack Obama administration cited a decline in over 18,000 tariffs imposed on US exports by foreign countries, producing a state-by-state report of products that would benefit from increased sales to the other eleven economies. Most US businesses with significant foreign sales accordingly supported the TPP. Opponents, especially smaller businesses that sell primarily in the domestic market, emphasize the TPP-mandated reduction in US tariffs that would harm US firms competing against imports.

The tariff reductions contained in the TPP are less relevant for these distributional effects than those of earlier trade accords, however, because tariffs no longer constitute the chief barrier to export growth nor the principle protection against imports. For example, Japan charges no tariffs on US automobiles, yet for decades the US auto industry has complained that many other aspects of Japanese markets not addressed by the TPP add more than $10,000 to the price of US-made automobiles in Japan. The US auto industry cites as evidence that US manufacturers sell about 13,000 cars per year in Japan, while Japanese companies sell more than that in the United States *per day*. The US trade deficit with Japan in the auto sector alone exceeds $50 billion per year.

While both Ford Motor Company and the unions that represent its workers oppose the TPP because it eliminates US tariffs of 25 percent charged against Japanese light trucks, their most vehement criticism is that the TPP does not address the unfair manipulation of currency exchange rates that make US products expensive abroad and foreign products cheap in the United States. The prominence of this issue derives from concern that the TPP will eventually add new members that are notorious for currency manipulation, especially China and Thailand.

Since the TPP would benefit export sectors and harm import-competing sectors in all twelve countries, some governments plan to offset the damage to vulnerable groups with increased spending designed to purchase political support. In Japan the Shinzo Abe administration has proposed $30 billion in aid to Japanese agriculture, and Canada plans $4.3 billion in support of dairy farmers who will lose tariff protection.

In the United States the greatest controversy over distributional consequences mirrors the opposition to NAFTA, namely that US workers would be forced into direct competition with foreign workers who earn markedly less and enjoy poorer working conditions and fewer rights. This is the so-called race to the bottom that has motivated virtually all US labor unions to oppose most trade accords, including the TPP. As a consequence, most Democrats—with the notable exception of President Obama—oppose the TPP, and most Republicans (save Donald Trump) align with business in supporting it. This partisan pattern is familiar from the NAFTA debate, and is also echoed in Canada, New Zealand, and Australia, where liberal groups are wary of the accord and conservatives support it. As one trade unionist put it, "the TPP is a dream for corporations, but a nightmare for workers" (CWA 2015).

The 6,000-page TPP agreement also poses familiar dilemmas involving competing values and national sovereignty, with critics especially concerned that democratic processes were circumvented in the secretive negotiation process and will be similarly sidestepped in its implementation. During the six years of negotiations, the only input from the American public came through twenty-eight advisory committees, whose composition was heavily tilted toward corporate interests. The *Washington Post* reported that of the 566 committee members, 480 (85 percent) were from private industry and their trade associations, while only 31 came from labor organizations and just 16 from nongovernmental organizations. More than half of the committees were made up entirely of corporate representatives, and another quarter contained only a single noncorporate member. For example, given that the intellectual property rights advisory committee included representatives of pharmaceutical companies but no noncorporate members, it is hardly surprising that the TPP requires all twelve nations to extend copyright protections that greatly increase prices for life-saving drugs.

If critics were concerned by the drafting of the TPP outside the open political processes expected in a democratic nation, they are even more alarmed by provisions of the TPP that replace domestic institutions with international ones. At issue are the mechanisms to be used in adjudicating disputes that inevitably arise in any business transaction, but are especially common in international trade matters that involve multiple government jurisdictions. Businesses are understandably reluctant to rely upon judicial proceedings in foreign countries, especially when a foreign government is a party to the dispute. Thus they have pressed for so-called investor-state dispute settlement systems to be incorporated into all recent trade agreements. Modeled after WTO tribunals, the TPP permits corporations to challenge government policies that erode their profits in specially convened expert panels consisting of three private lawyers rather than domestic courts.

Critics see this as a violation of national sovereignty and an interference with democratic processes. For example, consumer groups note that the TPP will result in increased imports of food from countries with suspect safety standards, especially seafood from Malaysia. Such concerns about food safety are hardly new, and US law consequently requires that certain categories of meat contain labeling information on the country of origin so that consumers might judge that risk for themselves. However, in 2012 an expert panel ruled that that US law violates WTO rules. Since the TPP would greatly expand the number of corporations eligible to pursue such remedies, critics fear that all manner of consumer protections may be swept away.

Environmentalists have been on the leading edge of such criticism. "The TPP as a whole is a frontal assault on environmental and climate safeguards" (Norton 2015), said Friends of the Earth president Erich Pica, raising the specter of corporate profits dominating all other values that nations may legitimately wish to pursue. The Sierra Club has noted that ExxonMobil and Chevron have used similar rules in past agreements to challenge policies including a natural gas fracking moratorium in Canada, a court order to pay for oil pollution in Ecuador, and environmental standards for a coal-fired power plant in Germany. Such challenges would be heard by trade tribunals that could order governments to pay fossil fuel firms for the profits they hypothetically would have earned if the climate protections being challenged had not been enacted.

In short, the TPP offers the undeniable benefits of expanded trade, but these benefits are not free. They come at the expense of compromises with dilemmas involving distributional effects, alternative values, and limitations on national sovereignty.

Choices for Nations and Individuals

Few would deny the contention of liberal theory that trade permits a higher level of aggregate consumption than would be possible if consumers were prevented from purchasing foreign products. It is hard to imagine modern life without the benefits of trade. Of course, it does not follow that trade must be utterly unrestricted, because the aggregate economic effect tells only part of the story. As mercantilists remind us, trade also carries with it important social and political implications. Trade shapes the distribution of income and wealth among individuals, affects the power of states and the relations among them, and constrains or enhances the ability of both individuals and nations to achieve goals built on other values. Thus, trade presents a dilemma for nations: no policy can avoid some of trade's negative consequences without also sacrificing some of its benefits. That is why most governments have sought to encompass elements of both liberalism and mercantilism in fashioning their trade policies. The same is true for individuals, because every day each individual must—explicitly or implicitly—assume a stance on the dilemmas identified in this chapter. In turn, trade forces individuals to consider some of the following discussion questions, questions that require normative judgments as well as a keen understanding of the empirical consequences of trade. We must always remember to ask not only what trade policy will best achieve our goals but also what our goals should be.

Discussion Questions

1. Are your views closer to those of a liberal or a mercantilist?
2. Is it patriotic to purchase domestic products? Why or why not?
3. Does one owe a greater obligation to domestic workers and corporations than to foreign ones?
4. Should one purchase a product that is cheap even though it was made with slave labor or by workers deprived of human rights?
5. Should a country surrender some of its sovereignty in order to receive the benefits of joining the WTO?
6. Should one lobby the US government to restrict the sales of US forestry products abroad because these products compromise the environment?

Suggested Readings

Alston, Julian M., Daniel A. Sumner, and Henrich Brunke (2007) *Impacts of Reductions in US Cotton Subsidies on West African Cotton Producers*. Boston: Oxfam America.

Chen, Shaohua, and Martin Ravallion (2004) "How Have the World's Poorest Fared Since the Early 1980s?" Washington, DC: World Bank.

Easterly, William (1999) "The Lost Decades: Explaining Developing Countries' Stagnation, 1980–1998." Washington, DC: World Bank.

Fallows, James (1993) "How the World Works." *Atlantic Monthly* (December).

Judson, Ruth (2012) "Crisis and Calm: Demand for U.S. Currency at Home and Abroad from the Fall of the Berlin Wall to 2011" (November). www.federalreserve.gov.

Moon, Bruce E. (1998) "Exports, Outward-Oriented Development, and Economic Growth." *Political Research Quarterly* (March).

——— (2000) *Dilemmas of International Trade*. 2nd ed. Boulder: Westview.

Nager, Adams B., and Robert D. Atkinson (2015) "The Myth of America's Manufacturing Renaissance: The Real State of U.S. Manufacturing." www2.itif.org.

Pierce, Justin R., and Peter K. Schott (2012) "The Surprisingly Swift Decline of U.S. Manufacturing Employment" (December). www.nber.org.

Polanyi, Karl (1944) *The Great Transformation.* New York: Farrar and Reinhart.

Ricardo, David (1981) *Works and Correspondence of David Ricardo: Principles of Political Economy and Taxation.* London: Cambridge University Press.

Smith, Adam (1910) *An Inquiry into the Nature and Causes of the Wealth of Nations.* London: Dutton.

US Bureau of Economic Analysis (2015) "Table 1: U.S. International Trade in Goods and Services." www.bea.gov.

US Treasury (2015) "Foreign Portfolio Holdings of U.S. Securities." www.treasury.gov.

World Bank (annual) *World Development Indicators.* New York: Oxford University Press.

11

Ending Poverty, Reducing Inequality

Don Reeves

- Poverty is a mother watching her kids get sick too often, or die for lack of a vaccination that would cost a few pennies.
- Poverty is to live crowded under a piece of plastic in Calcutta, huddled in a cardboard house during a rainstorm in São Paulo, or homeless in Washington, D.C.
- Poverty is a job application you can't read, a poor teacher in a rundown school, or no school at all.
- Poverty is watching your crop in Ethiopia made worthless by farm programs in the United States and Europe.
- Poverty is being locked for long hours inside a garment factory or working long hours only as needed in someone else's field.
- Inequality is being aware of others who have access to resources a hundred or a thousand times greater than what would provide the basic needs for your family.
- Poverty and inequality are to feel powerless—without dignity or hope.

Dimensions of Poverty

Poverty has many dimensions. Religious ascetics may choose to be poor as part of their spiritual discipline. Persons with great wealth may ignore the needs of those around them or may miss the richness and beauty of nature or great art and remain poor in spirit. But this chapter is about poverty as the involuntary lack of enough resources to provide or exchange for basic necessities—food, shelter, healthcare, clothing, education, and opportunities to work and to develop the human spirit.

Globally, poor people disproportionately live in Africa. The largest number live in Asia. A significant number live in Latin American and Caribbean countries. Three-quarters of the people in several sub-Saharan Africa countries and Haiti are poor. Depending on the threshold chosen, at least one in four or nearly half of all people in developing countries are poor. The poverty situation worldwide is shown in Figure 11.1.

But no place in the world is immune to poverty. The United States, some European countries, and Australia also have large blocks of poor people. With few exceptions, the incidence of poverty is higher in rural than in urban areas, but is shifting toward the latter. Nearly everywhere, women and girls suffer from poverty more than do men and boys. Infants, young children, and elderly people are particularly vulnerable. Cultural and discriminatory causes of poverty are immense, especially among minorities and indigenous peoples. The difficulties in changing long habits and practices should not be underestimated.

This chapter looks first at ways in which poverty is measured. It then turns to approaches to reducing poverty in the context of a global economy, especially the relationship between economic growth, inequality, and poverty, both in the United States and globally. Finally, the chapter reviews a few among many policy choices that might help reduce poverty and inequality.

Measuring Poverty and Inequality

Poverty is not the same in the United States or Poland or Zimbabwe. It is often described differently by supporters or critics of a particular regime. Poverty does not lend itself to an exact or universal definition. Deciding who is poor depends on who is measuring, where, and why.

Poverty Thresholds

Poverty is usually measured by income or consumption. The World Bank estimates poverty using two thresholds. In 2015, it estimated that over 800 million people were living on incomes equivalent to less than $1.90 per day. More than 2 billion were living on less than $3.10 per day (World Bank 2015d). The entire first group and the majority of the latter chronically lack some or all basic necessities. The rest live so close to the edge that any emergency—illness, work layoff, drought—pushes them from just getting by into desperation.

In the United States, poverty is officially defined as income less than three times the value of a "thrifty food plan" devised by the US Department of Agriculture and adjusted for family size—$24,250 for a family of four in 2015 (*Federal Register* 2015). The thrifty food plan was devised in the early 1960s to address short-term emergencies, and was not intended to be

Figure 11.1 Number and Percentage of Poor People Worldwide, 1990–2015

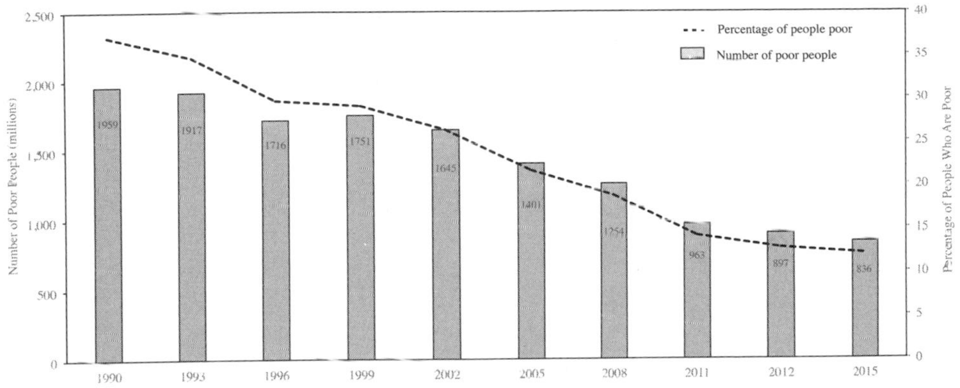

Source: World Bank (2015d).

used for longer-term food budgeting. Although it is adjusted annually for changes in food prices, other costs, particularly housing, have grown faster than food costs since the plan's base year (1955), so the threshold has represented a gradually declining standard of living. Some critics say the threshold is higher than necessary, partly because benefits from certain government programs—such as Medicare, food stamps, housing subsidies, and child-related tax credits—are not counted.

In 2011, the US Bureau of the Census introduced a "supplemental poverty" measure. This new measure adds cash income and federal cash or in-kind benefits that families can use to meet basic needs, such as food stamps and tax credits. It also subtracts certain unavoidable expenses, such as taxes, work expenses such as childcare, and out-of-pocket medical expenses. The net effect of these adjustments increases somewhat the overall incidence of poverty. It lowers it for families with children, who benefit more from the assistance programs, but raises it for elderly, who have more medical expenses. The new measure will not replace the official calculation of poverty, but will be used for continuing research, such as measuring the effect of poverty-targeted assistance programs. Regardless the measure used, poor people themselves feel hard-pressed.

Relative Poverty vs. Absolute Poverty

Low-income people living among others who are as poor as them do not feel as deprived as persons who have the same income but live among others who are better-off. This is reflected in many nations' definition of poverty as one-half of median income, or some other measure of relative poverty—a threshold based on a comparison with a defined group within a particular country. For example, the newly introduced supplemental poverty measure for the United States is related to expenditures for food, clothing, shelter, and utilities by families at the thirty-third percentile of family expenditures.

Absolute poverty, on the other hand, is measured on the basis of a fixed amount of income or purchasing power. The Word Bank threshold for extreme poverty is set at $1.90 per person per day, and is adjusted periodically for inflation. The US poverty threshold—$24,250 for a family of four in 2015—is another example of an absolute measure of poverty. The level fixed for an absolute poverty threshold often makes a dramatic difference in the observed poverty rate. In what may seem a small difference, from $1.90 per day to $3.10 per day, the World Bank's count of poor people more than doubles.

Gross National Income

Gross national income (GNI) per capita is the most widely used measure in comparing national incomes. GNI is the value of all goods and services produced within an economy plus or minus cash transfers into and out of the economy, such as profit paid to foreign investors or money sent home by citizens working abroad.

Among the world's economies, large and small, the World Bank counts thirty-one low-income economies with an annual per capita GNI of $1,045 or less as of 2014. By its count, fifty-one lower-middle-income economies have per capita GNIs ranging from $1,046 to $4,125, and fifty-three upper-middle-income economies have per capita GNIs ranging from $4,126 to $12,735. Sixty-eight high-income economies have per capita GNIs of $12,736 or more (World Bank 2015d).

GNI provides a quick measure of the capacity of an economy overall to meet people's needs. It also represents the pool from which savings and public expenditures can be drawn. But GNI is seriously flawed as a measure of poverty or well-being, because it gives no information about the quality of production or the distribution of income within the country.

First, GNI fails to distinguish among types of economic activity. Manufacturing cigarettes, making bombs, and running prisons are scored as contributing to GNI the same as making bicycles, teaching school, building homes, or conducting scientific research. Second, many goods and services generate costs that are not reflected in their prices—polluted air from manufacturing, or illness from overconsumption, for example. Third, many nurturing and creative activities—parenting, homemaking, gardening, and home food preparation—are not included, because they are usually not bought and sold. At best, GNI includes only estimates for food or other goods consumed by producers, unpaid family labor, and a wide range of other economic activities lumped together as the "informal" sector. Illegal or criminal activities, such as drug-dealing or prostitution, are generally not included in estimates but nonetheless contribute to some people's livelihood.

Purchasing Power Parity

GNI figures for various countries are usually compared on a currency exchange basis. In 2014, the per capita GNI in Bangladesh, 90,580 taka, could be exchanged for $1,080. But 90,580 taka would buy more in Bangladesh than $1,080 would buy in the United States, primarily because wages there are much lower. To overcome this disparity, the World Bank and the United Nations Development Programme (UNDP) have adopted a measure—purchasing power parity (PPP)—that estimates the number of dollars required to purchase comparable goods in different countries. Bangladeshi PPP is estimated at $3,330, rather than $1,080 (World Bank 2015d).

PPP estimates, as used throughout this chapter, make country-to-country comparisons more accurate and realistic and somewhat narrow the apparent gap between wealthy and poor countries. Even so, vast disparities remain. PPPs in Norway, Switzerland, and the United States, ranging from $55,860 to $65,970 per capita, are thirty-seven to eighty-five times those of Burundi and Ethiopia, at $770 and $1,490 (World Bank 2015d).

Inequality

Estimates of poverty and well-being are based on country averages of gross national income per capita, which is a crude measure at best. Because poverty is experienced at the household and individual levels, the distribution of national income is crucial.

Detailed and reasonably accurate information is necessary for targeting antipoverty efforts and particularly for assessing the consequences of policy decisions. But census data as comprehensive as those for the United States are a distant dream for most poor countries. Many of them have trouble keeping such basic records as birth registrations. They may have only a guess as to the number of their citizens, let alone details about their conditions. Representative household surveys are the only viable tool for most countries for the foreseeable future.

Household surveys, to be useful—especially for comparison purposes—need to be carefully designed, accurately interpreted, and usable for measuring comparable factors in different times, places, and circumstances. Private agencies, many governments, and even some international agencies are tempted to shape or interpret surveys to put themselves in the best light. Users of survey results need to be keenly aware of who conducted each survey and for what purposes.

Global inequality. Globally, we accept gross income inequality. The most-used measure of inequality compares the income or consumption of the richest one-fifth, or quintile, of each population, with that of the lowest quintile. Measured in PPP values, the wealthiest one-fifth of the world, about 1.5 billion people, account for more than three-quarters of the world's consumption (see Figure 11.2), about $60 trillion; the bottom half, over 3.6 billion people, for about $5 trillion. Within the latter group, the poorest one-fifth, about 1.4 billion people, share less than $1 trillion (Shah 2010).

Recent surveys of household studies covering nearly all the developing countries since 1975 conclude that there is no clear overall trend in comparisons based on purchasing power from 1981 to 2015. Review again the trend line in Figure 11.1. The number of people in developing countries living on less than $1.90 per day (PPP 2011) has dropped dramatically over this period. But the number living on less than $3.10 per day (PPP 2011) has fluctuated around just over 2 billion, although the proportion has dropped because of increasing population.

Two further caveats are necessary. First, nearly all of these gains occurred in China early in this period, and in China and India in more recent years. Without China's and India's gains, the number of extremely poor has risen, especially in Africa. Second, the people below the $1.90 per day threshold are on average much worse off, again especially in Africa, but also elsewhere, even in China and India.

Meanwhile, the incomes of a very small proportion of nearly every nation's population have skyrocketed. World Bank economist Branko Mi-

Figure 11.2 Distribution of World Population and Global Income, 2008

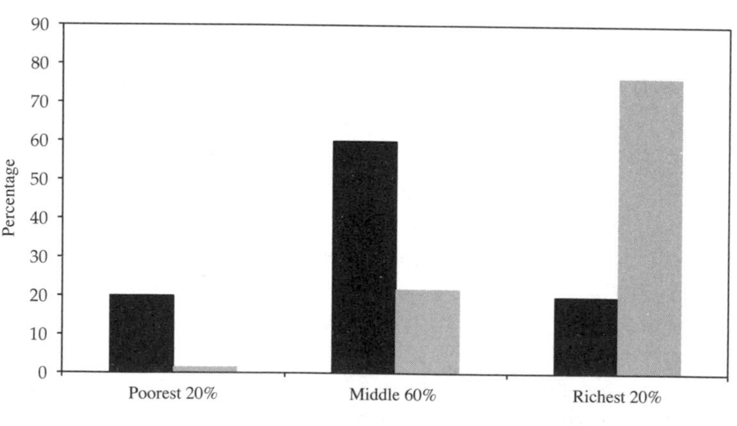

Source: Shah (2010).

lanovic estimated that the ratio between the income of the top 5 percent and the bottom 5 percent of people in the world was 185 to 1 in 2005, up from 78 to 1 in 1988. The world's richest people, less than 2 percent, have as much income as the bottom three-quarters of the world's population (Milanovic 2006). The disparity may have flattened a little during the Great Depression, as wealthy persons suffered loss in investment income, but there seems to be consensus that since then, the wealthy have captured nearly all the gains in income (Stiglitz 2015).

Inequality in the United States. The poverty gap between the richest and almost everyone else in the United States is widening rapidly. Since the late 1970s, the share of national income going to the top quintile has climbed from about 44 percent of US aggregate income to over 51 percent in recent years. The share to the lowest quintile has dropped from just over 4 percent to barely 3 percent, and the share has also dropped for everyone in between. Whereas in 1980 the top households had 10.5 times the income of the bottom quintile, since 2010 they have had 16 times as much. Since the Great Depression, more than all the gains have accrued to the top income categories. After inflation adjustments, the average worker is no better off than in the late 1970s (Stiglitz 2015).

The poorest are getting even poorer. The richest are getting much richer. (For a broader discussion of these trends and possible responses, see Figure 11.4.) The UNDP uses per capita income instead of household income to compare income shares. At varying dates in the past decade, it found the ratio between the income of the richest quintile and the income of the poorest quintile in the United States to be the highest among industrial nations, about double the ratio for the Scandinavian countries. (Compare the ratio for the United States with those for other countries in Table 11.1).

Inequality within developing countries. Among the low-income countries for which income estimates are available, the ratios between the top and bottom quintiles at varying recent dates in the past decade ranged from 5.0 to 1 for India and 5.8 to 1 for Indonesia, up to 16.8 to 1 for Brazil and 17.5 to 1 for Colombia (see Table 11.1).

Differences in income distribution make a big difference to poor people. Measured in PPP$, Colombia's per capita GNI is more than twice India's, but India's poor have more purchasing power. Egypt's GNI is barely half of Chile's, but Egypt's poor people have more purchasing power. Thailand's per capita GNI is less than Brazil's, but Thailand's poor have nearly twice the purchasing power. In China, which has been the fastest-growing economy in the world for twenty-five years, the income share of the richest quintile has grown, while everyone else's has shrunk. There, purchasing power for the poor has barely budged.

Table 11.1 Poverty Impact of Income Distribution, Selected Countries, 2014

	GNI per Capita (PPP$), 2014	Income per Capita (PPP$)		Ratio of Highest 20 Percent to Lowest 20 Percent
		Lowest 20 Percent	Highest 20 Percent	
Norway	65,970	31,006	124,024	4.0
United States	55,860	8,658	142,443	16.5
South Korea	34,620	13,675	64,913	4.7
Malaysia	23,850	5,366	61,414	11.4
Chile	21,570	4,853	55,004	11.3
Brazil	15,900	2,703	45,474	16.8
Thailand	13,950	4,743	32,573	6.9
China	13,130	3,086	30,921	10.0
Colombia	12,600	2,079	36,477	17.5
Egypt	11,020	5,124	22,205	4.3
Indonesia	10,250	3,895	22,396	5.8
Philippines	8,300	2,449	20,626	8.4
India	5,760	2,448	12,326	5.0
Nigeria	5,680	1,534	13,888	9.1
Bangladesh	3,340	1,486	6,914	4.7

Source: World Bank (2015d).

Estimating a Base for Measuring Changes in Inequality

Until about two centuries ago, nearly all the world was poor. In many nations, there were a few wealthy or very wealthy families. In a few nations, over time, these wealthy families or clans grew strong enough to dominate those around them and establish empires. Think of ancient Egypt, Persia, Greece, Rome, or China at intervals over the past 4,000 years. But even within these conquering nations, nearly all the people remained very poor, to say nothing of the people in nations they conquered. This remained true through the early stages of the European empires established during the sixteenth and seventeenth centuries.

Using 1820 as a proxy for earlier eras, and for each of several intervals since then, World Bank researchers estimated the minimum subsistence income for everyone in a nation—those resources necessary just to keep people alive. Next they estimated the total national income for each nation at the same time. Finally, they calculated the ratio between a bare-subsistence national budget and their best estimate of national income. From these calculations, they estimate that national incomes over a long period through 1820 were on the order of five times this minimum subsistence allowance, with considerable variations and fluctuations, of course. In this exercise, they identified as "surplus" the resources above those needed for bare subsistence. Over this long period, they estimated that the few wealthy families on average captured about three-quarters of the available "surplus." This was generally true for the world as well as individual nations. Nearly all the people were very poor, in each nation and the world (Milanovic 2011).

Since the advent of industrialization and the emergence of a middle class in industrial economies, however, a difference has emerged in the location of the poor and rich quintiles of people. Incomes among countries diverged. Most of the global increase in wealth and income was in the industrial countries of Western Europe, the United States, and later Japan. Whereas in earlier periods the differences in wealth and income were within countries, by the middle to late twentieth century the major differences in income distribution were between countries—a rich country–poor country divide had emerged.

Globally, the ratio between subsistence and total production has widened from about 5 to 1 in the earlier period to nearly 20 to 1 at the beginning of the twenty-first century. But overall, nearly three-quarters of the "surplus" today is still captured by the wealthy. Until very recently, most of these wealthy people lived in the industrial countries, while most very poor people lived in poor countries. By now, with few exceptions, wherever economies are growing, there has emerged a wealthy elite (Milanovic 2011). In China, for example, several hundred million people have moved from extreme poverty into lower-middle and middle class, but the gap between the poorest sectors and the very top has widened dramatically (Stiglitz 2015).

Direct Measures of Well-Being

Other indicators measure well-being even more directly than income or poverty rates—for example, infant or under-five mortality rates, life expectancy, educational achievement, and food intake.

Hunger. The Food and Agriculture Organization (FAO) of the United Nations estimates shortfalls in food consumption. The FAO estimates that the absolute number of people in developing countries who consume too few calories stood at about 1 billion in 1990–1992, and had dropped to under 800 million by 2015. Because population has grown over the same period, however, the proportion of hungry people in developing countries declined from about 26 percent to about 14 percent. The slow steady decline in hunger was interrupted during high food prices in the mid-1990s, showing the extreme vulnerability of poor people to volatile food prices (FAO 2015d).

The most dramatic gains in reducing hunger over the period were in East and Southeast Asia, most notably China, where the percentage of hungry people dropped from 30 percent to less than 10 percent and the number fell from 289 million to 134 million (see Figure 11.3). Less dramatic gains by both measures were recorded in the Middle East and North Africa. In South Asia and Latin America and the Caribbean, the proportion declined, but the absolute number increased slightly over the period. In

Figure 11.3 Projected Number of Undernourished People by Region (millions), 2014–2016

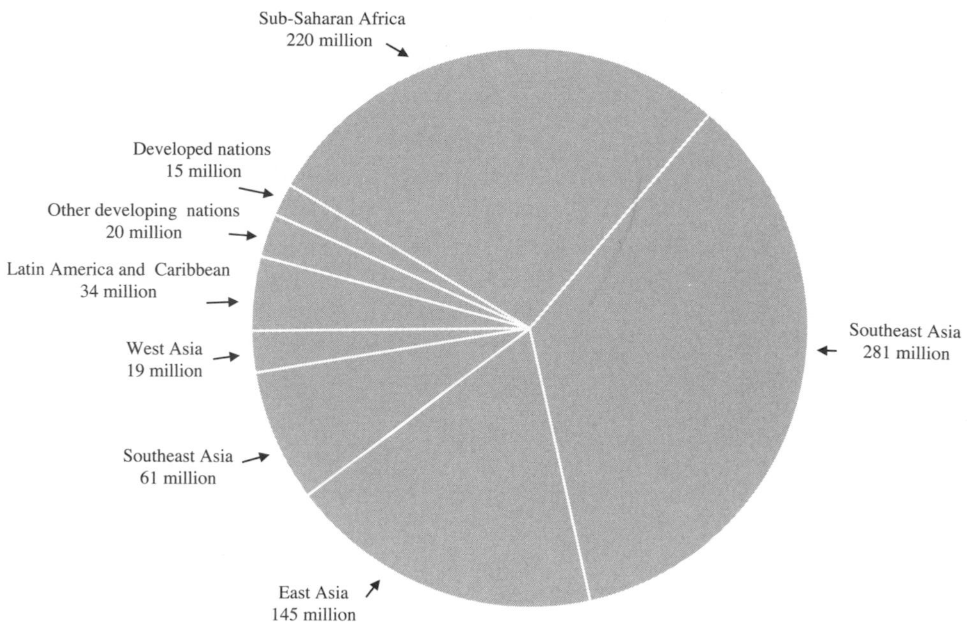

Source: FAO (2015).

Africa, the percentage of hungry people dropped slightly, while the number grew from 182 million to 220 million (FAO 2015d).

In 2008 and 2009, as the global financial recession deepened, food insecurity in the United States increased sharply from recent years. In 2006 and 2007, 11 percent of US households (12.9 million) were food-insecure, meaning that they did not have access at all times to enough food for active, healthy life for all household members. By 2009, nearly 15 percent of households (17.4 million) were food-insecure. Of these, about one-third had very low food security, meaning that food intake of one or more household members was reduced or otherwise disrupted because the household lacked money or other resources for adequate food. Also, between 2007 and 2009, households using food pantries rose by 44 percent, from 3.9 to a record 5.6 million households. Alas, the trend has not reversed. Need, as measured by food pantries, has continued to climb ever since (BFWI 2015).

The Human Development Index. In 1990 the UNDP created the Human Development Index (HDI), which gives equal weight to three factors of development: life expectancy at birth, educational attainment (based on the adult literacy rate and mean years of schooling), and per capita purchasing power.

People's lives can be improved if even limited resources are focused on nutritional programs, public health, and basic education. China and Sri Lanka, for example, have invested relatively heavily in education and healthcare. They rank with many industrial countries in life expectancy and educational attainment, higher on the HDI scale than other nations with comparable per capita incomes.

Other nations rank much lower on the HDI scale than on a per capita GNI scale. The oil-rich nations of the Middle East rank low in both longevity and educational attainment, particularly because of the status of women in these societies. Several African nations have extremely low educational attainment and longevity indicators, for varied reasons. Angola and Namibia have been engulfed in long independence struggles and civil war. Botswana and Gabon, although relatively rich in natural resource income, have not devoted proportional resources to education and healthcare services (UNDP 2014b).

It is significant that the United States is among the nations that rank lower on the HDI scale than on a per capita GNI scale. Even though GNI in the United States is higher than in all but a handful of other nations, the United States lags Canada and most European nations in healthcare, educational attainment, and strength of social safety nets.

An Emerging Dream: Eliminating Poverty and Hunger

After this extensive exploration of how poverty and inequality are measured, let us now turn to a review of efforts to reduce or eliminate poverty and inequality over the past fifty years. The hope that most or all the people in a particular society, or the whole world, might escape from extreme poverty and hunger is a relatively recent concept, enabled by the Industrial Revolution of the nineteenth century and more recent developments. It became a feasible worldwide goal only in the second half of the 1900s. Increasing attention to inequality and meeting specific basic needs strengthens the hope.

At the close of World War II in 1945, world leaders (among wealthy nations) were focused on recovery and preventing a repeat of the experience of two world wars and a severe global depression. Several steps were taken. The United Nations was created as a more viable organization than the League of Nations, attempted after World War I. Recognition of the growing linkages in international finance led to creation of the World Bank and the International Monetary Fund. An international trade organization was attempted (what would eventually become the World Trade Organization), but took another forty years to actually get started. Beginning at the same time, and over the next two decades, dozens of former European colonies around the world declared their independence.

The initial focus of the new financial institutions was on recovery from the severe damages of war in Europe and Japan. Recovery was actually more rapid than expected by many, and by the 1960s, attention began to turn to the former colonies and other poor states that had never been colonized, or had achieved independence earlier, collectively referred to as the less-developed countries (LDCs), or developing countries.

Flush with relative prosperity, the international community began to consider the notion that at least the basic needs of every person on the planet might be met. The international financial institutions shifted their focus in this direction. Even after global recession and widespread severe global hunger in the early 1970s, US secretary of state Henry Kissinger spoke for many when he declared the goal of "eliminating world hunger in a decade" at the first World Food Conference in Rome in 1976. Progress since has been uneven, often disappointing.

The Setting for Reducing Poverty and Inequality

Efforts to reduce or eliminate poverty and inequality over the past six decades must be set in the context of the Cold War over much of that period and several developments since its decline:

- Globalization—the evolution of a single worldwide network for producing and exchanging money, goods, and services.
- The shift from resource-based economies to knowledge-based economies.
- A rapidly increasing global work force, from barely 1 billion early in this period to over 3 billion today, with prospects of reaching 4 billion by 2050, with nearly all the increase occurring in developing countries.
- Lagging education and skills training in much of the added work force.
- By the 1990s, the near-dominance of market-based liberal political economics as the conventional wisdom in international financial and development matters.
- Since about 2000, lessening emphasis on a structural approach to development, and greater emphasis on specific development goals.

Globalization and the shift to knowledge-based economies are inextricably linked. New information, communication, and transportation technologies have dramatically changed the way many businesses are managed (remote access to real-time market information, on-time delivery of manufacturing components on a global basis, digital voice transcription, international call centers, and automatic transmission of orders and billing). These same technologies have also spawned whole new industries (distance learning, medical consultation, online markets, and the gathering and "mining" of megadata). This immense capacity to process information has enabled new scientific advances (mapping of the human genome, medical and space research, cross-species bioengineering). The knowledge factor outweighs the resource factor in an increasing number of endeavors.

Globalization and Poverty

Globalization has had mixed effects on employment, poverty, and income distribution. Hundreds of thousands of new jobs have been created in poor countries as standardized manufacturing and information technology jobs have been moved to Asia and, more recently, to Africa. By the standards of more-developed nations and human rights advocates, many of these jobs are not very desirable. But for most of the workers, they are an improvement over any alternative. Meanwhile, a comparable number of jobs in the United States and other richer countries have been eliminated; wages for the majority of workers have stagnated or declined.

Low-wage jobs, by themselves, are not enough to build thriving economies (Stiglitz 2015). Will poor nations be able to emulate South Korea and Taiwan from a generation ago, with increasingly sophisticated products and services for themselves as well as for export? Where will the resources to educate and train new workers come from, particularly in the poorer countries, and for increasingly sophisticated jobs? How will any gain, or savings, from globalization be distributed, within nations and worldwide?

Structural Approaches to Development

Through the 1960s and 1970s, developing countries generally attempted to grow their economies by copying one of the two main structural approaches in vogue in that era, expecting that if the right "system" were adopted, good results would follow. Many nations opted for some version of a centrally planned or state-directed economy (communism or socialism). Others opted for some version of liberal democracy and market capitalism, many entailing sizable international loans that were often poorly administered or looted by corrupt officials. Much of the competition was ideologically driven, as part of the Cold War. Regardless of the structural approach, results were judged primarily by the criterion of growth in national income, with little attention to its distribution.

When the number of centrally planned economies peaked in the 1970s, they included about 40 percent of the world's population. By the turn of the twenty-first century, with a couple of minor exceptions, these countries had all introduced market-oriented reforms. Some, such as China, began to introduce such reforms gradually. Others, such as the Soviet Union, held on until their economies collapsed, then made a dramatic conversion, often with a sharp drop in income and well-being and slow fitful recoveries.

The dominance of market-based economic thought was partly the default of competitive systems, but was believed by many to be a victory for market-based democratic economies. In 1989, political economist Francis Fukuyama wrote a well-received essay titled "The End of History?" in which he observed that we may have reached "the end point of mankind's ideological evolution and the universalization of Western liberal democracy as the final form of human government" (1989: 4).

Led by the United States, this version of economic liberalism dominated the international financial institutions, under the rubric of the Washington Consensus. These principles were translated into a set of conditions that developing nations were required to adopt to be eligible for financial assistance: repayment of debts, austerity in social and safety-net programs, openness to foreign investment and freer trade, and reliance on market-based economies.

But most poor nations did not prosper under this sort of regimen. With a few notable exceptions, their economies did not grow; too few new jobs were created. Where there were gains from economic growth or sale of scarce natural resources, they were too often captured by an already wealthy elite, as in much of Latin America. Most people remained poor and hungry, many desperately so.

A few countries have shown that it is possible to have both economic growth and decreasing inequality if the right policies are in place. In South Korea, for example, where per capita income grew rapidly through the 1960s and 1970s, today the richest fifth of the population has about five times as much income as the poorest fifth. The ratio has narrowed slightly over the past four decades; poor people have shared in the rapid growth. That is, their incomes have increased more than average on a percentage basis, although the absolute increase in income has been greater for wealthier persons (Stiglitz 2015).

Despite rhetoric, no nation has attempted, or is attempting, a true free market economy. Debates about political economies are usually about deciding which functions can be left to markets and which cannot, or shaping the context or rules under which markets function. A central question is how market-oriented political economies might contribute more to reducing poverty or reducing inequality, especially in the poorest countries.

Changing Emphases for Economic Development

Although the Washington Consensus dominated international financing for development from the 1970s through the 1990s, it was never completely accepted. Beginning in the 1960s, several Asian economies (South Korea, Taiwan, and Indonesia) adopted market-based economic models, but governments played a heavy role in allocating capital toward favored industries, often referred to as state capitalism. These countries emphasized education and took other steps along the lines outlined here to ensure reasonably equitable income distribution. Their success and prosperity has encouraged other developing countries to adopt similar policies.

China began to depart from a centrally planned path (in fact, if not in name) in 1979, after three decades of communist rule that included a completely state-dominated economy. But the permitting of market-based reforms in China was gradual, and strictly controlled. First, farmers were permitted to form teams who could sell their produce in open markets, once they had delivered the requisite rental portion to the local and national governments. In the early 1980s, foreign firms were invited to set up joint ventures with state-owned manufacturers to create goods for export. Two areas of competition accompanied these openings: goods for export, which had to meet international standards for quality; and international partners, which helped improve operational efficiency compared to the relatively low productivity of many state-owned Chinese firms. Some of the joint partnerships appear to have been set up primarily to acquire technological innovations.

Gradually, over the next two decades, more and more private Chinese businesses were permitted. Some were tiny—small shops to sell produce, goods, or services; others, primarily manufacturing, grew rapidly to immense proportions, especially export businesses. Some state-owned businesses were sold, either to workers or to private entrepreneurs.

But most of these changes remained under government control, particularly any large investments of capital, whether from the Chinese state banks or from outside China. Such strict controls over capital ran counter to the prevailing Washington Consensus—that notion that capital should be permitted to flow freely, both within and between nations.

China, as a nation, prospered under this regime. Its economy has grown rapidly, to become the second largest in the world. Four hundred million people have been lifted out of extreme poverty, an accomplishment unprecedented in all of human history.

Other challenges to the Washington Consensus have emerged, especially since the 1997 financial crisis that began in Asia and spread elsewhere. In retrospect, the relatively harsh conditions demanded by the International Monetary Fund for emergency assistance in that crisis are now seen to have made recovery more difficult than it otherwise would likely have been. Since then, throughout the developing world, nations have increased their international reserves and put more controls in place over the flow of foreign capital.

In other respects, developing countries have introduced different approaches that seem to have produced better results during the first decade of the twenty-first century than earlier. Rather than depending on market forces to allocate national resources, more and more developing nations are directing resources to areas of perceived need. Some approaches involve direct government investment, often through state-controlled banks; others involve direct or indirect subsidies; and still others address infrastructure needed by particular sectors.

In the past decade, Mexico and Brazil have introduced transfer schemes targeted to poor households, in which transfer payments to poor families are conditioned on families keeping their children in school or meeting other conditions. Inequality among their populations has begun to decrease. China has turned some attention toward addressing growing income inequality, particularly toward developing a retirement scheme for an aging population comprising fewer workers and more retirees. More attention is being paid to several aspects of the "social contract" between governments and their citizens. But the trends have not yet reversed. Incomes for the very wealthy are growing faster than for any other group (Stiglitz 2015).

Promising changes are taking place in Africa as well. Steven Radelet, in *Emerging Africa: How 17 Countries Are Leading the Way* (2010), discusses five ways in which these leading nations have changed that have allowed them to raise incomes while reducing poverty and inequality:

1. Democratization and increased accountability of elected governments, especially when compared to the "big man" governments that prevailed earlier; since 1989, twenty-five African nations have moved to democratically elected governments.
2. Shifts toward more sensible economic policies: careful budgeting and targeting of public expenditures, curtailing of military expenses, and caution regarding external capital flows and international indebtedness.
3. Ending of the debt crisis and freeing of resources to promote education and healthcare, often with cooperation and assistance from both public and private overseas partners.
4. Spreading of new technologies, particularly cell phones and the Internet, that are essential to marketing agricultural and other products, distance education, and healthcare.
5. The emergence of a new generation of political, economic, and social leaders (the "cheetah generation"), many of whom are educated abroad.

Unfortunately, the political climate in the United States has hampered its move away from the Washington Consensus. See Figure 11.4, below.

Figure 11.4 Poverty and Inequality Trends in the United States

In his 2014 book *Capital,* French economist Thomas Piketty documents that the ownership, inheritance, and favorable taxation of property and other capital investments contribute to increasing inequality. He looks at all available data from about twenty countries, especially France, Britain, and the United States, going back nearly 300 years. With the exception of the mid–twentieth century, income from capital has nearly always exceeded that for wages, and has been a major source of continuing high inequity.

Poverty in the United States declined from the 1940s through the mid-1970s, largely as a result of policy changes begun under Franklin D. Roosevelt's New Deal. Changes included the creation of Social Security; the GI Education Bill for World War II veterans; support for strong labor unions; Medicare; food and housing assistance programs; assurance of civil rights; minimum wages and overtime bonuses; progressive income and estate taxes; and insured, but regulated, financial institutions. Workers shared in the gains from increasing productivity.

Over this period, inequality in the United States decreased dramatically. In 1928, the top 1 percent of US households garnered 23 percent of the nation's income. During the mid-1970s, their share was only 9 percent, as the income shares of every other sector had increased.

Beginning in the mid-1970s, and at least partly in response to increasing global competition, business began to organize itself to reshape the US political economy, in a domestic version of the Washington Consensus. In 1971, there were 145 businesses represented by registered lobbyists in Washington, D.C.; by 1982, there were 2,445, and the number continues to climb. They have persuaded Congress to lower taxes on corporations and wealthy individuals—especially for capital gains; business regulations were reduced, leading to riskier financial activities; and new rules made it easier to block union organizing. Concurrently, political civility declined, and gerrymandering of election districts protected incumbents (Packer 2011).

Over the next generation, business managers and owners captured nearly all the gains from increasing productivity. Compensation for workers grew very slowly or not all, while compensation for top management grew exponentially. The ratio of median income for CEOs compared to median income for workers grew from about 35 to 1 in the mid-1970s to 295 to 1 since 2010. The share of national income going to the top 1 percent climbed back to its 1928 peak (Stiglitz 2015).

Since the 1980s, each successive recession has required a longer recovery period. Since the Great Recession of 2008, many fear that employment will never return to its pre-recession level. Claims that lower taxes for the wealthy and austerity in public spending would lead to economic recovery and growth are not supported by the record of the past decade (Stiglitz 2015).

From about 1980 until 2007, the inevitable consequences of this skewing of national income were postponed by middle-class families maintaining their consumption and market demand through three coping mechanisms: more

(continues)

Figure 11.4 continued

two-income families, longer working hours, and increased debt, through both credit cards and repeated borrowing against the inflated values of homes. When the housing bubble collapsed in 2007–2008, the ensuing recession was tragic. Millions of families lost their jobs and many lost their homes. The crisis was made much worse by the gambling on these substandard mortgages by financial institutions that bundled and sold them around the world. Most of the bigger financial institutions were rescued from their folly; most families were not.

Other factors have contributed to increasing inequality. Educational achievement has declined. The United States is near the bottom of developed countries in high school completion rates and in reading and math testing. Although college enrollment is up, so is the noncompletion rate. Opportunities for good jobs with decent pay have diminished. Stability has declined for many families. Many are burdened with heavy debts, often related to healthcare emergencies or educational efforts. Noted sociologist Robert Putnam details this diminishing opportunity for low- and moderate-income families in *Our Kids: The American Dream in Crisis* (2015). The hope is fading for many that anyone, regardless of their beginnings, can work hard and achieve success.

Few recognized that the rapid shift of income to the wealthy would lead to a greatly weakened economy. Wealthy families spend less of their income in ways that create market demand and associated employment. But they have been able to maintain their political power, which has made the necessary reforms more difficult. It remains to be seen whether the hard-pressed middle class can recover their political clout, and change the rules of the game, to help regain their former share of economic returns.

Top 1 Percent Share of US Total Income, 1913–2012

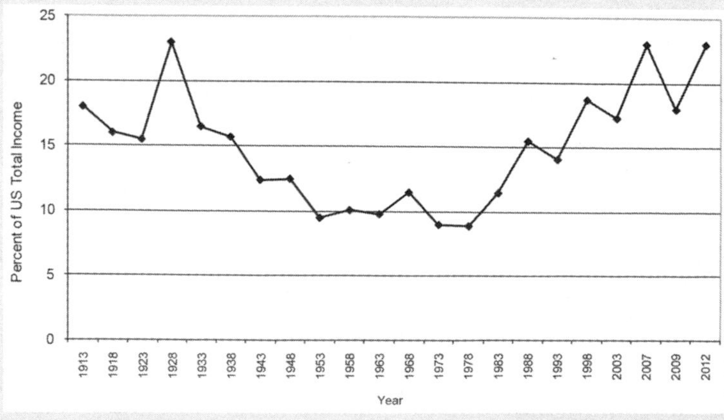

Source: Saez (2013).

The Framework for Sustainable Development

The discussion in this chapter until this point, as in the two previous chapters of Part 2, on the global economy, has been framed primarily in economic terms: the growth of each nation's and the world's economic activity, and its allocation. A brief review of hunger and scattered reference to other aspects of development have hinted that development is a much broader topic. In the remainder of this chapter, let us try to link the preceding discussion to several emerging themes of sustainable development.

During the 1970s, widespread concern developed that human economic activity must come to terms with Earth's carrying capacity in ways that did not compromise the ability of future generations to meet their own needs. By around 2000, formulations of sustainable development also began to include phrases such as "social development" or "social inclusion."

This threefold definition of sustainable development—economic growth, environmental sustainability, and social inclusion—was embodied (if not named) in the eight Millennium Development Goals (MDGs) adopted by the United Nations in 2000, to be achieved by 2015:

1. Eradicate extreme poverty.
2. Achieve universal primary education.
3. Promote gender equality and empower women.
4. Reduce child mortality.
5. Improve maternal health.
6. Combat HIV/AIDS, malaria, and other diseases.
7. Ensure environmental sustainability.
8. Undertake a global partnership for development.

These goals were refined into twenty-one specific, quantified targets, with approximately sixty detailed indicators. Only one MDG target was fully achieved: "Halve, between 1990 and 2015, the proportion of people whose income is less than $1 a day" (later amended to $1.25 and, going forward, $1.90 a day). But considerable progress was made on nearly all the goals (UN 2015a).

Encouraged by the significant progress toward the Millennium Development Goals, in September 2015 the United Nations adopted bolder, more comprehensive Sustainable Development Goals (SDGs), to be achieved by 2030, more fully described in Chapter 14 (UN 2015c).

Selected Policy Issues

The substance of several of the seventeen new Sustainable Development Goals is taken up in various chapters of this book. But several of the newly stated goals seem especially relevant to this discussion.

Goals 1 & 2: No Poverty, End Hunger

While extreme poverty has been cut by more than half since 1990, over 800 million people still live on less than $1.90 a day. About the same number (not always the same persons) are still hungry. Including these, roughly half of all people in developing nations live on the equivalent of $3.10 per day or less. Global unemployment hovers around 200 million workers. For most of these, an escape from poverty and hunger will come from access to better education and a decent job for at least some members of each family.

Goal 4: Quality Education

Investments in basic education complement those in healthcare and improved nutrition, and contribute to payoffs in both developing and industrialized nations. Better education for youth, especially girls, leads to improved health awareness and practices for their families on a lifelong basis. In addition to completing universal access to primary education, greater efforts and global assistance are necessary to expand secondary education and lifelong learning opportunities. Improved cognitive and other skills improve productivity, enable better management of resources, permit access to new technologies, and (usually) result in higher incomes. In an upward spiral, higher incomes enable families to invest even more in human capital—more education and better healthcare for their (usually fewer) children.

These investments should also enhance participation in democracy. Although it seems questionable at times in the face of entrenched interests, widespread participation in political as well as economic activity over time reduces the likelihood of enacting bad policies and permits their earlier correction (Birdsall, Pinckney, and Sabot 1996).

Goal 8: Decent Work, Economic Growth, and Infrastructure

Even in the face of environmental constraints, the UN estimates that nearly 500 million additional jobs will be needed for currently unemployed workers and new entrants into the labor market between 2016 and 2030 (UN 2015c). Education, healthcare and increased food production, as noted earlier, all call for more good jobs. Building more adequate infrastructure (transportation, communication, finance and credit—especially for small businesses), plus development of renewable energy and other measures to reduce carbon emissions, could employ millions of these current and new job seekers. More stable income to low-income families nearly always has a multiplier effect on local economies, because these families usually spend nearly all their income.

Goal 10: Reduced Inequalities

The Sustainable Development Goal of "reducing inequality" had no counterpart in the Millennium Development Goals, although it has been hinted at in discussions of social inclusion. Even in the face of reductions in extreme poverty, about 75 percent of households in developing countries today live in countries where income is more unequally distributed than it was in the 1990s (UN 2015c). A very high proportion of the gains from economic growth in these nations over this period have accrued to a few wealthy parties, parallel to the outcome in more wealthy countries, notably the United States. Gains from increased productivity have been captured by business owners and especially by managers. Millions of new jobs in this era have paid so little that even people with full-time jobs have not escaped the ravages of poverty. Undue political power has shaped the rules of each nation's economy and the global economy to the benefit of a very small sector—usually fewer than the upper quintile, or even fewer than the top 5 percent in many instances.

Economic policies that would reduce both poverty and inequity are known, and used in some nations, both rich and poor. Some of these policies set the rules for markets and investments, based on fairness and transparency—beginning with financial firms. In addition to a credit infrastructure that serves small and new businesses, government bailouts for excessive risk-taking by banks and other financial firms should be curbed. In a global economy, fair trade rules are crucial for both developing countries and the environment (Stiglitz 2015).

Other economic policies, coupled with progressive tax systems that are enforced, should promote social investments in people, including especially healthcare and education. They should also undergird social protection networks, focused on children, the elderly, the disabled, and those often discriminated against.

Goal 16: Peaceful and Inclusive Societies, Justice, and Accountable Institutions

The framework for sustainable development outlined earlier—economic development, social inclusion, and environmental sustainability—will not be realized without the successful inclusion of a fourth dimension: good governance. Just as some actors in the marketplace can take advantage of their economic power, they and other powerful political actors can sway policies to their own self-interest, whether at the local, national, or international level. Meanwhile, poor people, whose well-being is the strongest evidence of whether policies are effective, often lack political access or clout.

Jeffrey Sachs (2015), a key figure in developing the Sustainable Development Goals, names four elements of good governance:

1. *Accountability*. Regardless of the economic or political organization, both governments and businesses must be accountable for their actions.
2. *Transparency*. With few exceptions, decisions and policies set by both public officials and private entities must be open, to ensure accountability.

3. *Participation.* Regardless the system, citizens and stakeholders need access to, and must take responsibility for, participation in shaping and enforcing policies of government and business entities.

4. *Responsibility.* Individuals, businesses, and governments have a responsibility not to harm others, including through pollution. This might be framed as the "do no harm" or "polluter pays" principle.

Bureaucratic Integrity and Competence

As the emphasis continues to shift from a structural approach to development toward more-focused goals in overcoming poverty and inequality, the role of public officials becomes even more crucial. Administrative skills and basic integrity rise in importance. Political courage, backed by a well-informed citizenry, is necessary to undertake new policies or programs, or end those that are not working, especially if changes challenge entrenched interests.

Conclusion

Extreme poverty and very low incomes—the lack of resources or income to command basic necessities—is the condition of nearly one-third of the world's population, largely in poor nations, even after significant gains in recent decades. Relative poverty still affects too many in the United States and other developed countries.

Poor countries need economic growth to overcome poverty, but other conditions are critical everywhere. Relatively egalitarian distribution of national income among and within households matters greatly. Gains must be sustainable. Decisionmaking must be broadly shared. Integrity and competence of public officials, backed by an educated and well-informed citizenry, is crucial.

Creating good jobs or business opportunities is the biggest single challenge for this generation. Many of the economic and policy tools to generate more equitable growth have been successfully demonstrated in recent decades, particularly in East and Southeast Asia. Very recent developments in some African countries look promising. Meanwhile, some of the worst effects of poverty have been, and should continue to be, offset by public and private interventions. Infant mortality and overall hunger have declined, and literacy and longevity have increased in many instances, even in the face of continued poverty.

Adapting these tools and programs to particular circumstances is of utmost concern to everyone. In an increasingly global economy, the well-being and security of each person or community or nation is inescapably linked to that of every other. All the world's nations have adopted the bold new Sustainable Development Goals. Reaching these goals will require a large measure of the one ingredient that seems in shortest supply: the political will to do so.

Discussion Questions

1. Are you more inclined to measure poverty in terms of absolute income, income distribution, or the capacity to reach more specific objectives such as the Sustainable Development Goals?
2. What would you consider a reasonable goal for the ratio between the top and bottom income groups within an economy? Within a business firm? What policies would be necessary to move toward these goals?
3. To what extent should government policies undertake or encourage the redistribution of national, or global, income? Using what mechanisms?
4. Which antipoverty or inequity-reducing policies would you give highest priority? What might be your role in changing or maintaining these policies?
5. Why is the United States falling behind Canada, Japan, and many European countries in educational attainment and healthcare?
6. How was your family affected by the Great Depression? Have you recovered from its effects by now?
7. Are you optimistic that poverty and inequality can be reduced or overcome? Do you think that the well-being of everyone is inescapably linked, and that the principal missing ingredient in overcoming hunger is political will?

Suggested Readings

Bread for the World Institute (2015) *Annual Report on the State of World Hunger.* Washington, DC.

Congressional Budget Office (2011) *Trends in the Distribution of Household Income Between 1979 and 2007.* Washington, DC. www.cbo.gov.

Food and Agriculture Organization (2015) *The State of Food Insecurity in the World.* www.fao.org.

Milanovic, Branko (2006) "Global Income Inequality: What It Is and Why It Matters?" DESA Working Paper no. 26. Washington, DC: World Bank.

Picketty, Thomas (2014) *Capital in the Twenty-First Century.* Cambridge: Harvard University Press.

Putnam, Robert D. (2015) *Our Kids: The American Dream in Crisis.* New York: Simon and Schuster.

Radelet, Steven (2010) *Emerging Africa: How 17 Countries Are Leading the Way.* Washington, DC: Center for Global Development.

Reich, Robert B. (2010) *Aftershock: The Next Economy and America's Future.* New York: Knopf.

Sachs, Jeffrey (2015) *The Age of Sustainable Development.* New York: Columbia University Press.
Stiglitz, Joseph E. (2012) *The Price of Inequality: How Today's Divided Society Endangers Our Future.* New York: Norton.
——— (2015) *The Great Divide: Unequal Societies and What We Can Do About Them.* New York: Norton.
United Nations (2015) *The Millennium Development Goals Report.* New York www.unmillenniumproject.org.
——— (2015) *2015 Time for Global Action, for People and Planet.* New York www.un.org.
United Nations Development Programme (2014) *Human Development Report.* www.undp.org.
World Bank (annual) *World Development Report.* Washington, DC.
——— (2015) *World Development Indicators 2015.* Washington, DC. http://data.worldbank.org.

12

Challenges of Population Growth and Migration

Ellen Percy Kraly, Caroline Anderson, Fiona Mulligan, and Kristen Weymouth

COMING TO GRIPS WITH THE IMPLICATIONS OF CURRENT POPULATION trends is an extremely important dimension of global studies. The process is neither easy nor comforting, because a significant population increase is an inevitable characteristic of the global landscape in the first fifty years of the twenty-first century. It is critical that students interested in global issues should appreciate both the causes of population growth and the consequences of population change for society and the environment. Such an appreciation will serve in developing appropriate and effective responses to population-related problems emerging globally, regionally, and locally.

This chapter addresses the interconnections among population change, environmental issues, and social, economic, and political change in both developing and developed regions of the world. Because population growth has momentum that cannot be quickly altered, it is important to begin by considering fundamental principles of population or demographic analysis, and to place recent global and regional population trends in historical perspective. Divergent philosophical and scientific perspectives on the relationships among population, society, and environment have been applied to past and current patterns of population growth, and also influence visions of the future. Debates on the implications of current growth have also influenced discussions about routes for population policy.

Principles and Trends

Demographic Concepts and Analysis

Demography is the study of population change and characteristics. A population can change in size and composition as a result of the interplay of three demographic processes: fertility, mortality, and migration. These components of change constitute the following equation for population change (P) between two points in time:

P = (+) births (–) deaths (+) in-migration (–) out-migration

On the global level, the world's population grows as the result of the relative balance between births and deaths, often called natural increase. The US population is currently increasing at about 0.7 percent per year; natural increase accounts for about two-thirds, and net international migration constitutes about one-third, of this relatively low level of population growth.

Many people seeking routes to sustainable development advocate a cessation of population growth, often referred to as zero population growth. When viewed from a short-term perspective, zero population growth means simply balancing the components of the population equation to yield zero change in population size during a period of time. In a long-term perspective, however, population scientists usually consider zero population growth by examining a particular form of a zero-growth population: the stationary population, one in which constant patterns of childbearing interact with constant mortality and migration to yield zero population change. In such a case, fertility is considered "replacement" fertility, because one generation of parents is just replacing itself in the next generation. In low-mortality countries, replacement-level fertility can be measured by the total fertility rate, and is approximately 2.1 births per woman to achieve a stationary population over the long term.

It takes a relatively long time, perhaps three generations after replacement fertility has been achieved, for a population to cease growing on a yearly basis. Large groups of persons of childbearing age, reflecting earlier eras of high fertility, result in large numbers of births even with replacement-level fertility. Hence an excess of births over deaths occurs until these "age structure" effects work themselves out of the population. This is known as the "momentum" of population growth. Using medium assumptions of future population growth, the United Nations Population Division estimates that by 2030, world population levels will grow to 8.5 billion, and projects a global population of up to 9.7 billion by 2050, an increase due in part to the momentum of population growth in the developing world (UNPD 2015).

Age structure is an important social demographic characteristic of a population. Both the very young and the very old in a population must be supported by persons in the working-age groups. The proportions of persons in different age groups in a population are depicted in a *population pyramid*. Figure 12.1 shows population pyramids for two countries, the Netherlands and Niger, as estimated by the United Nations Population Division for 2015. The pyramid for Niger reveals a youthful population, with well more than one-third under ten years of age (37.3 percent). This reflects high fertility. In the Netherlands, a low-fertility country, only about 11 percent of the population is under ten years of age. At the other end of the age spectrum, only 2.6 percent of the population of Niger is over the age of sixty-five years, compared to 18.2 percent of the population of the Netherlands (UNPD 2015). Migration plays a large role in the Netherlands' population composition and age structure, with 11.7 percent of the total population composed of foreign-born persons as estimated by the UN for 2013, compared to 0.7 percent for Niger in the same year (UNPD 2013a). These two age pyramids illustrate the history of past levels in fertility and migration as well as the different demands on society to support the young and the old.

Historical and Contemporary Trends in Population Growth

At mid-2015, the world's population was estimated at 7.3 billion and to be increasing at a rate of approximately 1.2 percent per year (UNPD 2015). These data represent a cross-sectional perspective on population characteristics—a snapshot that fails to capture the varying pace of population change worldwide and regionally. Over most of human history, populations have increased insignificantly or at very low annual rates of growth, with local populations being checked by disease, war, and unstable food supplies. Between the sixteenth and eighteenth centuries, population growth appeared to become more sustained as a result of changes in the social and economic environment: improved sanitation, more consistent food distribution, improved personal hygiene and clothing, political stability, and the like.

The world's population probably did not reach its first billion until just after 1800. But accelerating population growth during the nineteenth century dramatically reduced the length of time by which the next billion was added. According to the United Nations (UNDESIPA 1995; UNPD 2015), world population reached

- 1 billion in 1804
- 2 billion in 1927 (123 years later)
- 3 billion in 1960 (33 years later)
- 4 billion in 1974 (14 years later)
- 5 billion in 1987 (13 years later)
- 6 billion in 1999 (12 years later)
- 6.9 billion in 2010 (11 years later)
- 7.3 billion in 2015 (5 years later)

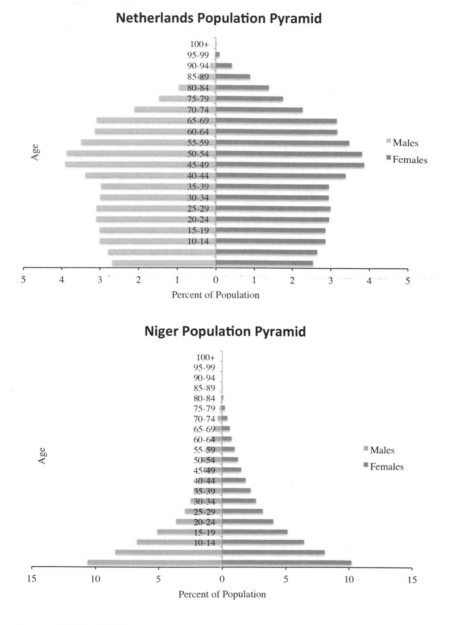

Figure 12.1 Population Pyramids for the Netherlands and Niger, 2014

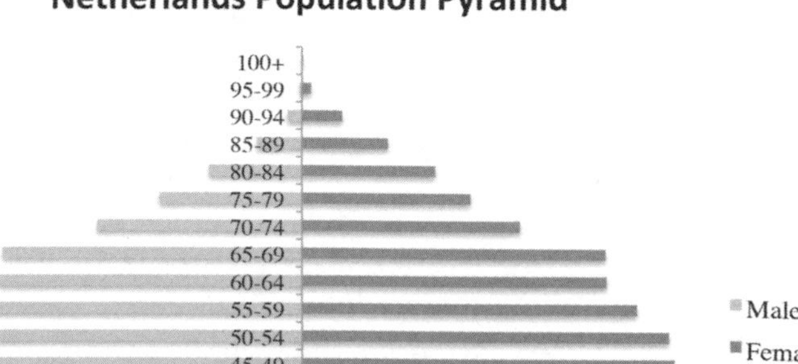

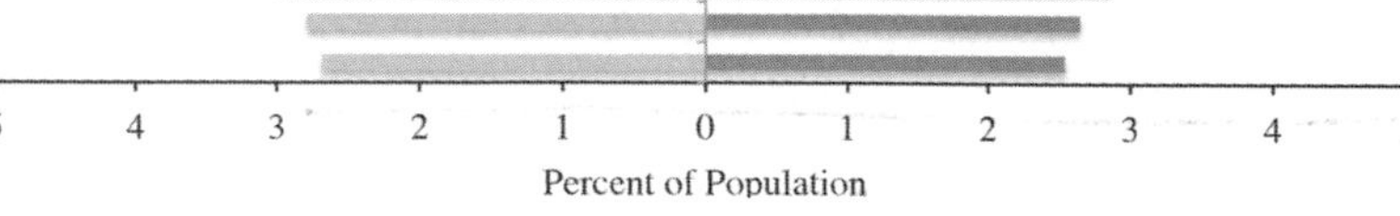

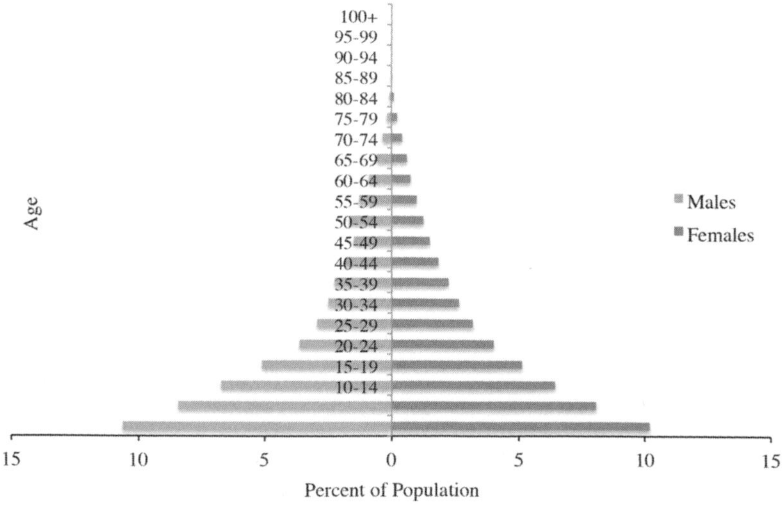

Source: UNPD (2015).

Rapid population growth occurred on a global scale during the second half of the twentieth century. Population data for years since 1955 are shown in Figure 12.2. Between 1955 and 2015, the world's total population more than doubled, increasing from 2.76 billion to 7.35 billion. The difference in height of the bars in the figure reveals the momentum of population growth that results in continued additions to the world's population, albeit in decreasing numbers. To illustrate, between 1985 and 1990, approximately 91 million persons were added to the world's population each year; between 2010 and 2015, the annual increase was estimated at 84 million (UNPD 2015), or 7 million persons less than annual increases twenty-five years before.

It is important to note, however, that despite these large additions to the world's population, the rate of population growth is *decreasing*. The average annual rate of global population growth reached an all-time high, of about 2.2 percent, between 1962 and 1964. Since that time, the pace of growth of the world's population has decreased to the current rate of approximately 1.2 percent per year (UNPD 2015).

Patterns of population growth differ significantly between more- and less-developed regions of the world. Table 12.1 provides greater geographic detail and summarizes population size and distribution for major regions of the world for selected years since 1955. Dramatic shifts in the geography of

Figure 12.2 World Population for Development Categories, 1955–2015

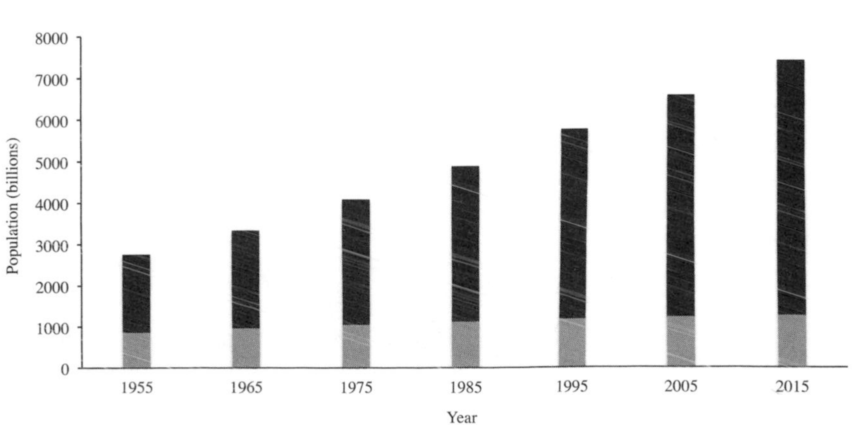

Source: UNPD (2015).

world population have occurred during the past five decades and are expected to continue well into the future. In 1955, over two-thirds of the world's population was located in less-developed countries; by 2015, this proportion had increased to 83 percent, over four-fifths. Asian countries make up nearly 60 percent of the world's population; nearly one-fifth, 1.376 million or 18.7 percent, of the global village live in China, and another 1.311 million or 17.8 percent live in India (data not shown in Table 12.1). Africa's share has increased from 9.2 percent in 1955 to over 16 percent of the world's current population. European populations constitute 10 percent of the world's population, a decline from 21 percent in 1955. Western Hemisphere regions—North America, Latin America, and the Caribbean—include approximately 14 percent of the world's population as of 2015.

Population growth is fueled by levels of fertility, mortality, and net migration. The rapid population growth that occurred in the post–World War II era reflected significant declines in mortality that resulted in large part from public health advances and the transfer of medical technology from more- to less-developed countries.

The total fertility rate measures the average number of births per woman of childbearing age and is a strong indicator of overall population growth. In the period 2010–2015, based on a United Nations Population Division analysis of available national measures, the total fertility rate for the world as a whole is estimated at 2.51 births per woman, representing a significant decline from 4.48 in 1970–1975. Fertility in more-developed countries has been below replacement for some time and is estimated at 1.67 births per woman. In less-developed countries, the rate has dropped from 5.42 in 1970–1975 to 2.65 in 2010–2015. Much of this decline is weighted by the aggressive fertility control campaign in China and by significant declines in fertility throughout Southeast Asia and in Latin America. Total fertility in India has also declined, from 5.26 in 1970–1975 to 2.65 for 2010–2015. Fertility in least-developed countries, including many in sub-Saharan Africa, has declined in past decades, yet still remains high, at 4.27 births per woman, well above replacement (UNPD 2015). Figure 12.3 provides a cartographic view of levels of fertility for countries of the world as estimated by the UN for 2010–2015.

Perspectives on Population Growth

Reflections on the relationship between population and society can be found in the early history of many cultures. In early Greece, Plato wrote about the need for balance between the size of the city and its resource base; in China, Confucianism emphasized the social and economic advantages of large families. Concern about the implications of population growth for social progress became a focus of social theory in the nineteenth century and continues in contemporary debates on the global effects of current levels of population growth.

Table 12.1 Population of More- and Less-Developed Countries Compared to World and Geographic Regions, 1955–2015

	1955	1965	1975	1985	1995	2005	2015
Population (millions)							
World	2,758	3,322	4,061	4,853	5,735	6,520	7,349
More-developed countries	863	966	1,047	1,114	1,170	1,209	1,251
Less-developed countries	1,895	2,357	3,014	3,739	4,565	5,311	6,098
Africa	254	322	416	550	720	920	1,186
Asia	1,534	1,875	2,378	2,897	3,475	3,945	4,393
Europe	577	635	677	708	728	729	738
Latin America and Caribbean	193	254	326	406	487	564	634
Northern America	187	219	242	267	296	329	358
Oceania	14	18	21	25	29	33	39
Percentage of world population							
World	100.0	100.0	100.0	100.0	100.0	100.0	100.0
More-developed countries	31.3	29.1	25.8	22.9	20.4	18.5	17.0
Less-developed countries	68.7	70.9	74.2	77.1	79.6	81.5	83.0
Africa	9.2	9.7	10.3	11.3	12.6	14.1	16.1
Asia	55.6	56.4	58.6	59.7	60.6	60.5	59.8
Europe	20.9	19.1	16.7	14.6	12.7	11.2	10.0
Latin America and Caribbean	7.0	7.6	8.0	8.4	8.5	8.6	8.6
Northern America	6.8	6.6	6.0	5.5	5.2	5.0	4.9
Oceania	0.5	0.5	0.5	0.5	0.5	0.5	0.5

Source: UNPD (2015).
Note: Numbers for individual regions have been rounded.

Figure 12.3 Total Fertility Rates by Country, 2010–2015

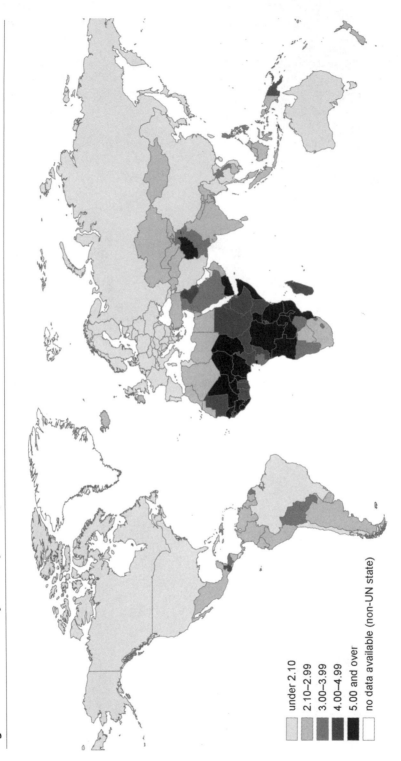

Source: UNPD (2015).

One of the most influential thinkers in the realm of population growth was Thomas Malthus, who published an essay on the principle of population in 1798 (Malthus 1826), which was significantly expanded over several popular editions. Malthus was a reactionary against the mercantilist philosophy that dominated eighteenth-century Europe and emphasized the value of large and increasing populations for economic growth and prosperity. Malthus instead argued that the inescapable human desire to reproduce would lead to starvation, poverty, and human misery if not halted by the "positive checks" of famine, war, and epidemics. Unlike today's neo-Malthusians, Malthus, a clergyman, was opposed to contraceptives as a means to limit family size and instead endorsed delayed marriage and abstinence.

Malthus's theories have permeated the population debate throughout the decades, and the two lines of thought that have traditionally dominated the arena are the *neo-Malthusian* and the *Cornucopian* perspectives. The neo-Malthusian perspective has remained much the same, while the Cornucopian perspective emphasizes the role of technological innovations and market forces, which through economics will manage the use of natural resources. This would allow for population growth to actually solve global problems through increased economic productivity and capacity for economic progress.

A third and increasingly referenced perspective on population growth requires a focus on the *structural dimensions* of social change, including processes such as population displacement, health and disease, food security, and environmental issues as outcomes of broader social and economic structural processes and institutions. Population growth, in particular high fertility, thus becomes more of a consequence than a cause of slow economic development and restricted social and economic opportunities. In addition, there is increasing attention to the relationships among government, leadership and authority structures, and population processes on both the local and the global scale. Moreover, in spite of, or perhaps because of, processes of globalization addressed by many chapters in this volume, nation-states continue to exercise authority in areas of international migration, trade and employment, political enfranchisement, and human rights (Bailey 2005).

Although these perspectives might initially appear incongruent, there are a number of common themes that connect all models of thought, mostly regarding ways in which to address the issue of population expansion. Thus the reduction of poverty, the improvement of life choices and the status of women, the increasing sustainability of food production, the improvement in water quality, and other aspects of social welfare all become strategies for reducing population growth. The reduction of barriers to effective fertility regulation methods is consistently associated with rapid fertility decline (Campbell, Prata, and Potts 2009). Similarly, there is an emerging recognition that slowing and ultimately ceasing world and regional population growth will eventually improve standards of living, stabilize food supplies, and halt environmental degradation (UNDP 2001; National Research Council 1986).

Coupled with these perspectives and theories of population growth are models of historically based expectations about the trajectory of population growth. The *demographic transition* model relies heavily upon the differences between developed and developing nations; it was initially advanced to describe population growth patterns in Europe and North America in the nineteenth and early twentieth centuries. It predicts that as societies undergo industrialization and urbanization, death rates will fall, followed by a lag of declining fertility, during which population growth continues to occur until norms and values shift from large-family to small-family ideals. Immigration contributes to diversity within society through the mixing of people of religions, cultures, and ethnic origins as well as educational levels and occupations. This transition stage is already apparent among developed countries that began the demographic transitions early.

The demographic transition model has been widely criticized and revised, particularly in recognition of the fact that it depends on the experiences of non-Western societies mirroring or converging with those of Europe and North America. Revisions allow for a clearer understanding of the ways in which family size is influenced by cultural beliefs and gender, particularly educational opportunities for girls and young women. Ron Lesthaeghe (2010) argues for an additional demographic model known as the *second demographic transition*. Once nations achieve low levels of fertility and mortality in the first demographic transition, they are able to achieve a second transition that involves a change in values that are often characterized by secularization, egalitarianism, and individuality. These changes have led to postponement of marriage and fertility, which influences declines in overall levels of fertility and contributes to the declining rate of population growth. However, it is important to note the differences within particular nations and within particular cultures that would affect socioeconomic status and fertility levels, and there may not be one demographic transition model that is universally applicable.

Expectations About Future Population Growth

Theories of population change guide analyses of future population growth, usually in the form of population projections. Most demographers are quick to state that population projections are not predictions but rather represent a calculation of future population size based on a set of assumptions or variants. Shown in Figure 12.4 are population estimates and projections prepared by the United Nations Population Division in its most recent projection series, for 1950–2050 (UNPD 2015). The world totals reflect the sum of projections conducted separately for each of the countries in the United Nations; the "fan" of population figures represents the four projection variants for the projection period 2010–2050. These variants reflect different assumptions about the pace and pattern of fertility change and also the severity and geographic extent of the HIV/AIDS epidemic.

The approach by the UN to modeling future population growth has changed to represent uncertainties in the trajectory of fertility decline among high-fertility countries and also the patterns of fertility increase among very low-fertility countries. The medium-fertility projection prepared by the United Nations Population Division for the 2015 revision represents a probabilistic-model fertility decline based upon past trends. Over the long run (through 2100), global fertility moves to just below replacement level fertility, a total fertility rate of 2.0 with assumed mortality decline. In the high-fertility projection, fertility follows a path of 0.5 children *above* that projected for each country in the medium variant; in the low variant, fertility is projected at a level of 0.5 children *below* that in the medium variant. The constant-fertility variant represents the status quo by assuming that fertility levels for 2010–2015 are maintained throughout the projection period. These

Figure 12.4 Projected World Population by UN Variants, 1955–2050

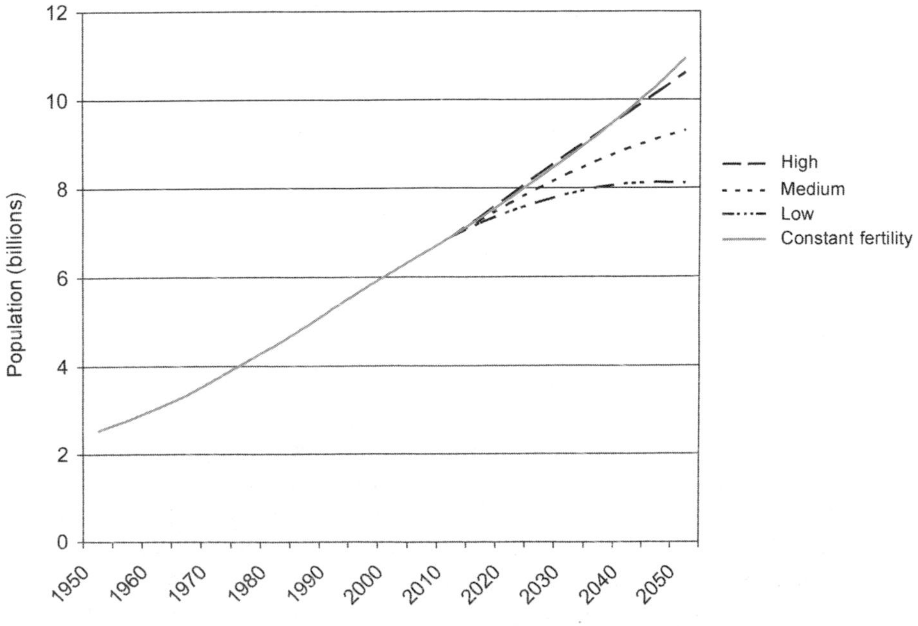

Source: UNPD (2015).

two variants provide useful points of comparison in depicting the extremes of fertility (un)likelihoods. In all four projections, mortality levels decline, although at a slower pace in those countries where mortality is already low. In those countries in which the HIV/AIDS epidemic is severe, a slower pace of mortality decline is assumed. While the projection series as a whole does not demand precise convergence among countries in terms of fertility and mortality, the results can be considered within the theoretical context of the demographic transition model. It is important to note, however, that greater variation among countries in pattern and pace of change in demographic rates is characteristic of these most recent UN projections, and significantly, fertility settles at *below* replacement fertility (2.0) in 2095–2100 (UNPD 2015).

The high-fertility variant results in growth in world population from 7.3 to 10.8 billion between 2015 and 2050, an increase of 3.6 billion, or almost 50 percent. The low-fertility variant projects an increase to 8.7 billion by 2050, an increase of well above 1 billion, or about 20 percent, over the 2010 population. Thus, even with a declining trajectory of fertility, the world's population will continue to grow through midcentury as a result of the momentum of population growth. The medium variant results in an increase to 9.7 billion by 2050, an increase of about 2.5 billion, or 34 percent, over the current population (UNPD 2015).

The projections also reveal the future impact of the HIV/AIDS epidemic. The 2012 revision of the UN's *World Population Prospects* (UNPD 2013b) identified thirty-nine countries as being most severely affected by the disease—that is, as having a prevalence of HIV/AIDS of more than 1 percent in recent years; it is important to note that this number represents a decrease from the forty-eight countries considered in the 2010 UN projection. Of the countries identified as most severely impacted by the disease, thirty-two are in Africa, one is in Asia, and six are in Latin America and the Caribbean (UNPD 2013b). Among highly affected countries in southern Africa, the demographic impact has been felt in overall decreases in life expectancy at birth, declining from sixty-two years to fifty-two between 1995 and 2005. This patterns seems to have been reversed in the most recent decade with life expectancy increase to fifty-seven years by 2015. Importantly, the prevalence of HIV/AIDS has begun to decline in recent years with the expanding access to antiretroviral therapy and increased efforts to control the further spread of HIV (UNPD 2015).

Shifts in the geographic distribution of the world's population are evident in all of the projections, as seen in Table 12.2. Referring to the medium-variant projection, the population in African countries, primarily in sub-Saharan regions, will increase from 16.1 percent in 2015 to nearly 25.5 percent of the world's population by 2050, and the population of Europe is expected to decline from just 10.0 percent to 7.3 percent of the world's population. Countries in North America and Latin America and the Caribbean (com-

Table 12.2 Projections of World Population for More- and Less-Developed Countries and for Geographic Regions, 2015 vs. 2050

	2015	Low Fertility, 2050	Medium Fertility, 2050	High Fertility, 2050	Constant Fertility, 2050	Instant Replacement Fertility, 2050
Population (millions)						
World	7,349	8,710	9,725	10,801	10,872	9,279
More-developed countries	1,251	1,162	1,286	1,416	1,260	1,382
Less-developed countries	6,098	7,548	8,439	9,385	9,612	7,898
Africa	1,186	2,236	2,478	2,731	3,170	1,732
Asia	4,393	4,698	5,267	5,873	5,676	5,444
Europe	738	638	707	779	687	769
Latin America and Caribbean	634	696	784	879	848	827
North America	358	391	433	477	430	452
Oceania	39	51	57	62	61	56
Percentage of world population						
World	100.0	100.0	100.0	100.0	100.0	100.0
More-developed countries	17.0	13.3	13.2	13.1	11.6	14.9
Less-developed countries	83.0	86.7	86.8	86.9	88.4	85.1
Africa	16.1	25.7	25.5	25.3	29.2	18.7
Asia	59.8	53.9	54.2	54.4	52.2	51.0
Europe	10.0	7.3	7.3	7.2	6.3	8.1
Latin America and Caribbean	8.6	8.0	8.1	8.1	7.8	7.4
North America	4.9	4.5	4.5	4.4	4.0	4.1
Oceania	0.5	0.6	0.6	0.6	0.6	0.5

Source: UNPD (2015).
Note: Numbers for individual regions have been rounded.

bined) will decrease by about 1 percent in the region's share of world population. Asian countries will continue to hold the largest share of the world's population, although decreasing from over 60 percent in 2015 to approximately 54 percent by 2050. It is important to consider two Asian countries in particular, China and India, whose population policies are considered later in this chapter. The population of China is projected to peak in size at 1.42 billion in 2030 then a decrease to 1.35 billion by 2050; in contrast, India's population is projected to continue to increase to 1.71 billion by 2050, thus overtaking China as the largest national population in the world and following a different trajectory of growth (data not shown in Table 12.2). Thus we can expect significant shifts in the world geography of population based on these projections (UNPD 2015).

Social and Environmental Dimensions of Geographic Mobility

As well as influencing population change, the movement of persons within and among countries is both a cause and a consequence of social, economic, political, and environmental factors. Geographic mobility is the general concept covering all types of human population movements. Migration is generally considered to refer to moves that are permanent or longer-term; internal migration within a country is distinguished from international population movements; international migration into a country is immigration, and international migration out of a country is emigration. Reasons for moving, such as labor migration, refugee migration, and seasonal migration, are often included in migration concepts. Internal and international population movements are processes that are increasingly linked through the geographic and social dimensions of global economic development.

Internal Migration and Urbanization

A corollary of the demographic transition model is growth in the size of cities as well as increasing proportions of populations living in cities and metropolitan areas—that is, urbanization. The UN estimates that 54 percent of the world's population was living in urban areas in 2014; the difference between more- and less-developed countries, 78 percent versus 48 percent urban, respectively, is dramatic (UNPD 2014b). Of these developing countries, certain cities have some of the largest populations in the world: Delhi has 25 million people; Shanghai, 23 million; and São Paulo, Mumbai, and Mexico City, 20 million (UNPD 2014b). India, however, has over half of its population currently living in rural areas. Recent trends suggest that these mega-cities' rates of population growth are slowly declining, and that the midsize cities will absorb the majority of the future urban population growth (Aggarwal 2014).

Demographers anticipate a shift in this rural-urban balance in the very near future. Cities will grow as a result of population growth and rural-to-urban migration throughout regions of the world. By 2050, for example, the level of urbanization in more-developed countries is expected to increase to 85 percent and in less-developed countries even more steeply to 63 percent, representing a dramatic shift in patterns of residence and economic activity (UNPD 2014b). The US Census produces age-specific migration rates, with young professionals ages twenty to twenty-four moving to urban areas within the United States for housing and job-related reasons, providing implications for the reasons for migration to urban areas by age. The addition of children to families often results in relocation of households to suburbs to meet housing and lifestyle needs. Immigrants from abroad and migrants from rural areas settle in distinctive locations in urban communities. Rising income also results in urban residents seeking housing with more conveniences and space. Thus, cities worldwide undergo patterns of demographic change according to social mobility, family dynamics, and migration. It is important to note, however, that there is no universal definition of what constitutes an urban environment. The criteria for classifying an urban area differ across countries, combining different characteristics of urban areas, such as population density, presence of infrastructure, and presence of education or health services, to identify urban environments (UNPD 2014b).

The causes of urban growth have varied among regions and during different historical periods. In Western societies, urbanization has been fueled in large part by technological change in both agricultural and industrial sectors, resulting in both a push from rural communities and a pull to emerging industrial centers (Harper 1995). In developing societies, rural-to-urban migration has been driven by many factors, including increasing population density (caused by high fertility rates) in rural areas, environmental degradation from practices such as overgrazing, and the pursuit of gainful employment in urban areas. In many developed countries, the pull of employment and higher wages is so great that levels of unemployment in Western cities are very high. Evidence of underemployment is shown in the large numbers of persons, including many children, attempting to earn livelihoods in what has been called by some the informal economy—for example, street vendors, curbside entertainers, and newspaper boys and girls. Slums are also a problem in rapidly urbanizing areas in developing countries. Issues such as poor nutrition, poverty, and disease arise from poor urban infrastructure and housing conditions. Employment possibilities in urban areas, however, outweigh the unfortunate living conditions in these areas (Kumar and Sinha 2009; Mudege 2009).

Environmental degradation also contributes to out-migration from rural areas. Western regions of China, in particular, are experiencing serious environmental problems, making it difficult for people to continue to support themselves through agriculture and herding. Approximately 1.2 million migrants were displaced from fragile environments in western China between 2000 and 2005 (Tan and Guo 2009). In 2013, Typhoon Haiyan displaced over 4 million people in the Philippines, which was over 1 million more people than the displacements of those in Africa, Europe, the Americas, and Oceania combined during the same year (Yonetani 2014). Because of climate change, natural disasters are becoming more frequent each year, leaving more people homeless and without security, which influences higher levels of environmentally induced migration.

International Population Movements

One of the most visible manifestations of globalization is the increasing scale of international population movements throughout all regions of the world. Migration from the global South to the global North has been the main driver of international migration trends, but South-North and South-South migrations have reached similar scales (see de Lombaerde, Guo, and Povoa Neto 2014). According to scholars Stephen Castles, Hein de Haas and Mark Miller: "International migration is part of transnational shift that is reshaping societies and politics around the globe. The old dichotomy between migrant-sending and migrant-receiving countries is being eroded—if this dichotomy was ever valid at all. Most countries experienced both emigration and immigration. Today, migration comes in new forms" (2013: 13–14).The consequences of international population movements for both the sending and the receiving nations and communities will have significant implications for emerging global issues.

Countries in both Western and Eastern Europe have been faced with large numbers of persons seeking political asylum from both European regions as well as from geographically distant sources, including East Africa and Southeast Asia. Migration forced by conflicts in the Middle East has reached a level unseen since the displacements of World War II and seem to carry a momentum of flight. Significant labor migration flows have emerged between South and Southeast Asia and oil-producing regions of the Middle East, and throughout the Asia Pacific region. The United States has grappled with issues concerning large numbers of undocumented migrants originating from Mexico and many other source countries. Refugee migration and population displacement are spatial characteristics of political, economic, and environmental change in many regions of Africa.

Castles, de Haas, and Miller (2013) identify six "general tendencies" of contemporary international population movements that they expect to continue well into the twenty-first century. First, international population movements will involve an increasingly large number of countries, both as sending and as receiving regions, hence resulting in the globalization of migration. Second, the directions of international migrations can be expected to continue to change with Europe becoming a major region of in-migration. Third, international migration will continue to become differentiated by including a wider variety of migrants—for example, seasonal migrants as well as migrants seeking permanent resettlement. Fourth, the number of countries historically characterized by emigration that will shift to countries of immigration will increase, thus expanding the geographic reach of the migration transition. Fifth, as women throughout the world become increasingly involved in the global work force, international migration will become more feminized. Women face unique situations in their migration experience. They play a particular role in labor markets and social contexts and migrate under different conditions than do men. Women often experience discrimination and work long hours with little time off, making their migration situations particularly challenging. And sixth, without a doubt, international migration will become a more significant political issue, both on the international stage as well as in the politics of individual nations.

The significance of the scale of refugee migration and displaced populations in global population issues cannot be overstated. The international definition of a refugee is a person who, "owing to a well-founded fear of being persecuted for reasons of race, religion, nationality, membership of a particular social group or political opinion, is outside the country of his nationality, and is unable to or, owing to such fear, is unwilling to avail himself of the protection of that country" (UNHCR 2012). Refugees seek safety from war and oppression, but can also be a source of political and economic instability in border regions and countries of asylum. For instance, Afghanis seeking refuge following the US military response to the September 11, 2001, terrorist attacks faced resistance in neighboring Pakistan.

At the end of 2014, the United Nations High Commissioner for Refugees (UNHCR) identified nearly 55 million persons throughout the world who were of concern to the organization as refugees, asylees, or internally displaced persons. This level of forced population displacement is 51 percent higher than just five years earlier. Of this extraordinary number, 14 million were recognized as refugees living in asylum in other countries; the remainder were persons who were internally displaced within their own countries for complex political, economic, and environmental reasons, and persons outside their home countries living in refugee-like situations. Table 12.3 shows refugees and other persons of concern to the UNHCR by region or origin. Many refugee settlements or camps have existed for many years. Some refugees have been repatriated to their homelands—for example, Guatemalans who had sought refuge in Mexico and Muslims who had fled Myanmar (formerly Burma); others, including many Vietnamese during the 1970s and 1980s, have been permanently resettled in other countries such as Canada, Australia, and the United States; in total number, the United States accepts the most refugees for permanent resettlement. The majority of the world's refugees are women and children, whose voices are often not heard in discussions about programs to aid and resettle refugees (UNHCR 2014).

Table 12.3 Refugees and Other Persons of Concern to the UNHCR, by Geographic Region of Origin, End of 2014

	Total	Refugees	Asylum Seekers	Returned Refugees	Internally Displaced Persons	Internally Displaced Returned	Other Persons of Concern
Population (thousands)							
World	54,945	14,380	1,796	127	32,275	1,823	4,545
Africa	17,756	4,127	699	97	9,920	1,541	1,372
Asia	25,940	7,942	258	29	15,180	281	2,251
Latin America and Caribbean	3,889	1,495	580	1	1,131	0	682
Europe	6,670	353	33	0	6,044	—	241
North America	621	416	205	—	—	—	—
Oceania	70	47	23	—	—	—	—
Percentage of world population							
World	100.0	100.0	100.0	100.0	100.0	100.0	100.0
Africa	32.3	28.7	38.9	76.4	30.7	84.6	30.2
Asia	47.2	55.2	14.4	23.1	47.0	15.4	49.5
Latin America and Caribbean	7.1	10.4	32.3	0.5	3.5	0.0	15.0
Europe	12.1	2.5	1.8	0.0	18.7	—	5.3
North America	1.1	2.9	11.4	—	—	—	—
Oceania	0.1	0.3	1.3	—	—	—	—

Source: UNHCR (2015a).
Note: Numbers for individual regions have been rounded.

Recent turmoil in countries of the Middle East and North Africa has resulted in a significant surge in the scale of population displacement and forced migrations toward the European Union. In mid-2014 the UNHCR projected a need for the resettlement of nearly 1 million persons seeking refuge from violence and insecurity projected to continue into the near future (UNHCR 2014).

Population Policies

A population policy may be defined as a deliberately constructed or modified institutional arrangement or specific program through which a government influences demographic change, directly or indirectly (Demeny and McNicoll 2003). According to a 2013 UN survey of government policies, seventy-two less-developed countries have policies or programs to reduce population growth; in contrast, twenty-four more-developed countries have goals to increase growth. Many more countries have indirect population policies that, while not targeting population growth, have clear implications for mortality, fertility, or migration (UNPD 2014a). The United States, for example, has not yet adopted a formal statement of goals concerning national population growth, but does have a long-standing policy for the permanent resettlement of immigrants and refugees, which in turn results in net additions to the population through international migration.

International Efforts to Address Population Issues

International population conferences bring together government delegations and representatives of nongovernmental organizations (NGOs) to discuss goals concerning population and to develop strategies for achieving those goals (see Kraly 2011). The most recent conference was held in Cairo in 1994. At each of these gatherings, there has been a general recognition, though not universal agreement, that rapid population growth fueled by high fertility poses a challenge to economic development in less-developed countries, that mortality should be reduced regardless of the effect on population growth, and that international migration is an appropriate arena of national policy and control (Weeks 2005). Over the past three decades, however, important shifts in thinking about population growth have occurred, affecting population policies and programs within countries.

The 1974 World Population Conference in Bucharest produced the first formal expression of a global population policy. The World Population Plan of Action, however, embodied a wide range of perspectives on the ways to reduce population growth within developing societies. Some countries, notably the United States, advocated fertility control, specifically family planning programs, to reach population growth targets. Other countries, primarily in the developing world, emphasized the role of development in leading to fertility decline (hence "development as the best contraceptive"). The 1984 International Population Conference in Mexico City found the United States reducing its support for family planning (which was linked in turn to the Ronald Reagan administration's views on abortion) and identifying population growth as having little hindrance on economic and social development. Many developing countries by this time, however, had instituted family planning programs in an effort to slow the retarding effects of rapid population growth on improving standards of living and educational levels and reducing mortality (Weeks 2012).

The 1994 International Conference on Population and Development recognized the global dimensions of population change. In its action program, the conference identified the connections among population processes, economic and social development, human rights and opportunities, and the environment, thus shifting attention away from targets concerning population growth to goals concerning sustained development, reduction of poverty, and environmental balance. The central role of women in the goals and programs to achieve sustainable development is underscored in the final conference report: "The key to this new approach is empowering women and providing them with more choices through expanded access to education and health services, skill development and employment, and through their full involvement in policy- and decision-making processes at all levels" (UNDESIPA 1995: 1). Twenty years later, the UN General Assembly convened to review the implementation of its action program, creating a new framework for beyond 2014 based on five pillars: dignity and human rights, health, place and mobility, governance and accountability, and sustainability (Yonetani 2014).

While an international conference on population that involves the convening of world governments has not occurred in the twenty-first century, the United Nations set forth its Millennium Declaration in 2000 and endorsed Millennium Development Goals in areas of human welfare, development, and the environment, including issues concerning population: reduction of child mortality, improvement of maternal health, and achievement of universal primary education. The United Nations Development Programme has charted progress toward achievement of each of the eight goals and twenty-one targets (UN 2015a). Additionally, the International Union for the Scientific Study of Population has its quadrennial conference to discuss developments in topics regarding population. The most recent conference occurred in 2013 in Busan, South Korea, and popular policy topics surrounded that of regulating fertility decline (particularly in China) through family planning and reproductive health, gender discrimination in health access, and strategies for addressing population aging.

Over many decades, the US government has implemented programs abroad concerning population, development, and human welfare. As mentioned earlier, US support for international family planning programs has wavered depending on the particular president's ideological lens. Under President Ronald Reagan, US support for fertility control programs was barred from any country that permitted women access to legal abortion (the so-called Mexico City policy). This restriction on US foreign aid was lifted in the early days of the Bill Clinton administration, reinstated under President George W. Bush, and again removed by President Barack Obama in 2009.

On the international scale, the emphasis on connecting population issues to the status of women has represented a significant step forward in embedding population analysis into broader discussions of the quality of human life and the balance between society and environment at local, national, and global levels.

Given the demographic trends and patterns discussed here, three additional population issues are likely to become major policy concerns in the near future: population aging, rapid population growth in already large metropolitan areas, and excess deaths due to HIV/AIDS.

Population aging presents a challenging set of issues in developed countries and is also emerging as a population issue in developing countries that have experienced rapid fertility decline. With smaller cohorts of young people entering the labor force, support for older age groups is constrained. An aging population requires social policy to support elderly age groups. Costs and geographic distribution of healthcare for the elderly are one clear set of policy concerns deriving from population aging. Less tangible are questions about the relationships among generations who have fewer siblings to care for parents; economic growth, productivity, and innovation fueled by competition; and politics and political participation.

The growth of cities (urban growth) as well as increasing proportion of the population living in cities (urbanization) will have a number of effects on population dynamics and standards of living, such as increasing competition in employment, environmental hazards, and reclassification of rural areas as urban places. With the expanding metropolitan areas, governments will need to implement policies that ensure that the benefits of urban growth—greater access to healthcare and education, improvements in water and sanitation within densely populated areas—are shared equitably and sustainably.

Though much of the focus in current demography continues to address the consequences of high levels of population growth in many less-developed countries, population decline is also a problem in certain regions of the world. Depopulation due to low birth rates or high rates of emigration has lasting effects on the labor force, aging populations, and political, economic, and social welfare. This issue requires unique adaptation by governments, communities, and households. Some scholars argue that depopulation may have benefits for the environment and sustainability because fewer resources will be consumed and pressure on habitats may be reduced. Other scholars identify benefits from low but positive population growth for economic progress and increasing standards of living.

National Population Policies

Most countries that have formal population policies seek to reduce population growth by reducing fertility. Beginning in the 1950s, providing contraception through family planning programs was initiated in many developing countries—often with significant contributions from developed countries, NGOs and foundations, and, in subsequent decades, international organizations such as the United Nations Fund for Population Activities (UNFPA). Increasingly, policies aimed at fertility reduction have encompassed broader perspectives on population dynamics, incorporating goals to increase the status of women through better health, enhanced educational and employment opportunities, greater access to credit, and so on.

The record of family planning programs has been variable throughout the developing world. India's national family planning program, maintained since 1952, has met with fertility trends that vary significantly throughout regions within the country and between rural and urban areas. In 1973, Mexico instituted a national policy to reduce population growth, with a focus on the reduction of fertility through maternal and child health programs, family planning services, sex education, and population information programs.

China's fertility control policy began in 1971 as a set of policy goals (*wan xi shao*) concerning delayed marriage (*wan*), longer intervals between births (*xi*), and fewer children (*shao*), following which the one-child policy was implemented in 1979. During the 1970s the Chinese birthrate declined significantly, reflecting the provision of contraception in combination with social and economic incentives to delay and reduce fertility. The birth control program also coincided with a general decline in fertility, which had been evident since the early 1960s. The Chinese fertility policy has been criticized harshly, however, for being coercive and for leading to selective abortion, abandonment, and infanticide of female infants. The level of fertility in China is estimated to be 1.55 births per woman for 2010–2015 (UNPD 2015).

The demographic implications of rapid fertility decline in China can be anticipated using population projections. Under assumptions of the medium-fertility population projection, the Chinese population is expected to increase from 1.376 billion in 2015 to 1.416 billion in 2028, but decline thereafter to 1.348 billion in 2050. Changes in population size will be accompanied by significant shifts in age composition: in 2015, 9.6 percent of the Chinese population was over sixty-five years of age; by 2050, this proportion is projected to more than triple, to 27.6 percent; by contrast, the proportion of the US population over sixty-five years old in 2015 was estimated by the UN at 14.8 percent, and is projected to increase to 22.2 percent in 2050 (UNPD 2015). Joining aging populations throughout the world, Chinese society will be facing increasing challenges in the support and care for the elderly.

International Migration and Refugee Policies

The UN's Universal Declaration of Human Rights recognizes the basic right of people to leave their homelands. The converse of this right to emigrate, however, is not recognized; that is, nation-states have the sovereign right to control the entry of nonnationals into their territory. Nearly all countries have clear policies concerning international migration and travel. The very few countries that continue to allow international migration for permanent resettlement include the United States, Canada, Australia, and New Zealand, often considered the traditional immigrant-receiving nations. A much larger range of countries provide humanitarian assistance to refugees in the form of permanent resettlement, political asylum, refugee camps, and financial and other resources for international organizations that seek to respond to refugee situations.

The demand for international migration, temporary labor migration, refugee resettlement, and temporary asylum can be expected to continue to grow in the next decade, with those who seek to move originating overwhelmingly from developing regions. Emerging and persistent patterns of undocumented migration throughout both the developed and the developing world are symptoms of the motivation of people to seek better opportunities. Matched with this demand are national doors that are gradually closing to international migrants. In the traditional receiving countries, concerns over the social, economic, political, and security effects of immigration have moved high up the political agenda at both the national and the state or provincial levels, often, but not always, alongside efforts to tighten migration controls, reduce immigration levels, and constrain access of immigrants to national and local social programs.

Worldwide, the United States accepts the largest number of immigrants for permanent resettlement. Since 2006, immigration has hovered around 1 million persons per year. In fiscal year 2010, Mexico, China, India, the Philippines, and the Dominican Republic provided the largest numbers of immigrants admitted to the United States (USDHS 2014). Highly skilled immigrants to the United States are predominantly Indian and mostly male (Jasso 2009).

US immigration policy is organized around several principles. First, the policy gives priority to close relatives of US citizens and, to a lesser extent, to relatives of immigrants already in the country. Second, the policy gives priority to persons with occupations, skills, and capital that will benefit the US economy. This dimension of US immigration policy may contribute to the loss of highly skilled and professionally trained persons from developing countries (referred to as "brain drain"). However, many scholars today are arguing that brain drain may not be entirely negative, because it also results from emigrants who return to their home countries after gaining valuable education, skills, and experience abroad. Third, immigrants to the United States must be admissible on the basis of a long list of personal characteristics (for example, good health, lack of criminal background, and sufficient economic resources). Fourth, there are annual numerical limits on the major categories of immigration to the United States.

Refugees are resettled in the United States if they meet the criteria of the international definition provided previously. The numbers of persons admitted as refugees reflect international need as identified by the US State Department in consultation with Congress. In the mid-1990s, an average of 80,000 refugees were admitted annually, largely from Bosnia-Herzegovina, countries of the former Soviet Union, and Vietnam (USDHS 2003). In the years following the terrorist attacks of September 11, 2001, refugee arrivals to the United States were sharply curtailed. Since 2004, refugee arrivals have steadily increased, with an average of nearly 60,000 persons arriving annually; major countries of origin include Burma, Bhutan, and Iraq (USDHS 2014).

The United States also issues hundreds of thousands of nonimmigrant visas each year to persons visiting the country for specific purposes, such as tourism and business, university study, consulting, and temporary employment. One effect of the September 11 terrorist attacks has been much greater scrutiny of visa applications, both permanent and temporary, including refugee applications. The relationship between international migration and homeland security has become a significant dimension of the US immigration debate.

There is no doubt that a growing world population has implications for climate change. As the number of people on Earth increases, so does consumption of fossil fuels and other natural resources. In particular, a still-increasing world population in the wake of increasing droughts across the world will create stress on the demand for water and its accessibility. Though the United States is a major producer of the world's carbon dioxide output, experts say newly industrializing countries are contributing significantly to the world's carbon dioxide emissions. These countries, like China and India, have large populations that will continue to grow over the next several decades. Though all nations are responsible for climate change, rapid population growth is a significant factor; a world population over 9 billion by 2050 will certainly hold consequence for global and regional environments. Climate change will disproportionately affect those living in poorer societies at all scales—local, national, and international—as certain societies have the resources to adapt to climate change while others who do not suffer. A popular solution for addressing climate change is to reduce population growth, but this raises issues concerning the freedom of choice regarding fertility. Particularly salient to the relationships among population, climate, and environmental change are geographic patterns of settlement, migration, and urbanization.

Transitional Demographies

Current demographic trends have led to distinctive shifts in social norms and patterns on a global scale. A rapid period of population growth followed closely by a swift decrease in fertility rates has contributed to unusual changes in social structure, and will in turn lend itself to continued phases of transition in the future. As indicated by John Weeks:

> The past was predominantly rural and the present is predominantly urban. . . . [T]he past was predominantly pedestrian . . . and the present is heavily dependent on the automobile. . . . The past was young . . . whereas the present is older. . . . In the past, people lived in households with more people than today . . . and the average person in each household was considerably less well educated than today, with only 10 percent of those in 1900 achieving a high school education, compared to 80 percent now. (2012: 4)

Put simply, the world is changing quickly—a transformation that is both influenced by and influencing demographic change.

Population trends and patterns within countries and regions hold fundamental and inescapable implications for the full spectrum of global issues addressed in this book. While the annual rate of world population growth has been declining in recent decades, significant increases in population size, particularly in countries in the developing world, will continue into the near future. Understanding the sources of population change, specifically declines in fertility and patterns of migration, is a critical dimension of efforts to attain sustainable development, reduce poverty, and protect the global environment. Population scientists are directing world attention to the specter of HIV/AIDS and other infectious diseases, and also to the rapid urbanization under way throughout many regions of the developing world.

Present trends in fertility, mortality, and migration hold the key for the future trajectory of world population growth. Population policy decisions made today—locally, nationally, and internationally—will influence that trajectory and ultimately the size and distribution of global population.

Discussion Questions

1. Is population growth a major global problem?
2. Do you agree more with the Cornucopians or the neo-Malthusians regarding population growth?

3. What population problems arise from rapidly growing cities?
4. Should countries open their borders to refugees fleeing political persecution and those seeking economic opportunity?
5. Was the Chinese government's one-child policy justified? Should governments be involved in population control?
6. Should the US government give foreign aid to reduce world population growth? Should the aid be conditional?
7. To what groups of immigrants should countries give preference?
8. How are human rights considered in population policy making?

Suggested Readings

Aggarwal, S. (2014) "Emerging Global Urban Order and Challenges to Harmonious Urban Development." *Transactions of the Institute of Indian Geographers* 36, no. 1.

Castles, Stephen, Hein de Haas, and Mark J. Miller (2013) *The Age of Migration: International Population in the Modern World.* 5th ed. New York: Guilford.

Commoner, Barry (1992) *Making Peace with the Planet.* New York: New Press.

de Lombaerde, Philippe, Gei Guo, and Helion Povoa Neto (2014) "Introduction to the Special Collection: South-South Migrations: What Is (Still) on the Research Agenda?" *International Migration Review* 48.

Harper, Charles L. (1995) "Environment and Society: Human Perspectives on Environmental Issues." Upper Saddle River, NJ: Prentice Hall.

Internal Displacement Monitoring Centre (2015) "Global Estimates 2014: People Displaced by Disasters." www.internaldisplacement.org.

Kraly, Ellen Percy (2011) "Population Policy: Issues and Geography." In Joseph Stoltman, ed., *21st Century Geography: A Reference Handbook.* Thousand Oaks, CA: Sage.

Lesthaeghe, R. (2010) "The Unfolding Story of the Second Demographic Transition." *Population and Development Review* 36, no. 2.

United Nations Development Programme (2014) "Frameworks of Action for the Follow-Up to the Programme of Action of the International Conference of Population and Development Beyond 2014." http://icpdbeyond2014.org.

United Nations High Commissioner for Refugees (2014) "UNHCR Global Resettlement Needs: 2015." Geneva.

——— (2014) "UNHCR Global Trends 2013." Geneva.

United Nations Population Division (2013) "International Migration Stock: The 2013 Revision." www.un.org.

——— (2013) "World Population Prospects: The 2012 Revision—Highlights." http://esa.un.org.

——— (2014) "World Population Policies Database." http://esa.un.org.

——— (2014) "World Urbanization Prospects." http://esa.un.org.

——— (2015) "World Population Prospects: The 2015 Revision—Highlights and Data Files." http://esa.un.org.

US Department of Homeland Security (2013) *Yearbook of Immigration Statistics: Refugees and Asylees.* www.dhs.gov.

Yonetani, M. (2014) "Global Estimates 2014: People Displaced by Disasters." www.internal-displacement.org.

13

Recognizing the Role of Women in Development

Jennifer Dye and Laura Dudley Jenkins

IN OUR OWN RESEARCH, WE HAVE COME ACROSS STRIKING EXAMPLES of women being left behind by development or fighting to shape future development. Laura once saw three women in rural Maharashtra, India, cutting down the one tree left in a barren, arid landscape. This act of economic desperation challenged her preconception of women as protectors of nature. Other women in India had been the original "tree huggers," protesting logging by embracing trees during the Chipko movement of the 1970s. This contrast inspired her to consider what kinds of development could benefit both women and nature. Jennifer's research on large-scale land acquisitions in Tanzania and Ethiopia opened her eyes to both the lingering impact of colonial property rights and the current collusion between modern agribusiness and political leaders. Governments selling or leasing huge swaths of land to foreign investors sidelined women, who constituted a substantial percentage of agricultural workers, from agricultural policy decisionmaking.

Despite such challenges, women continue to press for some of the most innovative changes in policies to achieve development, including political, economic, and social development. National development usually means structural changes emphasizing economic growth, which is often assumed to lead to greater wealth and power. However, as this chapter will demonstrate, this concept of development in practice does not lead to greater wealth, power, or growth for everyone. Half the population—women—are often left out of the development conversation; this chapter examines this problem and some possible solutions. Finally, this chapter aims to equip the reader with analytical tools that facilitate alternative narratives and views of development and of women.

What Is Development?

In many ways, development emerged as a concept as people in the United States and Europe tried to explain the opposite of development—or what they called underdevelopment. Emerging at the end of colonialism, the breaking up of colonial empires, and the period of reconstruction after World War II, the idea of development, or rather underdevelopment, was solidified with US president Harry S. Truman's 1949 inaugural address. In this address, Truman stated that the benefits of scientific advances and industrial progress should be passed on to underdeveloped areas; in addition, "what we envisage is a program of development based on the concepts of democratic fair dealing" (Esteva 2010: 1–2; see also Rai 2011; Woolcock, Szreter, and Rao 2009). This speech emphasizes industrialization, scientific progress, and democratization as key components of development. The speech is also an example of a growing view of a developed West and underdeveloped non-West, a dichotomy that originated in Western nations. While other nations have influenced the conversation on development, it is still steered by influential governments and international organizations dominated by the most powerful countries.

The United Nations Development Programme defines the term *development* as social, economic, and political structures and processes that allow opportunities for all members of society to have education, employment, civil participation, and social and cultural fulfillment as human beings (UNDP 1996; see also Soubbotina with Sheram 2000). Many people understand development as economic growth and assume that such development will also combat poverty. The UNDP (1996), for instance, cites economic growth as the "means" to accomplish the "end" goal of human development.

However, many development projects adversely affect those in poverty and can actually increase poverty, in some cases causing those who were not impoverished before the project to become impoverished afterward. This is more likely when development is done in the name of modernization, progress, and economic growth but without democratic consultation with those immediately impacted by the policy or project. Modernization, progress, and economic growth are legitimate goals, but when policies are designed or carried out without consulting women and various other marginalized groups, they can easily create negative or skewed results.

Questioning the Idea of Development

The origins of the idea of development provided a framework for conceptualizing development theoretically and carrying out development policies or projects. However, these frameworks and policies provoked more and more questions. For instance, what global and local causes led to underdevelopment, and what can be done about it? Is development, implying evolution toward an idealized, Western model, a useful concept? Which development goals and policies are selected? Who decides to pursue these goals and policies? How are these goals and policies carried out and implemented? Do they have the intended effects? Who is impacted by these policies? Are the outcomes positive? In sum, how is development pursued—and contested? Critics, many from the global South, have challenged development ideas and practices by posing these and other questions. Their approaches range from postmodernism to postcolonialism, dependency theory, world systems theory, and feminism. We will focus on the latter.

One significant feminist critique debunks the assumed universality and gender neutrality of development. Development is far from universal and gender-neutral; as a concept and in practice, development is couched in a very gendered reality, where gender relations are entrenched throughout societies' social, economic, and cultural structures and processes. In other words, different institutions, structures, and processes within society are not gender-neutral; they are hierarchical and reinforce gender relations, rather than acting as neutral or objective components or as corrective or balancing components of society. This affects development; it is addressed, practiced, and carried out within these gendered structures and processes. For instance, women are the majority of the world's food producers, but men are often the recipients of agricultural aid, such as credit and tools. Gender relations still act as a source of social differentiation and influence access to land and other resources in many parts of the world (Behrman, Meinzen-Dick, and Quisumbing 2011; Boserup 1970, 2011; Cotula 2013; Wanyeki 2003). Focusing on women is important because women's voices are so often left out of development decisions; gender relations affect development policies and outcomes, and development can affect gender relations.

Alternatives and Tools of Analysis

Feminist scholars spearheaded the critique of development and its gender blindness, and from these critiques important contributions to the study of development—its meanings, priorities, and analyses—have emerged. One significant contribution to reconceptualizing development is the capabilities approach. This approach, advocated by Amartya Sen and Martha Nussbaum, emphasizes the capabilities of individuals to choose "to achieve outcomes that they value and have reason to value"; for instance, poverty is thus understood as capability-deprivation (Sen 1999: 291). People using a capabilities approach examine development at a micro level, focusing on individual capabilities, such as the ability to engage in economic transactions or to participate in political activities. In sum, the capabilities approach examines individuals' abilities and opportunities, taking into account relevant cultural, personal, and external factors that inhibit or promote those capabilities.

The capabilities approach is now widely accepted as a development paradigm and has led to the creation of several capabilities-based indices to measure development, including women's development. Martha Nussbaum says human capabilities are "what people are actually able to do and be" (2000: 5). She lists central functional human capabilities, including life, health, bodily integrity, senses, imagination, thought, emotions, practical reason, affiliation with other people and other species, play, and political and material control over one's environment. She discusses the many ways women around the world are prevented from doing and being as much as men (Nussbaum 2000). The focus on capabilities in the study of international development moves our attention from national economic indicators toward the abilities of men and women to live their lives with dignity.

Building upon the capabilities approach and feminist scholarship, three tools of analysis are particularly significant and useful when examining women and issues related to development: structure, agency, and intersectionality. These three tools allow for meaningful examination of development, both as a process and as a site of contestation, and highlight the impact and role of women and other marginal groups.

Structure. Structure is how society is organized, including societal processes, laws, and cultural norms that influence or limit the choices, opportunities, and rights available to people. Essentially, structure is the context of opportunities and constraints placed on individual actions and choices. A structural analysis highlights the hierarchies and oppressions that are inherent in a system. Structures include institutions and hierarchies based on systems of patriarchy—systems where men hold primary power and privilege politically, socially, and economically.

Structure may not be obvious on a daily basis, but it is an important analytical concept because it allows us to examine structural constraints or opportunities women face (Everett and Charlton 2014). To illustrate, in many countries, women are structurally constrained by laws concerning land and its use. In southern Uganda, under customary law, a woman can work land that is allocated to her by her husband's family to produce goods to feed the family or sell. However, the woman cannot choose to sell or rent the land without the permission of her husband's family. These structural constraints are important; they hinder the economic empowerment of women, which ultimately affects the development for their families and communities (Veit 2011).

Agency. Here, agency is defined broadly as the ability to act independently and make choices that align with one's values and preferences, or as Jana Everett and Sue Ellen M. Charlton eloquently state, agency is "the ability of people individually and collectively to adapt to, influence, resist, or change the dominant structures" (2014: 7). Simply put, agency is what individuals can and will make of their lives within their structural context. Agency is related to capability, or what people can be and do. For women, agency is often restricted by social, economic, and political structures.

For instance, Oxfam has reported that almost half of the countries in the world still have gender disparities in primary and secondary education; maternal mortality has only slightly improved; and women's work in homes is often left out of national economic statistics like income and gross domestic product (GDP) (Oxfam 2014). Women's work, especially in the home, is often left out of national economic statistics because activities like fetching water, carrying firewood, tending animals, and caring for children, sick, and elderly persons are often unpaid and thus not accounted for in the formal economy. This is because national economic statistics like GDP do not take into account unpaid labor and services or other activities that do not involve actual money. As a result, national economic statistics (and policies based on them) do not account for a large amount of women's activities and work. On the other hand, people exercising their agency also influence structures. As Amartya Sen states:

> What people can positively achieve is influenced by economic opportunities, political liberties, social powers, and the enabling conditions of good health, basic education, and the encouragement and cultivation of initiatives. The institutional arrangements for these opportunities are also influenced by the exercise of people's freedoms, through the liberty to participate in social choice and in the making of public decisions that impel the progress of these opportunities. (1999: 5)

Intersectionality. Already, one can see that various factors, like agency and structure, are interconnected, and these interactions are essential to understanding development and women. Intersectionality is also about interconnectivity. This feminist concept begins with the premises that all individuals have multiple and layered identities based on social relations, histories, and structures, and that the interconnections among these various identities and related institutions must be considered all together. All women are in some ways subjected to forms of discrimination, but other factors such as sexual orientation, sexuality, skin color, race, ethnicity, age, religion, ancestry, ability, class, culture, and status as migrant, refugee, or indigenous person, among other identities, combine to determine one's social location and status.

Intersectionality is an important concept when considering women and development because it provides an analytical tool for understanding and exposing how these intersections create unique experiences of both oppression and privilege. And by doing so, it helps identify meaningful, substantive distinctions and similarities and shows how development problems, policies, programs, and services impact various individuals differently (AWID 2004;

Crenshaw 1989, 2004). Thus, intersectionality is the recognition that all individuals have different experiences of agency and structure based on their identities. For instance, a woman from an indigenous group in Ethiopia with darker skin color has a very different experience of her own agency and faces different structural constraints and opportunities than a woman from the highlands of Ethiopia. Recognizing these differences can help development processes and programs become more successful and meaningful.

* * *

These three concepts—structure, agency, and intersectionality—help researchers to approach development in ways that are inclusive of women and other marginalized groups. We will now utilize these concepts by applying them to three significant development issue areas to examine the role of gender, gender relations, and gendered systems and structures in development. The first issue area is representation and the political agency of women, which will include discussion of Rwanda as well as the global spread of legislative quotas, a structural approach that has largely benefited women. Next, women's agency related to health and livelihoods is discussed along with the idea of "food sovereignty" and the La Via Campesina movement in Latin America. Finally, we turn to the issue of education for girls and women, the structural impediments faced by many, and the remarkable agency, despite the odds, of student-activist Malala Yousafzai of Pakistan.

Key Issues and Related Activism: Political Representation, Food Sovereignty, and Education

Women's Political Representation

Women have achieved the highest political offices in many countries of the global South. Female prime ministers or presidents have led most South Asian and several Latin American and African countries. Many legislatures in these regions contain higher percentages of female representatives than the US Congress or Senate, where women's representation has never come close to reaching the proportion of women in society. In a ranking of countries on the basis of the percentage of women in national legislatures, the United States is seventy-first. Rwanda is ranked first, followed by Bolivia. Women constitute a majority in the lower legislative houses of both these countries (see Table 13.1).

Electing women into public office, or successfully running for office themselves, increases women's capabilities. According to Nussbaum, the cen-

Table 13.1 Representation of Women in National Parliaments by Region, 2001–2015 (percentages)

	2001	2005	2008	2011	2015
World (average)	14.0	16.2	17.8	19.2	22.6
Americas	15.3	19.7	21.4	22.6	27.2
Europe	15.9	18.4	20.3	21.4	25.5
Sub-Saharan Africa	12.1	16.5	17.8	19.3	23.2
Asia	15.5	15.9	16.7	18.0	18.4
Pacific	13.6	13.9	15.0	14.8	15.7
Arab states	3.6	6.8	9.0	11.7	17.9

Source: IPU (2015).

tral human functional capabilities include "being able to participate effectively in political choices that govern one's life [and] having the right of political participation, protections of free speech and association" (2000: 80). Increasing the number of women in elected office contributes to development by increasing the political agency of women. In other words, women voters can elect candidates who may be more likely to represent their interests. Sometimes women candidates and officeholders bring distinctive development priorities to the table, prioritizing access to water, food, or education, as will be discussed in more detail later. Women may be more cognizant of the impact of other types of development policies on women and girls. Thus, advancing women's representation can increase the agency of the women who become part of elected governments as well as the agency of the women they represent by giving voice to concerns neglected by male politicians.

Despite their slowly increasing representation in some countries and larger leaps in others, women remain extremely underrepresented in legislative, executive, and judicial institutions around the world. This dearth of women cannot be explained away by stereotypes about women's supposedly "natural" reticence to become involved in politics. Studies of political-party strategies, systemic opposition to women by incumbent legislators, and electoral systems demonstrate that these and other structural factors, rather than women's personal preferences, explain women's lower representation (Hawkesworth 2005). For example, research on political parties shows that male "gatekeepers" often "structure candidate selection processes to prevent women from being chosen for open, safe or winnable seats," and that if women manage to gain formal positions in a political party, male incumbents tend to shift decisionmaking from formal to informal mechanisms (Hawkesworth 2005: 150). Such structural factors are keeping women out of elected offices and leadership roles around the world. In contrast, one structural initiative that increases women's agency through increased political representation is legislative quotas for women.

Legislative quotas function in different ways, but they all require that women constitute a certain percentage of candidates or that women hold a certain percentage of legislative seats. The seats are still contested, meaning multiple candidates from different political parties vie for seats, and voters are given choices. Gender quota systems deliver a degree of intersectional diversity in legislatures by ensuring that women are included, in addition to any other forms of diversity already occurring through the electoral system. For instance, an election may facilitate ideological diversity through a competitive political-party system and geographic diversity through electoral districts. With the addition of gender quotas, female candidates from varied parties and districts may join the legislative process, leading to a more representative cross section of society in public office (see Figure 13.1).

On the other hand, those who oppose quotas can also draw on the idea of intersectionality to critique these policies. In India, some critics argue that a proposed national women's quota in the parliament would be filled by numerically or socioeconomically dominant social groups—that upper-

Figure 13.1 Beijing+20: The Global Spread of Gender Quotas

Gender quotas spread around the world after the UN World Conference on Women in Beijing in 1995. At that conference, Hillary Rodham Clinton famously stated: "Human rights are women's rights and women's rights are human rights." Government officials and activists from around the world met in Beijing to discuss a variety of problems and policies relating to women's rights and development. Some discussed and learned about the possibilities of legislative quotas for women, which had been successful in countries such as Argentina. Many national governments signed on to the Beijing Platform for Action in 1995, and gender quotas subsequently became one popular mechanism to implement their new commitment to "take measures to ensure women's equal access to and full participation in power structures and decision-making" (UN 1995).

This pivotal meeting, as well as pressure and encouragement from a variety of organizations, activists, and scholars at local and global levels, led to a ripple effect as quotas spread throughout the world (Krook 2010). As of 2015, twenty years after the Beijing conference, 128 countries had "constitutional, electoral or political party quotas" for women (Quota Project 2015). In other words, this total includes constitutionally mandated quotas, electoral rules requiring quotas, and (largely voluntary) political party quotas. Since 1995, the percentage of women in legislatures worldwide has doubled, from 10 percent to 20 percent (Staudt 2014). Still, most countries have a long way to go to achieve anything approaching gender balance in the political sphere.

class, upper-caste Hindu women would dominate the women's seats. In part due to such arguments, the Indian government has not expanded legislative quotas for women, currently used in India's local government councils, to the national parliament (Jenkins 1999). At the local level in India, however, this intersectional critique has inspired intersecting quotas. In addition to quotas for women, there are quotas for lower castes and a rule that, within the women's quota, certain seats are for women of the lowest castes, officially listed by the government as "scheduled castes." Although the complex web of quotas needed to achieve a comprehensive cross-section of society is not feasible, this type of policy is an innovative way to try to put intersectionality into action.

How does Rwanda lead the world in women's representation? Rwanda leads the world in the representation of women. Rwanda's most recent elections resulted in women being elected to 64 percent of seats in the lower house (in 2013) and to 39 percent of seats in the upper house (elected in 2011); in contrast, the most recent elections in the United States (in 2014) resulted in 19 percent women in the Congress and 20 percent in the Senate (IPU 2015). One secret of Rwanda's success is women's quotas.

After the 1994 genocide in Rwanda, the country underwent a political transformation, including a gender transformation. The Rwandan genocide was an intense period of violence during which an estimated half to 1 million people were killed over a period of about a hundred days. In the aftermath of this violence, which also decimated political and economic institutions, Rwandan women took on an increasingly important role in the rebuilding of the country. Initially involved as 17 percent of the Transitional National Assembly after the genocide, women of different political parties united in the Forum of Rwandan Women Parliamentarians, "the first group to cross party lines in a country sharply and dangerously split" (Wilber 2011). Such cooperation could have reassured Rwandans worn down by violence that more women in politics would contribute to better conflict resolution.

Rwanda's 2003 constitution guaranteed women 30 percent of posts in decisionmaking organs. By the 2008 parliamentary elections, women held 56 percent of seats in the lower house of parliament, exceeding their quota and "making Rwanda the first country in the world with a female majority in a national legislative chamber" (Debusscher and Ansoms 2013: 1117). The reformulation of political institutions through a new constitution provided an opportunity to introduce quotas. The dramatic change in politics and gender relations also can be attributed to the disruption of traditional gender relations during wartime, followed by the active roles played by the Rwandan women's movement and by political leaders committed to women's rights in the postconflict period (Debusscher and Ansoms 2013).

What difference does women's representation and participation in politics make? In their study of women as political role models, Christina Wolbrecht and David Campbell (2007) found that in countries where more members of parliament are women, women and girls are more likely to discuss and participate in politics. In their study of India, Raghabendra Chattopadhyay and Esther Duflo showed that quotas for women in local legislatures led to more investment in the development priorities of women, such as access to drinking water in contexts where collecting water is primarily women's responsibility. They concluded that "correcting imbalance in political agency does result in correcting inequities in other spheres as well" (2004: 985).

Quotas do not solve the problems of all women, though. Through interviews in Rwanda, Debusscher and Ansoms considered "the transformative potential of Rwanda's gender equity policies" (2013: 1113). In other words, did women transform development policies or processes, or simply become integrated into existing structures? They found that while women in formal politics and the formal economy have a voice in government, the government continues to neglect women in the informal economy, such as subsistence agricultural and care workers. Civil society organizations advocating for women have few opportunities to voice the concerns of nonelite Rwandan women or shape development priorities. In short, taking an intersectional view, they concluded that one must heed "class, location, and ethnicity" to truly "realize gender equality in Rwanda" (2013: 1131).

Women's political representation has advanced in much of the world, in part due to the international spread of legislative quota systems. In fact, several countries in the global South have leapfrogged over the global North and now have higher percentages of women in elected office. Although women in many countries remain untouched by this quota trend, in countries where the policies exist, voting for female candidates or serving in elected office has given millions of women new political agency. This female agency has led to a recalibration, if not transformation, of development priorities.

Food Sovereignty

Food and agriculture relate to several aspects of development, including the livelihoods, health, and nutrition of women across the globe. Women significantly contribute to the rural economy of developing countries as farmers, laborers, and entrepreneurs. In fact, women make up about 43 percent of the agricultural labor force in developing countries (FAO 2015b). However, women have less access than men to agricultural assets, inputs, services, and other rural employment opportunities. This gender gap has several dimensions: women operate smaller farms, earn less from their livestock, have greater overall workloads, including low-productivity activities (like fetching water and firewood), have less education and less access to agricultural information, use less credit, are less likely to purchase agricultural inputs like fertilizer, seeds, and mechanical equipment, and receive lower wages for the same work (FAO 2011).

Beyond the realm of small-scale agriculture, women face marginalization as agribusiness expands. As history shows, industrialization leads to a decline in the agricultural work force; the proportion of the population involved in agriculture is well below 10 percent in Western Europe and North America, but in many African, South Asian, and Central Asian countries, more than 50 percent of the work force is employed in agriculture (Everett and Charlton 2014). Industrialization, globalization, and international markets have fostered large agribusiness or for-profit agricultural "developments," ranging from seed engineering to livestock breeding and large-scale landholding. While there could be potential opportunities for women to participate in this type of agriculture, to date, "equal access to these markets is still limited" (World Bank 2009: 1).

Thus, as is the case with small-scale agriculture, in industrialized large-scale agriculture women face inequality and limited agency due to a number of structural forces. In small-scale agriculture or agriculture used primarily for subsistence, women face inequality in terms of access to agricultural information, access to credit, and access to agricultural inputs like fertilizer, seeds, and mechanical equipment. In large-scale agriculture, or largely mechanized or nonsubsistence agriculture, women are not even participants. This gap between the large contributions of women to agriculture and the amount of agricultural services, inputs, and opportunities available to them is due to a number of structural forces, including the world food system, the rise of large-scale agribusinesses, and the societal, cultural, and economic forces that shape gender roles, equality, and agency. Ultimately, understanding power and control in the current food system, as well as the movements that challenge this system, illuminates the links between gender, food, and agriculture.

The predominant approach to agriculture and the food system is one of food security, which primarily addresses freedom from hunger. Food security is defined as ensuring that all people at all times have adequate physical and economic access to "sufficient, safe and nutritious food to meet their dietary needs and food preferences for an active and healthy life" (FAO 2003). While its definition does indicate that there are social and political dimensions to food security, critics of this approach to agriculture and food systems say it ignores the political nature, and the local, regional, and national contexts, of the agriculture and food system. Instead, food security tends to emphasize a model focused on increasing production and growth. As a result, food security as a framework downplays questions of power and agency, structural constraints, and intersectional analysis within the agricultural and food system. These weaknesses led to the creation of an alternative framework—that of food sovereignty.

As a concept, food sovereignty means that nations and people have the right to control their own food systems, including markets, modes of production, food culture, and environment, and recognizes that there are political and economic dimensions inherent in food and agricultural systems (Wittman, Desmarais, and Wiebe 2010). Advocates of food sovereignty, such as the La Via Campesina movement (see Figure 13.2), both expose and reconfigure the linkages among food, agriculture, and gender. This was achieved in part by critically examining and analyzing women's agency and the structural constraints placed on them within the agricultural and food system, but also through the recognition of intersectionality—that not all women faced the same constraints and opportunities based on their identities within their society. The concept and the movement for food sovereignty emerged during the 1990s from the experiences and critical analyses of those most affected by agricultural policies as a way to address the inequalities in agriculture—both industrial and small-scale.

Food sovereignty offers an alternative framework and approach to the agriculture and food system. Instead of emphasizing increasing productivity per plant or animal, or yields per acre, food sovereignty focuses on agroecological agriculture—approaching agriculture holistically based on traditional knowledge and local food system experiences, linking ecology, culture, economics, and society to decide how agricultural production is carried out. Additionally, food sovereignty emphasizes people's access to and control of natural resources. Essentially, food sovereignty means that people and communities' rights to food and control over food production are more important than global markets, trade balances, and the sheer quantity of yields and production. Thus, food sovereignty highlights the role of agency, structure, and intersectionality within the agricultural and food system.

This focus on inequalities blows open the role of gender and the prioritization of rights. For instance, take women's rights to property—access to land and other resources is an integral part of achieving equality for women, especially in regard to agriculture and food. Focusing on attaining women's rights to property is important, but attaining this right is not sufficient. As Raj Patel states: "In a country with equal rights to property for all, the fact that some have more resources than others, and therefore are able to command more property than others, reflects underlying and persistent inequalities in power that make the ability to [own and sell] property a comparatively trivial right" (2010: 194). Essentially, gaining property rights or other rights is not sufficient if there are structural inequalities in power. The concept of food sovereignty seeks to address this power inequality; it recognizes the structural forces at play that create inequalities in the agriculture and food systems, and works to resituate power, control, and agency back within the hands of those most directly affected by and involved in agriculture and food production.

Figure 13.2 La Via Campesina and Women

Created in 1993, La Via Campesina, a transnational peasant movement that addresses inequalities in the current agriculture and food system, is one of the most politically important agrarian movements in the world today (Desmarais 2011; Borras and Franco 2010). In the 1980s, changing trade policies favored export-oriented agriculture and structural adjustment programs increased privatization and cut government services and social safety net policies. These policies resulted in negative impacts on small-scale and rural farmers—most of whom were women—in many parts of the developing world. While La Via Campesina was not created specifically for the purpose of addressing gender inequality in agriculture, it has grown to recognize that addressing this is a key component to making agricultural development more equitable for all.

La Via Campesina recognized gender equality from its inception, but it was not until after its second international conference in 1996 that it began to address gender issues systematically and formed a special committee, the International Women's Commission, to develop strategies and mechanisms to ensure women's equal participation and representation at all levels of the movement (Desmarais 2011). This marked a turning point for women; it created an international political space for women to organize themselves to address patriarchal systems at the local, national, and international levels of agriculture and food production.

Since the creation of the International Women's Commission, women have gained significant space and influence within the movement. The commission has achieved this by creating a network of workshops, exchanges, and gatherings for women to share their experiences and insights and to learn how to enhance their involvement in policies about agriculture and food. Through information-sharing, it has broadened the understanding and knowledge bases of the women and men in the movement—from advocating the idea of "food sovereignty" to practical applications like marketing strategies and modes of alternative production.

By the 2000 conference in Bangalore, the work of the International Women's Commission led to an organization-wide Gender Position Paper, a critical analysis of the role of gender in the restructuring and globalization of agriculture. La Via Campesina's recognition of gender equality did not end there. Recent issues addressed include the violence within the predominant agricultural system, including violence against women, once again situating gender equality and women at the heart of agriculture and food systems (Desmarais 2011; Wittman, Desmarais, and Wiebe 2010).

Work by transnational organizations like La Via Campesina has inspired and popularized reconceptualizations of development, such as food sovereignty, which emphasizes egalitarianism, tackling structural inequalities, and increasing the agency of those closest to food and agricultural production. Such activism results in meaningful steps toward recognizing and rectifying gender inequality in the global food and agricultural system. Attention to women and food sovereignty means acknowledging that women have had a substantial role in agriculture, that some forms of agricultural "development" harm women's livelihoods, and that gender inequalities permeate local, national, and international agriculture and food systems.

Educating Girls and Women

Education for girls and women is not only a development goal in its own right but also an achievement that enables and even drives other forms of development—social, economic, and political. For example, educating girls and women can increase life expectancy for children, contribute to local economies, and make women more informed and involved citizens.

How does educating girls impact their lives and their communities positively? Education gives girls and women more agency, or the freedom and ability to make decisions and act on them without being completely restricted by economic, sociocultural, or other structures. The agency they gain by staying in school is correlated with many other positive developmental goals (Sen 1999: 189–203). For instance, educated women tend to delay childbirth and have fewer children, which can result in healthier families and economies. Why might female education lead to lower birthrates? There are several possible explanations. Family members may recognize that educated women are valuable to the family beyond their roles as mothers and not insist on early procreation. Educated women may develop enough voice within their families to delay their age of marriage or childbirth. Girls may learn about reproduction and family planning in school and, with further education, gain enough status within their marriage to be able to choose to use birth control and enough economic resources to pay for it.

If education for girls is important in its own right and good for the community too, why do female literacy rates and education levels continue to lag behind men's in many developing countries? To answer this question it is helpful to draw on analytical tools including structure/agency and intersectionality.

From a structural perspective, what are some of the economic and cultural impediments to girls' education? Sometimes economic factors cause a girl to drop out of school earlier than her brothers. At the family level, parents with very limited resources may want to educate all their children but choose to prioritize the education of sons due to lack of money and the expectation that sons may be a better investment in the family's uncertain economic future. Even "free" government schools often require school fees, supplies, and uniforms, expenses that are out of reach for the poorest families (Henderson and Jeydel 2010).

At the community level, a poor region may lack a school, a teacher, or necessary educational materials. Even if a school exists, it may lack resources to provide private and sanitary toilets for students, which means that girls are more likely to drop out when they start menstruating. Although outsiders looking at the numbers—a drop in rates of girls attending school after puberty—might blame this decline purely on cultural conservatism, in some cases the problem (lack of sanitation/privacy) would hinder students regardless of their cultural background. Although it would certainly not solve all girls' educational challenges, a practical change (more private and sanitary toilets) could help some more girls stay in school rather than staying home due to embarrassment or illness.

In other instances, cultural factors, such as patriarchal practices or worldviews, restrict female students' educational access. Patriarchy occurs all over the world and should not be equated with certain regions or religions but rather examined case by case. One widely held view in the West is that Islam restricts girls' education, in part because some movements or regimes do so in the name of Islam. Muslim advocates of women's education, on the other hand, can support their arguments by pointing to Muhammad's wife Khadijah, a savvy businesswoman, or to several passages in the Quran supporting their position. Moreover, in Saudi Arabia, the majority of university students are women.

In Pakistan, however, this is not the case, and some communities severely limit girls' education. Pakistani critics of girls' education attempt to justify these limitations in the name of Islam, but they may be more accurately described as local customs. Some Pakistanis conflate things that go against local "cultural norms, values or practices as being in contradiction with Islam" (Guneratne and Weiss 2014: 197). The vastly different female literacy and education rates in different Muslim-majority communities around the world suggest that the cultural structures we should be scrutinizing are more specific local patriarchies rather than general ideas associated with Islam (see Figure 13.3).

Various economic or cultural structures can impede girls' agency, by preventing them from going to, or staying in, school. On the other hand, even in countries in which females have low literacy rates, some girls and women are able to become highly educated. To understand these dynamics, we turn to intersectionality. Intersectional analysis reveals "overlapping systems of subordination" (MacKinnon 2013: 1020). Initially used to recognize the combined impacts of discrimination (racism and sexism) experienced by black women in the United States and the failure of the US legal system to adequately address these overlapping systems, intersectionality can be a revelatory concept in analyses of non-US contexts as well.

In Pakistan, for example, a girl may be more or less educated depending on her location (urban or rural? which region?), her ethnicity (associated with patriarchal practices in her locality?), and her social class (wealthy or poor?). These factors intersect to mean that a girl in a rural village with only one school in a region dominated by patriarchal leaders or

Figure 13.3 Malala Yousafzai

Malala Yousafzai won the Nobel Peace Prize in 2014 for her work as an activist fighting for girls' right to education in Pakistan. She won the prize jointly with Kailash Satyarthi, an Indian activist who focuses on child labor, another rights problem that keeps children out of school. The Nobel committee honored them "for their struggle against the suppression of children and young people and for the right of all children to education."

Malala was a fifteen-year-old Pakistani schoolgirl in 2012 when a member of a Taliban group active in northwest Pakistan shot her on the bus she took home from school. The Taliban is a collection of groups active in Pakistan as well as Afghanistan. When the Taliban ruled Afghanistan, they denied girls the right to go to school and tried to control the curriculum. In Pakistan's Swat Valley, they were trying to close girls' schools, including the one Malala attended, which was founded by her father. In her memoir *I am Malala,* she recalls: "I had started taking the bus because my mom was scared of me walking on my own. We had been getting threats all year," due to her family speaking out against the Taliban and for peace and the right to go to school (Yousafzai 2013: 4).

She writes: "It's hard for girls in our society to be anything other than teachers or doctors if they can work at all. I was different—I never hid my desire when I changed from wanting to be a doctor to wanting to be an inventor or a politician. Moniba [Malala's best friend] always knew if something was wrong. 'Don't worry,' I told her. 'The Taliban have never come for a small girl'" (2013: 4). Nevertheless, not long after this conversation, a gunman boarded their bus and shot Malala and two of her classmates. Malala recovered and continues to speak out for girls in her engaging and inspiring public appearances to promote education worldwide. Her *Daily Show* and other interviews are available on YouTube. She is the youngest person ever to receive the Nobel Peace Prize.

insurgents may not attend school at all, or for long, especially if her family is poor, faces intimidation, or needs to pay fees for multiple children. Indeed, Pakistan's literacy rates, especially for girls, are alarmingly low. A 2015 estimate of Pakistan's literacy rate (based on whether people age fifteen and older can read and write) was 58 percent, putting Pakistan near the bottom globally for this indicator, at 201 out of 217 countries ranked. Broken down by gender, the male literacy rate is 70 percent, and the female literacy rate is 46 percent (CIA 2015). Within Pakistan, women and girls are more likely to be illiterate, as are people living in rural areas or urban informal settlements (slums), the poor, ethnic minorities, refugees or nomadic persons, and people with disabilities (Choudhry 2005: 5–7). Being in more than one of these categories increases even more one's likelihood of not learning to read or write.

At the same time, a wealthy daughter of university-educated city dwellers might attend elite private schools and colleges in Pakistan or abroad and even, in the case of Benazir Bhutto, become the prime minister of Pakistan. Males outnumber females in primary, secondary, and higher education in Pakistan; notably, it is in higher education that the numbers are currently approaching parity. A small elite of less than 10 percent of Pakistanis (in the seventeen to twenty-one age group) have the opportunity to pursue higher education, and in this small group, the gender imbalance in education is much smaller than in primary and secondary schools (UNESCO 2015). An intersectional analysis of female education in Pakistan must focus, at a minimum, on social class and region, which are key factors related to a girl's chances of becoming educated (Haq 2015; Choudhry 2005).

In contrast with women in Pakistan, Saudi Arabian women, like women in the United States, are the majority of university students, yet many still face hurdles and challenges. Though Saudi Arabia ranks higher than Pakistan in terms of literacy (147 out of 217 countries ranked) with its much higher national literacy rate (95 percent), the literacy rate of its women (91 percent) still lags behind that of its men (97 percent). Again, intersectional analysis can reveal the combined impact of gender, class, and location on educational chances. Girls' dropout rates are higher in certain regions of Saudi Arabia, and the socioeconomic level and traditions of different communities can impact the age of marriage, which in turn correlates with the education levels of women (Hamdan 2005). In contrast, Rajaa Alsanea's novel *Girls of Riyadh* evocatively captures the privileges of upper-class, urban women attending university in Saudi Arabia:

> After Sadeem flunked out of school, which came as a huge surprise to everyone since she was known for her academic excellence, her father proposed that the two of them travel to London for some fun. Sadeem asked him, though, to let her go alone and stay in their flat in South Kensington. . . . After some hesitation, her dad agreed. . . . He urged her to occupy her free time by signing up for a computer or economics course of some kind so that she could benefit from her time away once she returned to her college in Riyadh. (2007: 61)

Despite this degree of privilege, Sadeem and the three other highly educated female characters in the novel experience the toll of patriarchy on their personal, educational, and professional lives due to expectations relating to gender, mobility, and marriage. Intersectional advantages may help in some spheres but do not solve all gender equity problems.

Educating girls and women not only is crucial for developing their own capabilities but also has positive ripple effects for their families, communities, and the world. Nevertheless, structural impediments, such as deficient resources or patriarchal practices, restrict girls' access to education and their opportunities even if educated. In societies where opportunities are limited, some women and girls have managed to attain education, sometimes enabled by their social class or geographic location. Even in regions where girls' education is most under attack by patriarchal political movements, as in northwest Pakistan, a few break through educational barriers, including Nobel Prize winner Malala Yousafzai (see Figure 13.3). She and others who manage to continue their schooling are proof that increasing the agency of women and girls is good for them as well as beneficial for their families and communities.

Conclusion

The idea of development has not always benefited marginalized and underrepresented groups like women. As Vandana Shiva states: "What goes by the name of development is a maldevelopment process, a source of violence to women and nature throughout the world" (2010: 65). However, some progress has been made by highlighting shortcomings of current conceptualizations of development, and ultimately reformulating policies to address these "maldevelopments."

Illustrated by the three areas of representation and political agency, agriculture and food sovereignty, and education, the conceptual tools of structure, agency, and intersectionality have helped make development approaches more inclusive of women and other marginalized groups. In the case of representation and political agency of women, these conceptual tools have led to a reevaluation of policy to include legislative quota systems. This has led to higher percentages of women in elected office in both the global North and the global South, and in turn this increased female agency has led to changes in priorities and policies in development. The area of agriculture is one in progress. Women compose the majority of food producers in rural, small-scale agriculture, and are largely absent from large-scale agriculture. Yet movements like La Via Campesina have worked to make agriculture and the food system more inclusive and egalitarian, especially for women. Finally, educating girls and women is crucial to development and has positive ripple effects for their families, communities, and the world.

In all these instances, critiques based on structure, agency, and insectionality highlight inequalities women face. Efforts to address these inequalities and to include women in the conversation on development can lead to increases in agency and capabilities for women around the world. Ultimately, approaching development critically to include analyses of structure, agency, and intersectionality—and to explore instances of maldevelopment and its root causes—will lead to inclusiveness and improvements for girls, women, and the rest of the world.

Discussion Questions

1. What are some ways feminists have reconceptualized "development"? Discuss new issues, emphases, or definitions that women have brought to development policy debates.

2. Of the "capabilities" discussed in this chapter, which would you prioritize? Why?

3. Consider a policy related to development from this book or from current events. How might you challenge or change the policy if you take "intersectionality" into consideration?

4. Why is women's agency important both for women's lives and for other aspects of development?

Suggested Readings

Basu, Amrita, ed. (2010) *Women's Movements in the Global Era: The Power of Local Feminisms*. Boulder: Westview.

Enloe, Cynthia (2014) *Bananas Beaches and Bases*. Berkeley: University of California Press.

Everett, Jana, and Sue Ellen M. Charlton (2014) *Women Navigating Globalization: Feminist Approaches to Development*. Lanham: Rowman and Littlefield.

Mertus, Julie A., and Nancy Flowers (2008) *Local Action Global Chance: A Handbook on Women's Human Rights*. Boulder, CO: Paradigm.

Nussbaum, M. (2004) "Promoting Women's Capabilities." In L. Benería and S. Bisnath, eds., *Global Tensions: Challenges and Opportunities in the World Economy*. New York: Routledge.

Patel, R. (2012) "Food Sovereignty: Power, Gender, and the Right to Food." *Public Library of Science (PLoS) Medicine* 9, no. 6.

Runyan, Anne Sisson, and V. Spike Peterson (2013) *Global Gender Issues in the New Millennium*. Boulder: Westview.

Visvanathan, Nalini, Lynn Duggan, Nan Wiegersma, and Laurie Nisonoff, eds. (2011) *The Women, Gender, and Development Reader*. London: Zed.

14

Achieving Sustainable Development

Pamela S. Chasek

DEVELOPMENT STRATEGIES IN THE EARLY PART OF THE TWENTY-FIRST century have been shaped by the increasing tensions between economic health and ecological health. Capitalism, the predominant economic system, depends on repetitive expansion. This process of expansion needs and supports industrial processes with insatiable appetites for resources such as oil, coal, wood, and water, and it depends on increasing use of land, sea, and atmosphere as sinks for the deposit of wastes. Clearly, there is a conflict between the economic system's relentless demand and the world's limited and shrinking supplies.

Although there is concern that the ravenous economy will gobble up and despoil the natural environment, some scholars and policymakers suggest that this catastrophe can be avoided: with sustainable development, we can have economic growth while protecting the environment (WCED 1987; UN 1992). Sustainable development involves many global actions—from the development of concepts, to the negotiation, monitoring, and financing of action plans. For over three decades, the United Nations and its member states have tried to implement a global program on sustainable development, with limited success (Rogers, Jalal, and Boyd 2006). However, in 2015 the international community began to take the concept of sustainable development to a new level in the UN's new development agenda and the adoption of a set of new global Sustainable Development Goals. This chapter examines the evolution of the concept of sustainable development and the contribution of the United Nations to understanding and implementing development that is economically, socially, and environmentally sound.

What Is Sustainable Development?

Concepts of sustainability and sustainable development appeal to many people because they hold out the promise of reconciling these divergent views about the relationship between economic development and environmental health. Yet, while one can argue that reconciling the tension between ecology and economy is the central goal of sustainable development, there is little agreement on what sustainable development actually means. As a result, sustainable development has a multiplicity of definitions. Generally, it implies that it is possible to achieve sound environmental planning without sacrificing economic and social improvement (Redclift 1987). Some definitions emphasize *sustainability,* and therefore the focus is on the protection and conservation of living and nonliving resources. Other definitions focus on *development,* targeting changes in technology as a way to enhance growth and development. Still others insist that sustainable development is a contradiction in terms, since development as it is now practiced is essentially unsustainable.

The Brundtland Commission underlined concern for future generations by asserting that sustainable development is development that "meets the needs of the present without compromising the ability of future generations to meet their own needs" (WCED 1987: 8). The commission, formally known as the World Commission on Environment and Development but commonly known by the name of its chair, Norway's Gro Harlem Brundtland, was convened in the 1980s by the United Nations to formulate a long-term agenda for action on the environment and development.

Definitions of sustainable development tend to focus on the well-being of humans, with little explicit attention to the well-being of nature. However, the International Union for the Conservation of Nature, the United Nations Environment Programme, and the World Wide Fund for Nature have proposed a definition that includes nature and highlights the constraints of the biosphere: sustainable development is "improving the quality of human life while living within the carrying capacity of supporting ecosystems" (IUCN, UNEP, and WWF 1991: 10). Although this definition observes the traditional hierarchy that places human beings above the natural world, it does emphasize our dependence on the biospheric envelope in which we live.

Over time, the concept of sustainable development has evolved. It has been recognized that efforts to build a truly sustainable way of life require the integration of action in three key areas: economic growth, conservation of natural resources and the environment, and social development. Essentially, according to Peter Rogers, Kazi Jalal, and John Boyd, economic criteria cannot be maximized without satisfying environmental and social constraints; environmental benefits cannot necessarily be maximized without satisfying economic and social constraints; and social benefits cannot be maximized without satisfying economic and environmental constraints (2006: 46).

All definitions of sustainable development require that we see the world as a system that connects space and a system that connects time. When we think of the world as a system over space, we begin to understand that air pollution from North America affects air quality in Asia, and that pesticides sprayed in Argentina could harm fish stocks off the coast of Australia. And when we think of the world as a system over time, we realize that the decisions our grandparents made about how to farm the land continue to affect agricultural practices today, and that the economic policies we endorse today will have an impact on urban poverty when our children are adults (IISD 2013).

We also must understand that quality of life is also part of a system (IISD 2013). While it is good to be physically healthy, what if you are poor and don't have access to education? You may have a secure income, but what if the air in your part of the world is polluted? And it is good to have freedom of religious expression, but what if you are not able to feed your family?

All of our activities are a small part of a larger system, the planet we live on. Viewing our human systems as operating within the larger ecosystem is crucial for achieving a sustainable relationship with the environment, and ensuring our own species' continued survival on the planet (Folke et al. 1994: 4).

Thus, if development is to be genuinely sustainable, policymakers need to make substantial modifications to their strategies and their assumptions. However, the difficulties of actually delivering on the hopes that many people around the world have attached to the idea of sustainable development have become increasingly evident. In part, these difficulties reflect political problems, grounded in questions of financial resources, equity (justice or fairness), and the competition of other issues, such as terrorism and war, for the attention of decisionmakers. In part, they reflect differing views about what should be developed, what should be sustained, and over what period.

The Evolution of Sustainable Development

Supportive ecosystems are the sole sources of the necessities of life, including air, fresh water, food, and the materials necessary for clothing, housing, cooking, and heating. In addition and equally important, it is only within ecosystems that vital life-supporting processes can take place: these include the regeneration of soil, pollination of plants, and global circulation of carbon, oxygen, and other elements necessary for life (Munro 1995). The vast majority of the world's peoples depend upon ecosystems that are often far from where they live. Trade and technology today bring produce of land and sea to shops from all over the world. For example, cotton grown in Egyptian soil with water from the Nile River ends up as undergarments in shops in the United States and Europe. Thus, in a sense, the Egyptian ecosystem supports US consumers. Phenomena that disrupt ecological processes have similar extended effects—ozone depletion, acid rain, and climate change affect everyone regardless of where they live on the planet, whether or not their emissions of chlorofluorocarbons, sulfur, or carbon dioxide have contributed to the problem.

Yet at the same time, the evolution of the concept of sustainable development is subject to the divergent views of the industrialized world and the developing world. Developing countries continue to insist that the industrialized countries, because of their historical dominance in the combustion of fossil fuels and production of toxic chemicals and hazardous wastes, are responsible for environmental problems and should bear the responsibility for any solution. More generally, they identify the high levels of consumption in industrialized countries as a key cause of global environmental degradation. For example, according to the United Nations Development Programme, today there are more than 900 cars per thousand people of driving age in the United States and more than 600 in Western Europe but fewer than 10 in India. US households average more than two televisions. In Liberia and Uganda, less than one household in ten has a television. Domestic per capita water consumption in the richest countries averages 425 liters a day, more than six times the 67 liters per day average in the poorest countries (UNDP 2011a: 27). The average person in an industrialized country, like the United States, accounts for nearly four times the carbon dioxide emissions of someone in China or India, and nearly thirty times that of someone in Kenya. The average British citizen accounts for as much greenhouse gas emissions that contribute to climate change in two months as a person in a least-developed country generates in a year (UNDP 2011a: 24). Therefore, many developing countries argue that industrialized countries in the North must adopt more sustainable consumption and production patterns and significantly reduce the use of natural resources and fossil fuels before the South follows suit.

As the international community became more concerned about the state of the environment and its relationship with economic development, this sense of crisis came to be reflected in a series of United Nations conferences held in 1972, 1992, 2002, and 2012.

The 1972 Stockholm Conference

The Stockholm Conference (formally known as the United Nations Conference on the Human Environment), held in 1972, was the first large-scale environmental conference to look beyond scientific issues to broader political, social, and economic issues. It put the environment squarely on the international agenda.

The Stockholm Conference took place at a time when issues of global equity were becoming more prominent in international forums. Developed countries clashed with developing countries over global economic relations and environmental politics. Before the conference, developed countries had identified a particular set of issues to be addressed—such as pollution, population explosion, conservation of resources, and limits to growth. But the developing countries wanted to enlarge the agenda to include issues such as shelter, food, and water. They were able to use their voting power in the UN General Assembly to press developed countries to adopt a more inclusive agenda (McCormick 1989).

The most significant institutional outcome of the Stockholm Conference was the creation of the United Nations Environment Programme. In the decades since the conference, UNEP has played a significant role in shaping the environmental policy agenda and in coordinating environmental policy within the United Nations system. The conference output also included the Declaration on the Human Environment, together with a declaration of principles and recommendations for action.

The Stockholm Conference put the environment firmly on the international political agenda and thereby paved the way for intensified multilateral environmental cooperation and treaty-making. By stressing that environmental issues inherently are political and need to be subject to political negotiations and decisionmaking, the Stockholm Conference rejected the earlier notion that environmental issues were primarily relevant only to scientists and other experts. The conference also identified a theme that has been at the center of international environmental discourse ever since: the possibility of simultaneously achieving economic development and environmental management.

The Brundtland Commission

While the Stockholm Conference successfully brought international attention to environmental issues, it did not resolve any of the inherent tensions in linking environmental protection with social and economic development. To bring back the focus on the broader issues of environment and development that had been discussed at the Stockholm Conference, in 1983 the UN General Assembly established an independent commission to formulate a long-term agenda for action. Over the next three years, the newly established Brundtland Commission held public hearings and studied the problem. Its 1987 report, *Our Common Future,* stressed the need for development strategies in all countries that recognized the limits of the ecosystem's ability to regenerate itself and absorb waste products. Recognizing "an accelerating ecological interdependence among nations," the commission emphasized the link between economic development and environmental issues, and identified poverty eradication as a necessary and fundamental requirement for environmentally sustainable development. In addition, the Brundtland Commission popularized the term *sustainable development,* describing it as "a process of change in which the exploitation of resources, the direction of investments, the orientation of technological development, and institutional change are all in harmony and enhance both current and future potential to meet human needs and aspiration" (WCED 1987: 46).

The 1992 Earth Summit

On the twentieth anniversary of the Stockholm Conference, governments gathered again, this time in Rio de Janeiro, Brazil, to move the sustainable development agenda forward. The Earth Summit, as it was popularly known (formally designated the United Nations Conference on Environment and Development [UNCED]), attracted greater official and unofficial interest than had the Stockholm Conference. More than 170 nations sent delegates, and 108 of these nations were represented by their heads of state or government. Thousands of nongovernmental organizations (NGOs) sent representatives, and nearly 10,000 members of the media attended (UNDPI 1997).

The summit and the preparatory work that preceded it showed that there were still significant differences between the developed and the developing world. Consequently, each group provided different inputs to the agenda-setting process: developed countries wanted to focus on ozone depletion, global warming, acid rain, and deforestation, while developing countries also wanted to explore the relationship between their sluggish economic growth and the economic policies of the developed countries. The concern was that an "environmentally healthy planet was impossible in a world that contained significant inequities" (Miller 1995: 9).

The major output of the Earth Summit was a nonbinding agreement called Agenda 21 (referring to the twenty-first century), which set out a global plan of action for sustainable development. In 294 pages, comprising 40 chapters covering 115 separate topics, Agenda 21 demonstrated the emergence of a clear international consensus on the issues affecting the long-term sustainability of human society, including domestic social and economic policies, international economic relations, and cooperation on issues concerning the global commons (see Figure 14.1).

The summit also produced two nonbinding sets of principles—the Rio Declaration of Environment and Development, and the Statement of Forest Principles—that helped create norms and expectations. Two legally binding treaties, the United Nations Framework Convention on Climate Change and the Convention on Biological Diversity, which were negotiated independently of the UNCED process on parallel tracks, were opened for signature

Figure 14.1 UNCED's Agenda 21

Section I: Social and Economic Dimensions

- International cooperation to accelerate sustainable development in developing countries
- Combating poverty
- Changing consumption patterns
- Demographic dynamics and sustainability
- Protecting and promoting human health conditions
- Promoting sustainable human settlement development
- Integrating environment and development in decisionmaking

Section II: Conservation and Management of Resources for Development

- Protection of the atmosphere
- Integrated approach to the planning and management of land resources
- Combating deforestation
- Managing fragile ecosystems: combating desertification and drought
- Managing fragile ecosystems: sustainable mountain development
- Promoting sustainable agriculture and rural development
- Conservation of biological diversity
- Environmentally sound management of biotechnology
- Protection of the oceans, all kinds of seas, and coastal areas; and protection, rational use, and development of their living resources
- Protection of the quality and supply of freshwater resources
- Environmentally sound management of toxic chemicals
- Environmentally sound management of hazardous wastes
- Environmentally sound management of solid wastes and sewage-related issues
- Safe and environmentally sound management of radioactive wastes

Section III: Strengthening the Role of Major Groups

- Women
- Children and youth
- Indigenous people
- Nongovernmental organizations
- Local authorities
- Workers and trade unions
- Business and industry
- Scientific and technological community
- Farmers

Section IV: Means of Implementation

- Financial resources and mechanisms
- Transfer of environmentally sound technology; cooperation and capacity building
- Science for sustainable development
- Promoting education, public awareness, and training
- National mechanisms and international cooperation for capacity building in developing countries
- International institutional arrangements
- International legal instruments and mechanisms
- Information for decisionmaking

at the Earth Summit and are often referred to as the Rio Conventions, along with the 1994 United Nations Convention to Combat Desertification, which was called for by Agenda 21.

The Earth Summit also marked a watershed in advancing the concept of sustainable development. As Tommy Koh, the diplomat from Singapore who chaired the UNCED preparatory committee, stated:

> It used to be fashionable to argue in the developing countries that their priority should be economic development and that, if necessary, the environment should be sacrificed in order to achieve high economic growth. The sentiment was to get rich first and to clean up the environment later. . . . Today, developing countries understand the need to integrate environment into their development policies. At the same time, developed countries have become increasingly aware of the need to cut down on their wasteful consumption patterns. The new wisdom is that we want economic progress but we also want to live in harmony with nature. (1997: 242)

The Millennium Development Goals

Concerns over globalization—the rapid growth and integration of markets, institutions, and cultures—and other emerging issues such as the HIV/AIDS pandemic added a new dimension to the sustainable development debate as the millennium approached. There was a growing recognition that the world was failing to achieve most of the goals for a more sustainable society set out in Agenda 21 and elsewhere. Between 1992 and 2000, official development assistance from industrialized countries plunged, while HIV/AIDS rolled back life expectancies in some countries to pre-1980 levels as the number of people living with the disease approached the 30 million mark. The world's population climbed above 6.1 billion in 2000, up from 5.5 billion in 1992—a significant increase in just eight years. The total number of people living in poverty dropped slightly—from 1.3 to 1.2 billion—but most of the gains were in Southeast Asia and virtually no progress was made in sub-Saharan Africa, where almost half the population was living in poverty. There remained at least 1.1 billion people lacking access to safe drinking water and 2.4 billion lacking adequate sanitation (UNDPI 2002).

To help prepare the United Nations to meet these challenges, the General Assembly in September 2000 adopted the Millennium Declaration, in which world leaders agreed on a far-reaching plan to support global development objectives for the new century (UN 2000). The world's leaders reaffirmed their commitment to work toward a world of peace and security for all, and a world in which sustainable development and poverty eradication would have the highest priority. The Millennium Development Goals (MDGs) evolved from the Millennium Declaration. They are eight international development goals that UN member states agreed to achieve by the year 2015. The first seven goals are directed toward eradicating poverty in all its forms: halving extreme poverty and hunger, achieving universal primary education, promoting gender equality, reducing the mortality of children under age five by two-thirds, reducing maternal mortality by three-quarters, reversing the spread of HIV/AIDS, halving the proportion of people without access to safe drinking water, and ensuring environmental sustainability. The final goal, that of building a global partnership for development, is viewed by some as developing the sort of North-South pact first envisaged in Rio in 1992.

These goals and the commitments of countries to achieve them were affirmed in the launch of the Doha Development Round of international trade negotiations under the World Trade Organization, which commenced in 2001; the Monterrey Consensus, which emerged from the United Nations Financing for Development Conference in March 2002; and the World Summit on Sustainable Development in September 2002.

The 2002 World Summit on Sustainable Development

Ten years after Rio, the United Nations convened the World Summit on Sustainable Development in Johannesburg, South Africa, to map out a detailed course of action for implementation of Agenda 21. The summit sought to overcome the obstacles to achieving sustainable development and to generate initiatives that would deliver results and improve people's lives while protecting the environment.

The World Summit on Sustainable Development opened on August 26, 2002, and brought together government representatives from over 190 countries, including 100 world leaders. An estimated 37,000 people attended either the summit or one of the many other gatherings held alongside the main event (UN 2002). As in Stockholm and Rio, there were divergent views among governments on how to tackle issues ranging from water and sanitation to desertification, climate change, biodiversity, oceans, health, education, science and technology, and trade and finance. The North continued to argue that development in the South needed to be environmentally sound, while the South continued to argue that development had to come first and that it was the responsibility of the North to help the South in this regard. After all, the North got rich while destroying its environment and was now asking the South not to do the same. This was seen, by some, as condemning the South to poverty. To put it simply, the idea in Rio was that the North should act first, shoulder most of the adjustment burden, offer access to environmental technology, and finally engage in some financial redistribution—then the South would come aboard and eventually share in commitments. Ten years later in Johannesburg, the South argued that the North had not fulfilled its part of the bargain and therefore that developing countries did not have to fulfill their commitments toward environmentally sound development.

The Johannesburg summit produced three key outcomes. The first was the Johannesburg Declaration, a pledge by world leaders to commit fully to the goal of sustainable development. The second was an implementation plan, which set out a comprehensive program of action for sustainable development and included quantifiable goals and targets with fixed deadlines. Finally, the summit produced nearly 300 voluntary partnerships and other initiatives to support sustainable development. Unlike the Johannesburg Declaration and the implementation plan, this major outcome was not the result of multilateral negotiations involving the entire community of nations. Instead, it involved numerous smaller partnerships composed of private-sector and civil society groups, as well as governments that committed themselves to a wide range of projects and activities.

Many of the commitments and partnerships agreed to in Johannesburg echoed the Millennium Development Goals. For example, countries agreed to commit themselves to halving the proportion of people lacking clean water and proper sanitation by 2015. On energy, countries committed themselves to expanding access to the 2 billion people lacking access to modern energy services. In addition, while countries did not agree on a target for phasing in renewable energy (e.g., a target of 15 percent of the global energy supply from renewable energy by 2010), which many observers said was a major shortcoming of the summit, they did commit to green energy and the phase-out of subsidies for types of energy that are not consistent with sustainable development.

On health issues, in addition to actions to fight HIV/AIDS, reduce waterborne diseases, and address the health risks of pollution, countries agreed to phase out, by 2020, the use and production of chemicals that harm human health and the environment. There were also many commitments made to protect biodiversity and improve ecosystem management: reduction in biodiversity loss by 2010, restoration of fisheries to their maximum sustainable yields by 2015, establishment of a representative network of marine protected areas by 2012, and improvement of developing countries' access to environmentally sound alternatives to ozone-depleting chemicals by 2010.

Yet among all the targets, timetables, commitments, and partnerships that were agreed upon at Johannesburg, there were no silver-bullet solutions to the fight against poverty and a continually deteriorating natural environment. In fact, as an implementation-focused summit, Johannesburg did not produce a particularly dramatic outcome—there were no agreements that would lead to new treaties, and many of the agreed targets had already been agreed to at other meetings, including the Millennium Summit. As then–UN Secretary-General Kofi Annan told the press on the last day of the World Summit on Sustainable Development: "I think we have to be careful not to expect conferences like this to produce miracles. But we do expect conferences like this to generate political commitment, momentum and energy for the attainment of the goals" (UNDESA 2002).

Back to Rio

A decade after Johannesburg, two decades after Rio, and four decades after Stockholm, the eyes of the world turned back to Rio in June 2012 for yet another global event. The United Nations Conference on Sustainable Development (also referred to as Rio+20) sought to build on past events and redirect efforts where the international community had found shortcomings with existing approaches. The evolution of the concept of sustainable development through the UN system reveals a story of different interpretations of sustainable development that have reflected the different priorities of the North and South. The objective of Rio+20 was to secure renewed political commitment for sustainable development, assess the progress to date and the remaining gaps in the implementation of the outcomes of the major summits on sustainable development, and address new and emerging challenges. The conference focused on two themes: a green economy in the context of sustainable development and poverty eradication, and the institutional framework necessary for sustainable development. Together these two themes reflect the continuing struggle to bring the three dimensions of sustainable development together: environmental, economic, and social sustainability.

In a sense, this conference asked: Where will the world be in terms of sustainable development by 2050? The global economic system depends on endless growth, which many believe is clearly unsustainable. The governments of industrialized countries support this economic system, because with growing economies they can pacify the less affluent members of their societies with a slice of a larger pie, instead of having to share the existing pie more equitably. Developing-country governments also want their economies to grow, and to that end many have embraced the Western model of development. However, the planet cannot support everyone in such a resource-intensive lifestyle. Hence there is a need for discussions and actions on the shift to a green economy.

According to UNEP, a green economy is one that results in improved human well-being and social equity, while significantly reducing environmental risks and ecological scarcities. In its simplest expression, a green economy can be thought of as one that is low-carbon, resource-efficient, and socially inclusive. A green economy is seen as one whose growth in income and employment is driven by public and private investments that reduce carbon emissions and pollution, enhance energy and resource efficiency, and prevent the loss of biodiversity and ecosystem services. These investments need to be catalyzed and supported by targeted public expenditure, policy reforms, and regulation changes. This development path should maintain, enhance, and, where necessary, rebuild natural capital as a critical economic asset and source of public benefits, especially for poor people whose livelihoods and security depend strongly on nature (UNEP 2011).

The green economy must be discussed within the context of poverty. The lack of employment opportunities for young people, gender inequality, rapid and unplanned urbanization, deforestation, increasing water scarcity, and high HIV prevalence are pervasive obstacles. Moreover, insecurity and instability in conflict and postconflict countries make long-term sustainable development extremely difficult.

With regard to the institutional framework for sustainable development, among other initiatives (see UN 2012), Rio+20 took a step that could have an impact on the definition of sustainable development for years to come: the call for defining a set of Sustainable Development Goals (SDGs) to help provide a "concrete approach that delivers means for measuring—in accordance with the contexts and priorities of each country—both advances as well as bottlenecks in efforts to balance sustained socioeconomic growth with the sustainable use of natural resources and the conservation of ecosystem services" (Ministry of Foreign Affairs 2012). Many agreed that the MDG experience demonstrated that when there are objectives to guide the international community's efforts toward a collective goal, it becomes easier for governments and institutions to work together to reach them.

Supporters believed that the SDG approach would generate a series of additional benefits. Internationally agreed objectives could eventually be underpinned by targets, as is the case with the MDGs, which reflect the realities and priorities at the national level and play a useful role in guiding public policies. In the end, the Rio+20 outcome document, titled *The Future We Want,* agreed to develop "sustainable development goals [that] should be action oriented, concise and easy to communicate, limited in number, aspirational, global in nature and universally applicable to all countries while taking into account different national realities, capacities and levels of development and respecting national policies and priorities" (UN 2012: 46–47).

From the MDGs to the SDGs: Operationalizing Sustainable Development?

When historians look back at 2015, they will likely note that it was a watershed year for sustainable development. As the MDGs expired and were replaced with the SDGs, or Global Goals for Sustainable Development as they became known, the international community embarked on a new path to actually operationalize sustainable development, after decades of grappling with exactly how to define the concept.

There is broad agreement that the MDGs provided a focal point for governments on which to hinge policies and official development assistance (foreign aid) to alleviate poverty and improve the lives of poor people, as well as provide a rallying point for NGOs to hold governments and the UN system accountable. In fact it could be argued that the MDGs saved the lives of millions and improved conditions for many more. As the 2015 *Millennium Development Goals Report* (UN 2015a: 4–7) indicated:

- Extreme poverty has declined significantly. In 1990, nearly half of the population in the developing world lived on less than $1.25 a day; that proportion dropped to 14 percent in 2015.
- Globally, the number of people living in extreme poverty declined by more than half, falling from 1.9 billion in 1990 to 836 million in 2015.
- The proportion of undernourished people in the developing regions fell by almost half since 1990, from 23.3 percent in 1990–1992 to 12.9 percent in 2014–2016.
- The primary school net enrollment rate in developing regions reached 91 percent in 2015, up from 83 percent in 2000.
- In Southern Asia, only 74 girls were enrolled in primary school for every 100 boys in 1990. In 2015, 103 girls were enrolled for every 100 boys.
- In 2015 women made up 41 percent of paid workers outside the agricultural sector, an increase from 35 percent in 1990.
- The number of deaths of children under five has declined from 12.7 million in 1990 to just over 6 million in 2015 globally.
- Since 1990, the maternal mortality ratio has declined by 45 percent worldwide, including a decline of 64 percent in Southern Asia and 49 percent in sub-Saharan Africa.
- New HIV infections fell by approximately 40 percent between 2000 and 2013, from an estimated 3.5 million cases to 2.1 million.
- Over 6.2 million malaria deaths were averted between 2000 and 2015, primarily of children under five years of age in sub-Saharan Africa.
- Between 2000 and 2013, tuberculosis prevention, diagnosis and treatment interventions saved an estimated 37 million lives. The tuberculosis mortality rate fell by 45 percent.
- 2.6 billion people have gained access to improved drinking water since 1990 and 2.1 billion people have gained access to improved sanitation. Globally, 147 countries have met the drinking water target, 95 countries have met the sanitation target and 77 countries have met both.
- The proportion of urban population living in slums in the developing regions fell from approximately 39.4 percent in 2000 to 29.7 percent in 2014.

Nevertheless, the MDGs have been criticized for being too narrow. The eight MDGs failed to consider the root causes of poverty and gender inequality, many of the underlying environmental issues, and the holistic nature of development. The goals made no mention of human rights, nor specifically addressed economic development. Thc MDGs were considered goals for developing countries to achieve, with financial assistance from industrialized states (Ford 2015).

In addition, although significant achievements have been made on many of the MDG targets, progress has been uneven across regions and countries, leaving significant gaps. Millions of people have been left behind, especially the poorest and those disadvantaged because of their sex, age, disability, ethnicity, race, or geographic location. As of 2015, about 800 million people still live in extreme poverty and suffer from hunger. Over 160 million children under age five are stunted (inadequate height for their age) due to malnutrition. Fifty-seven million primary school–age children are not in school. About 16,000 children die each day before celebrating their fifth birthday, mostly from preventable causes. The maternal mortality rate in the developing world is fourteen times higher than in developed countries. One in three people (2.4 billion) still have insufficient sanitation facilities, including 946 million who still practice open defecation. Over 880 million people are estimated to be living in slumlike conditions in the world's cities (UN 2015a: 8).

Clearly there is more work to be done. And it is from this vantage point that the SDGs were created.

The Sustainable Development Goals

Unlike the MDGs, which were crafted by a group of UN experts under the guidance of the UN Secretary-General, the SDGs were negotiated by governments in the Open Working Group on Sustainability Goals that met thirteen times between March 2013 and July 2014 to create this cornerstone of the UN's post-2015 development agenda. While it is inherently difficult for governments to negotiate a set of goals as concise as the MDGs, governments also had a much larger agenda. The new goals are universal, in other words an agenda that recognizes shared national and global challenges, and offers a much needed paradigm shift away from outdated global development assumptions of the past. The new goals are also supposed to, first and foremost, end poverty and hunger, and achieve sustainable development in its three dimensions through promoting inclusive economic growth, protecting the environment, and promoting social inclusion.

The goals also encompass human rights, gender equality, women's and girls' empowerment, and peaceful and inclusive societies. And, as often repeated throughout the negotiations, the SDGs, unlike the MDGs, are supposed to ensure that no country or person is left behind. The MDGs did not have to deal with these challenges, since they focused on economic and social issues in developing countries and gave limited attention to the structural causes of poverty and sustainable development, including inequality, pollution, and resource scarcity. The result of this process was a set of 17 goals and 169 targets (see Figure 14.2 and UN 2014). Some governments and nongovernmental organizations have complained that such a large number of goals is too unwieldy to implement or sell to the public. However, there is a general consensus that it is better to have more goals that include targets on women's empowerment, the environment, good governance, and peace and security, for example, than fewer goals that don't address these issues.

Figure 14.2 Sustainable Development Goals

1. End poverty in all its forms everywhere
2. End hunger, achieve food security and improved nutrition, and promote sustainable agriculture
3. Ensure healthy lives and promote well-being for all at all ages
4. Ensure inclusive and equitable quality education and promote lifelong learning opportunities for all
5. Achieve gender equality and empower all women and girls
6. Ensure availability and sustainable management of water and sanitation for all
7. Ensure access to affordable, reliable, sustainable, and modern energy for all
8. Promote sustained, inclusive, and sustainable economic growth, full and productive employment, and decent work for all
9. Build resilient infrastructure, promote inclusive and sustainable industrialisation, and foster innovation
10. Reduce inequality within and among countries
11. Make cities and human settlements inclusive, safe, resilient, and sustainable
12. Ensure sustainable consumption and production patterns
13. Take urgent action to combat climate change and its impacts (taking note of agreements made by the [UN Framework Convention on Climate Change] forum)
14. Conserve and sustainably use the oceans, seas, and marine resources for sustainable development
15. Protect, restore, and promote sustainable use of terrestrial ecosystems, sustainably manage forests, combat desertification and halt and reverse land degradation, and halt biodiversity loss
16. Promote peaceful and inclusive societies for sustainable development, provide access to justice for all, and build effective, accountable, and inclusive institutions at all levels
17. Strengthen the means of implementation and revitalise the global partnership for sustainable development

The SDGs were adopted as the cornerstone of the UN's new sustainable development agenda, titled *Transforming Our World: The 2030 Agenda for Sustainable Development,* at a summit of heads of state and government at UN headquarters in New York in September 2015. Replacing the MDGs, the SDGs and the sustainable development agenda will guide development for the next decade and a half. Already, numerous governments, UN agencies, and international and nongovernmental organizations are already adjusting their programs and plans to conform to the SDGs.

The preamble of *Transforming Our World* states: "We are resolved to free the human race from the tyranny of poverty and want to heal and secure our planet." It continues: "We are determined to take the bold and transformative steps which are urgently needed to shift the world onto a sustainable and resilient path. As we embark on this collective journey, we pledge that no one will be left behind" (UN 2015b).

However, like the MDGs and previous sustainable development action plans and programs, the SDGs have been subject to criticism. Some critics argue that this massive list of tasks is a recipe for failure, a set of goals that, although adopted with great fanfare, will be quickly forgotten.

As already mentioned, some are concerned with the number of goals. British prime minister David Cameron called for no more than twelve goals, preferably ten. "I appreciate the work of the open working group, and how difficult it is to deal with competing demands, but frankly . . . I don't believe they will cut it at 17. There are too many to communicate effectively," he said. "There's a real danger they will end up sitting on a bookshelf, gathering dust" (Ford 2014). Along these lines, *The Economist* argued: "The number of SDGs . . . shows what happens when a bureaucratic process runs out of control. The organisers sought to consult as widely as possible, with the result that each country and aid lobbyist got a target for its particular bugbear. . . . Something for everyone has produced too much for anyone. Making matters worse, some developing countries think each extra goal will come with a pot of money, so the more goals, the more aid" (2015b).

In response, others have said that the number of goals is necessary—that the SDGs reflect the complexity and interconnectedness of today's social, economic, and environmental challenges. To achieve sustainable development, these challenges must be addressed in an integrated way. Similarly, unlike the MDGs, the SDGs are deliberately the product of a more grassroots process, which began with input from a broader range of advocacy groups, everyday citizens, and governments than ever before. As Amina Mohammed, UN Secretary-General Ban Ki-moon's special adviser on post-2015 development planning, put it: "What we had with the SDGs was a paradigm shift in the way we formed an agenda" (LaFranchi 2015).

Anthony Pipa, the US State Department's special coordinator for the post-2015 development agenda, agrees: "The political inclusivity of this process and the breadth of the goals decided on together say that governments alone can't achieve this, that it really requires all hands on deck. This is development as a political enterprise." He adds: "It requires the participation of business and civil society [as well as] the political commitment of the leadership of countries" (LaFranchi 2015). Similarly, Irish ambassador David Donoghue noted that it was important to have political buy-in from as many countries as possible: "If you were to tamper with the 17 in any way, too many countries will be afraid that the whole thing might unravel" (Carswell 2015). This also reflects a nod to the "integrated" nature of development goals. In other words, it does not make any sense to try to reduce extreme poverty, while ignoring the role the environment and good governance play in building prosperity (LaFranchi 2015).

Other critics, like Jason Hickel from the London School of Economics, believe that the SDGs themselves are contradictory. Hickel (2015) argues that the new sustainable development agenda points to the necessity of achieving "harmony with nature" and "sustainable patterns of production and consumption." The SDGs, he continues, demand halting the loss of biodiversity, and ending overfishing, deforestation, and desertification. "All of this reflects an awareness that something about our economic system has gone terribly awry—that the mandatory pursuit of endless material growth is chewing through our living planet, and producing poverty at a rapid rate." However, he criticizes the SDGs because they rely on the old model of endless growth of gross domestic product and higher economic productivity across the board (see SDG 8 in Figure 14.2). Thus, he argues that "the SDGs call for both less and more at the same time" and asks how they can "expect to succeed with such a profound contradiction at their root." He continues: "The SDGs want to reduce inequality by ratcheting the poor up, but while leaving the wealth and power of the global 1 percent intact. They want the best of both worlds. They refuse to accept that mass impoverishment (and ecological crisis) is the product of extreme wealth accumulation and overconsumption."

Other questions about the SDGs and the 2030 agenda remain. For one, while the SDGs are universal and therefore apply to all countries, there is an ongoing debate as to what this means in practice. Developing countries consistently stress that while the SDG framework is universally relevant to all countries, the roles and responsibilities in the implementation of the goals should be differentiated with respect to the different national realities, capacities, and levels of development, as well as to national policies and priorities (Muchhala 2014). Also there are questions of financing and the relationship between public and private sources of finance and whether the developed countries will bear most of the cost.

Another criticism is that while many of the SDGs contain elements of the three dimensions of sustainability, the level of integration is far lower than justified from a science perspective and far lower than discussed in the preparation process (ICSU and ISSC 2015). A report by the International Council for Science, in partnership with the International Social Science Council, states that the goals are presented using a "silo approach"—that is, they are addressed as separate elements, mostly in isolation from each other. However, these goal areas do overlap, many targets may contribute to several goals, and some goals may conflict. Since the SDG framework does not reflect interlinkages and cannot ensure that development takes place within sustainable levels of resource use at either the global or regional scale, it is possible that the framework as a whole may not be internally consistent—and as a result not be sustainable (ICSU and ISSC 2015).

The New Path to Sustainable Development

Can the universal Sustainable Development Goals be achieved by 2030? Is the planet on a path to sustainable development, or disaster? While the Earth Summit set out a vision of sustainable development, and established goals and principles for achieving it, turning goals into action is much more challenging. While the forty-year period between Stockholm and Rio+20 was characterized by growth in scientific understanding of environmental problems and the relationship between people and the planet, there was just as much that did not change that still remains today. Mistrust and suspicion still govern relations between North and South, governments still tenaciously embrace traditional views of national sovereignty, and tension between the long-term vision necessary for ecologically sound planning and the short-term concern for economic growth and political stability still preoccupies most governments (Conca and Dabelko 2010). Global consumption of goods and services has increased, but is still as unequal as ever, despite China's phenomenal economic growth in recent years. These divisions highlight the political challenges that remain, just like sustainable development issues themselves.

Despite the apparent tensions between economic health, social health, and ecological health, in the long run economic health is dependent on social and ecological health. The global economy cannot thrive in the face of the total devastation of our biospheric envelope, nor can it survive in the face of increasing poverty and disease. If we accept this fact, then there are only two ways to resolve this tension: we can let it continue until the integrity, the ecology, and the economy deteriorate and snap like old rubber bands, or we can make the economic, social, and cultural changes that are needed to support sustainable development at the community, national, and global levels.

The Sustainable Development Goals may mark the essential move toward realizing a world where people, planet, prosperity, peace, and partnership come together. The universal nature of the SDGs commits all countries to take action both within their own borders and in support of wider international efforts. It is hoped that individual national commitments will add up to a worldwide result that helps all people, especially those living in extreme poverty, and ensure a healthy environment. For the first time, a UN development plan recognizes the interlinkages among sustainability of ecosystem services, poverty eradication, economic development, and human well-being. However, it is comparatively easy to agree that the shift to sustainable development is necessary. The challenge is for governments to muster the political will to make this shift and for the people of the world to demand change.

Discussion Questions

1. What are key elements of the North-South debate over sustainable development? Why are these issues so difficult to reconcile?
2. How has the concept of sustainable development evolved since the 1980s?
3. What are some of the tensions between the three pillars of sustainable development?
4. What are the key differences between the Millennium Development Goals and the Sustainable Development Goals?
5. Do you think sustainable development is possible? Should it be a priority? Why or why not?

Suggested Readings

Chasek, Pamela S., David L. Downie, and Janet Welsh Brown (2016) *Global Environmental Politics*. 7th ed. Boulder: Westview.

Conca, Ken, and Geoffrey D. Dabelko (2014) *Green Planet Blues: Critical Perspectives on Global Environmental Politics*. 5th ed. Boulder: Westview.

Dodds, Felix, et al., eds. (2015) *Governance for Sustainable Development: Ideas for the Post 2015 Agenda*. www.article19.org.

Kjellen, Bo (2008) *A New Diplomacy for Sustainable Development: The Challenge of Global Change*. New York: Routledge.

Najam, Adil, David Runnalls, and Mark Halle (2007) *Environment and Globalization: The Five Propositions*. Winnipeg: IISD.

Rogers, Peter P., Kazi F. Jalal, and John A. Boyd (2006) *An Introduction to Sustainable Development*. Cambridge: Harvard University Press.

Sachs, Jeffrey D. (2015) *The Age of Sustainable Development*. New York: Columbia University Press.

15

Confronting Climate Change

Mark Seis

THERE IS LITTLE DOUBT THAT EARTH IS WARMING AND THAT LEVELS OF carbon dioxide in the global atmospheric commons are increasing. The ten warmest years on record have all occurred since 1998, with 2014 being the warmest year on record. July of 2015 was the hottest month in recorded history (NOAA 2015a). The global concentration of carbon dioxide in the atmosphere has now reached over 400 parts per million from 280 pre-industrialization. Our atmospheric commons has become the CO_2 dumping ground for countries pursuing industrial economic growth around the world.

In Garret Hardin's 1968 article "The Tragedy of the Commons," he argued that common property will be destroyed by human greed and exploitation. Hardin used the hypothetical example of cattle herders on a pasture (not owned by any particular individual). He argued that if an unsustainable number of cattle were added in an effort to maximize profits, then the pasture would eventually be overgrazed and thus destroyed. The problem is that as the herders individually attempt to maximize their profits and add more cattle, collectively they end up working against one another in their ability to maximize profit. Individual restraint is unlikely, because each herder knows that if he or she does not increase the number of cattle grazing, they will lose potential profits, at least in the short term, while other herders will continue to make profits from unsustainable grazing practices. The end result is the "tragedy of the commons." This example is what makes promulgating an international policy on reducing climate changing gases so difficult.

The two major approaches to addressing the destruction of the commons by pursuit of profit maximization are complete privatization and government regulation. In the former, a private actor controls the pasture that has been privatized. So, for example, in the case of a pasture that has been transformed from a commons to private property owned by a single herder family with the intention of owning the land forever, the owner would want to ensure that he or she could continue to graze cattle on the land. Therefore, theoretically, the family would use it sustainably. Conversely, if the government took control of the previously community-controlled pasture and regulated the land, then it would need to establish laws to regulate its use and to ensure that it is developed sustainably.

Hardin's concept of the commons, however, has been seriously criticized for mistaking what were actually community-regulated public lands for "open access regimes in which anything goes" (Athanasiou and Baer 2002: 145). Historically, socially regulated commons have been maintained by subsistence-based economics guided by cultural practices and a spiritual sense of belonging to the land that "stabilize[s] people's relationship with their ecosystems" (Cronon 1983: 12). Many people feel that the only way to preserve the atmospheric commons is "to convert it from an open-access resource into a commons, a limited socially regulated global commons in which access is appointed to us each in equal measure, by virtue of . . . our common humanity" (Athanasiou and Baer 2002: 145). Maintaining atmospheric stability as an essential component to all life on this planet is an example of a socially regulated commons that affirms our relationship with our biosphere. Conversely, some support the idea of converting the atmospheric commons into private property. Treating air as private property assumes that rationing air through markets is superior to cultural practices that ensure quality air for all. An example of the privatization approach is the creation of carbon dioxide trading regimes (discussed later in this chapter).

This chapter explores the threat of climate change and the accompanying consequences to human civilization, as we know it. It will examine specifically the global warming threat, causes, contributors, victims, history of climate change policies, and the prospects of geoengineering.

The Threat of Global Warming

Scientific research on carbon dioxide is over 150 years old. John Tyndall in the mid–nineteenth century recognized carbon dioxide as a greenhouse gas, which traps heat in our atmosphere (Oreskes and Conway 2010). Swedish geochemist Svante Arrhenius realized in the early twentieth century that the burning of fossil fuel could in fact change the climate, and Guy Callendar, a British engineer, "compiled the first empirical evidence that the 'greenhouse effect' might already be detectable" (Oreskes and Conway 2010: 170). US scientists in the 1960s warned Lyndon Johnson and other political leaders that increasing levels of carbon dioxide could impact our climate (Oreskes and Conway 2010).

In 1958, Roger Revelle procured research money for his colleague Charles Keeling to set up laboratories at the South Pole and in Hawaii to measure rising carbon dioxide levels (Oreskes and Conway 2010). Keeling was awarded the National Medal of Science for discovering what is now known as the Keeling curve. The Keeling curve shows the steady rise of carbon dioxide in the atmosphere since 1958. From 1960 to 2010, the atmospheric concentration of carbon rose from just under 320 parts per million to over 400. Most scientists agree that Earth can only sustain about 390 parts per million. Carbon dioxide levels based on samples of air bubbles trapped in ice cores from the Antarctic show that carbon dioxide levels have not been this high in 800,000 to 15 million years (Freedman 2013). Among the overwhelming majority of climate scientists, there is widespread concern that increased greenhouse gases are leading to an increase in Earth's temperature, known as global warming. The warming of the planet, in turn, leads to changes in the climate, referred to as climate change.

The scientific community is mounting a very strong case that human-generated greenhouse gases are warming the planet. "Ninety-seven percent of climate scientists agree that climate-warming trends over the past century are very likely due to human activities, and most of the leading scientific organizations worldwide have issued public statements endorsing this position" (NASA 2015b).

The World Meteorological Organization states that "the increase in temperature in the twentieth century is likely to have been the largest in any century during the past 1000 years" (WMO 2003). Since 1900, Earth's average temperature has risen by 1.6 degrees Fahrenheit, and "depending on if and when emissions are curbed, another 3 degrees to 9 degrees Fahrenheit of warming could be in store by the end of this century" (Thompson 2015a).

Despite the growing body of research documenting the changes occurring to our climate from increased greenhouse gases, a small number of skeptics remain. Some of these skeptics suggest that we do not possess enough data on a geological timescale to totally understand the natural cycles and fluctuations of Earth's climate. This claim has some merit, but for the 800,000 years of data that we do have, there is a relationship between higher levels of carbon dioxide and temperature increase, causing climate change. Others skeptics (Ray and Guzzo 1992; Michaels 1992; Lindzen 1993; Bellamy 2004, Robinson and Robinson 2012) question the actual amount of warming that will occur and the underlying projections of computer models. Others suggest that Earth's natural atmospheric process (for example, the interplay of oceans, forests, and sulfate aerosols) will be able to mitigate the greenhouse effect. However, the evidence is showing that Earth can no longer safely absorb the excess carbon humans are putting into the atmosphere as documented by the increasing carbon dioxide concentrations in the atmosphere. There are empirically observable changes that are happening to our planet that make it unequivocal that our biosphere is changing. Here is a summary (NASA 2015a) of major indicators documenting rapid changes to our planet:

- Global sea level rose about 17 centimeters (6.7 inches) in the past century. The rate in the past decade, however, is nearly double that of the past century.
- All three major global surface temperature reconstructions show that Earth has warmed since 1880. Most of this warming has occurred since the 1970s, with the twenty warmest years having occurred since 1981 and with all ten of the warmest years occurring in the past twelve years. Even though the first decade of the twenty-first century witnessed a solar output decline resulting in an unusually deep solar minimum in 2007–2009, surface temperatures continue to increase.
- The oceans have absorbed much of this increased heat, with the top 700 meters (about 2,300 feet) of ocean showing warming of 0.302 degrees Fahrenheit since 1969.
- Both the extent and the thickness of Arctic sea ice has declined rapidly over the past several decades.
- Glaciers are retreating almost everywhere around the world—including in the Alps, Himalayas, Andes, and Rockies, as well as in Alaska and Africa.
- The number of record-high temperature events in the United States has been increasing, while the number of record-low temperature events has been decreasing, since 1950. The United States has also witnessed increasing numbers of intense rainfall events.
- Since the beginning of the Industrial Revolution, the acidity of surface ocean waters has increased by about 30 percent. This increase is the result of humans emitting more carbon dioxide into the atmosphere and hence more being absorbed into the oceans. The amount of carbon dioxide absorbed by the upper layer of the oceans is increasing by about 2 billion tons per year.
- Satellite observations reveal that the amount of spring snow cover in the Northern Hemisphere has decreased over the past five decades and that the snow is melting earlier in the season.

Another group of skeptics do not dispute the warming trend, but believe that the global warming we are experiencing is a natural phenomenon, not a human-generated event. This is an extremely important distinction. If climate change is naturally occurring, then it makes no sense for humans to change the way they live. However, if humans are causing the problem, then changing the way we live may mitigate the effects of climate change.

Some of these skeptics argue that we are in a natural warming period due to more intense solar activity, which is not true according to data that suggest Earth is warming while we are in a period of solar decline (NASA 2015a). Another group of skeptics, who accept warming, argue that warmer temperatures are simply natural fluctuations in Earth's temperature. However, scientists reject this explanation based on the close relationship between global carbon dioxide levels and average global temperatures, and the fact that the increase in atmospheric carbon over the past 200 years is primarily a result of fossil fuel burning.

It should be reiterated that these skeptics are greatly outnumbered by the overwhelming majority of climate scientists who believe that the data suggest that humans are creating a change in our climate through the emission of fossil fuels. Hence, climate change is ultimately a political issue.

Causes and Consequences of Global Warming

Earth is constantly bombarded by solar radiation, some of which is absorbed and some of which is reflected back into space. This process is known as the greenhouse effect. When the natural carbon cycle is altered by fossil fuel burning (automobiles, power plants, industry, and heating are the most common fossil fuel–burning activities), large amounts of carbon dioxide are released into the atmosphere. The result is that more solar radiation is trapped in Earth's atmosphere and less is reflected, and therefore the planet begins to warm. Gases like carbon dioxide, chlorofluorocarbons (CFCs), methane, tropospheric ozone, and nitrogen oxides trap solar radiation and cause the atmosphere to warm. Carbon dioxide accounts for roughly 50 percent of the total greenhouse gases; chlorofluorocarbons, 20 percent; methane, 16 percent; tropospheric ozone, 8 percent; nitrous oxide, 6 percent (McKinney and Schoch 1996; NASA 2015a). As the atmosphere warms, it retains more water vapor due to evaporation. Water vapor is also a powerful greenhouse gas, because it traps long-waved solar radiation. This phenomenon was demonstrated by satellite measurements from the Earth Radiation Budget Experiments, which showed that as ocean surface temperatures increase, more infrared radiation is trapped in the atmosphere (Leggett 1990).

Increasing temperatures set into motion various positive feedback loops that escalate the problem of global warming. A warming planet means that there is less ice and snow in the mountain and polar regions to reflect back solar radiation. In addition, as Earth warms, large amounts of methane (which is a much more potent greenhouse gas than CO_2) are released from ice, tundra, and mud in the continental shelves. More methane means more greenhouse gases to trap solar radiation, which in turn results in hotter surface and ocean temperatures, and hotter temperatures mean more thawing and more melting of sea ice, which leads to more methane gas—creating a vicious cycle of warming.

With global warming and the ensuing changes in climate come increased precipitation in some areas, and drought in others. These changes are caused because of increased evaporation due to the heat and altered wind patterns. "Drought conditions in Australia have now lasted for over a decade, and parts of China, Portugal, Mexico, and high latitude South American countries all experienced their worst droughts in 50 years or more" (Mulrow 2010: 47). Throughout 2012, the US Drought Monitor indicated that two-thirds of the continental United States was in moderate to exceptional drought and that, with respect to the rest of the world, Russia, southeastern Europe, the Balkans, parts of China's Yunnan and southwestern Sichuan provinces, and Brazil experienced extreme drought. Brazil experienced its worst drought in fifty years (WMO 2012). As of 2015, California remains in a serious drought, enduring the driest three-year period in 1,200 years based on research ascertained from studying past climate through tree rings (Stevens 2014). For the first time in California's history, it has implemented water rationing and restrictions. Studies have shown that summers are becoming longer and warmer, serious storms are becoming more frequent and severe, and water shortages have become a chronic problem for eighty countries, constituting 40 percent of the world's population (Athanasiou and Baer 2002; Groisman and Knight 2008; Paskal 2010; Parenti 2011; Guzman 2013). In 2010, Pakistan experienced flooding that displaced 20 million people, and Russia experienced the greatest heat wave in its history, resulting in the loss of thousands of lives. Based on estimates by the World Health Organization, 150,000 people a year are now dying due to climate change (WHO 2015d).

The accelerated rate of warming is beginning to increase more extreme weather events according to a comprehensive report by the WMO titled *Atlas of Mortality and Economic Losses from Weather, Climate, and Water Extremes (1970–2012)*. The report documents more intense heat waves, droughts, floods, snow and extreme cold, and topical storms around the world (WMO 2014). It breaks the world down into various regions and for each region the data clearly demonstrate an increase in weather, climate, and water-related disasters. Authors Michel Jarrard and Dearati Guha Sapir write that climate-related disasters "are on the rise worldwide. Both industrialized and non-industrialized countries are bearing the burden of repeated floods, droughts, temperature extremes and storms. The escalating impact of disasters is due not only to their increasing frequency and severity but also to the growing vulnerability of human societies, especially those surviving on the margins of development" (WMO 2014).

Other consequences of climate change are rapidly changing habitats, which present significant obstacles to agriculture, damage ecosystems, and cause species extinctions (Knight 2010). Scientists estimate that climate change could drive one in six animal and plant species to extinction, while other researchers estimate that the numbers could be two to three times higher. Many species are already in the process of migrating and changing their ranges to more suitable habitats, with researchers finding among 1,700 plant and animal species a shift in their habitat of 3.8 miles per decade toward Earth's poles (Zimmer 2015). The number of vertebrate species has already fallen by over 30 percent since the 1970s, and as of 2000, dozens of livestock breeds have disappeared (Knight 2010). Studies suggest that we are entering the sixth great extinction (Wake and Vredenburg 2008). The resulting storm and drought damage may also lead to food shortages, especially when one considers the increase in human population (Cribb 2011).

Around the world, people are being driven from their homes because of climate-created catastrophes. Rising oceans and extreme floods are swallowing people's homes and farmland. Extreme drought is forcing small farmers to leave their lands in search of water. Based on some estimates cited by the United Nations (2009), the number of people fleeing due to climatic disruption in the form of sea-level rise, desertification, deluge, and water scarcity could range between 50 and 350 million people by 2050. There has been much dispute about the future estimates, but in 2008 the UN estimated that 20 million people were displaced by climate-related disasters (Barnes 2013). It is safe to assume that we are talking about millions of people who will be forced to relocate, especially with rising sea levels and more extreme weather events.

Currently there are no international recognized policies for people fleeing their homelands due to climate-related circumstances. While refugees fleeing from war-torn areas are recognized by international law, there are no such protections for climate refugees. The first appearance of the concept of environmental refugee appears in 1985 in a United Nations Environmental Programme report authored by Essam el-Hinnawi (Durkova et al. 2012). The recent coining of the term "climate refugees" is reason enough to recognize the urgency of the growing problem of the displacement of human beings from their homes by climate-related disaster.

Alaska is getting hotter faster than anywhere else in the continental United States. The permafrost is thawing, which means the ground is softening and, with the increased frequency and strength of winter storms, widespread coastal erosion is beginning to displace native communities occupying coastal lands and small islands (Argos 2010; Banerjee 2012). The sea is swallowing Shishmaref Inupiaq houses, and whole villages throughout Alaska have to be relocated due to the rising tides and sea levels; the

Shishmaref people are now facing the decision to move their community, which is projected to cost over $100 million (Argos 2010). These are poor communities. Rising sea levels are also inundating small island nations around the world like Tuvalu, the Maldives, and Halligen, and low-lying areas like Bangladesh.

Rising sea levels are not the only cause of climate refugees. People in landlocked African countries are also facing challenges from climate change. Chad, for instance, is undergoing rapid desertification caused by extended drought (Argos 2010). In Asia, the Himalayan watershed, which provides water to roughly 3 billion people, is facing duel threats of glacial melt and changing precipitation patterns (Paskal 2010). There are already problems in the area, specifically India, where 22 percent of Indians confront "absolute water scarcity" (Paskal 2010: 142). China is also heavily dependent on glacial melt for over 250 million people (Paskal 2010).

As climate continues to change, causing the problems outlined here, it becomes obvious that the problem of climate change is highly political. Basic resource issues like a lack of fresh water or too much water, coupled with potentially massive amounts of climate refugees, create a situation of global political instability. The potential for a new geography of violence caused by climate instability is a very real threat (Parenti 2011).

Major Contributors to Global Warming

Since the Industrial Revolution, scientists have measured a steady increase in carbon dioxide in the atmosphere. Preindustrial revolution levels of carbon dioxide hovered around 280 parts per million, and as previously noted Earth's atmosphere has now exceeded 400 parts per million. Carbon dioxide levels over the past ten years have been increasing at an average rate of 2 parts per million. There have also been significant increases in other greenhouse gases like methane and nitrous oxide (IEA 2014). Global carbon dioxide emissions for 2012 amounted to 31.7 metric gigatons. According to the International Energy Agency, "this represents a 1.2% year-on-year increase in emissions." Globally, carbon dioxide levels from 1990 to 2012 grew by 51 percent (IEA 2014: 8, 12).

Total carbon dioxide emissions vary widely by country. Some countries emit much more carbon than others, which has created problems in the international community with respect to formulating binding strategies for regulating greenhouse emissions. Table 15.1 shows the largest carbon-emitting countries, of which China and the United States far outpace the others. Another way to view carbon dioxide emissions is by the amount produced per person in a given country. Table 15.1 also shows the dramatic differences between carbon dioxide emissions in developed countries (the United States, Russia, Japan, Germany, Canada, and the United Kingdom) versus the developing countries (China, India, South Korea, and Iran). While China is the largest carbon-emitting country, due to its population of more than 1.3 billion people it only releases about 6.52 tons of carbon dioxide per person, while the United States releases an average 17.62 tons per person. Compare these numbers with a person from India, who releases 1.45 tons.

Higher carbon dioxide levels in wealthy countries are due to an obvious higher standard of living, involving the use of more electricity, larger houses, heavy reliance on automobile transportation, and heavily subsidized, low fuel costs. As the global South tries to emulate the wealthier North, it also begins to emit more greenhouse gases. The International Energy Agency has documented this fact by observing emission increases in Africa of 5.6 percent; Asia excluding China, 4.9 percent; the Middle East, 4.5 percent; and Latin America, 4.1 percent; while in North America emissions have dropped overall by 3.7 percent and in Europe by 0.5 percent (IEA 2014).

Table 15.1 Carbon Dioxide Emissions from Consumption of Energy, 2014

	Total Carbon Dioxide Emissions from Consumption of Energy (million metric tons)	Per Capita Carbon Dioxide Emissions from Consumption of Energy (metric tons per person)
China	8,715	6.5
United States	5,491	17.6
Russia	1,788	12.6
India	1,726	1.5
Japan	1,181	9.3
Germany	748	9.2
Iran	625	8.0
South Korea	611	12.5
Canada	553	16.2
Saudi Arabia	514	19.7
United Kingdom	497	7.9
Brazil	475	2.4
Mexico	462	4.1
South Africa	462	9.4
Indonesia	427	1.7
Italy	401	6.6
Australia	393	18.0
France	374	5.7
Spain	319	6.8
Poland	308	8.0

Source: UCSUSA (2014).

Most carbon dioxide emissions come from two major sources: electricity and heat generation. These two sectors taken together accounted for 42 percent of overall emissions, while transportation accounts for 23 percent, meaning that two-thirds of all emissions generated are for electricity, heat, and transportation. Industry accounts for another 20 percent, residential for 6 percent, and other, such as commercial/public service, agricultural/forestry, fishing energy industries, for 9 percent (IEA 2014: 10). According to the IEA, "carbon dioxide emissions from electricity and heat almost doubled between 1990 and 2012, driven by the large increase from coal" (2014: 10). Coal is used around the world to generate electricity and heat because there is an abundant supply, especially in countries like China, India, Australia, South Africa, and Poland. Unfortunately, coal is also the most carbon-intensive fossil fuel (IEA 2014: 10). From 2011 to 2012, "carbon dioxide emissions from electricity and heat increased 1.8% . . . while the share of oil in electricity and heat emissions has declined steadily since 1990, the share of gas increased slightly, and the share of coal increased significantly, from 65% in 1990 to 72% in 2012" (2014: 11). With respect to transport, carbon dioxide emissions from cars and trucks have increased 64 percent since 1990, accounting for three-quarters of 2012 transport emissions. Marine and aviation emissions have also increased: marine carbon dioxide emissions have increased 66 percent from 1990 levels and avaiton bunkers have increased by 80 percent from 1990 levels (IEA 2014: 11).

A Brief History of Climate Control Policies

In 1972, the United Nations Conference on the Human Environment, also known as the Stockholm Conference, was held. This conference brought together 114 governments and was attended by many nongovernmental organizations. It was the first time in history that those nations of the world came together to discuss issues surrounding the destruction of the environment (Switzer 1994; Valente and Valente 1995). The Stockholm Conference did not create any binding obligations, but served more as a catalyst to generate an international discourse on global environmental issues.

The first World Climate Conference was held in Geneva in February 1979, to discuss global warming and other related climate issues (Gupta 2010). Other political and scientific conferences followed: Villach, Austria, in 1985; Hamburg, Germany, in 1987; and Toronto, Canada, in 1988. Climate change was now in the spotlight and being treated as a global environmental and development problem (Gupta 2010). The Intergovernmental Panel on Climate Change (IPCC) was established in 1988 as a result of these conferences, and the first IPCC report was published in 1990. In 1989 the Netherlands held a high-level political meeting with heads of state for the sole purpose deliberating climate change, and the small island states held their first meeting to discuss the issue of climate change due to the fact they will be the first affected by rising water levels. By 1990, it was clear that climate change was an issue on the minds of scientists and nations (Gupta 2010). The IPCC report summarized all the collective science on climate change, suggesting at the time that carbon dioxide levels needed to be stabilized at 1990 levels, which would mean reducing all the greenhouse gas emissions significantly overtime to maintain the 1990 level.

The 1992 United Nations Conference on the Environment and Development, also known as the Rio Conference or Earth Summit, began serious global efforts to confront the problem of reducing carbon dioxide emissions. The Rio Conference was attended by 178 countries and 110 heads of state (Switzer 1994). One of the five major documents produced at the conference was the Framework Convention on Climate Change. Its purpose was the "stabilization of greenhouse gas concentrations in the atmosphere at the level that would prevent dangerous anthropogenic interferences in the climate system" (Flavin 1996: 36).

Although the United States, headed by the George H. W. Bush administration, was a major actor at the Rio Conference, it fought the binding of targeted carbon dioxide reductions to 1990 levels. Despite US reluctance to agree to the targeted carbon dioxide reductions, many industrialized European nations signed "a separate declaration to reaffirm their commitment to reducing their own CO_2 emissions to 1990 levels" (Gore 1992: xiv). In 1993, President Bill Clinton reversed the Bush administration's position, announcing that the United States would reduce carbon dioxide emissions to 1990 levels by 2000. But many of the efficiency initiatives enacted by the US Congress in 1992 (regarding appliance and lighting, for example) were weakened in 1994 and 1995, and remained severely underfunded (Flavin 1996).

Persuading the industrialized nations to make serious commitments to carbon dioxide reductions has become a major concern of the Alliance of Small Island States (AOSIS) and worldwide insurance companies. Insurance companies have become important actors in the climate change issue as well. The world's largest insurance companies, especially those dealing with property and casualty, obviously have a stake in any losses that may occur due to global warming. With sea levels rising and temperatures increasing, insurance companies expect greater losses. As noted previously, AOSIS is a small coalition of island nations that are extremely threatened by rising seas. A rise of one meter in sea level could flood their lands and destroy their economies. At the Conference of the Parties (COP) Berlin Conference, AOSIS proposed that industrial nations reduce their carbon dioxide emissions by 20 percent. This proposal was endorsed by seventy-seven non-AOSIS nations that participated in the conference, but was resisted by the majority of oil-producing states, like Kuwait and Saudi Arabia, and by larger carbon-emitting countries, like the United States and Australia (Brown 1996; Flavin 1996).

The primary objective of the Berlin Conference was to design measures that would reduce global emissions and to create a series of trial projects aimed at exchanging alternative low-carbon technologies among nations (Flavin 1996; Gupta 2010). Despite the fact that no legally binding carbon reduction targets were established, the Berlin Conference did provide a sense of renewed hope in formulating a global policy for mitigating climate change. The agreement reached at Berlin, known as the Berlin Mandate, instructs governments "to promote legally binding reduction commitments with regard to time horizons such as 2005, 2010, and 2020 to be adopted at COP-3 in 1997 at Kyoto" (Gupta 2010: 639).

The second IPCC report was published in 1996. The report noted that "the balance of evidence suggests a discernible human influence on the global climate" (Gupta 2010: 639). The Kyoto Protocol was adopted on December 11, 1997, and opened for signature on March 16, 1998. The protocol contains legally binding emission targets for key greenhouse gases, especially carbon dioxide, methane, and nitrous oxide. The agreement requires ratification by fifty-five countries; these fifty-five must include developed countries representing 55 percent of the carbon dioxide emissions of the ratifiers. According to the United Nations: "The overall commitment adopted by developed countries in Kyoto was to reduce their emissions of greenhouse gases by some 5.2 percent below 1990 levels by a budget period of 2008 to 2012. While the percentage did not seem significant, it represented emissions levels that were about 29 percent below what they would have been in the absence of the Protocol" (UN 1998).

One of the problems with Kyoto was the vagueness of negotiators in elaborating how countries could achieve reductions through emission trading (an alternative to socially regulated commons). Through emissions trading, a country that reduces its emissions below its allotted level can "trade" its unused emissions to countries that are achieving less success in reducing carbon emissions. Also vaguely elaborated at Kyoto was the degree to which carbon sinks—forests, rangelands, and croplands that absorb carbon—should count toward a country's effort to reduce global warming. It is also important to note here that the United States passed, prior to Kyoto, the Byrd-Hagel Resolution in 1997. The resolution forbid the United States from accepting any "future binding quantitative targets until and unless the key developing countries also participated meaningfully, especially because of the increased costs associated with taking action for the United States" (Gupta 2010: 643).

The third IPCC assessment report was published in 2000. The report affirmed previous climate change science and postulated that in light "of new evidence and taking into account the remaining uncertainties, most of the observed warming over the last 50 years is likely (66–90%) to have been due to the increase in [greenhouse gas] concentrations" (Gupta 2010: 643). At COP-6, the Hague Conference in 2000, the question of how to count reductions in carbon emissions remained the major obstacle. The United States, Canada, Japan, and Australia favored using flexible and creative approaches such as carbon sinks and market-based mechanisms, including emissions trading. Other European countries, however, interpreted the US advocacy of flexible methods as an attempt to avoid reducing emissions from cars, factories, and power plants. Many European countries wanted to reduce greenhouse gas emissions through the development of non–fossil fuel technology. However, according to one study of five European nations, only the United Kingdom and possibly Germany will meet Kyoto's emission reduction targets; also, it is unlikely that the United States will reach the targets, since it would have to reduce its emissions by 30 percent (Kerr 2000). In contrast to Europe, the United States wants to achieve the Kyoto targets without reducing greenhouse gases, because such cuts would likely involve increased coal and oil prices. Negotiations at the Hague Conference ultimately ended in deadlock over how to measure emission reductions.

In November 2001, negotiators from 160 countries met in Marrakech, Morocco, for COP-7 and agreed on the details of the Kyoto Protocol. In the resulting treaty, industrialized countries (with the glaring exception of the United States) agreed to reduce carbon dioxide by an average of 5.2 percent below 1990 levels by the end of 2012. The United States, under President George W. Bush, withdrew from negotiations ostensibly to protect its "economic best interest" (Athanasiou and Baer 2002: 117). Until the end of 2004, without the United States, negotiators had not been able to enlist the required support of countries responsible for generating 55 percent of carbon dioxide emissions, as required by the Kyoto Protocol. However, at the end of 2004, Russia, which had been reluctant to sign the treaty, announced its support for the Kyoto Protocol and ratified it. The protocol officially went into effect early in 2005.

The treaty combined emissions trading and carbon sinks as well as required emission cuts. Critics questioned the exemption of developing nations from the treaty, due to economic infeasibility and low levels of carbon dioxide emissions. They all questioned the significance of the treaty, given the absence of the United States.

The Kyoto Protocol, the world's only international treaty on global warming, was designed to expire at the end of 2012. At the 2007 summit of the Group of Eight (G8) industrialized nations in Germany, a major goal was to secure a commitment from the richest nations to prevent an average rise in global temperatures of more than 2 degrees Celsius (3.6 degrees Fahrenheit). The second phase of the Kyoto Protocol talks was also convened in 2007, in Bali (COP-13), to create a set of mandatory emission goals. A week before the G8 summit, however, President Bush announced that the United States would convene a series of meetings in the fall of 2007 to design a strategy to reduce greenhouse gas emissions. Bush's plan called for the ten to fifteen largest greenhouse gas–emitting nations to construct a post-Kyoto agreement that would set no mandatory or binding emission targets and focus only on technological solutions, with each country free to set its own goals and reduction targets.

Critics suggested that Bush was attempting to undermine existing efforts by the UN and the European Union to secure mandatory emission reductions. That charge was bolstered by a 2006 survey conducted by the Union of Concerned Scientists, which found that 58 percent of 279 scientists working in US federal agencies had been asked to eliminate terms like "climate change" and "global warming" from their reports. The survey also found that scientific reports were edited to change their meaning and that scientific findings were deliberately misrepresented. Over a five-year period, the survey reported 435 incidents of political interference (Monbiot 2007). In fact, the only agreement that came out of the G8 summit was to make "substantial cuts" in greenhouse gas emissions.

At the 2007 COP-13 Bali meeting, some progress was made, as the conference delegates agreed to a two-year process to generate a future post-Kyoto agreement. Countries also agreed in principle that "deep cuts in global emissions will be required" to reduce the effects of climate change. However, key obstacles still remain. The United States refused to go along with the European Union's proposal for mandatory cuts and wants key developing countries, like China and India, to be treated the same as developed countries. Also in 2007, the IPCC released its fourth assessment report, stating this time that it was 90 percent certain that observed increases in temperatures since the mid–twentieth century were the result of human-created greenhouse gases (Guzman 2013).

The December 2009 COP-15 Copenhagen Conference was based on ongoing negotiations from the 2007 Bali Action Plan. Hopes were high that President Barack Obama, who campaigned on building a new green energy infrastructure, would bring about change in US policy regarding climate change. President Obama did broker the Copenhagen Accord with a few key developing-nation leaders on the final day of the conference. There were a few governments that objected to the Copenhagen Accord because of its weaknesses. Some of the major provisions of the Copenhagen Accord include limiting the average rise in global temperatures to 2 degree Celsius; creating a process for countries to design specific emission reduction plans; creating criteria for reporting and verifying emission reductions; a commitment on the part of developed nations to generate $30 billion in additional resources in 2010–2012 to aid developing countries in reducing emissions, preserving forests, and adapting to climate change; and setting a goal of generating $100 billion to address the climate change needs of developing countries by 2020 (PCGCC 2009). Parties extended ad hoc working groups formed under the United Nations Framework Convention on Climate Change and the Kyoto Protocol in order to "continue negotiating toward a fuller agreement in late 2010 in Mexico" (PCGCC 2009).

Critics of the Copenhagen Accord note that it is not legally binding, there are no binding emission targets, and the amount of money targeted to help develop nations is far too low. On the upside, however, both China and India agreed to report to an international emission verification system. There were some criticisms of the US emphasis on the voluntary pledge of emission reduction rather than legally binding targets. One very positive aspect of the negotiations was the admission that the world cannot afford an average rise in global temperatures of 2 degrees Celsius above preindustrial levels (Vaughan and Adam 2009).

The 2010 COP-16 conference in Cancún, Mexico, built on the Copenhagen Accord with respect to the approving decisions regarding (nonbinding) national mitigation pledges, greater transparency, and establishment of a climate fund for developing nations. Also, an agreement was reached on a system of consultants to verify countries' data reporting. In Cancún, all the major economic powers agreed to reduce their emissions, which was a dramatic difference from the rancor that characterized Copenhagen. Cancún laid the groundwork for possibly establishing some binding emission reduction targets for the COP-17 conference in Durban, South Africa, in 2011.

The Durban meeting ended with some very modest and vague agreements. The agreements essentially renewed the Kyoto Protocol, but began movement toward a new framework that treats North and South the same (unlike Kyoto, which does not include the South). Furthermore, the Green Climate Fund for Developing Nations was established, which seeks to create an account of $100 billion per year beginning in 2020. The fund will assist Southern countries in developing green technology and preserving tropical forests (Broder 2011). Not surprisingly, critics blasted the Durban agreements from different sides. At one end of the spectrum were scientists and environmentalists who argued that the agreement did not go far enough. In contrast, the fossil fuel lobby and global warming deniers (including some US legislators) criticized the very assumption that humans were a contributor to climate change, in spite of overwhelming evidence of consistent warming.

The COP-18 climate negotiations in Doha, Qatar, in December 2012, agreed to the Doha Amendment, which creates a new commitment period under the Kyoto Protocol, maintaining the current legal and accounting models in which developed countries continue to lead the process to cut greenhouse emissions. The delegates agreed on a commitment to take unspecified action to reduce greenhouse gas emissions further. They established a timetable to adopt a universal climate agreement by 2015 wherein all parties would be held to legally binding actions, which would become effective in 2020. Delegates made some inroads on establishing financial and technological support for clean energy investment and sustainable growth in developing countries, but were vague on details.

Environmental critics of the Doha negotiations suggested that there is a real disconnect between the ambitions of the parties and what really needs to happen to combat climate change. The chair of the Alliance of Small Island States, Kieren Keke, noted that negotiations were "deeply deficient." The other major criticism entailed no specific mechanism for administering to vulnerable countries the financial and technical support agreed upon by the parties (Broder 2012).

The 2013 COP-19 climate change conference in Warsaw, Poland, produced some success but also much frustration. Participating governments agreed to communicate their respective contributions prior to the 2015 meeting in Paris to establish the Universal Climate Agreement. A breakthrough outcome on mitigating greenhouse emissions from forest degradation and deforestation was decided, and a mechanism was established for addressing "loss and damage" caused by climate change to poor nations. There was progress in finalizing the capitalization of the Green Climate Fund, which is designed to channel financing for the developing world to help it adapt to climate change. Criticisms mostly focused on a lack of details regarding timelines for developed nations to contribute to the Green Climate Fund, and debates raged on among developed and developing nations about who should bear the brunt of responsibility for the climate situation.

The IPCC released its fifth assessment report in 2014, succinctly concluding that "human influence on the climate system is clear, and recent anthropogenic emissions of greenhouse gases are the highest in history. . . . The atmosphere and oceans have warmed, the amounts of snow and ice have diminished, and sea level has risen" (IPPC 2014: 2). As evidence of climate change becomes unequivocal, international urgency to forge a universal climate agreement becomes paramount.

The COP-20 climate conference in Lima, Peru, in December of 2014, may have been the breakthrough that over two decades of international negotiations have been aiming to complete. The Lima Accord accomplished the feat of getting all nations, developed and developing, to agree to reduce their greenhouse emissions from the burning of fossil fuel. The accord requires every country to submit plans detailing how they are going to reduce their emissions after 2020 at home. The plans require a detailed strategy outlining domestic policies and laws aimed at achieving cuts in emissions based on each country's reduction percentage pledge. For example, the Obama administration has pledged that the United States will cut emissions by as much as 28 percent by 2025. The primary mechanism by which the

United States will accomplish this goal is to reduce emissions from transportation and power plants regulated through the Environmental Protection Agency (EPA). The Lima Accord requires that all nations submit their plans to the United Nations, which will make the plans available to the public.

The Lima Accord does not have binding targets or legal sanctions that can be enforced against any nation. In short, the accord is not a top-down mandate but an agreement designed to use peer pressure to encourage every nation to submit plans that amount to an overall reduction in the world's greenhouse gas emissions. There are no legal repercussions for failure to submit plans. The accord is not based on a scientific analysis of how much greenhouse gas emissions each country needs to cut in order to ensure we do not cross the 2 degree Celsius threshold. It is a political agreement, not a scientific one.

The December 2015 Paris meeting (COP-21) came on the heels of a 2014 agreement between the United States and China in which both pledged to future reductions of carbon emissions. The United States agreed to reduce its carbon emission levels by between 26 and 28 percent by 2025 compared to 2005, while China pledged to begin reducing its total emissions by 2030 if not sooner. Building on that momentum, 195 countries agreed in Paris to reduce their future greenhouse gas emissions through a mix of voluntary and mandatory actions. The agreement was made with an eye toward the 2 degree Celsius goal, but increased future cuts will need to be made to achieve that level. The North agreed to financially assist the South's emission reductions, but was not legally bound to do so at the $100 billion per year level the South desired. Other positive measures were new safeguards, including greater transparency, to prevent cheating by countries, and an agreement to reconvene every five years to seek more stringent cuts in greenhouse gas emissions. Of course, not all countries were pleased with the results. Countries at low sea levels sought deeper cuts and developing countries sought more commitment by wealthy countries. Others lamented the lack of mandatory cuts in emissions. Yet overall, delegates and observers regarded the COP-21 summit as movement in the right direction.

With respect to the United States, President Obama's climate change policies have been confusing and inconsistent. On the one hand, Obama has opened up vast areas of public lands for the drilling of oil and natural gas, and has opened some coastal areas and the arctic for offshore oil drilling. Obama has maintained that these policies are for the purpose of creating energy independence. On the other hand, Obama in a 2015 commencement address to the Coast Guard Academy claimed that "climate change, especially rising seas, is a threat to our homeland security—our economic infrastructure, and the safety and health of the America People." Obama went on to say: "I am here today to say that climate change constitutes a serious threat to global security, an immediate risk to our national security, and, make no mistake, it will impact how our military defends our country"

(Davis 2015). Obama also acknowledged that changing climatic conditions would create a surge in the number of climate change refugees. Obama's plan for dealing with the problem is based on new rules promulgated by the EPA to reduce carbon dioxide emissions by 28 percent from 2005 levels by reducing carbon emitted by coal-fired power plants and automobiles. The Republicans and the coal industry quickly criticized the plan, arguing that it was a huge executive overreach that would cost the economy jobs.

Substituting Alternative Energy for Fossil Fuel

Many nations are reducing their carbon dioxide output by replacing fossil fuel electric power generation with alternative energy, despite any international binding agreement. Currently, the majority of electricity in the world is generated by fossil fuels, 68 percent, with nuclear fission accounting for another 11 percent. Alternative energy production accounts for just over 20 percent of the total of the world's electricity production (Energies-Renouvelables 2013). The most-used alternative energies for generating electricity, constituting 20 percent of global electricity generation, are hydroelectricity, 78 percent; wind power, 11.4 percent; biomass, 6.9 percent; solar, 2.2 percent; geothermal, 1.5 percent; and marine energies, 0.01 percent (Energies-Renouvelables 2013).

Some countries are taking the lead in developing renewable energy. During the first seventy-five days of 2015, Costa Rica ran its entire nation on renewable energy with expectation that energy prices would decrease for consumers. Costa Rica generates most of its power with hydroelectric plants, geothermal, and some wind and solar, and uses fossil fuel only as backup. Costa Rica has set a goal to become carbon-neutral by 2021 (Siegel 2015).

Denmark, the United Kingdom, Germany, Scotland, and Ireland all set records for renewable energy production in 2014, relying mostly on wind and some solar. Denmark currently obtains 39 percent of its electricity from renewable energy sources and is expected to produce 50 percent of all its electricity from renewable energy by 2020. Wind power is also the cheapest form of electricity generation in Denmark. The United Kingdom now generates 9.3 percent of its electricity from wind, and can supply 6.7 million households with electricity from clean energy. Germany has made great strides in clean energy as well, using a combination of solar and wind power. Europe's largest economy, Germany now generates 26 percent of its electricity from clean energy sources. In 2014, wind power provided 100 percent of Scotland's household electricity for over six months of the year, and June and July sunshine provided 100 percent of the electrical power needs for the cities of Aberdeen, Edinburgh, Glasgow, and Inverness. Scotland's electric power grid could be completely generated by renewable energy by 2030. Ireland also set wind power electricity generation records in 2014 by providing 1.3 million homes with clean energy (Smith 2015).

The United States has also increased its clean energy capacity by generating 14 percent of its total electricity needs from renewable energy sources like biomass, geothermal, hydropower, solar, and wind, with hydropower accounting for 7 percent and the other renewable sources constituting the remainder. Wind power grew by 9 percent between 2013 and 2014, accounting for 5 percent of the nation's total electricity generation. Solar power also increased, rising in the first six months of 2014 by 116 percent, which is more than double from the previous year. Energy generated from biomass also increased, by 4 percent, from the previous year. The US Energy Information Administration was forecasting not so long ago that the United States would not reach 14 percent electricity generation from renewable sources until the year 2040 (Bossong 2014).

If it can be shown that renewable energy is cost-effective, which it is in the examples provided here, then we have an economic motivator to help wean ourselves off of fossil fuel electricity generation and switch to clean energy renewables. The United States is second in the world behind China in renewable energy investment (Smith 2015). The technology exists to produce 100 percent renewable energy electricity throughout most places in the world. The question is whether the world has the will to carry out this task with the expediency that is necessary to prevent further global warming and accompanying climate change. Not acting quickly enough may lead us down a much more risky and potentially catastrophic path of geoengineering.

The Geoengineering Option

Texas and Oklahoma recently endured historic flooding, leading to casualities and massive property loss, and India is undergoing a heat wave that has taken over a thousand lives with temperatures reaching 122 degrees Fahrenheit. If government action is not enough and the climate continues to become increasingly unstable, then many scientists, engineers, and politicians have advocated that we begin experimenting with geoengineering. Geoengineering is the planned manipulation of Earth's climate by engaging in a range of activities including manipulating the planet's cloud cover, changing the chemistry of the oceans to enable them to absorb more carbon, creating a planetary filter to reflect sunlight, and finding ways to capture and safely store carbon dioxide (Hamilton 2013). Geoengineering strategies tend to be divided into two categories: carbon dioxide removal and solar radiation management. Carbon dioxide removal is the process of extracting carbon from our atmosphere and storing it someplace else like in vegetation, the oceans, or underground. Solar radiation management entails limiting the amount of sunlight hitting Earth through increasing cloud cover and reflection (Hamilton 2013).

Some of the strategies for removing carbon from the atmosphere are liming the seas. "Climate engineering via enhanced weathering would aim to hasten the natural process. Rocks would be crushed and chemically transformed so that carbon dioxide gas in the air became embedded in an alkaline bicarbonate solution, which could then be mixed into seawater" (Clive Hamilton 2013: 41). This would increase the ocean's ability to absorb more carbon dioxide. Another strategy is to plant more vegetation, grow algae, and enhance soil to absorb more carbon dioxide. The goal is to sequester more carbon. Purifying the air through industrial processes involves "using water and chemicals, such as sodium hydroxide (caustic soda), to generate carbonate solids. The carbon dioxide is then extracted by heating, usually with natural gas" (Hamilton 2013: 47). In short, all of these strategies are aimed at increasing Earth's ability to absorb more carbon dioxide. It took Earth millions of years to store safely the carbon we are burning now. Every one of these strategies, with the exception of planting more vegetation, requires large-scale industrial infrastructure to combat industrial-scale production. While planting trees and creating large green spaces for vegetation to grow is always a good idea, it is always subject to carbon dioxide release due to natural causes like fire and human land development. As Clive Hamilton (2013) rightly points out, it makes much more sense to reduce our reliance on fossil fuel than to create a massive industrial infrastructure to combat the effects of our massive industrial infrastructure.

With respect to solar radiation management, some solutions being touted by scientists involve brightening clouds, modifying cirrus clouds, spraying sulfur, and tailoring solar filtration. These strategies involve reflecting sunlight away from Earth by modifying clouds or by creating a filter by spraying sulfate particles into the upper atmosphere much like what happens when a volcanic eruption occurs. As past volcanic eruptions have demonstrated, there are numerous problems associated with spraying sulfate aerosols, including shifts in climate that might affect food production, possible changes in monsoonal patterns, and further depletion of the ozone layer, which we are in the process of repairing. There are many unanswered questions with solar radiation management technology, especially if we have to rely on it indefinitely to control Earth's climate (Hamilton 2013).

It has been technology, spurred by the Industrial Revolution, that has brought us to the climate situation in which we now find ourselves. To turn to the technological treadmill to fix our complex climate, which has taken billions of years to evolve, is arrogant and extremely risky at best, and potentially catastrophic in a worst-case scenario. To engage in geoengineering is to go through the looking glass, from which there will be no return whatever the consequences. The big question to keep in mind is what could go wrong.

Conclusion

The weather is often the lead story in the evening news these days. Our climate is changing and the consequences are loss of human and nonhuman life, massive property destruction, and permanent displacement of human beings from their homes as climate refugees. Of course, there have always been weather-related disasters throughout history, but their frequency and severity are on the rise as the data demonstrate. Climate change is a product of human beings burning massive amounts of fossil fuels to live an industrial, consumer, capitalist lifestyle that has exceeded the natural process of Earth to mitigate our carbon footprint. Our lifestyle is no longer sustainable, meaning we cannot continue to live indefinitely as we are now, especially considering our growing population and increasing appetite for a consumer-based lifestyle without constraint. The evidence provided by the overwhelming majority of the scientific community is clear with respect to the fact that humans are the cause of our current climate problem.

Countries are working toward our first universal climate agreement, acknowledging that every nation has a role in reducing the world's carbon footprint. The big question is whether the efforts will be enough. Three decades ago, when the world was faced with the threat of a depleting ozone layer, countries cooperated to create an international environmental agreement that is responsible for preventing its further disintegration and promoting its eventual repair. Humans showed their wisdom by recognizing that there are limits to how we use our environment. It is time to consider the best science available and seek an international agreement that prevents us from destroying the habitat on which we all depend.

Refusing to take serious steps to limit our reliance on fossil fuels will result in the further destabilization of our climate and the possible need to consider geoengineering options. We are already beginning to see world conflicts on the rise due to drought, famine, access to fresh water, and rising sea levels. Both the CIA and the US military have openly acknowledged that climate-related issues are going to become a source of global conflict, especially if we do not begin to take serious actions to alter our global carbon footprint.

Discussion Questions

1. What are some of the ways the largest greenhouse-contributor nations could reduce their emissions?

2. What individual actions can you take to reduce your carbon footprint?

3. Will global conferences on climate change lead to a significant reduction in greenhouse gas emissions?

4. Does the North have an obligation to help the South develop in a more environmentally safe way? Does it have an interest in helping?

5. How seriously should countries consider geoengineering.

Suggested Readings

Climate Central (2012) *Global Weirdness: Severe Storms, Deadly Heat Waves, Relentless Drought, Rising Seas, and the Weather of the Future.* New York: Vintage.

——— (2015) "10 Warmest Years on Record Globally." www.climatecentral.org.

Darling, Seth B., and Douglas L. Sisterson (2014) *How to Change Minds About Our Changing Climate.* New York: The Experiment.

Hamilton, Clive (2013) *Earth Masters: The Dawn of the Age of Climate Engineering.* New Haven: Yale University Press.

Intergovernmental Panel on Climate Change (2015) "Climate Change 2014: Synthesis Report." www.ipcc.ch.

McKibben, Bill (2010) *Earth: Making a Life on a Tough New Planet.* New York: Times Books.

National Aeronautics and Space Administration (2015) "Global Climate Change: Vital Signs of the Planet." http://climate.nasa.gov.

National Oceanic and Atmospheric Administration (2015) "Global Analysis: March 2015" (April). www.ncdc.noaa.gov.

Part 3
Conclusion

16

Future Prospects

Michael T. Snarr and Megan L. Canfield

WHAT WILL THE FUTURE BE LIKE? WILL THINGS GET BETTER OR WORSE? Will humans organize themselves to more effectively confront global issues? Can the world work together to promote sustainable development or will poverty, gender disparities, climate change, and human rights violations continue to create obstacles to further cooperation? Possible scenarios for the world several decades into the future include world government, regionalism, decentralization, and the status quo.

World Government

Some scholars argue that a world government, consisting of a powerful central actor with significant authority, is the method by which we will organize ourselves in the future. The World Trade Organization's increasing consensus on economic issues, and the emergence of a multitude of free trade agreements, are often cited as evidence that some sort of weak world government is not out of the realm of possibility. Similarly, for those who argue that the world is moving toward a single global culture, a world government might not seem beyond reach. However, this possibility is not likely to occur, and certainly not anytime soon.

In theory, a world government would be more effective at addressing salient global issues, since power would be much more centralized. An obvious problem with the world government scenario, and the reason it will not be realized anytime soon, is the unlikeliness that the countries of the world would voluntarily give up their sovereignty. Furthermore, a world government would face many practical problems, such as who would be responsible for enforcing laws. Would a world government have a powerful military? If so, a justifiable fear of tyranny would result. If not, its enforcement capabilities would be questionable.

There are other possibilities in addition to a true world government. A *federation* would establish a relatively weaker world government, similar to the model of the United States, where the federal government shares power with the states. Even weaker would be a *confederation*, in which states would be the dominant actors but would give the world government some jurisdiction. Both federate and confederate systems would give a world government more power than the United Nations currently possesses.

Regionalism

In the regionalism scenario, countries would be organized into groups based on geographic proximity, perhaps following the pattern of current economic groupings like the North American Free Trade Agreement (NAFTA) countries, the European Union (EU), and the Asia Pacific Economic Cooperation (APEC) forum. As with a world government, countries would not completely relinquish their sovereignty, but it would be significantly reduced. Currently, the European Union is the leader in the movement toward economic and political cooperation. Not only has the EU drastically reduced barriers to economic integration and to the movement of people within its borders, but it has also adopted a single economic currency and made some progress toward a common foreign policy. Although NAFTA and APEC are relatively young in comparison to the EU, their formation represents the current popularity of regional arrangements.

Of course, the regionalism scenario also must deal with the reluctance of countries to relinquish their sovereignty, the fear of concentrating too much power in the hands of a central government, and the perception by some countries that others are behaving irresponsibly. The European Union's recent frustration over Greece's mishandling of its economic troubles is a case in point. However, these issues may be easier to resolve in smaller groupings of states than in a world government context.

On the positive side, regionalism would facilitate the coordination of regional policymaking on global issues such as the environment, human rights, and trade. Still, the enhanced ability of countries to coordinate policies within their respective regions would not necessarily translate into cooperation between regions. It could be argued that regionalism would simply transform a world in which *countries* compete into one in which *regions* compete, without solving pressing global problems.

Decentralization and Self-Reliance

At the same time that free trade and environmental agreements are being enacted, creating more centralized authority, there is significant movement toward decentralization of power. Historical movements mounted by strong separatist movements in Canada (by its French-speaking province of Quebec), the former Soviet Union, and the former Yugoslavia are prime examples of decentralization. More recently, East Timor, Montenegro, and South Sudan became independent countries after breaking off from Indonesia, Serbia and Montenegro, and Sudan, respectively. Although the various separatist movements have differing motives, many of them do have in common a desire for self-determination—that is, the desire to break away from the dominant culture and govern themselves. Consider that in the 1940s the world had just over 50 countries, but now it has nearly 200. The proliferation of decentralized terrorist cells can also be considered part of this movement toward greater local control.

This trend certainly casts doubt on a future involving "one world" or just a few regions. Each new country would of course be smaller and more culturally homogeneous than today's countries, which ideally would alleviate some of the nationalist tensions discussed in Chapter 4. However, this also would make achieving international consensus on issues like the environment, human rights, and nuclear proliferation more difficult.

There is, however, another type of locally oriented movement, commonly referred to as *civil society,* which has gained attention in recent years. In fact, many of the new hopeful prospects for the future that offer real improvements are civil society movements. Civil society comprises nongovernmental, nonprofit groups such as social service providers, foundations, neighborhood watch groups, and religion-based organizations. La Via Campesina (Chapter 13) and Inveneo (Chapter 5) are examples of civil society, as is the Bill and Melinda Gates foundation, which recently pledged $2 billion for green energy. In recent decades, more and more people have turned to civil society, rather than government, to solve their problems. Reading this book, you may have noticed the many global nongovernmental organizations (NGOs) mentioned. The number of NGOs has increased dramatically, from about 200 in the early 1900s to approximately 5,000 today. Their ranks include Amnesty International, Greenpeace, CARE, the Mennonite Central Committee, and the World Wide Fund for Nature. Composed of private citizens in more than one country, they focus on such global issues as the environment, poverty, human rights, and peace.

Those who are frustrated with government's inability to solve global problems insist that centralized governments are not the most effective way to deal with these problems. Governments, they argue, are simply too far removed from local communities to understand completely the nature of a particular problem and to offer effective solutions. Advocates of civil society are encouraged by the dramatic increase in NGOs. Critics, however, believe that local grassroots efforts will be insufficient to solve global problems like nuclear proliferation, terrorism, and climate change. They argue that governments are the only actors with sufficient resources to effectively confront these large-scale issues.

Some civil society movements are teaching individuals how to reduce their dependence on external actors. One such movement gaining recognition, in places like the United Kingdom and the United States, is the shift toward greater local reliance with respect to food; that is, more communities are seeking to "buy local" or eat more local food. This movement teaches people to rely more on those around them and therefore keeps money in the local economy. When consumers buy products from outside their community or drive out of the community for entertainment, their money immediately leaves with them. In contrast, buying local products from locally owned stores keeps a higher percentage of the money in the local community. The buying of local food operates on the same principle. Evidence for the popularity of local food can be seen in the rise of farmers' markets and community-supported agriculture (mentioned in Chapter 8). In the latter, consumers within a community pay a farmer in advance for fresh fruit and vegetables throughout the growing season. A unique aspect of this arrangement is that the consumers share the farmer's risks. In case of a poor harvest, the farmer will be financially secure, though the consumers will lose their payment. Farmers' markets and community-supported agriculture offer several benefits for the consumer. In addition to keeping more money in the local community, local food is touted as a way to build strong communities as consumers get to know the people who grow their food. Proponents also argue that local food tastes better due to less transportation time and is often safer since it is not produced in large factories, which are often responsible for tainted food.

Although these locally focused movements do not necessarily reject globalization, they are concerned about the vulnerability of people to global economic influences. Increasing the degree of one's local control over their food supply and economy can buffer against global economic shocks.

Status Quo

Perhaps the most likely scenario is one in which no dramatic changes occur over the next several decades. This is not to say that change will be absent, but that it will be only a gradual continuation of current trends toward globalization in the areas of economic integration, information flow among countries, the importance of nongovernmental actors (including multinational corporations), and cooperation among countries on environmental and other issues. Citizens will continue to pledge their allegiance to countries, not economic blocs; states, not groups of private citizens, will remain the dominant political actors; and short-term domestic interests will prevent states from surrendering their sovereignty.

Unfortunately, the status quo, while making some significant progress in combating various global issues, has made disappointing progress on areas such as climate change, peacemaking, and poverty.

The Future . . . It's Complicated

After over a dozen chapters of global issues, the reader has undoubtedly realized that we live in a world full of complex global issues. Confronted with these sometimes overwhelming issues, it is important to remember that positive advances are being made on many fronts. Smallpox has been eliminated. A global effort is now well under way to address sustainable development. Women have been increasingly successful in forming effective grassroots movements and making their voices heard. Fewer wars are being fought and fewer people are dying as a result of wars. Infant mortality rates are declining. The percentage of people in the world living on less than a dollar per day has declined, as has the percentage of malnourished people.

It is also worth remembering that these issues are interconnected. Take for instance the daunting issue of widespread poverty. Chapters 7 and 11 pointed out that health is directly related to poverty—that the poorer you are, the more likely you are to suffer from disease or malnutrition. Chapters 11 discussed how the number of children a woman bears will decrease as poverty is alleviated; and Chapter 13 revealed how education allows women to gain more control over their lives in an attempt to transcend poverty. Chapters 14 and 15 showed that for those who are desperately poor, issues of immediate survival must take precedence over concerns about the environment. Chapter 3 underscored the vast amounts of money spent on military budgets at the expense of social programs such as healthcare and education, and that these budget cuts can increase the burden on women, who tend to be responsible for providing healthcare and education for children (mentioned in Chapter 13).

Central to the issue of poverty is the unequal distribution of wealth, which appears to be getting worse. Chapter 11 addressed this problem. At the same time, as those who live in the North know, poverty is not simply a question of North-South relations—there are many pockets of poverty within the wealthy countries, and evidence suggests that the gap between the rich and poor is increasing within countries as well as between them.

So how can worldwide poverty be overcome? Well, in simple terms, it's complicated. The issue is connected with many other issues as discussed here, and its solutions are complex. At the domestic level, a country historically must achieve economic growth before income can be redistributed, but economic growth does not guarantee better income distribution. Chapter 11 explained how focusing on taxation, education, healthcare, and other such issues is necessary to foster a more favorable distribution of wealth; however, such an approach typically receives little support from those whose wealth would be transferred. The issue becomes even more complex if we confront the *global* distribution of wealth. An attempt to tax the wealthy countries in order to pay for social programs in poorer countries would meet a great deal of opposition, not only from the wealthy in the North, but also from the middle- and lower-income populations in the North. Historically, voluntary aid from North to South may have helped a little, but it has been insufficient to seriously address the poverty gap. And as Chapter 10 revealed, free trade often has the effect of exacerbating gaps between the rich and poor.

To complicate matters further, emerging technologies are changing the landscape. Chapter 2 highlighted the increasing role of technology in its case studies on cyber-warfare and autonomous weapons. However, technology can help provide answers if used correctly. Hopeful innovations have emerged in the past decade that may provide the spark the world needs to bring about positive changes. For instance, in Kenya, anonymous data locations, gathered from cell phone usage, are being used to track the spread of malaria. Tracking high levels of human traffic in travel hotspots may help medical professionals understand the transmission of the disease. On another front, solar and wind technologies are providing clean energy alternatives to fossil fuels and giving hope in the battle against climate change.

Another layer of complexity comes when considering the effects of gender on potential gains from certain technologies. Current statistics reveal that women in developing countries are much less likely to own mobile phones than men. When women have extra economic resources, they are less likely than men to spend them on, for instance, a mobile phone. More of their income will go to health and education for their family. While basic needs have to be a top priority, cell phones could increase access to information in the realm of healthcare, agriculture, financial credit, education, and the like (Dobush 2015). Research has also shown that cell phones may increase literacy for women in the developing world who don't have access to books (Rayman 2014). And with respect to the connection between cell phones and malaria, fewer women will be considered when tracking the spread of malaria. And so, it is clear that these issues and the way forward are complicated.

This section is not meant to discourage the reader, but rather to highlight the need for more holistic approaches. For instance, in order to alleviate poverty, women must be empowered, healthcare must be expanded, poor farming techniques must be reduced, and so on. Likewise, more interdisciplinary research must be carried out, and governments must have the political will to tackle these issues. Beyond governments, more action by nongovernmental actors is needed.

What Can I Do?

The good news highlighted throughout this book is the result of governments, NGOs, and individuals working together to solve problems and alleviate suffering. It is important to recognize that the future has not yet been written and that various actions undertaken today can have a critical effect on the issues discussed in this book. Assuming you agree that these issues deserve serious attention, whether on grounds of self-interest, a sense of patriotism, a religious view, or a sense of humanitarianism (see Chapter 1 for an elaboration of these perspectives), the practical question remains: What can I do to make a positive difference?

Common suggestions include: write to your government representatives, vote, buy recycled products, and so on. Another option is to form, join, or support an NGO like those mentioned throughout this book. Take, for example, Equal Exchange, Educating for Justice, Social Accountability International, and the Friends Committee on National Legislation. Each of these four NGOs, organized by a relatively small group of people, seeks to relieve the suffering of many. All four share a general concern for peace and social justice issues like poverty, human rights, inequality, and the like. In particular, they focus on peace and justice issues. Here is a brief look at these four NGOs.

NGO Case Study: Equal Exchange

Throughout the world, millions of people are engaged in growing, harvesting, and processing coffee. Most of the coffee growers are individuals who own small plots of land and sell their coffee to middlemen who export the coffee to markets in the North. As a result of the March 2000 coffee price collapse, the price paid to coffee farmers dropped to as low as four cents per pound in October 2001, the lowest price in a century. As a result, many coffee farmers were forced out of business. Although in subsequent years the prices crept back up to more than a dollar per pound, profits are still meager for coffee farmers.

Equal Exchange is one of several companies working to improve the lives of coffee farmers throughout the world. Since 1991 it has helped small coffee farms by creating a market for certified "Fair Trade" coffee. In the United States, Fair Trade food and beverage products are certified by TransFair USA and bear its seal. The TransFair designation means, among other things, that farmers will receive a fair price for their coffee. Currently, the minimum price paid to farmers for nonorganic Fair Trade coffee is $1.40 per pound. This is a significantly better price than they would receive otherwise.

Participating coffee farmers must organize themselves into a cooperative (a business owned by the farmers themselves) and make decisions democratically. The cooperatives are also expected to pursue sustainable development and reinvest much of their profits into improving living conditions in their communities (for example, healthcare, housing, education). Coffee farms are monitored by outside groups to ensure that these practices are followed. Companies committed to fair trading for all their imports use a business model that accepts smaller profits, which enables them to free up more resources for paying the higher coffee prices to farmers.

Due to consumer interest, some of the coffee bought by Starbucks and Dunkin' Donuts is fairly traded. Despite the rapid growth of Fair Trade coffee over the past few years, and interest among large companies like Starbucks, Fair Trade coffee represents only about 5 percent of US coffee sales (Rohrlich 2015). For this kind of market reform to continue, consumers will have to make a conscious decision to ask for and buy Fair Trade coffee and similar fairly traded products like chocolate, tea, or bananas. For more information, see the Equal Exchange website at www.equalexchange.com.

NGO Case Study: Educating for Justice

This case also deals with fair wages and individuals in the North seeking solidarity with workers in the South. The story of Educating for Justice's "Team Sweat" campaign began with Jim Keady, an assistant soccer coach at St. John's University seeking his master's degree in theology. While researching a paper on Nike labor practices in 1998, Keady discovered that Nike was violating several tenets of Catholic social teaching. Given St. John's Catholic identity, Keady saw a troubling contradiction in the process of the university's negotiation of a multimillion-dollar endorsement contract with Nike. After months of trying to seek change through the school's administration, he was essentially forced to resign his position because he could not, in good conscience, follow his boss's order to wear Nike-labeled apparel. In a lawsuit, he charged that because he had been forced to become "a walking billboard" for Nike (evidence indicated he was not given the choice of wearing a uniform without the Nike logo), his freedom of speech had been violated.

Although his lawsuit was unsuccessful, Keady has continued to increase awareness of what he feels is an exploitative wage paid to Nike workers in Southeast Asia. Nike has responded that nobody is forcing these people to work in the factories and that it does in fact pay a reasonable wage, better than many other Indonesian jobs. In reaction to Nike's claims, Keady offered to work in a Nike factory, manufacturing shoes, in order to judge the fairness of the company's wages. Nike refused the offer, so in 2000, Keady and Leslie Kretzu (cofounder of Educating for Justice) set off for Indonesia to try to live on $1.25 per day, the average wage for those working in Indonesian shoe factories at that time. They spent four weeks living with Indonesian workers, and conducted two subsequent research trips. Kretzu has since moved on from the work, but Keady has remained with the cause. He now travels to Indonesia regularly to conduct trainings for workers and update his research, and he continues to lecture across the United States telling the story of Nike's impoverished Indonesian work force.

Keady has targeted Nike because of its high profile and because it is the industry leader. Keady points out that Nike chairman Phil Knight has a net worth of more than $13.1 billion, making him the sixtieth richest person in the world, but he refuses to pay third world workers a living wage, which in most countries is three to four times the local minimum wage. Other activists criticize Nike for pulling jobs out of factories that have independent trade unions.

Educating for Justice's public education and advocacy program on this issue now flies under the campaign banner of "Team Sweat." Team Sweat is an international coalition fighting to make Nike a fair trade company where workers are paid living wages and have tri-party (workers, factory, Nike) union contracts. Team Sweat utilizes a multipronged approach to bring about the desired outcomes. Their activities include direct actions, online petitions, shareholder activism, grassroots education, and engagement with Nike executives and board members.

It appears that Educating for Justice/Team Sweat is making some progress in its crusade to win better conditions for workers in Asia. In 2012 and 2013, Keady and his trade union allies won major multi-million dollar wage settlements for Nike workers in Indonesia. Nike has also recently admitted some mistakes and has made some minor changes to its policies, but the fight for living wages and tri-party union contracts continues. To learn more, see Educating for Justice's Team Sweat websites at www.facebook.com/teamsweat and www.teamsweat.org, and on Twitter @TeamSweat.

NGO Case Study: Social Accountability International

Social Accountability International, a multistakeholder initiative, was established in 1997. It seeks to ensure that internationally accepted human rights pertaining to child labor, forced labor, health and safety, freedom of association, discrimination, discipline, working hours, and the like, are upheld in workplaces throughout the world.

Social Accountability International's workplace standards are referred to as "SA8000." A company certified as such demonstrates to consumers and other businesses that it provides a humane workplace. A growing number of companies have suppliers and facilities that are SA8000-certified, including Gap, Avon Products, Tchibo, Otto, Co-op Italia, Eileen Fisher, and Chiquita Brands International. Government programs in several exporting countries prefer or subsidize the use of SA8000 products.

Social Accountability International provides training programs and works to promote SA8000 certification in many countries around the world, including the United States, France, India, Germany, China, Honduras, Brazil, Italy, and Pakistan. Hundreds of thousands of people in over sixty countries, spanning North and South America, Europe, Africa, and Asia, are employed in workplaces that are SA8000-certified.

Consumers play an important role in ensuring the success of such voluntary programs. When individuals buy from certified companies, they help to protect workers' rights. Other businesses get the message that, in order to compete, they too need to respect workers' rights.

In addition to working with companies, Social Accountability International collaborates with a network of other NGOs, such as Amnesty International on the human rights front, as well as with labor organizations and governmental agencies. For more information, see the Social Accountability International website at www.sa-intl.org.

NGO Case Study: Friends Committee on National Legislation

The Friends Committee on National Legislation (FCNL) is a Quaker nonprofit, public interest lobby group. Lobbying groups are often viewed in a negative light and discredited because many have narrow, self-interest agendas. In contrast, the FCNL is run by a general committee comprising nearly 200 Quakers from across the country, rather than by a board of directors or shareholders.

The FCNL seeks to use Quaker values of peace, equality, and social justice to influence public policies for the good of all citizens, not just the interests of Quakers or any other specific group. Simply put, the members of this organization seek what they feel is best for the common good. In the words of the FCNL's mission statement, the lobbying group "seek[s] a world free of war and the threat of war . . . a society with equality and justice for all . . . a community where every person's potential may be fulfilled . . . [and] an earth restored" (FCNL 2013).

How does it do this? The FCNL has the largest group of registered peace lobbyists on Capitol Hill. These lobbyists focus their attention on issues such as climate change, demilitarizing US police forces, and countering mass incarceration. Of particular concern to the FCNL is the budget priorities of the United States: over 50 percent of the nation's discretionary spending—which does not include Social Security, Medicaid, Medicare—goes specifically toward military spending (NPP 2015).The FCNL community advocates for redistributing funds away from Pentagon spending into other budget priorities, such as reacting to climate change, advocating for universal human rights, and, of course, speaking out against continued war. The FCNL believes that all of these issues contribute to continuing conflict and inequality and that new policies will help prevent future violent conflict and protect civilians through spreading peace.

Related to the FCNL's attempt to reduce the US military budget is its peacebuilding program, which seeks to advocate US government policies that focus on preventing deadly conflicts in the future instead of fighting wars. According to the Global Peace Index, investing in peace around the world could reap a benefit of close to $9 trillion. The FCNL's program aims to "strengthen the conflict resolution capacity of local leaders, reinforce sustainable dispute resolution and increase trust through social, and economic programs . . . and by promoting tolerance and nonviolence" (FCNL 2015).

As part of this work, the FCNL also spotlights individuals around the world who are taking this message to heart and are standing up for peace and speaking out in their own communities. In the Central African Republic, Florence Ntakarutimana is working with Catholic Relief Services' Trauma Healing Program. She has been involved with trauma work for almost ten years in Kenya, Rwanda, Zimbabwe, the United States, and Canada. Similarly, Hussein Khalid is working in Haki Africa on human rights issues and youth empowerment. He was part of President Barack Obama's Summit on Countering Violent Extremism and is known to speak out in criticism of military response to violent extremism. It is important to realize that there are people all over the world working to support nonviolent resilience and peace in their own communities.

The FCNL community seeks to encourage the US government to do the same by mobilizing citizens around the country to lobby members of Congress on these issues. More information can be found at www.fcnl.org.

* * *

Although national and local (and perhaps regional) governments will continue to play important roles, we cannot depend solely on them to solve all of the problems discussed in this book. Hence, supporting the work of one of these NGOs, or buying products with social justice in mind, is an important action that concerned individuals can take. There are many, many choices—thousands of small groups, usually NGOs, working to make the world a better place. In fact, dozens, if not hundreds, of NGOs have organized around each issue discussed in this book. For instance, Fair Trade coffee is sold by several other groups, including Pura Vida Coffee, Just Coffee, and Green Mountain Coffee. Fair trade extends beyond coffee to food and clothing as well. Similarly, there are many NGOs, like Educating for Justice and Social Accountability International, that are involved in ensuring that the human rights of laborers throughout the world are respected.

It is up to each individual to work to create the world he or she prefers. Every time we make a purchase, we vote for one company and its values over another company and its set of values. We have a similar impact each time we choose to walk (instead of drive) or recycle. Thus, we are making many small decisions about the world we live in every day, and we should make these choices intentionally. When these actions are taken in concert with others, dramatic results at the global level can be realized. After all, if "citizens 'leave it to the experts,' they simply ensure that the expert's values and interests become policy" (Thompson 2003: 2).

It is important to remember that seemingly insurmountable obstacles have been overcome. Many thought that the scourge of smallpox, apartheid in South Africa, and legality of and widespread use of landmines would never end. However, each of these problems was overcome when groups of individuals organized themselves into social movements in the name of a better world. We hope readers will seek to learn more about the issues discussed in this book, educate others, and become active members for positive change in their community and the world.

Discussion Questions

1. Of the four future world scenarios discussed in this chapter, which do you think is most likely to emerge? Which do you think is most desirable?
2. Can you think of another possible world scenario?
3. Would a strengthened United Nations be desirable? Why or why not?
4. What do you think are the most serious challenges confronting humanity?
5. What can you do as an individual to make the world a better place?
6. Are there any farmers' markets or community-supported agriculture initiatives in your neighborhood or city? Have you purchased anything from them?
7. What do you think of the efforts of Equal Exchange, Educating for Justice, and Social Accountability International?

Suggested Readings

Clawson, Julie (2009) *Everyday Justice: The Global Impact of Our Daily Choices.* Downers Grove, IL: InterVarsity Press.

Frederking, Brian, and Paul F. Diehl (eds.) (2015) *The Politics of Global Governance: International Organizations in an Interdependent World.* Boulder: Lynne Rienner.

Karns, Margaret P., Karen A. Mingst, and Kendall W. Stiles (2015) *International Organizations: The Politics and Processes of Global Governance.* Boulder: Lynne Rienner.

Norberg-Hodge, Helena, Todd Merrifield, and Steven Gorelick (2002) *Bringing the Food Economy Home.* Sterling: Kumarian.

United Nations Development Programme (annual) *Human Development Report.* New York: Oxford University Press.

Worldwatch Institute (annual) *State of the World.* New York: Norton.

——— (annual) *Vital Signs.* New York: Norton.

Acronyms

ABM Treaty	Anti–Ballistic Missile Treaty
AFL-CIO	American Federation of Labor and Congress of Industrial Organizations
AFO	animal feeding operation
AI	artificial intelligence
AIDS	acquired immunodeficiency syndrome
AIIB	Asian Infrastructure Investment Bank
AOSIS	Alliance of Small Island States
APEC	Asia Pacific Economic Cooperation
BDS	Boycotts, Divestment, and Sanctions movement
BRIC	Brazil, Russia, India, and China
BRICS	Brazil, Russia, India, China, and South Africa
CC Dare	Climate Change Adaptation and Development
CFC	chlorofluorocarbon
COP	Conference of the Parties
CTBT	Comprehensive Nuclear Test Ban Treaty
CWC	Chemical Weapons Convention
DAC	Development Assistance Committee
DDoS	distributed denial of service
DOD	Department of Defense
DRC	Democratic Republic of Congo
ECOSOC	Economic and Social Council (United Nations)
ECOWAS	Economic Community of West African States
ECSC	European Coal and Steel Community
EPA	Environmental Protection Agency
EU	European Union

FAO	Food and Agriculture Organization
FCNL	Friends Committee on National Legislation
FDA	Food and Drug Administration
FDI	foreign direct investment
FPI	foreign portfolio investment
G8	Group of Eight
G-10	Group of 10
GATT	General Agreement on Tariffs and Trade
GDP	gross domestic product
GMO	genetically modified organisms
GNI	gross national income
GNP	gross national product
HDI	Human Development Index (United Nations)
HIV	human immunodeficiency virus
IAEA	International Atomic Energy Agency
IBRD	International Bank for Reconstruction and Development
ICBM	intercontinental ballistic missile
ICC	International Criminal Court
ICCPR	International Covenant on Civil and Political Rights
ICESCR	International Covenant on Economic, Social, and Cultural Rights
IGO	international governmental organization
IMF	International Monetary Fund
INGO	international nongovernmental organization
IPCC	Intergovernmental Panel on Climate Change
IS	Islamic State
ISIS	Islamic State of Iraq and al-Sham
LDC	less-developed country
MAD	mutual assured destruction
MDC	more-developed country
MDGs	Millennium Development Goals (United Nations)
MNC	multinational corporation
NAFTA	North American Free Trade Agreement
NATO	North Atlantic Treaty Organization
NGO	nongovernmental organization
NOAA	National Oceanic and Atmospheric Administration
NPT	Nuclear Nonproliferation Treaty
ODA	official development assistance
OECD	Organization for Economic Cooperation and Development
OPEC	Organization of Petroleum Exporting Countries
P-5	permanent five (United Nations Security Council)
PLO	Palestine Liberation Organization
PPP	purchasing power parity

PRC	People's Republic of China
R2P	responsibility to protect
SALT	Strategic Arms Limitations Treaty
SDGs	Sustainable Development Goals
SEATO	Southeast Asian Treaty Organization
SPLA	Sudanese People's Liberation Army
START	Strategic Arms Reduction Treaty
TB	tuberculosis
TNC	transnational corporation
TPP	Trans-Pacific Partnership
UAV	unmanned aerial vehicle
UDHR	Universal Declaration of Human Rights
UN	United Nations
UNAIDS	Joint UN Programme on HIV/AIDS
UNCED	UN Conference on the Environment and Development
UNDP	UN Development Programme
UNEP	UN Environment Programme
UNFPA	UN Fund for Population Activities
UNHCR	UN High Commissioner for Refugees
UNICEF	UN Children's Fund
UNOSOM	UN Operation in Somalia
UNPD	UN Population Division
UNPROFOR	UN Protection Force for Yugoslavia
UNRWA	UN Relief and Works Agency for Palestine Refugees in the Near East
USSR	Union of Soviet Socialist Republics
WHO	World Health Organization
WMD	weapons of mass destruction
WTO	World Trade Organization

Bibliography

Afify, Heba (2011) "Officers Get 7 Years for Killing That Helped Inspire Egypt's Revolt." *New York Times* (October 26).

Aggarwal, S. (2014) "Emerging Global Urban Order and Challenges to Harmonious Urban Development." *Transactions of the Institute of Indian Geographers* 36, no. 1.

AIC (American Immigration Council) (2014) "Refugees: A Fact Sheet." *Immigration Policy Center: American Immigration Council* (October 1). www.immigration policy.org.

al-Khalidi, Suleiman (2015) "Jordan, Israel Agree $900 Million Red Sea-Dead Sea Project." *Reuters* (February 26).

Alcock, Frank (2002) "Bargaining, Uncertainty, and Property Rights in Fisheries." *World Politics* 54, no. 3.

Alexander, Caroline (2015) "World Hasn't Had So Many Refugees Since 1945, Report Says" (June 17). www.bloomberg.com.

Alkema, Leontine, et al. (2015) "Global, Regional, and National Levels and Trends in Maternal Mortality Between 1990 and 2015, with Scenario-Based Projections to 2030: A Systematic Analysis by the UN Maternal Mortality Estimation Inter-Agency Group." *The Lancet* (November 12).

Alsanea, Rajaa (2007) *Girls of Riyadh*. New York: Penguin.

Alston, Julian M., Daniel A. Sumner, and Henrich Brunke (2007) *Impacts of Reductions in US Cotton Subsidies on West African Cotton Producers*. Boston: Oxfam America.

Altman, L. (1982) "A New Insulin Given Approval for Use in the U.S." *New York Times* (October 30).

Amery, Hussein A., and Aaron T. Wolf (2000) *Water in the Middle East: A Geography of Peace*. Austin: University of Texas Press.

Amnesty International (2008) *Amnesty International Report 2008: Foreward* (May 28). https://www.amnesty.org.

Amnesty International (2009) "Troubled Waters—Palestinians Denied Fair Access to Water: Israel-Occupied Palestinian Territories" (September 26). www.amnesty usa.org.

Angell, Norman (1909) *Europe's Optical Illusion*. London: Simpkin, Marshall, Hamilton, and Kent.
Arbatov, Alexei (2009) "Nuclear Disarmament and Non-Proliferation" (September). Speech transcript for the International Institute for Strategic Studies Review Conference.
Argos, Collectif (2010) "Climate Refugees." Boston: Massachusetts Institute of Technology Press.
Armstrong, Stuart (2014). *Smarter Than Us: The Rise of Intelligent Machines*. Berkeley: MIRI.
Arquilla, John, and David Ronfeldt, eds. (1997) *In Athena's Camp: Preparing for Conflict in the Information Age*. Santa Monica: RAND.
Ashley, Elizabeth, et al. (2014) "Spread of Artemisinin Resistance in *Plasmodium Falciparum* Malaria." *New England Journal of Medicine* (July 31). www.nejm.org.
Athanasiou, Tom, and Paul Baer (2002) *Dead Heat: Global Justice and Global Warming*. New York: Seven Stories.
AWID (Association for Women in Development) (2004) "Intersectionality: A Tool for Gender and Economic Justice." *Women's Rights and Economic Change*, 9. www.awid.org.
Awika, J. (2011) "Major Cereal Grains Production and Use Around the World." *Advances in Cereal Science: Implications to Food Processing and Health Promotion*. ACS Symposium Series. Washington, DC: American Chemical Society.
Bailey, Adrian (2005) *Making Population Geography*. New York: Oxford University Press.
Baker, Aryn (2015) "How Climate Change Is Behind the Surge of Migrants to Europe" (September 7). http://time.com.
Balbo, Laurie (2015) "Canada and USA Sign On to Rehabilitate the Jordan River." *Green Prophet: Sustainable News for the Middle East* (May 10). www.greenprophet.com.
Bamboo Grove (2008) "The Top Ten Reasons Why Bamboo Can Save the Planet." www.bamboogrove.com.
Ban Ki-moon (2007) "A Climate Culprit in Darfur." *Washington Post* (June 16).
Banco, Erin (2011) "Is Your Cell Phone Fueling Civil War in Congo?" (July 11). www.theatlantic.com.
Banerjee, Abhijit, and Esther Duflo (2011) *Poor Economics: A Radical Rethinking of the Way to Fight Global Poverty*. New York: PublicAffairs.
Banerjee, Subhankar, ed. (2012) *Artic Voices: Resistance at the Tipping Point*. New York: Seven Stories.
Barber, Benjamin R. (1992) "Jihad vs. McWorld." *Atlantic Monthly* (March).
Barkham, Patrick (2010) "The Real World of Oil Spills." www.oilspillsolutions.org.
Barnes, Hannah (2013) "How Many Climate Migrants Will There Be." *BBC News* (September 2).
Barringer, Felicity (2008) "Collapse of Salmon Stocks Endangers Pacific Fishery." *New York Times* (March 13).
BBC (British Broadcasting Corporation) (2009) "US to Resume Engagement with ICC."
Bebber, D. P., M. A. T. Ramotowski, and S. J. Gurr (2013) "Crop Pests and Pathogens Move Polewards in a Warming World." *Nature Climate Change* 3.
Becker, Anne E. and Arthur Kleinman (2013) "Mental Health and the Global Agenda." *The New England Journal of Medicine* (July 4).
Behrman, J., R. Meinzen-Dick, and A. Quisumbing (2011) "The Gender Implications of Large-Scale Land Deals" (January). www.ifpri.org.
Bellamy, David (2004) "Global Warming? What a Load of Poppycock!" *Daily Mail* (July 9). www.junkscience.com.

Bello, W. (2013) "Twenty-Six Countries Ban GMOs—Why Won't the US?" *The Nation* (October 29).

Bergen, Peter L. (2001) *Holy War, Inc.: Inside the Secret World of Osama bin Laden* New York: Free Press.

BFWI (Bread for the World Institute) (2015) *Annual Report on the State of World Hunger.* Washington, DC.

Bilmes, Alex (2014) "George Clooney: The Full Interview." *Esquire* (January 3).

Birdsall, Nancy, Thomas Pinckney, and Richard Sabot (1996) "Why Low Inequality Spurs Growth: Savings and Investment by the Poor." Working Paper no. 327. Washington, DC: Inter-American Development Bank.

Black, R. E., L. H. Allen, Z. A. Bhutta, L. E. Caulfield, et al. (2008) "Maternal and Child Undernutrition: Global and Regional Exposures and Health Consequences." *The Lancet* 371: 243–260.

Blanco-Canqui, H., and R. Lal (2008) "Principles of Soil Conservation and Management." New York: Springer.

Bloch, Sidney, and Peter Reddaway (1985) *Psychiatric Terror: How Soviet Psychiatry Is Used to Suppress Discontent.* http://www.law.virginia.edu/html/news/2006_spr/perlin.htm.

Boekhout van Solinge, Tim (2010) "Deforestation Crimes and Conflicts in the Amazon." *Critical Criminology* 18, no. 4 (December). http://link.springer.com.

Borger, Julian (2007) "Darfur Conflict Heralds Era of Wars Triggered by Climate Change, UN Report Warns." *The Guardian* (June 23).

Borras, S., Jr., and J. Franco (2010) "Food Sovereignty and Redistributive Land Policies: Exploring Linkages, Identifying Challenges." In H. Wittman, A. Desmarais, and N. Wiebe, *Food Sovereignty: Reconnecting Food, Nature, and Community.* Oakland: Food First.

Boserup, Ester (1970) *Women's Role in Economic Development.* New York: St. Martin's.

——— (2011) *Woman's Role in Economic Development.* New York: Earthscan.

Bosman, Philippe, et al. (2014) "*Plasmodium* Prevalence and Artiemisini-Resistant Falciparum Malaria in Preah Vihear Province, Combodia: A Cross-Sectional Population-Based Study." *Malaria Journal* (October 6).

Bossong, Kenneth (2014) "US Renewable Electrical Generation Hits 14.3 Percent" (August 27). http://ecowatch.com.

Broad, William J., David E. Sanger, and Thom Shanker (2007) "US Selecting Hybrid Design for Warheads." *New York Times* (January 7).

Broder, John M. (2011) "Climate Talks in Durban Yield Limited Agreement." *New York Times* (December 11).

——— (2012) "Climate Talks Yield Commitment to Ambitious, but Unclear, Action." *New York Times* (December 8).

Brown, Lester R. (1996) "The Acceleration of History." In Lester R. Brown, ed., *State of the World.* New York: Norton.

B'Tselem.org (2014) "Statistics: Fatalities." B'Tselem: The Israeli Information Center for Human Rights in the Occupied Territories.

——— (2015) "Settlements: Statistics on Settlements and Settler Population" (May 11). B'Tselem: The Israeli Information Center for Human Rights in the Occupied Territories.

Buehring, Gertrude, et al. (2015) "Virus in Cattle Linked to Human Breast Cancer." *Science Daily* (September 15).

Cakaj, Ledio (2011) "Too Far from Home: Demobilizing the Lord's Resistance Army" (February). www.enoughproject.org.

Calamur, Krishnadev (2015) "European Refugee Crisis: A 'Systematic' Violation of Human Rights." *The Atlantic* (October 22).

Callaway, Ewen, and David Cyranoski (2015) "Anti-Parasite Drug Sweep Nobel Prize in Medicine 2015." *Nature* (October 5).

Campbell, Martha M., Ndol Prata, and Malcolm Potts (2009) "The Impact of Freedom on Fertility Transition: Revisiting the Theoretical Framework" (September 27–October 2). Paper presented at the twenty-sixth International Population Conference, Marrakech, Morocco.

Carswell, Simon (2015) "Development Goals: The Tough Task of Drafting World's Wish-List." *Irish Times* (July 9).

Cassman, K. G., and S. Wood (2005) "Cultivated Systems." In R. Hassan et al., eds., *Ecosystems and Human Well-Being: Current State and Trends,* vol. 1. Washington, DC: Island.

Castles, Stephen, Hein de Haas, and Mark J. Miller (2013) *The Age of Migration: International Population in the Modern World.* 5th ed. New York: Guilford.

Causes (2011) "We'll Help You Change the World." www.causes.com.

Cavanaugh, John, et al., eds. (1992) *Trading Freedom: How Free Trade Affects Our Lives, Work, and Environment.* San Francisco: Institute for Food and Development Policy.

Cavelty, Myriam (2008) *Cyber-Security and Threat Politics: US Efforts to Secure the Information Age.* London: Routledge.

CBS News (2014) "The Most Polluting Protein? Environmental Impact of Beef, Pork, Poultry" (July 21).

CDC (Centers for Disease Control and Prevention) (2015) "HIV/ AIDS Basic Statistics." www.cdc.gov.

CGG (Commission on Global Governance) (1995) *Our Global Neighborhood.* New York: Oxford University Press.

CGS (Citizens for Global Solutions) (2004) "US Policy on the ICC" (December 3). www.globalsolutions.org.

Chang, Lulu (2015) "Anonymous Hacks ISIS Site, Replaces It with Viagra Ad" (November 27). http://finance.yahoo.com.

Chattopadhyay, Raghabendra, and Esther Duflo (2004) "Impact of Reservation in Panchayati Raj: Evidence from a Nationwide Randomised Experiment." *Economic and Political Weekly* 39, no. 9.

Chilcote, Ryan (2003) "Kuwait Still Recovering from Gulf War Fires" (January 3). www.cnn.com.

Choudhry, Muni Ahmed (2005) "Pakistan: Where and Who Are The World's Illiterates?" Paper commissioned for the 2006 UNESCO Education for All Global Monitoring Report *Literacy for Life.* http://datatopics.worldbank.org.

Christian Science Monitor (2011) "Ban Ki-moon: I Am Willing to Take Any Measures for Human Rights" (March 23).

CIA (Central Intelligence Agency) (2011) "The State Department Releases." *Country Reports on Terrorism 2010.* www.state.gov.

——— (2012) *The World Factbook.* www.cia.gov.

——— (2015) "Pakistan." In *The World Factbook.* www.cia.gov.

——— (n.d.) "Labor Force by Occupation." In *The World Factbook.* www.cia.gov.

Cirincione, Joseph, Jon B. Wolfstahl, and Miriam Rajkumar (2002) *Deadly Arsenals: Tracking Weapons of Mass Destruction.* Washington, DC: Carnegie Endowment for International Peace.

CNN (Cable News Network) (2010) "U.N. Blasts Global Response to Haiti Cholera Outbreak As Inadequate" (November 21). http://edition.cnn.com.

Cockerill, C. H. (2015) "STOP food waste at the TOP." Presentation at the sixth annual Food Symposium (April 8), Wilmington College, OH.

Cohen, Benyamin (2015) "Why Bono Should Win the Nobel Peace Prize." www.fromthegrapevine.com.

Cole, Matthew, and Mark Schone (2011) "Egyptian Blogger Who Posted Videos of Police Torture Is Arrested." *ABC News* (February 4).

Coles, Clifton (2004) "Water Without War." *The Futurist* 38, no. 2.

Conca, Ken, and Geoffrey D. Dabelko (2010) *Green Planet Blues: Environmental Politics from Stockholm to Johannesburg*. 4th ed. Boulder: Westview.

Cotula, L. (2013) *The Great African Land Grab? Agricultural Investments and the Global Food System*. New York: Zed.

Crenshaw, K. (1989) "Demarginalizing the Intersection of Race and Sex: A Black Feminist Critique of Antidiscrimination Doctrine, Feminist Theory, and Antiracist Politics." Chicago: University of Chicago Legal Forum.

——— (2004) "Intersectionality: The Double Bind of Race and Gender." *Perspectives Magazine* 12, no. 4.

Cribb, Julian (2011) *The Coming Famine: The Global Food Crisis and What We Can Do to Avoid It*. Berkeley: University of California Press.

Cronon, William (1983) *Changes in the Land: Indians, Colonists, and the Ecology of New England*. New York: Hill and Wang.

CSA (Committee on 21st Century Systems Agriculture) (2010) "Toward Sustainable Agricultural Systems in the 21st Century." Washington, DC: National Academies Press.

CSKR (Campaign to Stop Killer Robots) (2015) "Artificial Intelligence Experts Call for Ban" (July 28). www.stopkillerrobots.org.

CWA (Communications Workers of America) (2015) "CWA Statement on the Trans-Pacific Partnership Agreement Reached in Atlanta." *CWA News* (October 5). www.cwa-union.org.

Dadian, Margaret (2010) "Condom Sales Boom As Rwanda and Haiti Struggle to Rebuild." www.fhi.org.

Davies, Julian, and Dorothy Davies (2010) "Origins and Evolution of Antibiotic Resistance." *US National Library of Medicine National Institute of Health* (September). www.ncbi.nlm.nih.gov.

Davis, Julie (2015) "Obama Recasts Climate Change as a More Far-Reaching Peril." *New York Times* (May 20).

de Lombaerde, Philippe, Gei Guo, and Helion Povoa Neto (2014) "Introduction to the Special Collection: South-South Migrations: What Is (Still) on the Research Agenda?" *International Migration Review* 48.

de Waal, Alex (2007) "Is Climate Change the Culprit for Darfur?" www.ssrc.org.

Debusscher, Petra, and An Ansoms (2013) "Gender Equity Policies in Rwanda: Public Relations or Real Transformations?" *Development and Change* 44, no. 5.

Deconinck, Stefan (2004) "Israeli Water Policy in a Regional Context of Conflict: Prospects for Sustainable Development for Israelis and Palestinians?" http://waternet.ugent.be.

Deibert, Ronald, and Rafal Rohozinski (2010) "Risking Security: Policies and Paradoxes of Cyberspace Security." *International Political Sociology* 4, no. 1.

Delva, Joseph Guvler (2010) "Haiti Cholera Deaths Slow, but Spread Still Feared." *Reuters* (October 25).

Demeny, Paul, and Geoffrey McNicoll (2003) *Encyclopedia of Population*. Vols. 1–2. New York: Macmillan Reference.

Denning, Dorothy E. (1999) *Information Warfare and Security*. New York: ACM.

Desmarais, A. A. (2011) "The International Women's Commission of La Via Campesina." In N. Visvanathan, L. Duggan, N. Wiegersma, and L. Nisonoff, eds., *The Women, Gender, & Development Reader,* 2nd ed. New York: Zed.

Dey, Madan M., Manik Lal Bose, and Md Ferdous Alam (2008) "Country Case Study: Development and Status of Freshwater Aquaculture in Bangladesh." *WorldFish* 1.

Dobush, Grace (2015) "How Mobile Phones Are Changing the Developing World." Consumer Technology Association (July 27). www.cta.tech.

DOD (Department of Defense) (2011) "Strategy for Operating in Cyberspace." www.defense.gov.

——— (2012) "Department of Defense Directive: Autonomy in Weapon Systems" (November 21). www.dtic.mil.

——— (2013) "Unmanned Systems Integrated Roadmap." www.defense.gov.

Dodge, Robert (1994) "Grappling with GATT." *Dallas Morning News* (August 8).

Dolatyar, Mostafa, and Tim S. Gray (2000) "The Politics of Water Security in the Middle East." *Environmental Politics* 9, no. 3.

Dugger, Celia W. (2007) "CARE Turns Down Federal Funds for Food Aid." *New York Times* (August 16).

Durkova, Petra, et al. (2012) "Climate Refugees in the 21st Century." Regional Academy of the United Nations (December). https://fusiondotnet.files.wordpress.com.

D'Urso, Joseph (2015) "Child Death Rates Cut by Half, but U.N. Target Missed" (September 8). www.trust.org.

The Economist (2015a) "Ebola in Graphics: The Toll of a Tragedy" (August 27).

——— (2015b) "Unsustainable Goals" (March 25).

ECOSOC (2015) "Consultative Status with ECOSOC and Other Accreditations." NGO Branch. https://esango.un.org.

Ehrlich, P. R., and A. H. Ehrlich (1990) *The Population Explosion.* New York: Simon and Schuster.

Ekonu (2015) "Single Resource Economies & Conflict" (September 26). https://ekonuorg.wordpress.com.

Energies-Renouvelables (2013) "Worldwide Electricity Production from Renewable Energy Sources." www.energies-renouvelables.org.

Enough Project (2015) "Progress and Challenges on Conflict Minerals: Facts on Dodd-Frank 1502." http://enoughproject.org.

——— (n.d.) "Conflict Minerals 101." www.enoughproject.org.

Enzler, S. M. (2006) "Environmental Effects of Warfare." www.lenntech.com.

EPA (Environmental Protection Agency) (n.d.) "Animal Waste: What's the Problem?" www3.epa.gov.

Esteva, G. (2010) "Development." In W. Sachs, *Development Dictionary: A Guide to Knowledge as Power,* 2nd ed. New York: Zed.

Evans, Tony (2011) *Human Rights in the Global Political Economy.* Boulder: Lynne Rienner.

Everett, J., and S. E. M. Charlton (2014) *Women Navigating Globalization: Feminist Approaches to Development.* Lanham: Rowman and Littlefield.

Fallows, James (1993) "How the World Works." *Atlantic Monthly* (December).

FAO (Food and Agriculture Organization) (2001) "Genetically Modified Organisms, Consumers, Food Safety, and the Environment." Rome: Viale delle Terme di Caracalla.

Food and Agriculture Organization (2002) "Reducing Poverty and Hunger: The Critical Role of Financing for Development. Paper presented at the Interna-

tional Conference on Financing for Development, Monterrey, Mexico, March 18–22 March.
——— (2003) *Trade Reforms and Food Security: Conceptualising the Linkages.* Rome: Commodity Policy and Projections Service, Commodities and Trade Division. http://faostat.fao.org.
——— (2009) "High Level Expert Forum: How to Feed the World in 2050." Rome: Viale delle Terme di Caracalla.
——— (2010) "Global Forest Resource Assessment 2010." Rome: Viale delle Terme di Caracalla.
——— (2011) *The State of Food and Agriculture, 2010–11: Women in Agriculture.* www.fao.org.
——— (2012) "Climate Change: Livestock." www.fao.org.
——— (2013) "Food Waste Facts." www.unep.org/wed/2013/quickfacts/.
——— (2014) "The State of Food and Agriculture in 2014: In Brief." www.fao.org.
——— (2015a) "Livestock, Environment, and Development: Leading Livestock Development Toward Responsible Use of Natural Resources." www.fao.org.
——— (2015b) *Men and Women in Agriculture: Closing the Gap.* www.fao.org.
——— (2015c) "Save Food: Global Initiative on Food Loss and Waste Reduction." www.fao.org.
——— (2015d) *The State of Food Insecurity in the World.* www.fao.org.
——— (n.d.) "Farming Systems and Poverty." www.fao.org.
Farer, Tom (2002) "The United Nations and Human Rights: More Than a Whimper, Less Than a Roar." In Richard Pierre Claude and Burns H. Weston, eds., *Human Rights in the World Community.* Philadelphia: University of Pennsylvania Press.
FAS (Federation of American Scientists) (2002) "Military Aid Post September 11th." *Arms Sales Monitor Report* no. 48.
Fauci, Anthony, and Hilary Marston (2015) "Ending the HIV-AIDS Pandemic: Follow the Science." *New England Journal of Medicine* 373, no. 23 (December 3).
FCNL (Friends Committee on National Legislation) (2013) "The World We Seek: FCNL Legislative Policy Statement." http://fcnl.org.
——— (2015) "Peacebuilding Successes in Central African Republic." http://fcnl.org.
Federal Register (2015) "Annual Update of the HHS Poverty Guidelines." https://www.federalregister.gov.
FEWS NET (2015) "Drought in Ethiopia and Conflict in South Sudan and Yemen Sustain Food Security Emergencies." www.fews.net.
Flavin, Christopher (1996) "Facing Up to the Risks of Climate Change." In Lester R. Brown, ed., *State of the World 1996.* New York: Norton.
Foley, J. A., et al. (2005) "Global Consequences of Land Use." *Science* 309.
Folke, Carl, Monica Hammer, Robert Costanza, and AnnMari Jansson. (1994) "Investing in Natural Capital: Why, What, and How?" In AnnMari Jansson, Monica Hammer, Carl Folke, and Robert Costanza, *Investing in Natural Capital: The Ecological Economics Approach to Sustainability.* Washington, DC: Island.
Ford, Liz (2014) "UN Begins Talks on SDGs, 'Carrying the Hopes of Millions and Millions.'" *The Guardian* (September 24).
——— (2015) "Sustainable Development Goals: All You Need to Know." *The Guardian* (July 19).
Freedman, Andrew (2013) "The Last Time CO_2 Was This High, Humans Didn't Exist" (May 3). www.climatecenteral.org.
Friedman, Thomas L. (2005) *The World Is Flat: A Brief History of the Twenty-First Century.* New York: Farrar, Straus, and Giroux.

Fukuyama, Francis (1989) "The End of History?" *National Interest* (September–October).

Funk, C., and L. Rainie (2015) "Public and Scientists' Views on Science and Society" (January 29). www.pewinternet.org.

Gadsden, Chris (2008) "New Pacific Salmon Treaty." *Pacific Salmon Commission* (May 22). www.fishingwithrod.com.

Galtun, Johan (1994) *Human Rights in Another Key.* Cambridge: Polity.

Gettleman, Geffrey (2012) "The World's Worst War." *New York Times* (December 15).

Gladstone, Rick (2015a) "Dirty Water and Open Defecation Threaten Gains in Child Health." *New York Times* (June 30).

——— (2015b) "U.N. Reports About 200 Million Fewer Hungry People Than in 1990." *New York Times* (May 27).

Gladstone, Rick, and Mohammad Ghannam (2015) "Syria Deaths Hit New High in 2014, Observer Group Says." *New York Times* (January 1).

Glantz, Moshe (2014) "Foreign Investment in Israel Cut by Half in 2014." www.ynetnews.com.

Global Witness (n.d.). "Conflict Diamonds." www.globalwitness.org.

Goldstein, Joshua S. (2011) *Winning the War on War: The Decline of Armed Conflict Worldwide.* New York: Dutton.

Gore, Al (1992) *Earth in the Balance: Ecology and the Human Spirit.* Boston: Houghton Mifflin.

GPEI (Global Polio Eradication Initiative) (2015) "Polio the Week As of 9 December 2015." www.polioeradication.org.

GPF (Global Policy Forum) (2016) "US Opposition to International Criminal Court." www.globalpolicy.org.

Gray, Ellen (2012) "Landsat Top Ten: Kuwait Oil Fires." www.nasa.gov.

Grimmett, Richard F., and Paul K. Kerr (2012) "Conventional Arms Transfers to Developing Nations, 2004–2011." CRS Report for Congress no. R42678 (August 24). Washington, DC: Congressional Research Service.

Groisman, Pavel Ya, and Richard W. Knight (2008) "Prolonged Dry Episodes over the Conterminous United States: New Tendencies Emerging During the Last 40 Years." *Journal of Climate* 21, no. 9.

Guneratne, Arjun, and Anita M. Weiss (2014) *Pathways to Power: The Domestic Politics of South Asia.* Lanham: Rowman and Littlefield.

Gupta, Joyeeta (2010) "A History of International Climate Change Policy." *Wiley Interdisciplinary Reviews* 1, no. 5.

Guttmacher Institute (2013) "Unmet Need for Contraceptives in Developing World Has Declined, but Remains High in Some Countries." *International Perspectives on Sexual and Reproduction Health* 39, no. 3 (September).

——— (2014) "Adding It Up: Investing in Sexual and Reproductive Health" (December). https://www.guttmacher.org.

Guzman, Andrew (2013) *Overheated.* New York: Oxford University Press.

Hamdan, Amani (2005) "Women and Education in Saudi Arabia: Education and Achievements." *International Education Journal* 6, no. 1.

Hamilton, Clive (2013) *Earth Masters: The Dawn of the Age of Climate Engineering.* New Haven: Yale University Press.

Hamrouqa, Hana (2013) "Countries Engaged in Water Cooperation Do Not Go to War." *Jordan Times* (November 28).

Hanna, Attallah (2009) "Christian Population of Jerusalem Decreasing Under Israeli Scheme." *English Islam Times* (February 7).

Hansen, James M., et al. (2016) "Ice Melt, Sea Level Rise, and Superstorms: Evidence from Paleoclimate Data, Climate Modeling, and Modern Observations That 2º C Global Warming Is Highly Dangerous." *Atmospheric Chemistry and Physics Discussions* 16: 3761–3812.

Haq, Riazul (2015) "Education Woes: Pakistan Misses UN Target with 58% Literacy Rate." *Express Tribune* (June 5).

Hardin, Garrett (1968) "The Tragedy of the Commons." *Science* 162 (December 13).

Hareuveni, Eyal (2010) "By Hook or by Crook: Israeli Settlement Policy in the West Bank" (July). www.btselem.org.

Harper, Charles L. (1995) *Environment and Society: Human Perspectives on Environmental Issues*. Upper Saddle River, NJ: Prentice Hall.

Harris, J. M., and S. Kennedy (1999) "Carrying Capacity in Agriculture: Global and Regional Issues." *Ecological Economics* 29, no. 3.

Harvey, David (2005) *A Brief History of Neoliberalism*. Oxford: Oxford University Press.

Hawkesworth, Mary E. (2005) "Engendering Political Science: An Immodest Proposal." *Politics and Gender* 1, no. 1.

Hayes, Thomas C. (1990) "Confrontation in the Gulf: The Oilfield Lying Below the Iraq-Kuwait Dispute." *New York Times* (September 3).

Henderson, Sarah L., and Alana S. Jeydel (2010) *Women and Politics in a Global World*. New York: Oxford University Press.

Hertz, Noreena (2004) *The Debt Threat: How Debt Is Destroying the Developing World . . . and Threatening Us All*. New York: HarperCollins.

Hickel, Jason (2015) "The SDGs Fail to Offer the New Economy We So Desperately Need." *Eldis* (August 26).

Hochschild, Adam (1999) *King Leopold's Ghost: A Story of Greed, Terrorism, and Heroism in Colonial Africa*. New York: Houghton Mifflin.

Hoffman, Bruce (2006) *Inside Terrorism*. New York: Columbia University Press.

Hogendoorn, E. J. (1997) "A Chemical Weapons Atlas." *Bulletin of Atomic Scientists* (September–October).

Holm, Hans-Henrik, and Georg Sørensen, eds. (1995) *Whose World Order? Uneven Globalization and the End of the Cold War*. Boulder: Westview.

Homer-Dixon, T. F. (1991) "On the Threshold: Environmental Changes as Causes of Acute Conflict." *International Security* 16, no. 2 (Fall).

——— (1994) "Environmental Scarcities and Violent Conflict: Evidence from Cases." *International Security* 19, no. 1 (Summer).

——— (1999) "Environment, Scarcity, and Violence." Princeton: Princeton University Press.

House Hearing Before the Subcommittee on Basic Research (1999) "Genetically Engineered Foods." Testimony of James H. Maryanski, 106th Congress.

Howitt, R., D. MacEwan, J. Medellin-Azuara, J. Lund, and D. Sumner (2015) "Economic Analysis of the 2015 Drought for California Agriculture." Davis: Center for Watershed Sciences, University of California–Davis.

Huey, T. A. (2015) "Global and Local Food Systems in the GM Labeling Campaign." In D. E. Sahn, ed., *The Fight Against Hunger and Malnutrition: The Role of Food, Agriculture, and Targeted Policies*. Oxford: Oxford University Press.

Hunt, Lynn (2008) *Inventing Human Rights: A History*. New York: Norton.

Huntington, Samuel P. (1996) "The West: Unique, Not Universal." *Foreign Affairs* 75, no. 6.

——— (1998) *The Clash of Civilizations and the Remaking of World Order.* New York: Simon and Schuster.

Huppert, Daniel D. (1995) "Why the Pacific Salmon Treaty Has Not Brought Peace." Seattle: University of Washington, School of Marine Affairs. www.wsg.washington.edu/salmon/huppertreport.html.

Hussein, Hassen (2014) "Egypt and Ethiopia Spar over the Nile." *Aljazeera America* (February 6).

ICC (International Criminal Court) (2004) "Historical Introduction" (December 1). www.haguejusticeportal.net.

ICSU (International Council for Science) and ISSC (International Social Science Council) (2015) "Review of the Sustainable Development Goals: The Science Perspective." www.icsu.org.

IDF (International Diabetes Federation) (2015a) "China." www.idf.org.

——— (2015b) "India" www.idf.org.

IEA (International Energy Agency) (2014) "CO_2 Emissions from Fuel Combustion: Highlights." https://www.iea.org.

IES (Institute for Environmental Security) (2015) "IES Mission." www.envirosecurity.org.

IISD (International Institute for Sustainable Development) (2013) "What Is Sustainable Development?" https://www.iisd.org.

ILPI (International Law and Policy Institute) (2015) "The Status of Nuclear Weapons." http://nwp.ilpi.org.

IPCC (Intergovernmental Panel on Climate Change) (2014) "Climate Change 2014 Synthesis Report Summary for Policymakers." www.ipcc.ch.

IPU (Inter-Parliamentary Union) (2015) "Women in National Parliaments" (November 1). www.ipu.org.

IRC (International Rescue Committee) (n.d.) "Congo Crisis." www.rescue.org.

IUCN (International Union for Conservation of Nature), UNEP (United Nations Environment Programme), and WWF (World Wide Fund for Nature) (1991) *Caring for the Earth.* Gland, Switzerland: IUCN.

IWS (Internet World Stats) (2015) "Internet Usage Statistics the Internet Big Picture: World Internet Users and 2015 Population Stats." www.internetworldstats.com.

Izenberg, Dan (1997) "An Insider's View of the Jordan Rift." *Jerusalem Post* (May 9).

Jasso, Guillermina (2009) "Ethnicity and the Immigration of Highly-Skilled Workers to the United States" (September 27–October 2). Paper presented at the twenty-sixth International Population Conference, Marrakech, Morocco.

Jenkins, Laura Dudley (1999) "Competing Equalities: The Struggle over Reserved Legislative Seats for Women in India." *International Review of Social History* 44, no. 7.

Johnson, Dominic D. P., and Monica Duffy Toft (2014) "Grounds for War: The Evolution of Territorial Conflict." *International Security* 38, no. 3.

Jones, Simon, and Richard Beamish (2011) "Salmon Lice: An Integrated Approach to Understanding Parasite Abundance and Distribution." Chichester: Wiley.

Judson, Ruth (2012) "Crisis and Calm: Demand for U.S. Currency at Home and Abroad from the Fall of the Berlin Wall to 2011" (November). www.federalreserve.gov.

Juergensmeyer, Mark (2000) *Terror in the Mind of God: The Global Rise of Religious Violence.* Berkeley: University of California Press.

Juneau Empire (2004) "Report Recommends Cutting Fishing Fleet" (October 29). www.juneauempire.com.

Kahl, Colin H. (2012) "Not Time to Attack Iran." *Foreign Affairs* 91, no. 2. (March–April).

Kahn, R. E., D. F. Clouser, and J. A. Richt (2009) "Emerging Infections: A Tribute to the One Medicine, One Health Concept." *Zoonoses and Public Health* 56: 407–428.

Kang, Cecilia (2010) "Grameen, Gates Foundation Eye Mobile Technology for Development" (September 3). http://voices.washingtonpost.com.

Karim, Salim S. A. (2015) "Overcoming Impediments to Global Implementation of Early Antiretroviral Therapy." *New England Journal of Medicine* (August 27).

Kelland, Kate (2015) "Malaria Deaths Drop Below Half a Million, Africa Makes Progress." *Reuters* (December 9).

Kenworthy, Tom, and Steven Pearlstein (1999) "U.S., Canada Sign Accord on Salmon/Decades-Long Dispute over Fishing Rights, Limits." www.sfgate.com.

Kerr, Richard A. (2000) "Can the Kyoto Climate Treaty Be Saved from Itself?" *Science* (November).

Kimenyi, Mwangi (2013) "Can the International Criminal Court Play Fair in Africa?" www.brookings.edu.

Kirby, Peadar (2006) *Vulnerability and Violence: The Impact of Globalization.* Ann Arbor: Pluto.

Knight, Matthew (2010) "U.N. Report: Eco-Systems at 'Tipping Point'" (May 10). http://edition.cnn.com.

Knight, Sunny (2000) "Salmon Recovery and the Pacific Salmon Treaty." *Ecology Law Quarterly* 27, no. 3.

Koh, Tommy B. B. (1997) "Five Years After Rio and Fifteen Years After Montego Bay: Some Personal Reflections." *Environmental Policy and Law* 27, no. 4.

Koop, C. E., C. E. Pearson, and M. R. Schwarz, eds. (2002) *Critical Issues in Global Health.* San Francisco: Jossey-Bass.

Kopicki, A. (2013) "Strong Support for Labeling Modified Foods." *New York Times* (July 27).

Koplow, D. (2003) *Smallpox: The Fight to Eradicate a Global Scourge.* Berkeley: University of California Press.

Krakower, Douglas S., Jain Sachin, and Kenneth H. Mayer (2015) "Antiretrovirals for Primary HIV Prevention: The Current Status of Pre- and Post-Exposure Prophylaxis." *Science of Prevention* 12 (January 20).

Kraly, Ellen Percy (2011) "Population Policy: Issues and Geography." In Joseph Stoltman, ed., *21st Century Geography: A Reference Handbook.* Thousand Oaks, CA: Sage.

Kroenig, Matthew (2012) "Time to Attack Iran." *Foreign Affairs* 91, no. 1 (January–February).

Krook, Mona Lena (2010) *Quotas for Women in Politics: Gender and Candidate Selection Reform Worldwide.* New York: Oxford University Press.

Kumar, Kaushlendra, and R. K. Sinha (2009) "Understanding Women's Nutritional Status in Urban India: A Comparative Study of Slum Versus Non Slum Dwellers" (September 27–October 2). Paper presented at the twenty-sixth International Population Conference, Marrakech, Morocco.

Lackey, R. T. (2008) "Saving West Coast Salmon." Oregon: Stream Systems Technology Center.

LaFond, Kaye (2015) "Israel and Jordan Agree to Share Water, but Fall Short of Saving Dead Sea" (February 27). www.circleofblue.org.

LaFranchi, Howard (2015) "In New UN Goals, an Evolving Vision of How to Change the World." *Christian Science Monitor* (1 September).

Langley, Winston E. (1996) *Encyclopedia of Human Rights Issues Since 1945*. Westport: Greenwood.

Laurance, Edward J. (1992) *The International Trade in Arms*. New York: Lexington Books.

LaVal, R. K. (2004) "Impact of Global Warming and Locally Changing Climate on Tropical Cloud Forest Bats." *Journal of Mammalogy* 85, no. 2.

LEEDuser.com (2010) "NC-v2.2 MRc6: Rapidly Renewable Materials." www.leeduser.com.

Legatum Institute (2011) "The 2011 Legatum Prosperity Index." www.prosperity.com.

Leggett, Jeremy (1990) "The Nature of the Greenhouse Threat." In Jeremy Leggett, ed., *Global Warming: The Greenpeace Report*. New York: Oxford University Press.

Leitenberg, Milton (2011) "Deaths in Wars and Conflicts in the 20th Century." Cornell University Peace Studies Program, Occasional Paper no. 29. www.clingendael.nl.

Lele, Sharachchandra (2013) "Rethinking Sustainable Development." *Current History* (November).

Lendman, Stephen. (2014) "Israel Steals Palestinian Resources. Gaza Without Water and Electricity." *Global Research* (September 26).

Lesthaeghe, R. (2010) "The Unfolding Story of the Second Demographic Transition." *Population and Development Review* 36, no. 2.

Lewis, Bernard (1998) "License to Kill: Osama bin Ladin's Declaration of Jihad." *Foreign Affairs* (November–December).

Lewis, James, and Katrina Timlin (2011) *Cybersecurity and Cyberwarfare: Preliminary Assessment of National Doctrine and Organization*. Washington, DC: Center for Strategic and International Studies. www.unidir.org.

Lidman, Melanie (2015) "To Heal Defiled Jordan River, Activists Wade into Murky Regional Politics." *Times of Israel* (June 11).

Lindzen, R. (1993) "Absence of Scientific Basis." *Research and Exploration* (Spring).

Lipinski, B., et al. (2013) "Reducing Food Loss and Waste" (June). Washington, DC: World Resources Institute.

Look to the Stars (2015) "Angelina Jolie Charity Work, Events and Causes." https://www.looktothestars.org.

MacKinnon, Catherine A. (2013) "Intersectionality as Method: A Note." *Signs: Journal of Women in Culture and Society* 38, no. 4.

Mallin, Alexander (2015) "State Terror Report: Fatalities in Attacks Spiked by 81 Percent in 2014." *ABC News* (June 19).

Malthus, Thomas R. (1826) *An Essay on the Principle of Population*. 6th ed. London: Murray.

Mamdani, Mahmood (1996) *Citizen and Subject: Contemporary Africa and the Legacy of Late Colonialism*. Princeton: Princeton University Press.

Mantel, Barbara (2015) "Terrorism and the Internet." http://library.cqpress.com.

Marine Stewardship Council (2015) *Fish as Food*. https://www.msc.org.

Marks, G., N. Crepaz, and R. S. Janssen (2006) "Estimating Sexual Transmission of HIV from Persons Aware and Unaware That They Are Infected with the Virus in the USA." *AIDS* 20, no. 10 (June 26).

Marsh, Bob, et al. (2006) "Villagewide Wi-Fi: Wireless Internet in Africa" (May 22). www.time.com.

Massing, Michael (2015) "How the Gates Foundation Reflects the Good and the Bad of 'Hacker Philanthropy.'" *The Intercept* (November 25).

McCarthy, Michael (2010) "Oil Spill Could Be Among Worst Ever." *The Independent* (May 16).

McCormick, John (1989) *Reclaiming Paradise: The Global Environmental Movement*. Bloomington: Indiana University Press.

McGrath, Cam (2014) "Nile River Dam Threatens War Between Egypt and Ethiopia" March 22. www.commondreams.org.

McGwire, Michael (1994) "Is There a Future for Nuclear Weapons?" *International Affairs* 70, no. 2.

McKinney, M. L., and R. M. Schoch (1996) *Environmental Science: Systems and Solutions*. Minneapolis: West.

McNaugher, Thomas L. (1990) "Ballistic Missiles and Chemical Weapons." *International Security* 15, no. 2.

McVeigh, Tracy (2010) "Female Circumcision Growing in Britain Despite Being Illegal." *The Observer* (July 24).

McWilliams, Wane, and Harry Piotrowski (2014) *The World Since 1945: A History of International Relations*. 8th ed. Boulder: Lynne Rienner.

Michaels, P. (1992) *Sound and Fury: Science and Politics of Global Warming*. Washington, DC: Cato Institute.

Milanovic, Branko (2006) "Global Income Inequality: What It Is and Why It Matters?" DESA Working Paper no. 26. Washington, DC: World Bank.

——— (2011) *The Haves and Have-Nots: A Brief and Idiosyncratic History of Global Inequality*. New York: Basic.

Miller, Marian A. L. (1995) *The Third World in Global Environmental Politics*. Boulder: Lynne Rienner.

Mingst, Karen, and Margaret Karns (2000) *The United Nations in the Post–Cold War Era*. Boulder: Westview.

Ministry of Foreign Affairs, Republic of Colombia (2012) "Rio+20: Sustainable Development Goals (SDGs): A Proposal from the Governments of Colombia and Guatemala." www.uncsd2012.org.

Mockaitis, Thomas R. (2007) *The New Terrorism: Myths and Realities*. Westport: Praeger Security International.

Monbiot, George (2007) "There Is Climate Change Censorship and It's the Deniers Who Dish It Out." *The Guardian* (April 10).

Mondrus-Engle, M. (1982) "Two Unique Cattle Farming Programs in Costa Rica." *Rangelands* 4, no. 1.

Moon, Bruce E. (1998) "Exports, Outward-Oriented Development, and Economic Growth." *Political Research Quarterly* (March).

——— (2000) *Dilemmas of International Trade*. 2nd ed. Boulder: Westview.

Mooney, Chris (2015) "In the Last 25 Years, the World Lost a Forested Area the Size of South Africa." *Washington Post* (September 8).

Morris, Mary E. (1996) "Water and Conflict in the Middle East: Threats and Opportunities." *Studies in Conflict & Terrorism* 20, nos. 1–13.

Mowlana, Hamid (1995) "The Communications Paradox." *Bulletin of Atomic Scientists* 51, no. 4.

Moyo, Dambisa (2009) *Dead Aid: Why Aid Is Not Working and How There Is a Better Way for Africa*. New York: Farrar, Straus, and Giroux.

Muchhala, Bhumika (2014) "North-South Debate in the UN Within Context of Sustainable Development Goals" (March 14). www.twn.my.

Mudege, Netsayi (2009) "Forced to Stay: Migration and Satisfaction Among Urban Slum Migrants in Nairobi" (September 27–October 2). Paper presented at the twenty-sixth International Population Conference, Marrakech, Morocco.

Mulrow, John (2010) "Climate Change Proceeds Down Worrisome Path." In *Vital Signs*. Washington, DC: Worldwatch Institute.

Munro, David A. (1995) "Sustainability: Rhetoric or Reality?" In T. C. Trzyna, ed., *A Sustainable World*. London: Earthscan.
Nafziger, E. (2009) "Cropping Systems." In *Illinois Agronomy Handbook,* 24th ed. Urbana: University of Illinois Press.
Nager, Adams B., and Robert D. Atkinson (2015) "The Myth of America's Manufacturing Renaissance: The Real State of U.S. Manufacturing." www2.itif.org.
Napier, T. L., and C. H. Cockerill (2014) "Factors Affecting Adoption of Soil and Water Conservation Production Systems in Lesser-Scale Societies." In R. Lal and B. A. Stewart, eds., *Soil Management of Smallholder Agriculture*. Boca Raton, FL: Taylor and Francis.
NASA (National Aeronautics and Space Administration) (2015a) "Climate Change: How Do We Know?" http://climate.nasa.gov.
——— (2015b) "Global Climate Change: Vital Signs of the Planet." http://climate.nasa.gov.
National Archives (2003) "Britain and the Trade." www.nationalarchives.gov.uk.
National Research Council (1986) *Population Growth and Economic Development: Policy Questions*. Washington, DC: National Academy Press.
NECSI (New England Complex Systems Institute) (2011) "Concepts: Butterfly Effect." http://necsi.edu.
Net Squared (n.d.) "UC Berkeley Human Rights Center Mobile Challenge Winners." www.netsquared.org.
Neuhauser, Alan (2015) "75 Percent of Animal Specials to Be Wiped Out in 'Sixth Mass Extinction.'" *U.S. News & World Report* (June 19).
Newsweek (2014) "Special Issue: 100 Places To Explore Before They Disappear" (May 5)
NIAID (National Institute of Allergy and Infectious Disease) (2007) "Treatment of HIV Infection" (November). www.niaid.nih.gov.
Nickerson, Colin (1997) "Canadian 'Fish War' Catches US Tourists on an Alaskan Ferry." *Boston Globe* (July 22).
Nincic, Miroslav (1982) *The Arms Race: The Political Economy of Military Growth*. New York: Praeger.
NOAA (National Oceanic and Atmospheric Administration) (2011) "Five-Year Review of Endangered Species Act-Listed Salmon & Steelhead" (August 15). www.nwr.noaa.gov.
——— (2014) *Treaty Between the Government of the United States of America and the Government of Canada Concerning Pacific Salmon Basic Instrument for the Pacific Salmon Commission*. www.nmfs.noaa.gov.
——— (2015a) "Climate Monitoring: Global Analysis." www.ncdc.noaa.gov.
——— (2015b) "Fishwatch U.S. Seafood Facts: Managing Fisheries." www.fishwatch.gov.
——— (n.d.) "How Do We Know the Earth's Climate Is Warming?" www.noaa.gov.
Nordland (2015) "A Mass Migration Crisis, and It May Yet Get Worse." *New York Times* (October 31).
Norton, Ben (2015) "We've Sold Out the Environment and Our Jobs: The Ugly Truth About the 'Toxic' TPP." *Salon* (October 7).
Novartis (2010) "Novartis and Collaborators Discover Novel Antimalarial Drug Candidate" (September 3). www.novartis.com.
NPP (National Priorities Project) (2015) "Federal Spending: Where Does the Money Go." https://www.nationalpriorities.org.
Nussbaum, Martha (2000) *Women and Human Development*. New York: Cambridge University Press.

O'Byrne, Darren J. (2003) *Human Rights: An Introduction*. London: Pearson Education.

OECD (Organization for Economic Cooperation and Development) (2014) *Aid to Developing Countries Rebounds in 2013 to Reach an All-Time High*. www.oecd.org.

——— (2015) *Development Aid Stable in 2014 but Flows to Poorest Countries Still Failing*. www.oecd.org.

Ofori-Amoah, Abigail (2014) "Water Wars and International Conflict." http://academic.evergreen.edu.

O'Malley, Martin (2015) "U.N. Should Take Responsibility for Haiti's Deadly Cholera Epidemic" (August 17). www.cnn.com.

ONE (2011) "The Data Report 2011." www.one.org.

Oreskes, Naomi, and Erik M. Conway (2010) *Merchants of Doubt: How a Handful of Scientists Obscured the Truth on Issues from Tobacco Smoke to Global Warming*. New York: Bloomsbury.

Ouattara, Amed, and Matthew B. Laurens (2014) "Vaccines Against Malaria." *Clinical Infectious Diseases*. Vol. 60, Issue 6 (pp. 930–936). (December 1). http://cid.oxfordjournals.org/content/60/6/930.full.

Oxfam (2014) "Even It Up: Time to End Extreme Inequality." https://www.oxfam.org.

Packer, George (2011) "The Broken Contract." *Foreign Affairs* 90, no. 6.

Parenti, Christian (2011) *Tropic of Chaos: Climate Change and the New Geography of Violence*. New York: Nation.

Parker, Richard (2002) "From Conquistadors to Corporations." *Sojourners Magazine* (May–June).

Paskal, Cleo (2010) *Global Warring: How Environmental, Economic, and Political Crises Will Redraw the World Map*. New York: Palgrave Macmillan.

Patel, R. (2010) "What Does Food Sovereignty Look Like?" In H. Wittman, A. Desmarais, and N. Wiebe, *Food Sovereignty: Reconnecting Food, Nature, and Community*. Oakland: Food First.

Paul, T. V. (2000) *Power Versus Prudence: Why Nations Forgo Nuclear Weapons*. Montreal: McGill-Queen's University Press.

PBS Newshour (2014) "New Series Reveals 'The Cost of Not Caring' for Americans with Mental Illness" (May 23). www.pbs.org.

PCBS (Palestinian Central Bureau of Statistics) (2014) "The Palestinians at the End of 2014" (December 12). www.pcbs.gov.ps.

PCGCC (Pew Center on Global Climate Change) (2009) "Copenhagen Climate Conference: COP 15" (December). www.pewclimate.org.

Pearce, Fred (2015) "On the River Nile, a Move to Avert a Conflict over Water." *Yale Environment 360* (March 12).

Perkins, John (2005) *Confessions of an Economic Hit Man*. New York: Plume.

——— (2009) *Hoodwinked: An Economic Hit Man Reveals Why the World Financial Markets Imploded—and What We Need to Do to Remake Them*. New York: Crown Business.

Perlin, Michael (2006) "Human Rights Abuses in Mental Institutions Common Worldwide." *Virginia Law* (February 27).

Perlo-Freeman, Sam, et al. (2015) "Trends in World Military Expenditure, 2014." SIPRI Fact Sheet (April). http://books.sipri.org.

Peterson, Scott (2000) "Turkey's Plan for Mideast Peace." *Christian Science Monitor* (April 18).

Pierce, Justin R., and Peter K. Schott (2012) "The Surprisingly Swift Decline of U.S. Manufacturing Employment" (December). www.nber.org.

Piketty, Thomas (2014) *Capital in the Twenty-First Century.* Cambridge, MA: Belknap Press.

Pinker, Steven, and Andrew Mack (2014) "The World Is Not Falling Apart." www.slate.com.

Polanyi, Karl (1944) *The Great Transformation.* New York: Farrar and Reinhart.

Pomfret, Richard (1988) *Unequal Trade.* Oxford: Basil Blackwell.

Pounds, A., M. P. L. Fogden, and J. H. Campbell (1999) "Biological Response to Climate Change on a Tropical Mountain." *Nature* 398.

Pressman, Jeremy (2008) *Warring Friends: Alliance Restraint in International Politics.* Ithaca: Cornell University Press.

PSC (Pacific Salmon Commission) (2014) "About the Commission: The Pacific Salmon Treaty, 1985." www.psc.org.

Puddington, Arch (2015) *Freedom in the World 2015.* New York: Freedom House.

Putnam, Robert D. (2015) *Our Kids: The American Dream in Crisis.* New York: Simon and Schuster.

Quota Project (2015) "Global Database of Quotas for Women." www.quotaproject.org.

Radelet, Steven (2010) *Emerging Africa: How 17 Countries Are Leading the Way.* Washington, DC: Center for Global Development.

Rai, S. M. (2011) "The History of International Development: Concepts and Contexts." In N. Visvanathan, L. Duggan, N. Wiegersma, and L. Nisonoff, eds., *The Women, Gender, & Development Reader.* 2nd ed. New York: Zed.

Ralston, Keith, and Duncan A. Stacey (1997–1998) "Salmon Wars and the Crises of the Nineties." *Beaver* 77, no. 6 (December–January).

Ramsdale, Suzannah (2013) "Angelina Jolie: How She's Become an Inspiration to Us All." www.marieclaire.co.uk.

Ray, D. L., and L. Guzzo (1992) *Trashing the Planet.* New York: Harper Perennial.

Rayman, Noah (2014) "Cell Phones Could Help Millions in Developing Countries to Read." *Time* (April 23).

Redclift, Michael (1987) *Sustainable Development: Exploring the Contradictions.* New York: Methuen.

Reichman, Lee, and Janice Tanne (2002) "Timebomb: The Global Epidemic of Multi-Drug Resistant Tuberculosis." *New England Journal of Medicine* (April 18).

RHRC (Reproductive Health Response in Conflict) (2011) "Minimum Initial Service Package (MISP)." www.rhrc.org.

Ricardo, David (1981) *Works and Correspondence of David Ricardo: Principles of Political Economy and Taxation.* London: Cambridge University Press.

Robertson, Geoffrey (2000) *Crimes Against Humanity: The Struggle for Global Justice.* New York: Norton.

Robinson, G. Dedrick., and Gene D. Robinson III (2012) *Global Warming Alarmist, Skeptics, and Deniers: A Geoscientist Looks at the Science of Climate Change.* Abbeville, SC: Moonshine Cove.

Rodney, Walter (1983) *How Europe Underdeveloped Africa.* Washington, DC: Howard University Press.

Rogers, Peter P., Kazi F. Jalal, and John A. Boyd (2006) *An Introduction to Sustainable Development.* Cambridge: Harvard University Press.

Rohde, David, and David E. Sanger (2004) "Key Pakistani Is Said to Admit Atom Transfers." *New York Times* (February 4).

Rohrlich, Justin (2015) "Fair Trade, Free Markets, and the Bitter Fight Behind Your Morning Cup of Coffee." *VICE News* (May 8).

Rollins, John, and Clay Wilson (2007) "Terrorist Capabilities for Cyberattack: Overview and Policy Issues" (January 22). www.fas.org.

Romero, Simon (2010) "Poor Sanitation in Haiti's Camps Adds Disease Risk." *New York Times* (February 19).

Rose, John W., Maria Houtchens, and Sharon G. Lynch (n.d.) "Multiple Sclerosis." http://library.med.utah.edu.

Rueters (2010) "China May Not Issue New 2011 Rare Earths Export Quota Report." *Reuters* (December 30).

Rustad, Siri Aas, and Helga Malmin Binningsbo (2012) "A Price Worth Fighting For? Natural Resources and Conflict Recurrence." *Journal of Peace Research* 49, no. 4.

Sachs, Jeffrey (2005) *The End of Poverty: Economic Possibilities for Our Time.* New York: Penguin.

——— (2008) *Common Wealth: Economics for a Crowded Planet.* New York: Penguin.

——— (2015) *The Age of Sustainable Development.* New York: Columbia University Press.

Saenz, Aaron (2010) "South African Nanotech 'Tea Bag' to Filter Water for Pennies" (September 15). http://singularityhub.com.

Saéz, Almudena, et al. (2015) "Investigating the Zoonotic Origin of the West African Ebola Epidemic." *EMBO Molecular Medicine* 7, no. 1 (January).

Saez, Emmanuel (2013) "Striking it Richer: The Evolution of Top Incomes in the United States." *Pathways Magazine* (Winter 2008).

Sagan, Scott D. (1986) "1914 Revisited: Allies, Offense, and Instability." *International Security* 11, no. 2.

Saleh, Nivien (2010) *Third World Citizens and the Information Technology Revolution.* New York: Palgrave Macmillan.

Sanger, David E., and Michael R. Gordon (2015) "Deal Reached on Iran Nuclear Program; Limits on Fuel Would Lessen With Time." *New York Times* (July 14).

Sanger, David E., et al. (2013) "Chinese Army Unit Is Seen As Tied to Hacking Against U.S." *New York Times* (February 18).

Schaible, G., and M. Aillery (2012) "Water Conservation in Irrigated Agriculture: Trends and Challenges in the Face of Emerging Demands." *USDA Economic Information Bulletin* 99.

Scharre, Paul, and Michael Horowitz (2015) "An Introduction to Autonomy in Weapon Systems" (February). www.cnas.org.

Schmer, M. R., et al. (2007) "Net Energy Cellulosic Ethanol from Switchgrass." *Proceedings from the National Academy of Sciences of the United States of America* 105, no. 2.

Selman, Mindy, et al. (2008) "Eutrophication and Hypoxia in Coastal Areas: A Global Assessment of the State of Knowledge." http://pdf.wri.org.

Sen, Amartya. (1999) *Development as Freedom.* New York: Anchor.

Shah, Anup (2010) "Percent of People in the World at Different Poverty Levels." www.globalissues.org.

Sherman, Richard (2013) "Woodland Owners' Guide to Oak Management." www.extension.umn.edu.

Shiva, Vandana (2010) "Women in Nature." In Nalini Visvanathan, Lynn Duggan, Laurie Nisonoff, and Nan Wiegersma, eds., *The Women, Gender, & Development Reader.* London: Zed.

Shubber, Kadhim (2013) "Gallery: Humanity's Terrible Environmental Impact." *Wired* (April 22).

Shue, Henry (1980) *Basic Rights: Subsistence, Affluence, and U.S. Foreign Policy.* Princeton: Princeton University Press.

Siegel, R. P. (2015) "Costa Rica Went 100% Renewable—Then Saw Energy Prices Fall" (April 3). www.greenbiz.com.

Simmons, K. B., and M. I. Rodriguez (2015) "Reducing Unintended Pregnancy Through Provider Training." *The Lancet* (June 16).

SIPRI (Stockholm International Peace Research Institute) (2015) "SIPRI Military Expenditure Database." www.sipri.org.

Sivard, Ruth Leger (1991) *World Military and Social Expenditures 1991.* Washington, DC: World Priorities.

——— (1996) *World Military and Social Expenditures 1996.* Washington, DC: World Priorities.

Smith, Adam (1910) *An Inquiry into the Nature and Causes of the Wealth of Nations.* London: Dutton.

Smith, Tierney (2015) "5 Countries Leading the Way Toward 100% Renewable Energy" (January 9). http://ecowatch.com.

Sontag, Deborah (2010) "In Haiti, Rising Call for Displaced to Go Away." *New York Times* (October 4).

Soubbotina, T. P., with K. A. Sheram (2000) *Beyond Economic Growth: Meeting the Challenges of Global Development.* Washington, DC: World Bank. www.worldbank.org.

Spiers, Edward M. (2010) *A History of Chemical and Biological Weapons.* London: Reaktion.

Staudt, Kathleen (2014) "Women and Gender." In Peter Burnell, Lise Rakner, and Vicky Randall, eds., *Politics in the Developing World.* Oxford: Oxford University Press.

Steinberg, Gerald M. (1994) "US Non-Proliferation Policy: Global Regimes and Regional Realities." *Contemporary Security Policy* 15, no. 3.

Stevens, Matt (2014) "California Drought Most Severe in 1,200 Years, Study Says." *Los Angeles Times* (December 5).

Stiglitz, Joseph E. (2015) *The Great Divide: Unequal Societies and What We Can Do About Them.* New York: Norton.

Stilwell, Victoria (2015) "Obesity Is Hurting the U.S. Economy in Surprising Ways" (March 5). www.bloomberg.com.

Sullivan, Kathy (2015) "Water from a Stone: Jordanians Stretch Meager Resources to Sustain Syrian Refugees." *Frontlines* (July–August). https://www.usaid.gov.

Sun, Yun (2015) "The Sixth Forum on China-Africa Cooperation: New Agenda and New Approach." www.brookings.edu.

Sung, J. J., et al. (2005) "Increasing Incidence of Colorectal Cancer in Asia: Implications for Screening." www.ncbi.nlm.nih.gov.

SWIE (Stanford Woods Institute for the Environment) (n.d.) "Consequences of Increased Global Meat Consumption on the Global Environment: Trade in Virtual Water, Energy, and Nutrients." https://woods.stanford.edu.

Switzer, Jacqueline Vaughn (1994) *Environmental Politics: Domestic and Global Dimensions.* New York: St. Martin's.

Takle, E. (2008) "Global Warming: Impact of Climate Change on Global Agriculture." *AgDM Newsletter.* Ames: Iowa State University Extension and Outreach.

Tan, Yan, and Fei Guo (2009) "Environmentally Induced Migration in West China" (September 27–October 2). Paper presented at the twenty-sixth International Population Conference, Marrakech, Morocco.

Tannenwald, Nina (2005) "Stigmatizing the Bomb: Origins of the Nuclear Taboo." *International Security* 29, no. 4 (Spring).

TED (Trade and Environmental Database) (2000) "The Economic and Environmental Impact of the Gulf War on Kuwait and the Persian Gulf." www1.american.edu/ted/kuwait.htm.

Thompson, Andrea (2015a) "May CO_2 Peak Shows Trend Is Up, Up, Up" (May 15). www.climatecenteral.org.

——— (2015b) "2015 May Just Be Hottest Year on Record." *Scientific American* (August 20).

Thompson, J. Milburn (2003) *Justice and Peace: A Christian Primer*. 2nd ed. Maryknoll, NY: Orbis.

Tilman, D., et al. (2002) "Agricultural Sustainability and Intensive Production Practices." *Nature* 418.

Trout Unlimited (2009) "Mixed Reviews for Pacific Salmon Treaty." www.tu.org.

Tucker, Jonathan B. (2000) "Chemical and Biological Terrorism: How Real a Threat?" *Current History* (April).

Tumulty, Brian (1994) "US Industry Confronts Cost of Implementing GATT." *Gannett News Service* (July 18).

UCSUSA (Union of Concerned Scientists USA) (2014) "Each Country's Share of CO_2 Emissions." www.ucsusa.org.

UN (United Nations) (1992) *Agenda 21: Programme of Action for Sustainable Development*. New York.

——— (1995) *The United Nations Fourth World Conference on Women: Platform for Action*. www.un.org.

——— (1998) "United Nations Press Briefing on Kyoto Protocol" (March 16). www.unfccc.int.

——— (2000) *United Nations Millennium Declaration*. www.un.org.

——— (2002) *Report of the World Summit on Sustainable Development*. www.johannesburgsummit.org.

——— (2009) *World Population Prospects: The 2008 Revision—Highlights*. New York.

——— (2010) "UN Establishes High-Level Commission to Track Results and Resources for Women's and Children's Health" (December 16). www.un.org.

——— (2011) "Global Issues: Women." www.un.org.

——— (2012) *Report of the United Nations Conference on Sustainable Development*. www.uncsd2012.org.

——— (2013) *Responsibility to Protect: State Responsibility and Prevention*. Report of the Secretary-General. New York.

——— (2014) *Open Working Group Proposal for Sustainable Development Goals*. New York. https://sustainabledevelopment.un.org.

——— (2015a) *The Millennium Development Goals Report 2015*. www.un.org.

——— (2015b) *Transforming Our World: The 2030 Agenda for Sustainable Development*. https://sustainabledevelopment.un.org.

——— (2015c) *2015 Time for Global Action, for People and Planet*. www.un.org.

——— (n.d.) *Current Peacekeeping Operations*. www.un.org.

UN News Centre (2010) "UN and Partners Use New Mobile Phone Application to Enable Refugees to Trace Families" (September 9). www.un.org.

UNAIDS (Joint United Nations Programme on HIV/AIDS) (2007) "UNAIDS Policy and Practice." www.unaids.org.

——— (2015a) "Fact Sheet 2014: Global Statistics." www.unaids.org.

——— (2015b) "How AIDS Changed Everything: Fact Sheet." www.unaids.org.

UNCTAD (United Nations Conference on Trade and Development) (2015) *World Investment Report 2015*. http://unctad.org.

UNDESA (United Nations Department of Economic and Social Affairs) (2002) "The Johannesburg Summit Test: What Will Change" (25 September). www.un.org.

UNDESIPA (United Nations Department for Economic and Social Information and Policy Analysis) (1995) *Global Population Policy Data Base*. New York.
UNDP (United Nations Development Programme) (1994) *Human Development Report 1994*. New York.
——— (1996) *Human Development Report 1996*. New York.
——— (2001) *Human Development Report 2001*. New York.
——— (2011a) *Human Development Report 2011: Sustainability and Equity—A Better Future for All*. New York: Palgrave Macmillan.
——— (2011b) *The Millennium Development Goals Report 2011*. New York.
——— (2014a) *Human Development Report: Sustaining Human Progress—Reducing Vulnerabilities and Building Resilience*. New York.
——— (2014b) *Human Development Report 2014*. New York.
UNDPI (United Nations Department for Public Information) (1997) "Earth Summit Review Ends with Few Commitments" (July). New York.
——— (2002) "Press Summary of the Secretary-General's Report on Implementing Agenda 21" (January). New York.
UNEP (United Nations Environment Programme) (2007) "Environmental Degradation Triggering Tensions and Conflict in Sudan" (June 22). www.unep.org.
——— (2009) "Rainwater Harvesting: A Lifeline for Human Well-Being." www.unwater.org.
——— (2011) "What Is the Green Economy?" www.unep.org.
UNESCO (United Nations Education, Scientific, and Cultural Organization) (2015) "Country Profiles: Pakistan, Education." www.uis.unesco.org.
UNGA (United Nations General Assembly) (2015) "Countries in Arrears in the Payment of Their Financial Contributions Under the Term of Article 19 of the UN Charter." www.un.org.
UNHCR (United Nations High Commissioner for Refugees) (2012) "Refugees." www.unhcr.org.
——— (2014) *UNHCR Global Resettlement Needs: 2015*. Geneva.
——— (2015a) "Global Trends: Forced Displacement in 2014." www.unhcr.org.
——— (2015b) "2015 UNHCR Country Operations Profile: Democratic Republic of the Congo." www.unhcr.org.
UNHCR (2015c) "UN Gaza Inquiry Finds Credible Allegations of War Crimes Committed in 2014 by both Israel and Palestinian Armed Groups." http://www.ohchr.org/en/NewsEvents/Pages/DisplayNews.aspx?NewsID=16119&LangID=E.
University of Arizona (2015) Dark Web and Geopolitical Web Project. https://ai.arizona.edu/research/dark-web-geo-web.
UNPD (United Nations Population Division) (2013a) *International Migration Stock*. www.un.org.
——— (2013b) *World Population Prospects*. http://esa.un.org.
——— (2014a) *World Population Policies Database*. http://esa.un.org.
——— (2014b) *World Urbanization Prospects*. http://esa.un.org.
——— (2015) *World Population Prospects*. http://esa.un.org.
US Bureau of Economic Analysis (2015) "U.S. International Trade in Goods and Services." www.bea.gov.
USDA (US Department of Agriculture) (2013) "National Agricultural Statistics Service: California Agricultural Statistics—2012 Crop Year." Sacramento, CA.
——— (2015) "Economic Research Service: California Drought: Food Prices and Consumers." www.ers.usda.gov.
USDHS (US Department of Homeland Security) (2003) *2002 Yearbook of Immigration Statistics*. Washington, DC: US Government Printing Office.

——— (2014) *Yearbook of Immigration Statistics: Refugees and Asylees*. www.dhs.gov.

USDS (US Department of State) (2002) "US-Canada Yukon River Salmon Agreement Signed" (December 4). Washington, DC.

——— (n.d.) "Glossary." www.state.gov.

USITC (2003) "Steel-Consuming Industries: Competitive Conditions With Respect To Steel Safeguard Measures." (September). https://www.usitc.gov/3632.htm.

US Treasury (2015) "Foreign Portfolio Holdings of U.S. Securities." www.treasury.gov.

Valente, C. M., and W. D. Valente (1995) *Introduction to Environmental Law and Policy: Protecting the Environment Through Law*. Minneapolis: West.

Vaughan, David, and David Adam (2009) "Copenhagen Climate Deal: Spectacular Failure—or a Few Important Steps?" *The Guardian* (December 24).

Veit, P. (2011) "Women and Customary Land Rights in Uganda" (April). www.focusonland.com.

Wake, David B., and Vance T. Vredenburg (2008) "Are We in the Midst of the Sixth Mass Extinction? A View from the World of Amphibians." *Proceedings of the National Academy of Sciences* 105 (August 11).

Wallach, Wendell (2015) *A Dangerous Master: How to Keep Technology from Slipping Beyond Our Control*. New York: Basic.

Walton, David, and Louise Ivers (2011) "Responding to Cholera in Post-Earthquake Haiti." *New England Journal of Medicine* (January).

Wanyeki, L. M., ed. (2003) *Women and Land in Africa: Culture, Religion, and Realizing Women's Rights*. New York: Zed.

Watts, Jonathan, and Dan Collyns (2014) "Ecuador Indigenous Leader Found Dead Days Before Planned Lima Protest." *The Guardian* (December 6).

WCED (World Commission on Environment and Development) (1987) *Our Common Future*. Oxford: Oxford University Press.

WDF (World Diabetes Foundation) (2011) "Diabetes Facts" (June 5). www.worlddiabetesfoundation.org.

WDFW (Washington Department of Fish and Wildlife) (2015) "WDFW Help: Why Do Native Americans Have Their Own Separate Hunting and Fishing Seasons?" http://wdfw.wa.gov.

Weeks, John R. (2005) *Population: Introduction to Concepts and Issues*. 9th ed. Belmont, CA: Wadsworth.

——— (2012) *Population: An Introduction to Concepts and Issues*. 11th ed. Belmont, CA: Wadsworth.

Welch, Ashley (2015) "Amid Crisis, Refugees Face Numerous Health Risks." *CBS News* (September 25).

Weston, Burns H. (1992) "Human Rights." In Richard Pierre Claude and Burns H. Weston, eds., *Human Rights in the World Community*. Philadelphia: University of Pennsylvania Press.

White House (2009) "Remarks by President Obama in Prague" (April 5). www.whitehouse.gov.

WHO (World Health Organization) (2001a) "Fact Sheet 218." www.who.int.

——— (2001b) "Mental Health, Human Rights, and Legislation: WHO's Framework." www.who.int.

——— (2006) "Nutrition." www.who.int.

——— (2007) "Re-Defining 'Health.'" www.who.int.

——— (2012) "Voluntary Medical Male Circumcision for HIV Prevention" (July). www.who.int.

——— (2014a) "Fact Sheet on the World Malaria Report 2014" (December). www.who.int.

——— (2014b) "Female Genital Mutilation." Fact Sheet no. 241. www.who.int.

——— (2014c) "The Top 10 Causes of Death." Fact Sheet no. 310. www.who.int.

——— (2015a) "Depression." Fact Sheet no. 369. www.who.int.

——— (2015b) "Diabetes." Fact Sheet no. 312. www.who.int.

——— (2015c) *Global Tuberculosis Report.* 20th ed. www.who.int.

——— (2015d) "The Health and Environment Linkages Initiative (HELI)." www.who.int.

——— (2015e) "Health Workforce: Density of Physicians." http://gamapserver.who.int.

——— (2015f) "Malaria." Fact Sheet no. 94. www.who.int.

——— (2015g) "Maternal Mortality." Fact Sheet no. 348. www.who.int.

——— (2015h) "Nutrition for Health and Development." www.who.int.

——— (2015i) "Obesity and Overweight." Fact Sheet no. 311. www.who.int.

——— (2015j) "Schizophrenia." Fact Sheet no. 397. www.who.int.

——— (2015k) "Under-Five Mortality." www.who.int.

Wilber, R. (2011) "Lessons from Rwanda: How Women Transform Governance." *Solutions: For a Sustainable and Desirable Future* 2, no. 2.

Wild Salmon Center (2004–2015) "Factsheet: Hatchery Salmon Interactions with Wild Salmon Populations." www.wildsalmoncenter.org.

Wittman, H., A. Desmarais, and N. Wiebe (2010) "The Origins and Potential of Food Sovereignty." In H. Wittman, A. Desmarais, and N. Wiebe, *Food Sovereignty: Reconnecting Food, Nature, and Community.* Oakland: Food First.

WMO (World Meteorological Organization) (2003) "Extreme Weather Events Might Increase" (July 2). www.wmo.ch.

——— (2012) "Record Arctic Sea Ice Melt, Multiple Extremes, and High Temperatures." Press Release no. 966. www.wmo.int.

——— (2014) "Atlas of Mortality and Economic Losses from Weather, Climate, and Water Extremes: Better Disaster Data Enables Better Decisions." Press Release no. 998. www.wmo.int.

Wolbrecht, Christina, and David E. Campbell (2007) "Leading by Example: Female Members of Parliament as Political Role Models." *American Journal of Political Science* 51, no. 4.

Wolf, Aaron T. (2000) "'Hydrostrategic' Territory in the Jordan Basin: Water, War, and Arab-Israeli Peace Negotiations." In Hussein A. Amery and Aaron T. Wolf, eds., *Water in the Middle East: A Geography of Peace.* Austin: University of Texas Press.

Wood, Graeme (2015) "What ISIS Really Wants." *The Atlantic* (March).

Woolcock, M., S. Szreter, and V. Rao (2009) "How and Why Does History Matter for Development Policy?" Working Paper no. 68. Manchester: Brooks World Poverty Institute, University of Manchester.

World Bank (2009) *Gender and Agriculture Sourcebook.* Washington DC.

——— (2011a) "Advancing Food Security in a Changing Climate." http://web.worldbank.org.

——— (2011b) "Data by Country: Kenya." http://data.worldbank.org.

——— (2015a) "Data: Indicators, Foreign Direct Investment, Net (BoP, Current US$)." http://data.worldbank.org.

——— (2015b) "Gross National Income per Capita, 2014, Atlas Method and PPP" (September 18). http://databank.worldbank.org.

——— (2015c) "World Bank Forecasts Global Poverty to Fall Below 10% for the First Time; Major Hurdles Remain in Goal to End Poverty by 2030" (October 4). www.worldbank.org.

——— (2015d) *World Development Indicators 2015.* http://data.worldbank.org.

Wu, Mark, and James Salzman (2014) "The Next Generation of Trade and Environment Conflcits: The Rise of Green Industrial Policy." *Northwestern University* 108, no. 2.

Yaghi, Abdulfattah (2004) "Water Public Policy: A Study on the Near East Countries." Unpublished paper.

Yonetani, M. (2014) "Global Estimates 2014: People Displaced by Disasters." www.internal-displacement.org.

Yousafzai, Malala, with Christina Lamb (2013) *I am Malala: The Girl Who Stood Up for Education and Was Shot by the Taliban*. London: Orion.

Zimmer, Carl (2015) "Study Finds Climate Change As Threat to 1 in 6 Species." *New York Times* (April 30).

The Contributors

Caroline Anderson recently completed her master's degree in public health at the Johns Hopkins University Bloomberg School of Public Health.

Mary Ellen Batiuk is professor emeritus of social and political studies at Wilmington College.

Melissa M. C. Beaudoin teaches political science at Northern Virginia Community College at the Manassas campus.

Megan L. Canfield is a student at Wilmington College.

Pamela S. Chasek is professor and chair of government and politics at Manhattan College. She is also cofounder and executive editor of the International Institute for Sustainable Development's *Earth Negotiations Bulletin,* a reporting service on UN environment and development negotiations.

Coreen H. Cockerill is associate professor of communication arts and agricultural communication at Wilmington College.

Deborah S. Davenport has taught courses on global issues at Georgia State University and Mississippi State University, and in the United Kingdom.

Jennifer Dye teaches in the Department of International Affairs at the University of Cincinnati.

Audrey Ingram is a journalist based in Madison County, Ohio.

Laura Dudley Jenkins is associate professor of political science at the University of Cincinnati.

Lina M. Kassem is assistant professor of international affairs at Qatar University.

Ellen Percy Kraly is William R. Kenan Jr. Professor of geography and environmental studies at Colgate University.

Jeffrey S. Lantis is professor of political science at the College of Wooster.

Joe Lehnert is a PhD student at the University of California, Santa Cruz (UCSC), focusing on the fields of international relations and political theory.

Bruce E. Moon is professor emeritus in the Department of International Relations at Lehigh University.

Fiona Mulligan is on the staff of the Environmental Investigation Agency in Washington, D.C.

Michael D. Newman has participated in multiple missions with Médicins Sans Frontières (Doctors Without Borders), providing surgical treatment in conflict settings including Liberia, Nigeria, Sri Lanka, Syria, and South Sudan.

Don Reeves has served as general secretary of the American Friends Service Committee; economic policy analyst for Bread for the World Institute; and legislative secretary for the Friends Committee on National Legislation.

Mark Seis is associate professor of sociology at Fort Lewis College.

D. Neil Snarr is emeritus professor of social and political studies at Wilmington College.

Michael Snarr is professor of political science at Wilmington College.

Anthony N. Talbott is a lecturer in political science and human rights studies and interim director of the Human Rights Studies Program at the University of Dayton.

Christina L. Veite is studying medicine at Ohio University's College of Osteopathic Medicine.

Kristen Weymouth is studying international relations and geography at Colgate University.

Index

About the Book

HOW IS NEW TECHNOLOGY—CYBERWARFARE, DRONES, AND MORE—affecting global security? Are the 2015 Sustainable Development Goals having an impact? What progress are governments making in dealing with climate change? Is there a viable solution to the Syrian refugee crisis? How do we reconcile the concepts of universal human rights and national sovereignty? These are among the difficult questions addressed in this new, fully revised and updated edition of *Introducing Global Issues*.

The material has been successfully designed for readers with little or no prior knowledge of the topics covered. Each chapter provides an analytical overview of the issue addressed, identifies central actors and perspectives, and outlines past progress and future prospects. Discussion questions are posed to enhance students' appreciation of the complexities involved, and suggestions for further reading additionally enrich the text.

Michael T. Snarr is professor of political science at Wilmington College.
D. Neil Snarr is professor emeritus of sociology at Wilmington College.